Minority Education:
From Shame to Struggle

Multilingual Matters

MULTILINGUAL MATTERS 40
Series Editor: Derrick Sharp

Minority Education: From Shame to Struggle

Edited by
T. Skutnabb-Kangas and
J. Cummins

MULTILINGUAL MATTERS LTD
Clevedon · Philadelphia

127405

Library of Congress Cataloging in Publication Data

Minority education: from shame to struggle/edited by T. Skutnabb-
Kangas and J. Cummins.—1st ed.
   p.   cm.—(Multilingual Matters; 40)
Bibliography: p.
Includes index.
   1. Children of minorities—Education—United States. 2. Children
of minorities—Education—Europe. 3. Education, Bilingual—United
States. 4. Education, Bilingual—Europe. 5. Power (Social
sciences) I. Skutnabb-Kanghas, Tove. II. Cummins, Jim, 1949–
III. Series.
LC3731.M559 1988
371.97′00973—dc19

British Library Cataloguing in Publication Data

Minority education: from shame to struggle.
   (Multilingual Matters; 40).
   1. Developed countries. Ethnic minorities.
Education. Sociological perspectives
I. Skutnabb-Kangas, Tove II. Cummins, Jim,
1949–
370.19′342′091722

   ISBN 1-85359-004-5
   ISBN 0-85358-003-7 Pbk

Multilingual Matters Ltd.
Bank House, 8a Hill Road   &   242 Cherry Street
Clevedon, Avon BS21 7HH   Philadelphia, PA 19106-1906
England   USA

Typeset by Mathematical Composition Setters Ltd., Salisbury.
Printed and bound in Great Britain by WBC Print, Bristol.

Contents

Introduction
Jim Cummins and Tove Skutnabb-Kangas 1

I   SOCIOPOLITICAL ANALYSES

1   Multilingualism and the education of minority children
     Tove Skutnabb-Kangas 9

2   Language policy and language rights in the United States:
     Issues in bilingualism
     Eduardo Hernández-Chávez 45

3   The language education of immigrant workers' children in
     The Netherlands
     René Appel 57

4   The jewel in the crown of the Modern Prince:
     The new approach to bilingualism in multicultural education
     in England
     Arturo Tosi 79

5   Active bilingualism—the Swedish goal for immigrant
     children's language instruction
     Gunnar Tingbjörn 103

6   From multicultural to anti-racist education: An analysis of
     programmes and policies in Ontario
     Jim Cummins 127

II   EXPERIENTIAL PERSPECTIVES

7   Mother tongue and identity
     Nobody could see that I was a Finn
     Antti Jalava 161

Poems by:
Theodor Kallifatides
Binnie Kristal-Andersson
Pirkko Leporanta-Morley
Guilem Rodrigues da Silva
Rauni Magga Lukkari
Mazisi Kunene

Living with two languages
Jukka Kalasniemi 177

Returning to Sami identity
Johannes Marainen 179

III   COMMUNITY STRUGGLES FOR EDUCATIONAL RIGHTS

8   Rights and claims of indigenous people: Education and the
     reclaiming of identity. The case of the Canadian Natives, the
     Sami and Australian Aborigines
     Deirdre F. Jordan 189

9   The Pajaro Valley experience: Working with Spanish-
     speaking parents to develop children's reading and writing
     skills through the use of children's literature
     Alma Flor Ada 223

10   Finnish children in Sweden strike for better education
     *Tuula Honkala, Pirkko Leporanta-Morley, Lilja Liukka and
     Eija Rougle* 239

11   Resource power and autonomy through discourse in conflict -
     a Finnish migrant school strike in Sweden
     Tove Skutnabb-Kangas 251

12   Parents, schools and racism: Bilingual education in a
     Northern California town
     Jan Curtis 278

13   The Carpinteria language minority student experience:
     From theory, to practice, to success
     S. Jim Campos and H. Robert Keatinge 299

14   Beyond cultural inclusion: An Inuit example of indigenous
     educational development
     Arlene Stairs 308

15   Nine years of Finnish-medium education in Sweden—what
     happens afterwards? The education of minority children in
     Botkyrka
     Tom Hagman and Jouko Lahdenperä 328

IV   THE GLOBAL CONTEXT

16   Linguicism: Structures and ideologies in linguistic imperialism
     Robert Phillipson 339

17   Racism, ethnicism and etharchy or not?
     The principles of progressive control and transformative
     change
     Chris Mullard 359

18   Monolingual myopia and the petals of the Indian lotus:
     Do many languages divide or unite a nation?
     Debi Prasanna Pattanayak 379

19   Concluding remarks: Language for empowerment
     Tove Skutnabb-Kangas and Jim Cummins 390

Notes on Contributors 395

Index 399

Introduction

JIM CUMMINS and
TOVE SKUTNABB-KANGAS

During the past 15 years a large number of volumes have appeared on issues related to the education of ethnic minority students in international settings (e.g. Bullivant, 1981; Churchill, 1986; Devetak, Klopčič & Novak-Lukanovič, 1986; Edwards, 1984; Fishman, 1976; Rothermund & Simon, 1986; Skutnabb-Kangas, 1984; Spolsky, 1986; Spolsky & Cooper, 1978) and many more have analysed specific situations in individual countries. Why then another volume on this topic?

First, and most obviously, the educational issues remain largely unresolved, both at a theoretical level and especially at the level of policy and practice, while the number of minority students continues to increase dramatically. Even in situations (e.g. western European countries) where the numbers of new labour migrants have significantly decreased, the second and third generation minority population in schools has risen significantly. In other situations (e.g. the United States, Canada) continuing legal immigration and refugee settlement is supplemented by large numbers of undocumented workers. In the majority of immigration countries controversy continues unabated about appropriate ways of educating minority students, as the papers in this volume document. With the partial exception of Sweden (and Finland), policies, programmes and public debate remain notably uninformed with respect to the large amount of research that has been conducted on issues related to minority education. Not surprisingly, the victims of this confusion are the minority students who leave school as an undereducated underclass with minimal prospects for jobs or social opportunity. The probability of social disruption as a result of this massive miseducation has so alarmed governments of western industrialized countries that issues of minority education have been a focus of concern for the Organization for Economic Co-operation and Development (OECD) during the past five years (Churchill, 1986; OECD, 1986). The analyses in the present volume attempt to provide both a theoretical context for understanding the nature of the issues and strategies for reversing the current trends.

A second general reason why we conceived this book was our concern about many previous articles and edited volumes on minority/bilingual education. While there is much valuable material in these analyses, most attempt to be non-ideological in overt orientation, although implicit and covert ideologies are seldom far beneath the surface. Most treatments of the issues tend to reflect a "balanced" liberal approach to minority education in which vague principles of "multicultural education" are endorsed as a direction for policy and practice. We have no quarrel with the goals of promoting greater cross-cultural understanding among students and greater sensitivity to the cultural attributes of minority students on the part of teachers. However, as documented in several papers of this volume, "multicultural" or "intercultural" education has resulted in few significant changes for the education of minority children. The interactions between educators, on the one hand, and minority children and communities on the other, continue to reflect the power structure in the wider society where minority communities are disempowered. Our argument with the implicit perspective in most previous volumes dealing with minority education is that the societal power structure is ignored both as the context for and the fundamental causal factor (or set of factors) in minority students' educational failure. We believe that the causes of this failure cannot be understood unless the educational questions are considered in the context of the historical and current power relations between dominant and dominated groups. Strategies for change are futile unless they are founded upon a theoretically coherent (and empirically supported) understanding of why minority students have experienced and continue to experience academic difficulties, despite apparently serious attempts at educational reform. This type of understanding is not possible when the issues are analysed within a liberal ideological framework and, consequently, it is not surprising that initiatives which have emanated from this type of analysis (e.g. multicultural/intercultural education, transitional bilingual education in the United States, etc.) have frequently served only to erect a veneer of change that has left the underlying disabling structure intact. The hysterical/paranoid reaction that even these minimal changes evoke from the extreme right (e.g. the "US English" movement in the United States) reinforces the illusion that real change has occurred.

In contrast to most previous volumes, the contributions in the present volume by and large reflect an explicit rejection of a liberal ideological stance in favour of a "conflict" perspective (Paulston, 1980) in which consideration of the educational issues is rooted in an analysis of the inter-class and inter-ethnic conflicts or power struggles in society at large (see Skutnabb-Kangas, 1986, for a detailed discussion of research paradigms in minority education). Thus we analyse the educational problems of minority students as manifestations of institutionalized racism/ethnicism/ classism/linguicism in society (and in the schools that reflect the broader society) rather than only as a function of educators' lack of sensitivity to students' needs.

The contributions in the present volume, however, do not stop at the level of academic analysis. All of us are convinced that real change *is* possible in the education of minority children and we are committed to promoting such change; the theoretical analyses thus constitute, in Aronowitz and Giroux' (1985) terms, "a language of possibility" for the education of minority students. The experiences and programmes described by the contributors suggest that our "radical optimism" (Skutnabb-Kangas, 1986) is not totally naive. We hope that our theoretical analyses have identified at least some of the real barriers to change which have tended to be obscured by liberal attempts at reform.

A third reason for bringing together the contributions in this volume is that most previous analyses have excluded the perspectives of the minorities themselves. The individual and collective voices of those at the wrong end of the power relationships have (predictably) not been heard and have consequently had minimal influence on the policies and programmes being developed "to meet their needs". Most of the contributors to the present volume are themselves members of minority groups and have experienced directly what they are writing about.

In addition, a wide variety of disciplinary and experiential perspectives are represented. Most papers, in fact, attempt to integrate, to some extent, sociopolitical and psycho-educational approaches, since analysis of both is required to understand the educational disabling of minority students and directions for reversing this pattern. The analyses in the first section tend to focus on specific countries, the United States (Hernández-Chávez), The Netherlands (Appel), Britain (Tosi), Sweden (Tingbjörn), and Canada (Cummins), while a more general integration of sociopolitical and psycho-educational issues is provided by Skutnabb-Kangas. In all the contexts analysed, liberal reforms (e.g. programmes to teach the school language, quick-exit bilingual programmes, etc.) have been implemented with only limited success; the mixed results of these reforms tend to reinforce the underlying assumption against which the liberal reforms were ostensibly directed: namely, that it is the minority children and their parents who are deficient rather than the schools and societies. What other conclusion is possible when minority students continue to fail despite the best efforts of concerned educators? The theoretical analyses attempt to show the fallacies of this view by locating the problem not in the minority children or communities but in the societal institutionalized racism that is mirrored in the educational system. The dimensions of this racism are analysed in several of the chapters (Skutnabb-Kangas, Cummins, Phillipson, Mullard, Pattanayak) and specific strategies for change are outlined in the light of the theoretical analyses.

The change strategies discussed in the more theoretical papers are not simply abstract academic recommendations. They reflect a convergence of anti-racist change strategies derived from both the theoretical analyses and the lived experiences of communities and educators who have struggled to implement such changes. Examples of struggles by communities and educators from Europe, North America and Australia to implement anti-racist education are described in Section III, *Community struggles for educational rights*. These accounts show that changes at varying levels of the educational hierarchy *are* possible and can have dramatic effects both on minority students' educational achievement and on the ways in which communities and students perceive their own identities. The initiative for change may come from either the community, as in the case of the strike by Finnish school children in Stockholm (Honkala *et al*.), or from educators, as illustrated by Alma Flor Ada's account of the family literacy experience in the Pajaro Valley School District. However, whatever the catalyst for change, the process will involve, in Freire's (1985) term, conscientization both of the minority community and of (at least some) educators, as well as genuine collaboration between them as partners in children's education. This collaborative relationship represents a reversal of the domination and institutionalized racism that is imposed on the minority community in the society at large. In short, effective interventions by communities and/or educators inevitably go beyond the minimal dictates of liberal reform and begin to address the power relations that are manifested in the interactions between educators on the one hand, and minority children and communities on the other.

The policy and programme issues analysed formally in the theoretical and empirical papers are also addressed in the poems, stories and personal accounts. These speak eloquently of the shame, confusion and self-doubt that minority children (and adults) often feel as a result of their "education". The writers also describe the gradual emergence of the critical consciousness (conscientization) necessary both to analyse what has been done to them and to begin the struggle for identity, self-respect and self-determination. The experiential process described in these accounts is the individual realization of the collective process experienced by minority communities who rediscover their identities and begin to assert their children's right to grow fully as human beings in an education system free from violence.

To majority educators, whether their ideological orientation is liberal reformist or conservative, it may appear extreme to talk of educational violence and the shame it engenders in minority students. For minority groups, however, the violence is still very real, despite the fact that the overt violence that historically has characterized the education of minorities in virtually all western countries has become largely covert, with one or two exceptions (e.g. the torture of children in South Africa). The structure of interactions that leads minority students to internalize shame remains intact. An example will illustrate the point; in his autobiographical novel *How Green Was My Valley*, Richard Llewellyn gives an account of the operation of the "Welsh not", a wooden placard hung around the neck of any child caught speaking Welsh in school (introduced in the middle of the nineteenth century):

> "I heard crying in the infants' school as though a child had fallen and the voice came nearer and fell flat upon the air as a small girl came through the door and walked a couple of steps towards us ... About her neck a piece of new cord, and from the cord, a board that hung to her shins and cut her as she walked. Chalked on the board, in the fist of Mr. Elijah Jonas-Sessions, I must not speak Welsh in school ... And the board dragged her down, for she was small, and the cord rasped the flesh on her neck, and there were marks upon her shins where the edge of the board had cut." (Llewellyn, 1968:267).

Although physical violence for speaking the mother tongue seldom occurs any longer in most western countries, it is still extremely common for educators (who see themselves as being well-intentioned) to reprimand minority children for speaking their mother tongue and to advise their parents to use the school language in the home. The message is the same as in the example of the "Welsh not", namely, to survive in this society your identity must be eradicated; and the results as far as internalization of shame by children and parents are also similar. The results may be even more devastating since the institutionalized racism is hidden and the violence covert. When children's (or communities') identities become shrouded in shame they lose the power to control their own lives in situations where they interact with members of the dominant group (e.g. in classrooms). Consequently, they perform in school the way educators expect them to perform—poorly—thereby reinforcing educators' perceptions of them as deficient.

We have brought together the contributions in this book in order to help educators and communities uncover and dismantle the structure of institutionalized racism that disables minority students in schools. The struggle is still in its early stages.

References

ARONOWITZ, S. & GIROUX, H. A. 1985, *Education under siege: The conservative, liberal, and radical debate over schooling.* South Hadley, Mass.: Bergin & Garvey.

BULLIVANT, B. 1981, *The pluralist dilemma in education.* Sydney: George Allen & Unwin.

CHURCHILL, S. 1986, *The education of linguistic and cultural minorities in the OECD countries.* Clevedon, England: Multilingual Matters.

DEVETAK, S., KLOPČIČ, V. & NOVAK-LUKANOVIČ, S. 1986, *Education in multicultural societies.* Ljubljana: Institute for Ethnic Studies.

EDWARDS, J. 1984, *Linguistic minorities, policies and pluralism.* London: Academic Press.

FISHMAN, J. A. 1976, *Bilingual education: An international sociological perspective.* Rowley, Mass.: Newbury House.

FREIRE, P. 1985, *The politics of liberation: Culture, power and liberation.* South Hadley, Mass.: Bergin & Garvey.

LLEWELLYN, R. 1968, *How green was my valley.* Toronto: Signet.

OECD, 1986, *Immigrants' children at school. Vol. 1 & 2.* Unpublished report, Paris: Organization for Economic Co-operation and Development.

PAULSTON, C. B. 1980, *Bilingual education: Theories and issues.* Rowley, Mass.: Newbury House.

ROTHERMUND, D. & SIMON, J. 1986, *Education and the integration of ethnic minorities.* London: Francis Pinter.

SKUTNABB-KANGAS, T. 1984, *Bilingualism or not: The education of minorities.* Clevedon, England: Multilingual Matters.

—— 1986, Who wants to change what and why—Conflicting paradigms in minority education and research. In B. SPOLSKY (ed.), *Language and education in multilingual settings.* Clevedon, England: Multilingual Matters.

SPOLSKY, B. (ed.) 1986, *Language and education in multilingual settings.* Clevedon, England: Multilingual Matters.

SPOLSKY, B. & COOPER, R.L. 1978, *Case studies in bilingual education.* Rowley, Mass.: Newbury House.

Section I: Sociopolitical analyses

Section I, *Sociopolitical analyses*, provides a general framework (Skutnabb-Kangas), followed by more detailed descriptions and analyses of the history and/or present state of minority education in the United States (Hernández-Chávez), Canada (Cummins), The Netherlands (Appel), the United Kingdom (Tosi) and Sweden (Tingbjörn).

1 Multilingualism and the education of minority children [1]

TOVE SKUTNABB-KANGAS

"A linguistic science which is aware of these political involvements can only be militant. And it is the duty of linguists in their respective countries and regions to assume responsibility for this task, this struggle for the defence and development of their own language and culture."
(Postface to L.-J. Calvet, *Linguistique et Colonialisme*.)

Introduction

The topic of multilingualism and the education of minority children is fascinating to work with in several different ways:

— it is a socially important—and controversial—topic, with immediate implications for most societies in the world. It forces the researcher to penetrate questions of ethics and the philosophy of science more deeply than do many other areas of inquiry, when pondering over the relationship between research and policy.

— it is multidisciplinary and problem-oriented, and forces the researcher to familiarize herself with many disciplines, in addition to her original one(s), and to ponder over the relationship between the definitions of social reality inherent in different disciplines.

In this chapter it is possible only to introduce some of the issues. I hope, though, that both their fascination and their complexity become clear and that the reader is intrigued and wants to find out more. The chapter starts by presenting the tension between the fact that a majority of the fewer than 200 states of the world are officially monolingual (have one official language only), and the fact that these states contain speakers of some

4–5,000 languages. Is state monolingualism, then, a stupid and irrational state of affairs, or a rational necessity? Is monolingualism in fact a reflection of an ideology, akin to racism, namely *linguicism*, the domination of one language at the expense of others (see a more detailed definition later), or is it a sign of a mature state which has reached far in an inevitable but at the same time desirable development?

Those individuals whose mother tongues do not happen to be official languages in the countries where they live, *have* to become bilingual (or multilingual). If they want to be able to speak to their parents, know about their history and culture, know who they are, they have to know their mother tongue. If they want to get a good education (which is usually not available in their own language, at least not to the same extent as in the official language) and if they want to participate in the social, economic and political life of their country, they have to know the official language. It should be the duty of the educational systems to help them become bilingual, since bilingualism is a necessity for them, and not something that they themselves have chosen. The next question is: Does education in fact try to do so or not? In order to examine this question, definitions of both a mother tongue and of bilingualism/multilingualism are needed. The definitions used by the educational authorities are then examined, so as to see whether or not they reflect linguicism. In order to counteract the threat of linguicism, a declaration of children's linguistic human rights is proposed.

The next section of the chapter introduces a way of comparing the success of educational programmes in different countries in reaching the goal of bilingualism, which is a necessary goal for minority children. First it presents several types of programmes, and then it goes on to compare them in terms of factors which are necessary as preconditions for succeeding in making children bilingual. The analysis shows that most European and Europeanized countries do not organize the education of minority children so that they will succeed in becoming bilingual.

The last section before the conclusion examines who has been blamed for the failure, the children themselves (and their parents, their group and their culture) or the linguicist societies—and the conclusions are not especially flattering for us. At the same time I hope that they will be provocative enough for the reader to start to examine her/his own society and its linguicism.

Monolingualism or multilingualism?

The large majority of the countries in the world are *de facto multi-*

lingual (in the sense that several languages are spoken natively inside their borders, like Nigeria, with over 500 languages, or India with over 1,600 mother tongues claimed by its people). It is inevitable that most countries should be multilingual: the number of independent countries is less than 200, while the number of languages spoken in the world probably is between 4,000 and 5,000, depending on how a language is defined.

An example of a *monolingual* country (where only one language is spoken natively) is Iceland, with its 240,000 inhabitants. There are no indigenous minorities and no immigrants. Even people who come to stay because they are married to Icelanders mostly learn Icelandic, and their children become native speakers of Icelandic (even if some of them hopefully become native speakers of another language in addition to Icelandic). But this type of monolingual country is an exception in our world.

Just like countries, individuals can be monolingual or bi- and multi-lingual. A monolingual is a person who "knows" only one language, whatever that means. Obviously almost everybody, excluding very small children, knows at least a few words of other languages, but they would not call themselves multilingual because of that. Maybe it is easiest to define a monolingual in a negative way: a monolingual is a person who is NOT bi- or multilingual. We shall define bilingualism later in the chapter. There are more multilinguals than monolinguals in the world. Monolingual people are thus a minority in the world, but many of them belong to a very powerful minority, namely the minority which has been able to function in all situations through the medium of their mother tongue, and who have therefore never been forced to learn another language. The majority of multilinguals are multilingual *not* because they thought that multilingualism was so desirable that they consciously wanted to become multilingual. It is rather because all those people whose mother tongues have no official rights in their country have been *forced* to learn other languages in addition to their own. But since they have been forced precisely because of their powerless status (= they have not been able to demand official rights for their own language), this means that they as a group have less power than monolinguals. Reagan does not need to know any of the languages spoken in the USA except English, while native Americans and Chicanas need to learn English in addition to their mother tongues.

But perhaps those who are monolingual in the present world need not learn other languages because their mother tongues (English, Chinese, Russian, French, etc.) are so much better and so much more developed than other languages? Perhaps "smaller" languages are small because they are in fact somehow more primitive? From a *linguistic* point of view all languages spoken natively by a group of people have equal worth. All are logical, cognitively complex and capable of expressing any thoughts, provided enough resources are devoted to cultivation (creation of new lexical items, among other things). There is no such thing as "primitive languages". On linguistic grounds *all languages could have the same rights*, the same possibility of being learned fully, developed and used in all situations by their speakers. But in practice we know that this is far from the case. Different languages have different political rights, not depending on any inherent linguistic characteristics, but on the power relationships between the speakers of those languages.

The political rights or lack of rights of any language cannot be deduced from linguistic considerations. They are part of the societal conditions of the country concerned, and can only be understood in their historical context, by studying the forces which have led to the present sociopolitical division of power and resources in the societies concerned.

This is also true of cultural attitudes towards monolingualism and multilingualism. These vary on a continuum: at one end monolingualism is seen as a desirable norm; at the other end multilingualism is seen as the normal state of affairs. Granted the number of languages in the world, most countries and people should, of course, be closer to the multilingualism end of the continuum in their attitudes, and in fact most countries might be placed there. But there are some very powerful exceptions, namely most European countries and, especially, most Europeanized countries. It seems that the extreme monolingualist ideology is very strong in Europeanized countries, those countries which have been colonized by European settlers to such an extent that a virtual extinction of the indigenous populations has been attempted, either "only" physically (like parts of Australia, for instance Tasmania, or some parts of Latin America) or both physically and linguistically/culturally (North America, New Zealand, Australia). Likewise, this strong monolingual ideology also prevails in most former imperial European countries which are the sources of the languages of the former colonizers (Britain, France, etc.).

These negative attitudes towards multilingualism pertain both in relation to official multilingualism in a country (which is seen as divisive for the nation) and to individual multilingualism. Being bilingual has in several countries, especially the United States, been used almost as a synonym for being poor, stupid and uneducated. And it is true that coming from a linguistic minority in a monolingually oriented country has often meant misery and non-education.

For an *individual*, monolingualism almost inevitably means *monoculturalism* and *monoculism*, being able to see things with one pair of glasses only and having a poorly developed capacity to see things from another person's or group's point of view. It mostly means knowing not more than one culture from the inside, and therefore lacking relativity.

For a *country*, official monolingualism in the majority of cases means that *all the minorities are oppressed and their linguistic human rights are violated*.

To me monolingualism, both individual and societal, is not so much a linguistic phenomenon (even if it has to do with language). It is rather a question of a psychological state, backed up by political power. Monolingualism is a psychological island. It is an ideological cramp. It is an illness, a disease which should be eradicated as soon as possible, because it is dangerous for world peace. It is a reflection of *linguicism*.

Linguicism

Linguicism is akin to the other negative -isms: racism, classism, sexism, ageism. Linguicism can be defined as *ideologies and structures which are used to legitimate, effectuate and reproduce an unequal division of power and resources (both material and non-material) between groups which are defined on the basis of language (on the basis of their mother tongues)*.

D. P. Pattanayak, the Director of the Central Institute of Indian Languages, says in a powerful article (1986) that the Western way of looking at multilingualism is something like this: a country should ideally be monolingual. If it is officially bilingual, that is a pity but one can live with it. If it has three or more languages, it is underdeveloped and barbaric. In order to become civilized, it should strive towards becoming monolingual.

But if there are many more languages than countries, and if many countries decide to be officially monolingual, what happens to all the other languages and to their speakers? Should the speakers of these languages become monolingual, too? And if so, in which language should they become monolingual, their own or the language that the power élite in the country has decided should be THE language of that country? The last alternative would mean that thousands of languages would become extinct. Or should the speakers of other languages become bilingual? If so, what is the best way of becoming bilingual for a minority language speaker? Specifically, in which language should the minority child be taught, predominantly in her own language, or predominantly in the majority language, in order to become a competent bilingual?

The controversy about this, both about the *goal* (monolingualism or multilingualism) and about the *means* (operationalized as mother tongue medium education or second/foreign language medium education) is the main topic of this chapter. While we go along, we shall examine both the goals and the means in order to see the extent to which they reflect linguicism.

We could tentatively present the positions in Europe and Europeanized countries in the following, extremely simplified way:

Minorities (like many non-European and non-Europeanized countries) think that genuine multilingualism is a perfectly normal and desirable state. It is possible and desirable to have multilingualism as the linguistic goal in the education of all children. Mother tongue medium education is often a good way to bilingualism/multilingualism for minorities. Learning one's mother tongue is a human right which does not need any further legitimation.

Majorities[2] think that monolingualism in the majority language is the normal and desirable state. Societal multilingualism is divisive and should not be a goal. If individual multilingualism has to be accepted, the emphasis should be on the learning of the majority language. If mother tongue medium education for minorities has to be accepted, the only legitimation for it is that it leads to increased proficiency in the majority language.

The goal of education for linguistic minority children

If you want to have your fair share of the power and the resources (both material and non-material) of your native country, you have to be able to take part in the democratic processes in your country. You have to be able to negotiate, try to influence, to have a voice. The main instrument for doing that is language. You must be able to communicate with your fellow citizens, in order to be able to influence your own situation, to be a subject in your life, not an object to be handled by others. Language is the main instrument for communication. If you live in a country with speakers of many different languages, you have to share at least one language with the others, in order for a democratic process to be possible. And if the language most widely spoken by your fellow citizens (either because it is the mother tongue of the majority, or because the power élite[3] has decided that that will be the *lingua franca*) is NOT your mother tongue, you belong to a *linguistic minority* in your country. That means that *you have to become (at least) bilingual in order to participate.*

In a democratic country, it should be the duty of the school system to give every child, regardless of linguistic background, the same chance to participate in the democratic process. If this requires that (at least) some children (i.e. the linguistic minority children) become bilingual or multilingual, then it should be the duty of the educational system to make them bilingual/multilingual, as individuals (as opposed to the *country* being multilingual).

If Western attitudes really are inclined towards monolingualism (and I find no convincing arguments to refute Pattanayak's analysis), what are the chances that European and Europeanized countries will come up with good solutions to questions about the education of minority children, solutions which would promote multilingualism? Slight, as I see it. Monolingualism does *not* prevent *some* knowledge of other languages, provided these are "modern" and "European" and have been learned at school as part of becoming "educated". If monolingualism (with *some* knowledge of other languages) is the explicitly or at least implicitly desirable and accepted societal norm, there is an inherent conflict between supporting that norm, and organizing minority (or majority) education so that it would lead to high levels of bi- or multilingualism.

But this conflict is seldom discussed openly. In fact, most European countries have at least some passages in their declarations of goals for the education of minorities which refer to bi- or multilingualism. Mostly it is discussed as a societal phenomenon ("Britain is multilingual"), and here it means only that several languages are spoken in a country. This is often only stating a fact, not declaring a wish ("OK, there *are* several languages spoken in this country, and since we cannot really do much about it, we had better accept it and try to see if there is anything positive in it"). Bilingualism/multilingualism is seldom declared as a *goal* for the educational system. If it is, then the language learning *emphasis is put on the learning of the majority language* (L2 = language two, the second or foreign language) *by the minority children*. The part of their bilingualism which has to do with the *minority language* (L1 = the first language, the mother tongue), again states the fact, but does not declare a wish ("OK, they *do* speak that minority language, but obviously they need to learn L2, English/German/Dutch etc.: that is the most important thing in their education. If learning English makes them bilingual, then the goal of education must be to make them bilingual, because they *have* to learn English").

It thus seems that both minorities and majorities agree that minority children should be given the opportunity to learn the majority language in school. But they disagree about the learning of the minority mother tongue. Many minorities think that their mother tongues should have the same rights, also in schools, as majority people's mother tongues do. Majorities act as if minority mother tongues were of less value (cultural linguicism), and emphasize educational efforts geared towards the learning of the majority language (institutional linguicism).

Definitions of mother tongue

Before we can continue our discussion, we have to define what a mother tongue is. This gives us a better opportunity to assess whether minority and majority mother tongues have the same rights or whether majority mother tongues are given more institutional support (institutions in the abstract sense of laws and regulations, and in the concrete sense of day care centres, schools, etc.).

There are several different ways of defining a mother tongue. I use four different criteria for the definitions: Origin, Competence, Function and Identification (see Table 1.1).

TABLE 1.1   *Definitions of mother tongue*

Criterion	Definition
Origin	the language(s) one learned first
Competence	the language(s) one knows best
Function	the language(s) one uses most
Identification	
a. internal	the language(s) one identifies with
b. external	the language(s) one is identified as a native speaker of by others

(Skutnabb-Kangas, 1984: 18)

I have three theses about the definitions:

1. The same person can have different mother tongues, depending on which definition is used

2. A person's mother tongue can change during her lifetime, even several times, according to all other definitions except the definition by origin

3. The mother tongue definitions can be organized hierarchically according to the degree of linguistic human rights awareness of a society.

I am a good example of the first thesis myself. My mother tongue is Swedish according to the definition by origin, because both my bilingual parents spoke it to me when I was a baby. But I am bilingual in Finnish and Swedish according to the same definition (see page 21) because I myself used both languages side by side from the very beginning. My mother tongue is Finnish according to the definition by competence; I feel that it is the language I know best (even if I know Swedish, too, just as well as any monolingual Swedish academic). My mother tongue would be English (or possibly English and Danish) according to the definition by function (I speak mostly English—in addition to three other languages—at home, and read and write English more than other languages, and I live in Denmark). And according to all identification definitions I have two mother tongues, Finnish and Finland Swedish. This also illustrates the second thesis, because both English and Danish have come into the picture through emigration and marriage, i.e. changes.

The third thesis about the definitions is the most interesting one from the point of view of linguicism. According to my view, the definition by *function* is the *most primitive* one ("this Turkish child speaks German/Dutch/Danish/English all day long at the day care centre/in school, much more than Turkish, she even uses German with siblings, so German/Dutch/Danish/English must be the child's mother tongue"). Use of this definition does not consider the fact that most minority children are *forced* to use an L2 because there are no facilities in their mother tongue. The children and their parents have not themselves been given a chance to choose freely, from among existing alternatives, which language they would like to use in day care and school. This definition is, explicitly or implicitly, used in educational institutions in many European immigration countries.

When the degree of awareness rises a bit, the next definition, also pretty primitive, is used, namely the definition by *competence* ("the Turkish children could not even count in their so-called mother tongue" says a well-known linguist, implying that Swedish, in which the children had been taught how to count, was their mother tongue, because they knew it better than Turkish). Use of this definition fails to consider that a poor proficiency in the original mother tongue is a result of not having been offered the opportunity to use and learn the original mother tongue well enough in those institutional settings where the children spent most of their day (day care centres, schools, organized after-school activities). A poor competence in the original mother tongue (which is a result of the neglect of the mother tongue in institutions earlier on, i.e. a result of earlier oppression) is then often used to legitimize additional oppression. The child is labelled as a majority language speaker, or she is denied teaching in the original mother tongue on the grounds that she does not know it well enough or because she knows the majority language better.

Use of a combination of definitions by *origin* and *identification* shows the highest degree of linguistic human rights awareness: *the mother tongue is the language one has learned first and identifies with.*

Use of a definition of function or competence in educational institutions when defining a minority child's mother tongue reflects cultural and institutional linguicism. It can be open (the agent does not try to hide it), conscious (the agent knows about it), visible (it is easy for non-agents to detect) and actively action-oriented (as opposed to merely attitudinal). All this is typical of the early phases of the history of minority education, as described in the later sections of this chapter. Or it can be hidden, unconscious, invisible and passive (lack of support rather than active opposition), typical of the later phases of minority education development. Those countries which have developed the more sophisticated, culturally (rather than biologically) oriented forms of racism (ethnicism—see Mullard, 1985b), typically also exhibit this more sophisticated form of linguicism, a linguicism which blames the victim in subtle ways, by colonizing her consciousness.

Results of institutional and cultural linguicism for minority mother tongues

The above recommended mother tongue definition implies that the language identified with is the original mother tongue, the language learned first. But in a society with institutional and cultural linguicism and discrimination, not all minority children are allowed to identify positively with their original mother tongues and cultures.

Many minority children are being forced to feel ashamed of their mother tongues, their parents, their origins, their group and their culture. Many of them, especially in countries where the racism is more subtle, not so openly expressed, take over the negative views which the majority society has of the minority groups, their languages and cultures. Many disown their parents and their own group and language. They shift identity "voluntarily", and *want* to be German, Dutch, American, British, Swedish, etc.

Often this does not work either. The child's new majority identity is not accepted by everybody. This is generally expressed more openly in the years after the minority youngsters reach puberty, and it is more common with youngsters who do not look like the stereotype of what a "real" German, Dutch, Swede, Norwegian, etc. person "should" look like, and/or with youngsters whose accent does not sound "native". The minority youngster then often hears: "You are not one of us, you are not a real Swede/American/Dutch/German/Dane, etc. you are a Finnish devil/a Turkshit/a damn Paki, etc".

The child has then "voluntarily" disowned her original identity, but the new identity is not accepted by all the people from the majority group either. There is a conflict between the internal and the external identification. The youngster is not accepted, at least not unconditionally, by the majority group, with which she has been forced to identify (but whose language and culture she has not been given the opportunity to learn "fully": see Cummins, 1984). At the same time the road back to her own group is often closed too, not only psychologically (= she does not *want* to identify with the "dirty Turks" or "aggressive silent Finns"), but often also linguistically and culturally. The child no longer knows (or has never had the chance to learn) the original mother tongue "properly". Nor does she have all the components of cultural competence in the original culture (Phillipson & Skutnabb-Kangas, 1983).

Declaration of children's linguistic human rights

In order to avoid this type of situation, all those institutions, educational and otherwise, which now function in the way described above *vis-à-vis* minority children and their mother tongues, should be changed. Majority cultures, which now degrade minority children's languages and cultures, should be changed. In order to make the demands for change more concrete, we need a *declaration of children's linguistic human rights*.

The declaration of children's linguistic human rights

1. Every child should have the right to identify positively with her original mother tongue(s) and have her identification accepted and respected by others

2. Every child should have the right to learn the mother tongue(s) fully

3. Every child should have the right to choose when s/he wants to use the mother tongue(s) in all official situations
(Skutnabb-Kangas, 1986: 160)

Not to live up to these demands for minority children is linguicist. If Dutch, West German, Swedish, British, etc. day care centres and schools, actively or through passivity and lack of positive action, prevent minority children from being able to identify positively with their mother tongues, then they function in a linguicist way. If in the same vein they prevent minority children from learning their mother tongues fully and from using them in all official situations, including day care centres and schools, then these institutions also function in a linguicist way. If the education of minority children is not discussed in these terms, i.e. if the Swedes, Norwegians, Dutch, Germans, etc. are not even aware of or deny the fact that they are suppressing minority children's basic human rights every day, then the Dutch, German, Swedish, British, etc. cultures are linguicist *vis-à-vis* minority children and their languages.

All the demands formulated in the declaration of children's linguistic human rights are met to a very large extent in relation to majority children. Nobody questions their right to identify positively with their mother tongue, to learn it fully or to use it in official situations, for instance in schools. For majority children these rights are so self-evident that they may never think of them as human rights. Some people might think that it cannot be a human right to use one's mother tongue in all official situations, for instance. But even if one did not accept that the rights in the declaration are legitimate human rights, there is no way of denying the fact that majority and minority mother tongues do not enjoy the same rights in the educational systems of most European and Europeanized countries. Groups defined on the basis of their mother tongues thus have unequal access to educational resources, i.e. these educational systems reflect linguicism.

Definitions of bilingualism

Above we claimed that the majorities are mostly interested in the part of the bilingualism goal which has to do with the learning of the majority language by minority children. The mother tongues of the minority children are tolerated as parts of the curriculum only if the teaching of them leads to a better proficiency in the majority language. The minorities themselves, partly as a result of this, have to put a strong emphasis on the learning of the mother tongue as a linguistic human right. But the minorities do, of course, want their children to learn the majority languages fully too. We want our children to become bilingual, not monolingual or strongly dominant in either of the two languages. One of the confusing facts has been that many majority educational authorities claim that they want our children to become bilingual too. But when this claim is analysed, it transpires that the *definitions* used by majorities and minorities of bilingualism as the educational goal are different. That is one of the reasons why it is imperative to define "bilingual" every time the term is being used. There are literally hundreds of definitions. In Table 1.2 I organize them according to the same criteria which I used in the mother tongue definitions, and give a sample.

When majority educational authorities talk about bilingualism as a goal for the education of minority children, they seem to mean either a non-demanding competence definition (for instance 2d or 2e) or the most general function definition (uses two languages). We minorities would rather like to use a combination of 2, 3 and 4, a definition which makes sure that the speaker has the chance to learn and use *both* languages at a very high level and to identify positively with both. Again we see that the

TABLE 1.2 *Definitions of bilingualism*

Criterion	Definition
	A speaker is bilingual who:
1. *Origin*	a. has learned two languages in the family from native speakers from the beginning
	b. has used two languages in parallel as means of communication from the beginning
2. *Competence*	a. has complete mastery[4] of two languages
	b. has native-like control of two languages
	c. has equal mastery of two languages
	d. can produce complete meaningful utterances in the other language
	e. has at least some knowledge and control of the grammatical structure of the other language
	f. has come into contact with another language
3. *Function*	a. uses (or can use) two languages (in most situations) (in accordance with her own wishes and the demands of the community)
4. *Identification*	
internal	a. identifies herself as bilingual/with two languages and/or two cultures (or parts of them)
external	b. is identified by others as bilingual/as a native speaker of two languages

(Skutnabb-Kangas, 1984:91)

definitions used by the majority authorities confirm the picture of linguicism: there are almost no demands made on the minority child's
competence in her mother tongue.

My own definition is specifically planned to suit immigrant and
indigenous minority children. The goal of minority education should be to
make the children bilingual according to this definition:

> "A speaker is bilingual who is able to function in two (or more)
> languages, either in monolingual or bilingual communities, in accord-
> ance with the sociocultural demands made on an individual's com-
> municative and cognitive competence by these communities and by the
> individual herself, at the same level as native speakers, and who is able
> positively to identify with both (or all) language groups (and cultures)
> or parts of them." (Skutnabb-Kangas, 1984:90)

The implications of this definition for the educational system are far-
reaching, and should be compared with the implications of less demanding
definitions (for more detail see Skutnabb-Kangas, 1984).

In the next section we turn to an examination of concrete educational
programmes, in order to see to what extent there is a mismatch between the
goals and the means in the education of minority students. If the educational systems are organized to give minority students a fair chance of
becoming bilingual and succeeding in school, then the claims of linguicism
are unfounded. If, on the other hand, the education is organized to prevent
minority children from gaining access to the instruments (here operationalized in terms of high levels of bilingualism and a "good" education)
for claiming their fair share of power and resources, and if the mother
tongue (minority or majority language) plays a decisive part in the division
of children into those who do and those who do not gain such access, then
the educational system functions in a linguicist way.

Comparing the success of educational programmes in different countries in reaching the goal of bilingualism

Some of the educational programmes for minority and/or majority
children achieve a *high degree of success* (HDS) in making the children
bilingual and giving them a fair chance of good school achievement (see
Table 1.3). Others show a *low degree of success* (LDS): many children do
not learn any of the languages at the same level as monolinguals, or they
become strongly dominant in one of the languages, i.e. they fail to become
bilingual. They also show, as a group, low levels of achievement in schools,

often massive failure. One of the most frequently discussed factors in explaining the difference between the two groups is *which of the two languages has been used as the medium of education* (ME). Paradoxically, instruction through the medium of a mother tongue can lead to either HDS or LDS. Likewise, instruction through the medium of a second language can also lead to either HDS or LDS. In order to understand this we must look both at societal factors which determine what type of programme is chosen for different groups, and at cognitive, pedagogical, linguistic and sociological factors which determine the outcome of the instruction. It becomes abundantly clear from the analysis that "which language should a child be instructed in, L1 or L2, in order to become bilingual?" poses the question in a simplistic and misleading way. The question should rather be: "*under which conditions* does instruction in L1 or L2, respectively, lead to high levels of bilingualism?"

I will analyse different types of educational programmes in very concrete terms, in order to highlight the decisive factors, under four main headings: *segregation, mother tongue maintenance* (or language shelter), *submersion* and *immersion* programmes. In three instances it is necessary to treat separately the programmes meant for minorities and majorities. For each programme, I assess the *degree of success* (high or low), the *medium of education* (L1 or L2) and the *linguistic and societal goals* of the programme. The classification of the goals builds more on factual results achieved than on declarations of intention, and may therefore not always tally with the officially declared goals. Some of the discussion that follows is also found in Phillipson, Skutnabb-Kangas & Africa (1986).

My example of a *segregation* model for a *majority* population (in this case a powerless majority) is the Bantu education now given at the elementary level to Namibians in nine different L1s, in Namibia. Namibia is still illegally occupied by South Africa, despite the efforts of the United Nations (manifested in several declarations) to end this state of affairs. (To a certain extent also the education for Blacks in South Africa is of the same kind.) Segregation programmes produce poor results, meaning scholastic failure for the majority of those who start school (and many do not), and low levels of cognitive/academic proficiency (see Cummins, 1984) in both languages. This fits with the linguistic goal, dominance in L1, and the societal goal, perpetuation of apartheid.

My example of *segregation* for a *minority* is the education of migrant Turks in Bavaria, West Germany, through the medium of Turkish, again with low levels of success. The linguistic goal is dominance in Turkish. The societal goal is to prepare the migrant pupils for forced repatriation when

TABLE 1.3

| | L1 | | | | L2 | | |
| | Segregation: LDS | | Maintenance: HDS | | Submersion: LDS | | Immersion: HDS |
	Bantu	Turks	Uzbekistan	Finns, Chicanas	Zambia	W. Europe minorities	Canada
Organizational factors							
1 alternative programmes available	–	–	+	+	–	–	+
2 pupils equally placed *vis-à-vis* knowledge of ME	+	+	+	+	–	–	+
3 bilingual (B), trained (T) teachers	B	B or T	BT	BT	B	T	BT
4 bilingual materials (e.g. dictionaries) available	–	+	+	+	–	–	+
5 cultural content of materials appropriate for pupils	–	–	+	+	–	–	+
Learner-related affective factors							
6 low level of anxiety (supportive, non-authoritarian)	–	–	+	+	–	–	+
7 high internal motivation (not forced to use L2, understands & sympathetic with objectives, responsible for own learning)	–	–	+	+	–	–	+
8 high self-confidence (fair chance to succeed, high teacher expectations)	–	–	+	+	–	–	+

L1-related linguistic, cognitive, pedagogical and social factors

	B	B	W	W	B	B	W
9 adequate linguistic development in L1 (L1 taught well (W), badly (B) or not at all in school)	−?	+?	+	+	−	−	+
10 enough relevant, cognitively demanding subject matter provided	−?	+?	+	+	−?	−?	+
11 opportunity to develop L1 outside school in linguistically demanding formal contexts	+?	−	+	−	+	−	+
12 L2-teaching supports (+) or harms (−) L1-development	+	+	+	+	−?	−	+

L2-related linguistic, cognitive, pedagogical and social factors

	B	B	W	W	B	B	W
13 adequate linguistic development in L2 (L2 taught well (W), badly (B) or not at all in school)	B	B	W	W	B	B	W
14 L2 input adapted to pupils' L2 level	+	+	+	+	−?	−	+
15 opportunity to practise L2 in peer group contexts	−	−	+	+?	−	−	−
16 exposure to native speaker L2 use in linguistically demanding formal contexts	−	+	+	+	−	+	+

LDS = low degree of success
HDS = high degree of success

their parents' labour is no longer needed or when they themselves become "too expensive" or "too troublesome" for West Germany (for instance when resisting assimilation and racism by political or other means).

In contrast to segregation, mother tongue (MT) maintenance programmes which also use the children's mother tongues as ME, show high levels of success—because the linguistic goals (bilingualism) and societal goals (equity and integration) are different. An example of *maintenance* for a *majority* is the MT-medium education given in the Soviet republic of Uzbekistan to the seven main language groups, including the dominant group, the Uzbeks. Since the main groups are all in the same position educationally, with the same rights, they are here treated as together forming a majority. In Uzbekistan, where only a tiny élite was literate 70 years ago when the country was still under feudal conditions, all children now complete at least 10 years of education. The main groups have the right to education through the medium of their own languages, with Russian or another Uzbekian language as a second language.

Examples of *maintenance* for *minorities* are the Finnish-medium classes for the Finnish migrant population in Sweden (or Spanish-medium classes for the Chicana population in the USA), both still rare. The first three cohorts of Finnish youngsters who have gone through the whole comprehensive school (nine years) in Finnish in Botkyrka, a suburb of Stockholm, continue their education in upper secondary schools in the more academic streams to a somewhat greater extent than Swedish youngsters from the same schools (Hagman & Lahdenperä, this volume).

An example of *submersion*[5] for a *majority* is education through the medium of a former colonial language in many African countries, for instance Zambia (Chishimba, 1984). For the vast majority of the population the results are poor, both academically and linguistically (Africa, 1980). The linguistic goal achieved is dominance in English for the élite, and, for the masses, dominance in their mother tongues (which the school does nothing to develop) and limited proficiency in English.

Submersion programmes for *minorities* are still by far the most common way of educating both indigenous and immigrant minorities in most countries in the world. Even in Sweden, where we have come a long way, some 80% of the immigrant children are educated this way, through the medium of Swedish, regardless of the fact that *all immigrant organizations in every Scandinavian country demand mother tongue medium education*. Most migrants, for instance in the UK and West Germany (except Turks in Bavaria who are in segregation programmes and some Greek and other migrants in maintenance programmes), undergo submersion, resulting in dominance in the majority language at the expense of the mother tongue, and poor school achievement. Societally this means assimilation for some (depending on whether the country in question allows assimilation or not) and marginalization for the many. It should, perhaps, also be added that *transitional programmes*[6] belong to the submersion type, too; they are simply a version of submersion which is a bit more sophisticated than direct submersion (see my typology in Skutnabb-Kangas, 1984: 125–133).

By contrast, Canadian *immersion*[7] programmes, in which English-speaking *majority* children are educated through the medium of an L2 (mostly French, but several other languages are also in operation: see Lambert & Taylor, 1982), lead to high levels of bilingualism and success at school (Swain & Lapkin, 1982). The societal goals include linguistic and cultural enrichment for the power majority, and increased employment prospects and other benefits for an élite. As is clear from the definition of immersion programmes, the concept cannot, by definition, be applied to minorities.

To summarize so far, in all HDS contexts the *linguistic goal* has been *bilingualism*, and the *societal goal* has been a *positive* one for the group concerned. In all LDS contexts, the *linguistic goal* has been *dominance in one of the languages*, either L1 or L2. *NOT* bilingualism. The other language (non-ME) has been neglected or taught badly. The *societal goal* has been to *keep the group* (or at least most of them) *in a powerless subordinate position*.

Next we turn to how the programmes are organized, in order to see the extent to which they create optimal conditions for efficient L2-learning and bilingualism. The preconditions for learning L2 effectively and for becoming bilingual have been grouped into four categories, called *organizational* factors, *learner-related affective* factors, and *linguistic, cognitive, pedagogical and social L1-related and L2-related* factors, respectively. These factors are chosen to reflect the present views in different disciplines in relation to important or necessary preconditions for L2-learning and bilingualism.

How do different programmes support L2-learning and bilingualism?

We start with *organizational factors. Alternative programmes* (Table 1.3, factor 1) are available only in the HDS programmes, i.e. in maintenance and immersion contexts. These programmes are optional. An

Uzbek or Tadjik in the USSR, a Finn in Sweden or a Chicana in the USA who wants education through the medium of Russian, Swedish or English (instead of Uzbek, Tadjik, Finnish or Spanish, respectively), can opt for that. An English-speaking Canadian child can choose between English-medium education or a French-medium immersion programme. By contrast, children in segregation or submersion programmes have no choice. Either alternatives do not even exist, as in most submersion programmes, or, if they do, children in segregation or submersion programmes are precluded from them administratively or economically.

Factor 2 covers whether there are *in the same class both native speakers of the medium of education (ME) and pupils for whom the ME is an L2.* This is a normal situation in submersion programmes, disadvantaging the L2-*learners.* In Zambia, the pupils' class background and geographical location (urban or rural) has a decisive influence on their prior knowledge of English. In all the other programmes pupils are, in relation to prior familiarity with the ME, on an equal footing in that initially either they all know the language of instruction (segregation and maintenance) or none of them do (immersion).

The third factor shows that the HDS programmes have teachers who are *both bilingual and well trained.* For instance, in immersion programmes, the teacher understands everything that the English-speaking children say in English, even if she herself speaks only French to the children. Thus the children can communicate all their needs to the teacher initially in their L1, and only later start doing so in L2 when they feel confident enough. The LDS programmes have either well trained monolingual teachers who do not understand their pupils' mother tongues (submersion for minorities) or else the training of the teachers is inadequate, even if they are to some extent bilingual (for instance segregation, and submersion for majorities in Zambia). We consider, though, that a bilingual (mostly meaning minority group) teacher without any training is usually a better choice than a monolingual well trained teacher. This is especially so in second language contexts, where the pupil hears L2 outside school anyway. Especially in relation to small children, it is close to criminal, real psychological torture, to use monolingual teachers who do not understand what the child has to say in her mother tongue. Not giving minority teachers a good training, adjusted to the conditions in the receiving country, is one of the reflections of the institutional racism in the Western countries. At the same time it protects the employment prospects of majority teachers, and makes minority children's failure in schools look like the children's fault, instead of the deficiency of the school system which it of course is.

Factor 4 shows that most of the LDS programmes lack *bilingual materials*. The materials actually used (factor 5) in them are imported or racist or both, thus imposing alien cultural values.

The *learner-related affective factors* suggest that a supportive learning environment and non-authoritarian teaching reduce *anxiety* (6). *Internal motivation* (7) is increased when the pupil is not *forced* to use L2, and can start producing L2 utterances only when she feels ready for it. Again this stresses the importance of bilingual teachers, because the child is forced to use L2 if the teacher does not understand the child's L1. High motivation is also related to an understanding of and sympathy with the educational objectives and to sharing in responsibility for one's own learning (which is difficult without bilingual materials). *High self-confidence* (8) is related to whether learners have a real chance of succeeding in school, and to favourable teacher expectations. One of the conditions for this is that the teacher accepts and values the child's mother tongue and cultural group, and is sympathetic with the parents' way of thinking, even though the teacher might have a different class background from the parents. There is a positive correlation between a plus-rating on these three factors (low anxiety, high motivation and high self-confidence) and the successful programmes.

The final two sets cover *linguistic, cognitive, pedagogical and social language-related factors*. *Linguistic development in L1* (9) is inadequate when the MT is taught badly, as in most segregation programmes (which should not be blamed on the teachers!) or not at all, as in most submersion programmes. It should also be mentioned that a couple of hours a week of mother tongue instruction for a minority child is more therapeutic cosmetics than language teaching.

Enough *relevant cognitively demanding subject matter* (10) to promote the common underlying proficiency for all languages (CALP: see Cummins, 1984; Skutnabb-Kangas, 1984) is provided in the HDS programmes. This is done through the medium of L1 in maintenance and through L2 in immersion (where it is made sure that the children understand, and where it has been shown that they can transfer the knowledge: see Swain & Lapkin, 1982). The input may satisfy this criterion in some segregation programmes, because the pupils at least understand the instruction. In submersion, when both language and subject matter are unfamiliar, it is less likely (for details see Skutnabb-Kangas, 1984). If the child learns how to use language as an effective instrument for thinking and problem solving in one language (by gaining a lot of relevant knowledge and using it), this capacity can also be transferred to other languages.

In addition to L1-development in school, pupils also need the *opportunity to develop their MTs outside school in linguistically demanding formal contexts* (11). Otherwise they are restricted to being able to discuss everyday things in informal settings only. This opportunity exists at least to a certain extent for all indigenous groups, but not for immigrants. Some groups may therefore be able to compensate for inadequate school provision outside the school setting. A more general factor which influences whether the language learning situation is additive (Lambert, 1975: you *add* a new language to your existing linguistic repertoire, without losing your mother tongue) or subtractive (another language replaces the mother tongue) is the degree to which *L2-teaching supports or harms L1-development* (12). Only submersion programmes threaten the MTs in this way.

Linguistic development in L2 (13) is inadequate when the L2 is badly taught, as it is in all the LDS programmes. A teacher, monolingual in L2, can never be a really good L2 teacher! A good L2 teacher knows both languages.

Also relevant is the degree to which *L2 input is adapted to pupils' L2 level* (14). It is difficult to adapt the input in this way in immigrant submersion contexts, because the difference in the pupils' proficiency in the same class is too great. The task is relatively more feasible when no pupils are native speakers of the ME, as in Zambia.

Absence of the *opportunity to practise the L2 in peer group contexts outside school* (15) may be due to practicalities (immersion children do not meet many L2 children), to sheer racism (Turkish children are often avoided by German children), or to a shortage of L2 native speakers, as in Zambia, or as in Bantu education, where institutionalized racism and apartheid aggravate the situation.

Exposure to native speaker L2 use in linguistically demanding formal contexts (16) depends on the existence of L2 institutions staffed by native L2 speakers. Turks in West Germany cannot escape exposure to native German, whereas Zambians are exposed to a range of non-native Englishes, some of them appropriate regional models, some of them interlanguages (= languages spoken by learners of English) (but see Kachru, 1986).[8]

As we can see from the chart (Table 1.3), there is a clear difference between the programmes in that the HDS programmes with bilingualism as the linguistic goal and with positive societal goals have organized the teaching so that many of the preconditions for efficient L2 learning and bilingualism are met. The LDS programmes do so to a much lesser extent.

This comparison also functions as a validation of the way we attributed goals to the different programmes—otherwise it might have been claimed that we first looked at the results and then attributed positive goals to the HDS programmes and negative goals to the LDS programmes. Likewise, the comparison validates our claims about linguicism.

We can see that the situation for those who would want to organize minority children's education properly is tricky in those countries where the exploitation of a minority (or a powerless majority, as in Namibia) is open and brutal. Measures which under different, less oppressive conditions would be positive (like mother tongue medium education) can in the hands of an oppressive regime become instruments for segregation and apartheid.

We can also draw a conclusion by taking an example from the European situation. As long as West Germany uses Turkey as its Bantustan, from which it fetches workers (whose childhood and education costs have been paid by their parents and the Turkish society) when it needs them, and sends them back when it no longer needs them or when they become old, sick or unemployed, it seems difficult to do much by changing things in the schools in West Germany. Still, at the same time as progressive people work for the political changes needed in order to give minorities human conditions in West Germany, preparation for change is needed in schools, too. It is necessarily a defensive strategy, a defensive line of argumentation, that must be used, as long as societal conditions do not allow the type of offensive strategies we use in Scandinavia, and as long as the results of using an offensive strategy might be misused so as to strengthen the segregation.

We migrants in the Scandinavian countries, especially those of us who come from the other Scandinavian countries, *cannot be thrown out*, and that provides a different basis for our work. The defensive strategy, necessary in openly linguicist countries like West Germany, thus involves using arguments to legitimize the minority mother tongue in schools, which emphasize its instrumental value in learning the majority language. The offensive strategy used in Scandinavia emphasizes the human rights argument for legitimizing the minority mother tongues. The defensive line of argumentation may later on function as a negative boomerang, because the argument itself is linguicist. But choice of argument to be used is determined by the stage at which the society in question finds itself in the historical development of minority education.

In the final section we shall look at these stages. Who is to blame, according to the analyses on which different measures are based? Whose fault is it thought to be that minority children experience difficulties in school? Is it the child who is deficient, or is the society that controls the school "deficient", i.e. linguicist and racist?

Deficient children or deficient schools and societies?

We shall chart stages in the development of minority education in different countries. This is partly based on a report by Stacy Churchill for OECD, Centre for Educational Research and Innovation (CERI) (see Churchill, 1985). The readers are invited to look at the measures in their own countries and communities and try to place them in the scheme. What has been done, based on what problem definition, and with what goal? Table 1.4 summarizes the development.

When minority children experience problems in school, a *reason for the problems* is diagnosed, explicitly or implicitly. Then *measures* are suggested and taken to alleviate the problems. Behind the measures one can also discern an opinion about the *future of the minorities*: are these going to (be allowed to) maintain their languages and cultures, or are they going to disappear fast, or in some generations, to be assimilated into the majority? If they are not going to be assimilated immediately, is this seen as good and positive or bad and divisive for the society?

The first four phases in the development which most countries seem to be going through are based on *deficit theories*. There is *something wrong with the minority child* (1, L2-related handicap: the child does not know enough of the majority language), *the minority parents* (2, socially conditioned handicap: the parents are working class), *the whole minority group* (3, culturally conditioned handicap: the child's cultural background is "different"), *or all of these* (4, L1-related handicap: the child does not know her own language and culture properly, and this leaves her without a firm basis for L2-learning, and gives her poor self-confidence). To a small extent there may also be something lacking in majority *individuals* (not systems), peers and teachers who may discriminate, because they have not had enough information.

In these four phases it is envisaged that the minority should become majority-language-speaking fast (1, 2). But as long as the children still speak their original mother tongue, the school should help them to appreciate it (3, 4). The main measures depend on which specific handicap the child is thought to suffer from. It seems that the measures from earlier phases are continued when the school system moves to the next phase.

Different European countries seem to show a somewhat different course of development. In Scandinavia, especially Sweden, we have focused much on the language handicaps (1 and especially 4). This has been mainly because of us Finns. We are the largest immigrant group in Sweden, and our social structure and cultural traits are relatively close to those of Sweden, partly as a result of the 650 years of colonization by Sweden. We Finns differ from the Swedes mainly in relation to language. Swedish is Indo-European, Northern Germanic, Finnish is Finno-Ugric, not related at all. The United Kingdom/Queendom has focused on cultural differences (3), in addition to the L2-related handicap (1), and the mother tongue deprivation discussions have barely started. West Germany has focused more on the social handicap explanations (2), in addition to cultural and linguistic L2-related handicaps, especially in relation to the largest migrant minority group, people from Turkey.

When one looks at the measures on a pan-European level, most energy just now is being spent on measures based on the later phases in the cultural deficiency explanation. The interculturalism seen in government declarations and invading all European teacher in-service training courses and new curricula is important to analyse because it still represents deficiency models, even if the package in which it is served (ethnicism and linguicism) is much more appetizing than was the old "racism-based-on-biological-differences".

It is also important to note that many of the measures, taken on the basis of the different explanations of reasons for problems, may be needed in many ways. It is good for minority children to have additional tuition in L2 and to learn more about their own culture, and it is useful that majority children and teachers learn something about minority cultures. And it is, as we have shown, necessary for minority children to develop their mother tongues in MT-medium programmes. But it is the *basis* for these measures which is wrong. All of them, even the mother tongue deprivation model, see the *child* as deficient and lacking, and try to compensate for the "deficiencies", in order for the child to change to fit the school. It is still considered to be a deficiency in European schools to have another mother tongue and cultural background than the majority of the pupils and not to be middle class (and a boy).

The *enrichment theories* start from the conception that schools should be adapted to the children, not vice versa. The child's mother tongue and cultural and social background should be a positive starting point for the school. The existence of minorities is seen as costly but enriching for societies, and bilingualism/biculturalism is seen as beneficial and stimulating for the child. If minority children experience problems in school, these may be due to the extra work involved (5) or, in the last phase (6), either to similar reasons as for monolingual children or to these and racism, linguicism and discrimination. Only the last phase implies *transformative change* (see Mullard, 1985a); all the others are more or less liberal/reformist. And it is only the last phase which can start to combat linguicism.

TABLE 1.4

Reason for problems	Measure	Goal
Deficit theories		
1 *Linguistic L2-related handicap, learning deficit* (the child does not master L2 well enough)	*More teaching of MaL* (auxiliary teaching, ESL, introductory classes etc); compensatory	MI is to become MaL-speaking as fast as possible
2 *Social handicap, socially linked learning deficit* (the child's parents come from lowest social classes)	*More social and pedagogical help* (aids, tutors, psychologists, social workers, career advisers etc); in addition to measure 1; compensatory	Same as 1
3 *Cultural handicap, culturally linked learning deficit* (the child has a "different" cultural background; the child has low self-confidence; the child is discriminated against	*Inform MI-children about MA-culture/about their own culture;* inform all children about MI-cultures/ start multicultural/intercultural educational programmes; eliminate discrimination/racism in teaching materials; attitudinal courses for teachers; in addition to measures 1 and 2; compensatory	MiL in the family 1–2 generations; MI-children need help to appreciate MI-culture (until they become MaL-speaking)

4 Linguistic *L1-related handicap, learning deficit because of L1 deprivation* (the child does not know her own L properly and has therefore poor grounding for the learning of L2 CALP) (the child loses content while learning L2)	*Teaching of L1 as subject; elementary education through the medium of L1 with as fast a transition to L2-medium as possible.* MiL has no intrinsic value, it is therapeutic; compensatory (more self-confidence, better co-operation with home, gives better basis for MaL-learning, functions as bridge for transmission of content during L2-learning); in addition to measures 1 and 3	Same as 3

Enrichment theories

5 High levels of bilingualism beneficial for the individual but difficult to attain, demands much work and energy. The primary goal is to learn MaL properly; it is a prerequisite for equal opportunity	Teaching through the medium of MiL for several years inside MA-school; obligatory teaching of MaL; transition to MaL-medium teaching after elementary education	MiL is allowed to be maintained for private use; bilingualism necessary; MiL is allowed to exist (in a diglossic situation) as long as demographic basis exists
6 Bilingualism enhances development. If problems arise, the causes are similar to those of monolingual children; some problems may be caused by racism/discrimination	Separate, equal school systems for MI and MA children, L1 is medium for both and L2 obligatory (or possible to study) for both. Positive discrimination of the M1 economically (smaller units allowed)	Existence of minorities is enriching for the whole society. MiL has (at least some) official status and its use is encouraged, also for MaL-children

MI = minority; MiL = minority language; MA = majority; MaL = majority language.

The only labour immigrant minority in the world which has come to the first enrichment phase is Finns in Sweden. I am disregarding both (1) temporarily immigrated élites, NATO officers, diplomats, oil experts, international businesswomen and civil servants, etc., and (2) labour migrants who have set up their own schools at their own expense, without financial support from the receiving country. We are thus talking about education inside the ordinary state-supported educational system.

Very few minorities in the world have come to phase 6, if we think of minorities in terms of numbers. It is indicative that the best protected educational rights among this type of numerical minorities are enjoyed by present or former power minorities (such as white South Africans, a present power minority, or Swedish-speakers in Finland, a former power minority, descendants of former colonizers). It is thus indicative of the importance of political factors that until now not many countries have accepted the existence of minorities as an enrichment, unless these minorities have or have had the power to dictate the conditions. In some situations where there are equal minorities on both sides of the border (German-speakers in Denmark, Danish-speakers in Germany), this has been achieved. Some minorities in socialist countries have also succeeded. Many of these, for instance Yugoslavia, do organize the education of minorities in ways where the non-socialist countries have much to learn (see Bugarski (forthcoming); Göncz (forthcoming); Institute for Ethnic Studies, Ljubljana, 1985; Lük Necak, 1985; Mikes, 1984; Petrovic & Blagojevic, 1985). The USSR has done the same (see Drobizheva, 1986; Grigulevich & Kozlov (eds), 1981; Guboglo, 1986). Some minorities in a few Third World countries have come far, too, for instance in India (Ekka, 1984; Pattanayak, 1981). And some of the well-organized labour migrant minorities might succeed, too, if we know what we are doing and why. There is a wealth of international experience to share, because the linguicism is the same.

Conclusion

Trying to summarize extremely complicated matters in a short paper necessarily entails huge overgeneralizations, and the argumentation is to some extent crude shorthand (for a more detailed exposition see my *Bilingualism or not: the education of minorities*, 1984, 378 pages). A few general remarks in conclusion are of necessity even more shorthand.

High levels of bilingualism/biculturalism benefit every child, but for minority children bilingualism is a necessity. It is possible to achieve, if the main principle is followed, which seems to hold across different situations:

support via all institutional measures the language which is otherwise less likely to develop in the cognitively demanding decontextualized register.

This language which otherwise does not get the chance, is for the minority children their mother tongue, and for power majorities (such as English-speakers in Canada) a minority language. These are the "easy" cases. But what about the others?

If several minorities together form the majority, the choice of ME should reflect the power relations between the minority groups and the group whose language they want to learn as their second language. The weaker the minority groups, the stronger the emphasis on their own language. But being educated through the medium of one's own language and wanting to become bilingual necessitates either much contact with that second language *and* good teaching in it, given by bilingual well-trained teachers (as in the Uzbekistan case), or, if there is little contact with the second language (as in Zambia where there is little contact with native English-speakers), extremely good teaching in that language (which Zambia does not have). The absolute degrading of African languages during the colonial period and through neo-colonial economic politics and its con-comitant ideology has produced a colonized consciousness, where the African languages are in a weak position (and need all the support schools can give), even when the former colonial power is no longer physically present with armies (see Angula, 1984; Kalema, 1980, 1985; Mateene, 1980a and b, 1985a and b; Phillipson, 1986).

Very few educational programmes in Europe for migrant minorities try to make the children bilingual, even if many claim that they do. They practise linguicism, as we have shown. But why do they do that? If we as linguists tell them that all languages are of equal worth, and make them aware of the problems, might they not change? If we tell them how minority children should be educated in order for them to reach high levels of bilingualism and to achieve at school, would they not organize education accordingly?[9] Is it not a question of lack of information? The answer is a simple no.

Western industrial countries will need cheap labour at home in the future, too. The shitwork still needs to be done by somebody in Western countries.[10] The Third World produces much of the raw materials, food, clothing and equipment that we use. The exploitation of those countries now just takes different, more invisible forms than slavery and coloniz-ation, but it is at least equally severe. But we cannot export all of our cleaning, cooking, sweeping, public transport and washing up, or our sick and old, to be taken care of in the Third World, as easily as we export capital. Therefore, the industrial world needs to educate the children of the migrants, the great-grandchildren of the slaves from the colonies, for these jobs. Therefore, minority education needs to be racist and linguicist, in order to force the great-grandchildren of the slaves to continue to take the shitwork. In this it has succeeded.

Why so much fuss about language, then, if all these things are decided politically, anyway?—if what is best for a child linguistically, cognitively, pedagogically and socially does not count?—if language, in addition to that, can mislead our engagement so that we don't see how it is used in the interculturalism celebration to fool us, to prevent us from seeing the same old racism in its cultural clothes, in the assimilationist ethnicism?—and if power is all that matters anyway?

For three reasons, at least:

— we need our language for analysis. Without a thorough analysis we struggle in the dark

— we need our language for solidarity, both with our contemporaries, and across generations

— we need bilinguals as mediators. Those who are bi-something (bilingual, bidialectal, bicultural) have been forced to look at *two* different languages, dialects, cultures *from the inside*. It is easier for us bilinguals to *understand both parties*.

In a world at five to twelve (= on the verge of self-destruction) what is needed is *not* monolingual technical idiots (white, middle-class, male) who can make the missile and push the button. They are people who have never been forced to and who are probably not able to see matters from the inside from somebody else's point of view. You can obviously not discuss with a missile, but a real bilingual/bicultural might be able to mediate before the button is released, provided she has the instruments for analysis, and the solidarity.

It may be time for linguists also to realize that linguicism is not a bunch of ill-willed, misinformed individuals. It is not a question of information, but of power structure. Obviously, it is our job as linguists to produce information, but unless we know whose questions we ask in our research and why, we may unknowingly provide arguments for supporting linguicism and racism, especially the hidden, unconscious, invisible kind, which is the most difficult one to detect and to fight. A poster I have on my study door has, as a part of the devastating and beautiful picture by Malaquias Montoya, a text by G. R. Castillo: "One day the apolitical intellectuals of my country will be interrogated by the simplest of our people". Researchers are some sort of intellectuals, too, aren't we?

Notes to Chapter 1

1. Previously published in Phillipson, Robert and Skutnabb-Kangas, Tove, 1986, *Linguicism rules in education*, Roskilde, Roskilde University Centre, Institute VI, 42–72. Thanks to Eduardo Hernández-Chávez, Kahombo Mateene, Chris Mullard, D. P. Pattanayak, Markku Peura and Robert Phillipson for inspiring discussions and insights. Of course, none of them is responsible for the results. Thanks to Robert, too, for helping to nativize the language.

2. When using terms minority/majority, I define them in terms of power relationships, not (entirely) in terms of numbers. If "majority" is used to denote a numerically strong but politically weak group (like Blacks in South Africa), this is marked by calling them a powerless majority, implying that they have the capacity to become a "real" majority, i.e. to gain access to their fair share of power, which would be "more" than the power of the numerical minorities, among them the white power-minority. But using labels like "majority" and "minority" is unsatisfactory from another point of view, too: it obscures the class differences both between and, especially, within these groups, and makes them appear much more homogeneous than they are. The enormous heterogeneity of both "majorities" and "minorities" should be constantly borne in mind. Within each group there are contradictory and conflicting views, and this is one source of change in society.

3. Terms like "power élites" are often used in vague ways, as synonymous with "ruling class" or "decision-makers". The vagueness makes it difficult to distinguish between groups in power in less and more democratic political systems. Giddens (1973: 118–127) has an illuminating discussion of the differences, from the "strongest case" of a "ruling class" to the "weakest", i.e. most democratic, with "leadership groups". All of these groups can decide about the official language or the language of instruction. The decisions tend to be more beneficial for minorities in the "weaker" formations.

4. "Mastery", of course, has sexist connotations, in addition to its (for me) negative class connotations. Many of the words many of us use unawares every day are living examples of the hidden, unconscious sexism, racism and classism in our societies. There are many good

candidates even in this paper, and where they have been unavoidable (because explanations would be too long) I have at least tried to mark my distance (for instance when calling French, English and German "modern" "European" languages).

5. A *submersion*, or sink-or-swim programme, is a programme where linguistic minority children with a low-status mother tongue are forced to accept instruction through the medium of a foreign majority language with high status, in classes where some children are native speakers of the language of instruction, where the teacher does not understand the mother tongue of the minority children, and where the majority language constitutes a threat to their mother tongue—a subtractive language learning situation.

6. A *transitional programme* is a programme where linguistic minority children with a low-status mother tongue are instructed through the medium of their mother tongue for a few years and where their mother tongue has no intrinsic value, only an instrumental value. It is used only in order for the children to learn the majority language better, and in order to give them some subject matter knowledge while they are learning the majority language. As soon as they can function in the majority language orally, they are transferred to a majority language medium programme. A transitional programme is a more sophisticated version of submersion programmes, a more "humane" way of assimilating.

7. An *immersion* programme is a programme where linguistic majority children with a high-status mother tongue voluntarily choose (among existing alternatives) to be instructed through the medium of a foreign (minority) language, in classes with majority children with the same mother tongue only, where the teacher is bilingual so that the children in the beginning can use their own language, and where their mother tongue is in no danger of not developing or of being replaced by the language of instruction—an additive language learning situation.

8. The worldwide spread of English has led to local variants becoming established, first in North America, later in Third World countries. There is now an increasing tendency to regard such "nativized" forms as Indian English or West African English as authentic local norms. Native speakers of these variants represent the norm (Kachru, 1986) even in situations where they may have English as their second language. Thus "exposure to native speaker language" may be a more varied concept than the one implicit in the text (see also Phillipson, 1986).

9. You can often hear school administrators say that they would like to adhere to some of the principles referred to in this chapter, and indeed instruct minority children through the medium of their mother tongues. But it just so happens that they have 49 different languages in one single school (a situation which is not unusual), and therefore they can do nothing. It is impossible to justify that one group gets such instruction, when the 48 others do not. This is, with due respect to the practical difficulties involved, a false argument. There are many innovative ways of solving most of the problems, *if the political will exists* (small classes, age-integrated classes, bussing, firm long-term planning which guarantees instruction through the medium of certain languages at certain places for a long time so that people with those mother tongues can move to where they know there will be instruction, co-operation across school district (and even country) borders, summer camps, guaranteeing young minority people teacher jobs in advance if they promise to undergo training, etc., etc.). In most cases practical arguments are used to mask the real arguments, and the issue of principle is avoided.

10. It is sometimes claimed that there is a high correlation between the percentage of women on the labour market and the percentage of foreigners in the lower sectors of the dual labour market. Simplified: if domestic women go out to work and do not do the shitwork, foreigners have to be imported to do it, because domestic men refuse to do it. Good counter-examples are Finland and Saudi Arabia. In Finland most women are gainfully employed (around 48% of the total work-force is female) but there is virtually no migrant labour. In Saudi Arabia there are very few domestic women working outside their homes, but there is a big migrant labour force. Likewise, the welfare state is sometimes blamed: when people do not take care of their children, the sick and the old at home any longer, the new work thus created goes to migrants. Again, Finland and Saudi Arabia are counter-examples: Finland manages with the welfare state and without migrants, Saudi Arabia does not, regardless of the presence of migrants. Both arguments are parts of the conservative ideology, refusing to admit the function of migrants for capitalist societies.

References

AFRICA, H. 1980, *Language in education in a multilingual state: a case study of the role of English in the educational system of Zambia.* Ph.D. Dissertation, Toronto: University of Toronto.

ANGULA, N. 1984, English as a medium of communication for Namibia: Trends and possibilities. In COMMONWEALTH SECRETARIAT & SWAPO 1984, pp. 9–12.

BUGARSKI, R. (forthcoming), Language policy and language planning in Yugoslavia. To appear in French in J. MAURAIS (ed.), *L'aménagement linguistique comparé*. Quebec & Paris: Conseil de la langue française, le Robert.

CALVET, L. J. 1974, *Linguistique et Colonialisme*. Petit Traité de Glottophagie. Paris: Petite Bibliothèque Payot.

CHISHIMBA, M. M. 1984, Language policy and education in Zambia. *International Education Journal* 1984, 1:2, 151–180.

CHURCHILL, S. 1985, *The education of linguistic and cultural minorities in the OECD countries*. Clevedon: Multilingual Matters 13.

COMMONWEALTH SECRETARIAT & SWAPO 1984, *English Language Programme for Namibians*. Seminar Report, Lusaka, 19–27 October 1983.

CUMMINS, J. 1984, *Bilingualism and special education: Issues in assessment and pedagogy*. Clevedon: Multilingual Matters 6.

DROBIZHEVA, L. 1986, Social and psychological aspects of inter-ethnic relations in the USSR. In Y. V. ARUTIUNIAN (ed.), *Multilingualism: Aspects of interpersonal and intergroup communication in pluricultural societies*. Moscow: Institute of Ethnography of the Academy of Sciences of the USSR. pp. 19–31.

EKKA, F. 1984, Status of minority languages in the schools of India. *International Education Journal* 1984, 1:1, 1–19.

GIDDENS, A. 1973, *The class structure of the advanced societies*. London: Hutchinson.

GRIGULEVICH, I. R. & KOZLOV, S. Ya. (eds) 1981, *Ethnocultural processes and national problems in the modern world*. Moscow: Progress Publishers.

GÖNCZ, L. (forthcoming), Psychological studies of bilingualism in Vojvodina. In Yugoslavian General Linguistics.

GUBOGLO, M. 1986, Language and communication in Soviet society. In Y. V. ARUTIUNIAN (ed.), *Multilingualism: Aspects of interpersonal and intergroup communication in pluricultural societies*. Moscow: Institute of Ethnography of the Academy of Sciences of the USSR. pp. 3–18.

INSTITUTE FOR ETHNIC STUDIES (Ljubljana) 1985, Some Yugoslav experiences in the achievement of the equality of the nations and nationalities in the field of education. Paper presented at the National seminar on Education in multicultural societies. Ljubljana, 15–17 October.

KACHRU, B. B. 1986, *The alchemy of English. The spread, functions and models of non-native Englishes*. Oxford: Pergamon Press.

KALEMA, J. 1980, Report on functions and activities of the OAU Inter-African Bureau of Languages. In K. MATEENE & J. KALEMA (eds), 1980, pp. 1–8.

—— 1985, Introduction. In K. MATEENE, J. KALEMA & B. CHOMBA (eds), 1985, pp. 1–6.

LAMBERT, W. 1975, Culture and language as factors in learning and education. In A. WOLFGANG (ed.), 1975.

LAMBERT, W. & TAYLOR, D. 1982, Language in the education of ethnic minority immigrants: Issues, problems and methods. Paper presented to Conference on Education of Ethnic Minority Immigrants, Miami.

LÜK NECAK, A. 1985, Education in multicultural societies and its social implications. Paper presented at the National seminar on Education in multicultural societies. Ljubljana, 15–17 October.

MATEENE, K. 1980a, Introduction. In K. MATEENE & J. KALEMA (eds), 1980, pp. vi–vii.

—— 1980b, Failure in the obligatory use of European languages in Africa and the advantages of a policy of linguistic independence. In K. MATEENE & J. KALEMA (eds), 1980, pp. 9–41.

—— 1985a, Colonial languages as compulsory means of domination, and indigenous languages, as necessary factors of liberation and development. In K. MATEENE, J. KALEMA & B. CHOMBA (eds), 1985, pp. 60–69.

—— 1985b, Reconsideration of the official status of colonial languages in Africa. In K. MATEENE, J. KALEMA & B. CHOMBA (eds), 1985, pp. 18–28.

MATEENE, K. & KALEMA, J. (eds) 1980, *Reconsideration of African linguistic policies*. Kampala: OAU Bureau of Languages, OAU/BIL Publication 3.

MATEENE, K., KALEMA, J. & CHOMBA, B. (eds) 1985, *Linguistic liberation and unity of Africa*. Kampala: OAU Bureau of Languages, OAU/BIL Publication 6.

MIKES, M. 1984, Instruction in the mother tongue in Yugoslavia. *Prospects*, XIV:1, 1984, 121–131.

MULLARD, C. 1985a, Racism, ethnicism and etharchy or not? The principles of progressive control and transformative change. This volume, Ch. 17; originally presented as a plenary paper at the International Symposium on Minority Languages in Academic Research and Educational Policy, Sandbjerg Slot, Denmark, April 1985.

—— 1985b, *Race, power and resistance*. London: Routledge & Kegan Paul.

PATTANAYAK, D. P. 1981, *Multilingualism and mother tongue education*. Delhi: Oxford University Press.

—— 1986, Educational use of the mother tongue. In B. SPOLSKY (ed.), 1986, pp. 5–15.

PETROVIC, R. & BLAGOJEVIC, M. 1985, The educational structure of ethnic groups in Yugoslavia. Paper presented at the National seminar on Education in multicultural societies, Ljubljana, 15–17 October.

PHILLIPSON, R. 1986, *The rule of English*. In R. PHILLIPSON & T. SKUTNABB-KANGAS.

PHILLIPSON, R. & SKUTNABB-KANGAS, T. 1983, *Cultilingualism—papers in cultural and communicative (in)competence*. ROLIG-papir 28, Roskilde Universitetscenter.

——1986, *Linguicism rules in education*, 3 volumes, Roskilde University Centre, Institute VI: Roskilde.

PHILLIPSON, R., SKUTNABB-KANGAS, T. & AFRICA, H. 1986, Namibian educational language planning: English for liberation or neo-colonialism? In B. SPOLSKY (ed.), 1986, pp. 77–95.

SKUTNABB-KANGAS, T. 1984, *Bilingualism or not: the education of minorities*. Clevedon: Multilingual Matters 7.

——1986, Who wants to change what and why—conflicting paradigms in minority education research. In B. SPOLSKY (ed), 1986, pp. 153–81.

SPOLSKY, B. (ed.) 1986, *Language and education in multilingual settings*. Clevedon: Multilingual Matters 25.

SWAIN, M. & LAPKIN, S. 1982, *Evaluating bilingual education: A Canadian case study*. Clevedon: Multingual Matters.

WOLFGANG, A. (ed.) 1975, *Education of immigrant students*. Toronto: Ontario Institute for Studies in Education.

2 Language policy and language rights in the United States

Issues in bilingualism

EDUARDO HERNÁNDEZ-CHÁVEZ

On a cultural level, language is the symbolic expression of community, encoding a group's values, its folkways and its history. Socially, it is the most powerful means of interaction and communication, and it is through language that an individual or a group seeks and attains participation in society. The denial of a people's development and use of its native tongue is thus a denial of its participation in society and of its very peoplehood.

The concept of language rights, in its most general sense, refers to the right of a people to learn, to keep and to use its own language in all manner of public and private business. This is a human right.

But it is not always a civil right. In a given polity, where a people speaks a language different from that of a politically and economically dominant group, the language of intergroup interaction and the degree of participation in the dominant society by the subordinate group become issues of civil policy. The ethnic minority (or subordinate majority) demands the right to take part in the institutions that affect its well-being. The dominant society, on the other hand, has at stake control of those institutions and devises mechanisms to limit the access of subordinate groups to them. Language is one of the most effective means towards this end. Requirements to learn and to use the language of the dominant group bar from effective participation all those who have not acquired the dominant tongue to a level of proficiency that is usually very rigidly defined. (And to those who do acquire such mastery, other barriers to full access are in place.)

Even in liberal societies where universal participation is the ideal, similar processes are at work, though perhaps in more subtle ways. Such societies maintain an interest in developing political and philosophical unity among diverse groups and view linguistic and cultural homogeneity as an important ingredient of that process. Language rights are seen as contrary to these goals.

Justice Holmes, in a dissenting opinion in *Meyer v. Nebraska* (262 U.S. 390, 401–3, 1923) put the matter succinctly for language policy in the United States:

> "We all agree, I take it, that it is desirable that all citizens of the United States should speak a common tongue, and therefore that the end aimed at by the statute is a lawful and proper one."

The statute referred to was a Nebraska law which, responding to the anti-German feelings following World War I, prohibited the teaching of any subject in a non-English language below the eighth grade. Twenty-one States had passed similar legislation. Although the court majority found that these laws violated the due process protections of the Fourteenth Amendment, Holmes' dissent affirmed the popular sentiment of the period regarding language minorities:

> "Youth is the time when familiarity with a language is established and ... I am not prepared to say that it is unreasonable to provide that in his [the child's] early years he shall speak and hear only English at school."

Nearly 50 years later, the California Supreme Court in *Castro v. California* (2 Cal. 3d 223, 1970) declared,

> "The state interest in maintaining a single language system is substantial and the provision of ballots, notices, ballot pamphlets, etc., in Spanish is not necessary either to the formation of intelligent opinions on election issues or to the implementation of those opinions through the mechanics of balloting."

(In 1973, Congress passed Public Law 94-73 mandating bilingual education election materials, including ballots, in political subdivisions in which more than 5% of the voters were of a single language minority and had an illiteracy rate higher than the national average. By 1976, California, following the federal lead, required the posting of facsimile ballot measures and ballot instructions in Spanish in all precincts not covered by provisions of the federal law although actual ballots in Spanish were not universally required.)

The issue for American language minorities is thus joined. Both *Meyer* and *Castro* found that while the private use of a minority language could not be regulated, full participation in American society equal to that of the dominant group demanded mastery of English. Non-English languages had no standing in law.

Such a situation is—or should be—intolerable to Chicanos, for it ultimately entails either a perpetual inaccessibility to American institutions or the loss of our ethnic language with the concomitant weakening of cultural strengths and sense of community.

The latter assertion merits elaboration. Many scholars, including Chicanos, hold that Spanish is and will remain a viable language among Chicanos indefinitely into the future. (See, for example, Skrabanek, 1970; Fishman & Hofman, 1966.) The basis of this reasoning is the continuing large-scale immigration from Mexico and the growth of the Spanish-speaking population. Most projections estimate that Mexicans will be the largest ethnic minority by the end of the 1980s (Macias, 1977).

There exists also the widespread belief that the learning of English is merely additive, that Chicanos are becoming a nation of bilinguals who use English for some purposes and Spanish for others. English is the appropriate language for participation in general American society and Spanish (or a mixture of Spanish and English) is the language of the home and of the community. Even as astute an observer as California Appeals Court Justice Cruz Reynoso has noted that

"... as the years go by the Mexican-American people and people of other Latin-American cultures are going to be bilingual and bicultural, and we must all speak English as our first language. So there is no need to make Spanish an official language ..." (Humanities Network Newsletter 4: 1.9.1980)

However, recent analyses seriously question these assumptions (Thompson, 1974; Hernández-Chávez, 1978). Spanish is numerically very strong and growing stronger. But, torn from its Mexican foundations, it is structurally unsound and in danger of toppling. Mounting evidence demonstrates that the language is now being lost by second-generation Chicanos and, among large numbers of people, even within the first generation (Thompson, 1974; Laosa, 1975).

Were this linguistic acculturation accompanied by a stable bilingualism, the ethnic language would remain strong, and we would become a bilingual and bicultural society. But it is not. The necessity of using English for all important purposes in the society outside the family in the final analysis makes Spanish superfluous even within the family, the last bastion of its survival.

This erosion of language has its cause in the very denial of language rights enunciated by Justice Holmes, which is a fundamental tenet of language minority policies in the United States. Even the most basic contact with American institutions requires a destructive amount of linguistic acculturation.

The importance of language rights then becomes evident. For minority groups language rights should include the right to learn both the mother tongue and the majority language fully, i.e. to become fully bilingual.

Historical context

Official attitudes toward bilingualism in American society have historically depended upon the political and social status of particular language minority groups. If a group has been viewed as alien to the prevailing notions of American culture, harsh sanctions have invariably been imposed on language practices. That these sanctions are applied in conjunction with other legislative and administrative restrictions is a clear indication that the issues are much broader than language. They revolve around the rights of groups to participate fully in the economic and political life of the country and at the same time to retain their distinctive character as an ethnic group.

The United States does not have and has not had an official language policy. English is not established by the Constitution nor has Congress passed any law recognizing English as the national language of the United States. Nevertheless, the strong Anglo-Saxon traditions of the country, coupled with myriad state and federal laws imposing the language for particular purposes, have made English the *de facto* national language.

In recent years, there has been a growing movement, spearheaded by a group known as US English, to specify English in the Constitution as the sole official language of the United States. The movement gathers impetus from many sources. Japanese successes in the market-place, Arab control of oil supplies, and the taking of hostages in the Middle East, among other factors, create a sense of being under siege by foreigners. But the strongest and most immediate motivation is the deep apprehension about the greatest migration of Mexicans in North American history (to which are added large numbers of political refugees from El Salvador and Guatemala). As a consequence, the states bordering Mexico have been targeted by US English for constitutional amendments naming English as the only official language.

Successes in these states are expected to pave the road toward a national constitutional amendment. Already California, through Proposition 63 passed in November 1986, has incorporated such an amendment into its own Constitution.

Where no laws exist that govern linguistic practice, the assumption is always that English is to be the official language.

Historically, the vicissitudes of language policies have reflected the political and economic conditions prevailing in an era and the popular attitudes that these have engendered. The first several decades from the foundation of the republic were characterized by tolerance or even acceptance of other language groups. In particular, the Germans were strong allies of the English colonists in the War of Independence, and many documents, including the Articles of Confederation, were written in German and English. In the first third of the nineteenth century, new groups of German immigrants settled in the Midwest where they instituted German schools and engaged in political activity through German. They were a majority group in the areas they settled and were seen as patriotic and loyal to the United States, so their language and culture posed no threat to the English.

By the mid-nineteenth century, attitudes toward non-English groups began to change, and language became an important focus of inter-ethnic conflict and discrimination. The source of some of the conflict was religion and economic competition, as in the case of the Catholic Irish. Attempts to curb their political participation took the form of English literacy requirements for voting that were enacted in several states.

With the influx of European immigration reaching its peak in the latter half of the century, anti-foreigner bias extended even to the German population, many of whom were also Catholic. The use of German in the schools was discontinued in many midwestern cities and legislation was passed to force English to be used as the language of instruction in private as well as public schools.

In California during this same period, the conflict between Anglo-Saxons and Mexicans centred on land and mining rights. Although the Monterey Convention had official translators and provided for documents to be written in both Spanish and English, by 1855 a series of discriminatory laws and regulations was passed. All instruction in the schools had to be in English; the publication of laws in Spanish was suspended by legislation; court proceedings were required to be held in English. These laws had a clear economic and political basis and were intended to establish and maintain the control exercised by the Anglo group.

The sentiments against non-Anglo minorities continued unabated throughout the latter half of the century. In California, additional repressive laws were passed requiring all schools—public and private—to conduct instruction in English. Literacy requirements were enacted and English was mandated as the sole language of official proceedings.

In New Mexico, liberalism toward Mexicans prevailed for a longer period. As late as the 1880s, public elementary schools were conducted bilingually and state laws were written first in Spanish, then translated into English. However, by the last decade of the century, the struggle over land became acute, and this was accompanied by a spate of repressive legislation. All schools were now required to teach in English. The New Mexico Enabling Act instituted English as the language of instruction and required English literacy as a condition for holding public office.

With but brief lulls, xenophobic attitudes were played out against other groups and in other locales well into the present century. Beginning in the first decade of the century, political unrest in Mexico brought increasing numbers of Mexicans into Texas and other areas. Texas quickly passed laws requiring English to be the sole language of instruction and instituted segregated schools. Bills were introduced in Congress to limit immigration from Mexico, but these were defeated by agricultural and railroad interests.

World War I heightened anti-German and anti-foreigner feeling to the point of hysteria. German was banned as the language of instruction in 34 States and in some locales the use of German in public places was prohibited. Hawaii and California passed anti-Chinese and anti-Japanese statutes, such as the California Alien Land Law and the licensing and regulation of private schools in Hawaii.

The depression and World War II re-inflamed anti-foreigner sentiment, leading to such atrocities as the repatriation of Mexicans and the internment of the Japanese. The Nationality Act, directed at Mexicans and Japanese and passed on the eve of the United States' entry into the war, required the understanding, speaking, reading and writing of English as conditions of citizenship.

The period following the war brought new immigration from Mexico and from war-torn countries of Europe. Internal migrations of Mexicans, Puerto Ricans and others added to this and spawned a wide variety of repressive language legislation. States prescribed the exclusive use of English across a broad range of governmental activities. Official notices had to be in English and printed in English language newspapers; the right to vote or hold office was conditional on English literacy; licensing for business and professions required an examination in English; court and quasi-judicial proceedings had to be conducted in English, though in some cases interpreters were allowed. Only the statutes of Maryland and Tennessee made no reference to language (Leibowitz, 1969).

Some of these laws have been challenged, with little effect. For example, as noted above, the California Supreme Court ruled in *Castro v. California* (2 Cal. 3d 223, 1970) that the constitutional provision requiring English literacy for voting violated the equal protection clause of the federal constitution. Nevertheless, its ruling did not require the state to provide ballots or election material in non-English languages, only that Spanish speakers could vote—in English. Other challenges were even less successful. In *Carmona v. Sheffield* (475 F. 2d 738, 9th Cir. 1973), the court denied the right of Spanish speakers to have their claims for unemployment explained in Spanish. And in *Guerrero v. Carlson* (9 Cal. 3d 808, 1973), an injunction to prohibit the termination of welfare payments on the basis of English-only notice was denied.

It was only in the federal courts that linguistic minorities found a modicum of support for language rights. One of the earliest decisions came in *Meyer v. Nebraska* (262 U.S. 390, 1923). The court ruled that the prohibition on the teaching of a foreign language was unconstitutional, though at the same time it upheld the right of the state to require English. Similarly, the court later found the Hawaii statute restricting and regulating the language of instruction in private schools to be unconstitutional (*Farrington v. Tokushige*, 273 U.S. 284, 298, 1927). However, as late as 1959, the court upheld a provision of the North Carolina Constitution that required the ability to read the constitution (in English) as a condition of voting (*Lassiter v. Northampton Election Board*, 360 U.S. 45, 1959). This provision had been directed at Blacks, but the decision had an important impact on language minorities.

The civil rights movement of the 1950s and 1960s led to the first major relaxation of some of the discriminatory language legislation of the previous 100 years. The Voting Rights Act of 1965, for example, suspended literacy tests under certain conditions and specifically enfranchised speakers of languages other than English, provided that they had completed primary school. The constitutionality of the latter provision was challenged and found to be valid by the Supreme Court (*Morgan v. Katzenbach*, 384 U.S. 641, 1966).

In 1967, Title VII of the Elementary and Secondary Education Act was passed. This law provided funds for schools that wished to implement programmes of bilingual education designed for language minority students. There were several major forces that led to this legislation. Crucially important was the political necessity to respond to the unrest among ethnic minorities and their demands for equal opportunity. Also, the liberalism of the period permitted the legislation to pass rather easily. There was a growing awareness that the increasingly complex economic structure required a higher degree of education for minorities than had been achieved in the past. Moreover, the interest in foreign language courses that had been generated by the post-Sputnik National Defense Education Act had begun to wane. Both the American Council of Teachers of Foreign Languages and the Teachers of English to Speakers of Other Languages were mindful of the rapidly increasing numbers of Spanish speakers and the opportunity for jobs in bilingual education. Neither group had previously directed its efforts toward language minorities, but the changed conditions provided the incentive for them strongly to support Title VII.

In a regulation interpreting the Civil Rights Act of 1964, the Department of Health, Education and Welfare (HEW) required affirmative action to "rectify the language deficiency" of non-English speaking students. The Supreme Court in *Lau v. Nichols* (94 S. Ct. 786, 1974) upheld the right of HEW to issue such a regulation and ordered the San Francisco schools to provide a special programme of instruction for its Chinese pupils. The special instruction programmes did not have to be bilingual, but could involve intensive English instruction. The Office for Civil Rights, however, defined bilingual education as one of the remedies that would be approved under certain conditions.

Following the federal lead, many states, including California, soon enacted laws permitting or mandating a form of bilingual education. It is to be noted that all of these, as well as the federal law and regulations, emphasize the use of the native language as a bridge to English. The native language would be used to offset early educational retardation, but the principal goal of these programmes was to be the more effective teaching of English.

Bilingual educators are generally strongly in favour of these stipulations. Since the child does not immediately need to begin learning through a language she does not know, her confidence and self-concept are supported, and she has the opportunity to learn English at a less frantic pace. Educators also believe that bilingual education will enrich the child culturally and linguistically, producing a bilingual individual who will be able to function effectively in each of her languages. The slogan "Bilingualism Says Twice as Much" expresses this belief.

Opponents of the movement claim that the programmes are intended to maintain, at public expense, the language and cultures of ethnic minorities. This is based on the fact that legislation and Office for Civil Rights regulations include language permitting "bilingual/bicultural treatments" designed to develop and maintain necessary skills in each language. These critics insist that since the United States is an English-speaking country and all citizens will need English to function effectively, the major efforts of these programmes must be directed at achieving English fluency. Moreover, maintenance of the native language serves only as a crutch to children and poses the additional danger of developing a Spanish-dominant group that will have separatist tendencies in the manner of French Quebec.

Some of the groups opposing bilingual education are teacher organizations. They use familiar arguments about the great priority that must be given to English, claiming that only in this way can the child obtain a high level of education. However, in the sorts of legislation they have supported (e.g. the elimination of bilingual teacher certification requirements), it is clear that the main concern is not so much education as jobs.

The issues of separatism and jobs are false issues. The goal of language rights in education is not separatism but economic and political (though not sociocultural) integration. Further, separatist sentiments derive from repressive policies, and language may become their symbol. Language differences do not cause separatism.

The focus on jobs opposes the needs of teachers to those of children. And, in any case, the jobs issue relates much more to the matter of declining enrolments among English speakers than it does to bilingual education.

Neither the advocates nor the opponents of bilingual education addresses the central question, that of language as a right. The educational consequences of instruction through a second language are disastrous for most Chicano pupils. Because of the complexity of the language learning process, even after children learn to function with substantial skill in their second language, academic learning through that medium is immensely more difficult than for native speakers. And if the native language has not been developed, the child loses a powerful means of learning. In short, the child under these conditions is denied the right to an equal educational opportunity.

Equally as important, the failure to develop the home language is often a cause of alienation between children, their parents and their community. This failure is not the child's but can be laid directly on the doorstep of the English-oriented policies in education. For in this society the full development of language and culture is a central function of the school, and such policies are clearly prejudicial and destructive.

The maintenance of language and culture by the school, then, is not a frill. It is a matter of academic and social survival and must be considered a civil right. For these reasons, bilingual education must be supported, if at all, as a maintenance effort. Children must be educated by the best means available, and these include their native language. And the educational process may not weaken or destroy the children's inheritance, which links them to their family and community.

In addition to bilingual education and the bilingual ballot, a fair number of state and federal administrative departments make some provision for bilingualism. A leader in this regard is the Social Security Administration which translates many of its publications into Spanish. The Internal Revenue Service also provides tax forms and instructions in Spanish upon request. Welfare, unemployment offices, and other public services will often provide Spanish-speaking personnel in areas with large concentrations of Chicanos. And the courts will occasionally provide interpreters, though this is left to the discretion of individual judges.

Despite these kinds of gains, it is clear that the regulations and practices permitting limited official bilingualism are designed as stop-gaps. They provide minimal services under the pressure of political or bureaucratic necessity and are in no way intended to open governmental processes to the full participation of linguistic minorities. Indeed, the history of language rights legislation demonstrates that its function—even that of modern permissive laws and regulations—is to restrain the access of linguistic minorities to American institutions at the same time that it demands the acquisition and use of English for full participation in society.

In the late 1970s and continuing in the 1980s, we have entered a new era of retrenchment in the provision of language and minority rights. The great immigration of workers from Mexico and Latin America combined with serious problems in the national economy have brought once again to the surface the underlying ethnocentrism and xenophobic sentiments of the Anglo group. The recent demonstrations against Iranian immigrants and the violence against Indo-Chinese and Cuban refugees are symptomatic of this reactionism.

Calls for modification or outright repeal of bilingual voting and bilingual education laws are becoming ever more strident on the part of the media and public figures. Leaders among language minority groups themselves, fearful that the hard-won gains will be lost entirely, are seeking ways to blunt the reaction by compromise and accommodation to some of the demands.

Thus, as this brief review shows, the prospects for minority language rights are not very positive. The administrative practices employing bilingualism are minimal and are generally instituted to ease the administrative burden of the particular agency rather than to enhance the access of language minority people. They have little status in law.

Existing legislation is scant and was passed during a brief period of liberalism in reaction to social unrest and as a means to relieve political pressure.

The few court decisions that have addressed the question have dealt with it in the weakest possible way. Thus, *Meyer* simply upheld the private right to learn a foreign language; *Castro* permitted Spanish speakers to vote but reaffirmed the compelling state interest to conduct the electoral process totally in English; and *Lau* merely gave the executive the right to issue regulations. In each of these decisions, the court took pains to enunciate the State's interest and right to require English. There is no constitutional obligation for the State to provide services in non-English languages. The court upholds the State's interest in efficient government through the imposition of a common language which citizens may be required to know and invokes the principle of *concursus horribilium*, that if one group were allowed language rights, there would be no basis for denying them to others who will also want them.

For these reasons, it seems quite clear that language rights, in whatever arena, can be achieved only through political action and that this action must take place in the context of a sharp definition of the issues and the promulgation of these issues within language minority communities. Court decisions, legislative action and administrative practices basically respond to political conditions. Where these are unfavourable toward ethnic minorities, as they have been in the United States for all but brief periods in its history, repressive policies are to be expected. Relaxation of those policies has come about only as a result of concerted political activity by the minority groups themselves.

Therefore, language rights become at once an end and a means to full politico-economic participation. Without a broad spectrum of concrete and irrevocable minority rights, including those of language, inclusion in the political process will be slow and inevitably weak. Nor will the attainment of these rights result from the largesse of the State. They will be achieved only through a concerted political struggle that encompasses all segments of the Chicano people and other linguistic minorities and that is based on a solid ideological foundation.

Bibliography

ADAMS, C. F. 1973, "Citado a compadecer": Language barriers and due process—Is mailed notice in English constitutionally sufficient? *California Law Review* 61: 6, 1395–1421.

FISHMAN, J. A. & HOFMAN, J. E. 1966, Mother tongue and nativity in the American population. In J. FISHMAN *et al.* (eds), *Language loyalty in the United States*. The Hague: Mouton.

HERNÁNDEZ-CHÁVEZ, E. 1978, Language maintenance, bilingual education, and philosophies of bilingualism in the United States. In J. E. ALATIS (ed.), *International dimensions of bilingual education.* Proceedings of the 1978 Georgetown University Roundtable on Language and Linguistics. Washington D.C.: Georgetown University Press, pp. 527–550.

—— 1979, Meaningful bilingual/bicultural education: A fairy tale. In National Multilingual Multicultural Materials Development Center, *Language Development in a Bilingual Setting*. Pomona, California: California State Polytechnic University.

LAOSA, L. 1975, Bilingualism in three United States Hispanic groups: Contextual use of language by children and adults in their families. *Journal of Educational Psychology* 67: 5, 617–627.

LEIBOWITZ, A. 1969, English literacy: Legal sanction for discrimination. *Notre Dame Lawyer* 45: 7, 7–67.

MACIAS, R. F. 1977, Projections of the Chicano–Latino population in the U.S. to 2000. Mimeo.

SKRABANEK, R. L. 1970, Language maintenance among Mexican-Americans. *International Journal of Comparativ* Sociology 11, 272–282.

THOMPSON, R. 1974, Mexican American language loyalty and the validity of the 1970 census. In G. BILLS (ed.), *Southwest Areal Linguistics*. San Diego: Institute for Cultural Pluralism, pp. 65–78.

3 The language education of immigrant workers' children in The Netherlands

RENÉ APPEL

This chapter[1] deals with some aspects of the education of immigrant workers' children in The Netherlands. Attention will be focused mainly on the minority language issue. In the first section I shall give an overview of the (short) history of the educational situation of immigrant workers' children, and discuss the educational policy of the Dutch government towards these children. The second section deals with recent social-political and educational trends in The Netherlands. The socio-political trends can be summarized under the headings "get back" and "assimilate"; in education recent discussions have been concentrated on the concept of "intercultural education". In the third section, I shall present information on the following topics: minority language use of immigrant workers' children; attitudes of immigrant workers towards their language, and towards minority language education. In the last section I shall discuss the (limited) empirical evidence concerned with the effects of minority language education in The Netherlands.

It is my intention to describe in this chapter some aspects of the Dutch situation. Therefore, no comparisons are made with other countries, and no references to the international literature on this subject are included.

The education of immigrant workers' children

According to Miedema (1982), in 1982 about 650,000 people with a non-Dutch ethnic background lived in The Netherlands; that is about 5% of

the total population. Nearly 300,000 of them were people from Mediterranean countries which had labour migration contracts with The Netherlands. About 40% were Turkish and about 25% Moroccan. The second
largest group consisted of people from the former colony Surinam; their
number is estimated at nearly 200,000 (Vallen et al., 1982).

Mainly due to tensions on the job market (a shortage of unskilled
labourers) in the period 1960–1966, the first wave of immigrant workers
came to The Netherlands. In 1960 there were about 50,000 workers from
Mediterranean countries. In 1969–1972 immigrant workers were again
recruited, in a situation of economic expansion. The law regulating the
reunion of immigrant workers' families made it possible in the 1970s for
many women and children to come and join the men. Despite the fact that
the hiring of new immigrant workers had stopped, it has long been expected
that the number of immigrants would increase, because of new family
reunions and the high birth rate among immigrants (more than twice the
birth rate among Dutch people). In 1983 predictions could not be made so
easily. Many immigrant workers and their families had gone back to their
country of origin, or were planning to return, because of the unfavourable
social and economic situation in The Netherlands (see also the following
section). The number of immigrant workers' children (further: immigrant
children) went up very quickly in a short time. In 1972 there were 10,000
immigrant children in Dutch primary education, and in 1980 more than
40,000, Turkish and Moroccan children forming the largest groups (about
20,000 and 10,000 children respectively). In future the number of immigrant
children will probably continue to grow. Predictions about the population
of Amsterdam (which has the largest number of citizens with a non-Dutch
ethnic background) stated that in 1990 44% of the young people would have
a non-Dutch background, i.e. mainly Surinam, Turkish and Moroccan (De
Volkskrant, 5.11.1982). Kool et al. (1980) give as a prognosis that there will
be about 30,000 Turkish children of primary school age living in The
Netherlands in 1990, and also 30,000 Moroccan children. But these
predictions are probably no longer valid because of recent developments
(i.e. return to country of origin).

In 1980, immigrant children formed little more than 3% of the primary
school population. This percentage seems to be low, but one should realize
that the immigrant workers and their families live mainly in a few industrial
areas. Most of the immigrant children are to be found in the big cities
(Amsterdam, Rotterdam, The Hague, Utrecht, Eindhoven), in Twente, and
in the south of the Province of Limburg. In the cities, the immigrant
families are housed mostly in the so-called old working-class neighbourhoods. As a consequence, many schools in these neighbourhoods often have

more than 50% immigrant children, and some of them even more than 90%, the outcome of two opposite trends: an increasing number of immigrant children came to the schools (among other reasons because there was some expertise in the educational reception of these children), and an increasing number of Dutch children were sent to other schools by their parents, because they expected that teaching would deteriorate with so many immigrant children present.

In 1974, the Ministry of Education formulated for the first time main lines of educational policy regarding immigrant children (Penninx, 1979). This policy is often characterized as a "two track policy", but it can also be interpreted as an ambiguous policy. On the one hand, it was aimed at the integration of immigrant children in the Dutch educational system to guarantee as much as possible that they would have the same educational and social possibilities as Dutch children. On the other hand, it was taken into account that immigrant children might return to their country of origin sooner or later. "Integration with maintenance of minority identity" became a key notion. In fact, the educational policy concerning immigrant children was not supported by clear ideas about the position and the future of immigrant workers and their families in The Netherlands. Neither were there clear ideas on the re-organization of the form and content of the educational system to adjust it to the new situation with immigrant children. The main part of the policy was the so-called facilities arrangement. On the basis of this arrangement schools or groups of schools with a relatively large number of immigrant children could engage special teachers for the first reception and teaching of Dutch, and a foreign teacher to take charge of classes in the children's native language and culture (for about five hours a week). It should be noted that many schools did not use this opportunity, because reception of the immigrant children and integration in the Dutch classes provided too many problems already. Because the content and form of the education for immigrant children was not settled, schools everywhere experimented with the reception and teaching of immigrant children in a provisional, often not very well-thought-out way. In fact, "experiment" is not the proper word here; it was more improvising on the basis of more or less casual circumstances and the personal preferences of teachers. For example, nobody knew how to teach Dutch as a second language, how to teach reading and writing to older children, or how to integrate the classes in the children's own language and culture which were mostly considered to be superfluous extra baggage.

In the second half of the 1970s, the admission of immigrant children to Dutch schools was in nearly all cases educationally organized in one of the following two ways:

1. Immigrant children, directly from the country of origin or already in The Netherlands a few years, were placed at once in regular Dutch classes. Each day for about 30–45 minutes they received extra courses in Dutch language proficiency outside the regular classes, in small groups consisting of three to eight children. The Dutch courses were given by a special teacher (see above); it was called *aanspreekbaarheidsonderwijs*, which could be paraphrased as: courses which should ensure that children have enough passive knowledge of Dutch to participate in Dutch classes.

2. Immigrant children were placed together in a so-called reception class in which they received education from a special teacher. This "reception education" was also exclusively in Dutch. After about one year the children were placed in regular Dutch classes. This organization type was put into practice mostly in schools with many immigrant children who came directly from their country of origin.

In both organization types, courses in the children's own language and culture could be given by a foreign teacher for about four hours a week.

The further education of foreign children had roughly the following form. The children received the same education as Dutch children in regular classes. In addition to that, for the first two or three years their Dutch language proficiency was improved in extra courses with special teachers for about five hours a week; in these courses most attention was paid to reading and writing. Furthermore, in many schools there was also the opportunity to follow courses in the minority language and culture for about another five hours a week.

It must be stressed that the two aims of the educational policy for immigrant children could only be achieved in a minimal way. Integration in the Dutch classes was not very successful; the immigrant children could not participate fully in the activities of the Dutch children, because they had to spend a lot of time doing tasks which were set by the special teachers. Integration was also impeded by the fact that the immigrant children did not feel at ease in the Dutch classes. There was a pedagogical and didactic climate which they were not used to. Their self-confidence was undermined because many activities were going on in the classes which they did not understand, or could only partly understand. The realization of the second goal, maintenance of identity, was impossible in an educational situation with such a marginal share of minority language and culture teaching. In fact the children's identity was more or less destroyed, while insufficient provision was made to build a new one.

In 1981, the Ministry of Education published a new *Policy Paper on Cultural Minorities in the Educational System* (*Beleidsplan*, 1981). In this paper the basic assumption is that (most of) the immigrant families will stay in The Netherlands. The paper pleads for "intercultural education" to prepare all children, indigenous and non-indigenous, for their participation in a multicultural society (see the following section). Apart from the intercultural aims, the announced policy is in many ways a continuation of the existing educational practice: immigrant children integrate in Dutch schools; they receive compensatory courses in Dutch, and the teaching of the minority groups' own languages and cultures is possible for about five hours each week, which was to be reduced to two and a half hours in 1984 (this is also given a new legal status in the law regulating Primary Education).

Minority language and culture (MLC) teaching is motivated in the following way.

"[It] can contribute to the development of the student's self-concept and self-confidence. More knowledge of the culture of the country of origin makes it easier to maintain contacts with family and friends from and in the home country. At the same time it will simplify the re-integration in the educational system of the country of origin in case the family decides to return. Because only a small part of the indigenous minorities returns permanently, minority language and culture education should be aimed at the first two objectives." (*Beleidsplan*, 1981:8)

The main argument seems to be that MLC-teaching will facilitate the integration of immigrant children. Besides that, the minority language and culture education has only a marginal position in the school. In the Policy Paper the multi*cultural* society is taken as a starting point, but nothing is said about a multi*lingual* society. It is obvious that the public authorities have no opinion on language policy at all. The question of whether it is desirable, useful, necessary or possible for The Netherlands to have, for example, a stable, permanent Turkish–Dutch bilingual minority group in the future is not dealt with. But the proposed educational policy illustrates that there is perhaps an implicit language policy: Turkish, Moroccan-Arabic and other non-indigenous minority languages to disappear from the Dutch speech community.

With respect to minority language teaching, the situation of immigrant children (and other children from non-indigenous minority groups) differs strikingly from that of children from the only indigenous linguistic minority, the Frisians. In Appel (1983) the differences between these groups are analysed. It is concluded that Frisian–Dutch bilingual education (with Frisian as an obligatory subject, and with the possibility of using Frisian as the language of instruction throughout primary school) is commonly accepted because the Frisians do not cause sociopolitical problems; language maintenance efforts are not disputed and are officially supported. In contrast, bilingual education for non-indigenous linguistic minorities is stimulated when sociopolitical conflicts arise or are expected to arise. Language problems of non-indigenous minority groups are more readily recognized and officially acknowledged if the groups concerned are considered to be the cause of (potential) social or political conflicts.

This can be illustrated by the attitudes towards minority language teaching for Moluccan children. The Moluccans, who speak Moluccan-Malay, form a small but much discussed minority group (about 32,000 people). They came to The Netherlands in 1951, and only minimal measures were taken to try to solve the language and educational problems of the Moluccan children. The government seemed to realize that more facilities were needed to cope with these problems, when the political activities of the Moluccans, who are striving for an independent state in the Indonesian archipelago, escalated with the event in Bovensmilde in 1977, culminating in schoolchildren and their teachers being taken as hostages. Within one year, the government presented a paper on the problems of the Moluccan community in The Netherlands. One of the announced measures was the organization of instruction on Malay and Moluccan culture for Moluccans. The official attitude towards minority languages seems to be more or less ambiguous: minority language teaching is stimulated, but only in a limited way, because it is feared that the political and cultural identity will be strengthened too much, which might result in new sociopolitical conflicts.

In the early 1980s the characteristics of the group of immigrant children were rapidly changing. In the 1970s most of the immigrant children who entered Dutch primary schools came directly from their country of origin, or they had spent only a short time in The Netherlands. From about 1980 on, more and more immigrant children have already lived for years (or were born) in The Netherlands. At the end of this decade almost all of the immigrant children who enter primary school will have lived in The Netherlands all of their lives.

In nearly all cases these "second-generation" immigrant children are placed in regular Dutch school classes. According to the governmental facilities arrangement there are fewer possibilities of hiring extra teachers for these children than for children who have been in The Netherlands for only a short time; so there are fewer opportunities for the necessary educational support. The few extra teachers function more or less as remedial teachers, with their work sometimes integrated in the regular classes and sometimes in special classes for small groups of immigrant children. They try to support the children in their acquisition of Dutch (mainly reading and writing) and in other school subjects. If the parents want it, the second-generation immigrant children can follow courses in minority language and culture (MLC) given by a foreign teacher for, at most, two and a half hours a week. Till 1984 this was five hours a week, but it has been reduced by a governmental decision in favour of the Dutch part of the curriculum. Often children (with the same nationality) from different schools have to gather at one school for these courses. At some schools there are even no opportunities at all. According to a statement by Papatya Nalbantoğlu, a Turkish teacher in Amsterdam, less than 15% of the Turkish children in Amsterdam attend MLC courses (*De Volkskrant*, 26.10.1982). But it should be noted that, especially there, the position of minority language teaching is extremely weak. There are no general quantitative data on the participation in MLC courses.

Many schools (or School Boards) think that it is too complicated to organize MLC courses, because it is difficult to integrate them in the regular Dutch programme. It is also supposed that MLC teaching will diminish the (Dutch) educational possibilities of the immigrant children, or that it will promote segregation. One should realize that Dutch law makes MLC courses possible, but schools are not obliged to organize these courses, even if they have more than 80% immigrant children.

The conclusion must be that immigrant minority languages generally fulfil only a minor role in the Dutch educational system, and that recently this role has even been reduced.

New trends in the 1980s

In this section I shall deal with recent social-political and educational trends with regard to immigrant children. I am quite aware that it is difficult to state anything about the "value" of these trends; for example, how many people share certain opinions and what is their influence on social and political practices? What follows must be a more or less personal view of the situation in The Netherlands in the 1980s.

Social-political trends

Traditionally, Holland is considered to be a country rather tolerant towards foreigners and strangers. Apart from the question of whether this is true, one can observe that tolerance towards immigrants and immigrant workers is diminishing. There are different signs which point to this trend. For the first time since World War II, a fascist party (*Centrum-partij*) gained a seat in the Dutch Parliament (in the 1982 elections). The political viewpoints of this party are very Dutch ethnocentric; nearly all social and economical problems in Dutch society are "explained" by referring to the ethnic minority people who "take our houses, take our work, etc.". It is not concluded that immigrant workers and their families should be thrown out (that would mean a charge of racism) but it is surely implied.

Some polls on the views of Dutch people regarding immigrants are also signs of a growing intolerance. The facts both of these polls and of the results are significant. One poll reported that 39% of the Dutch people were of the opinion that unemployed immigrants should be forced to return to their countries of origin, but after more questions half of these people thought that it was not right to do this (*Buitenlanders Bulletin*, 1982, Vol. 7, nr. 9). According to the outcomes of a second poll nearly 29% of the Dutch people wanted unemployed immigrants to leave The Netherlands (*De Volkskrant*, 22.2.1983). A study among secondary school students pointed out that 17% of them held strong prejudices against ethnic minorities (*De Volkskrant*, 4.11.1982).

Different factors have contributed to this rising attitude towards immigrants (which in many ways is the continuation of an existing attitude). The economic recession can be considered an important cause. In a period of growing unemployment, immigrant workers are seen as unwelcome rivals on the job market. Additionally, people are eager to look for scapegoats, and the immigrant workers are good candidates for this role.

The second recent social-political trend I shall call the assimilation trend. Of course, the idea that immigrants should adjust themselves to the majority is traditional. But this idea seemed to be revitalized in the early 1980s. Couwenberg (1982a, b) pleads for the maintenance of Dutch national identity, which is threatened by ethnic minorities. He states that Dutch culture "... finds its inspiration in christianity and humanism", and he summarizes its political kernel with the notion of "liberal-democratic order" (Couwenberg, 1982b). This political kernel contains both the equality principle and the national right of self determination.

"The equality principle implies that equal cases deserve equal treatment, and that unequal cases should be treated unequally. Are indigenous (Dutch) people in the same position as non-indigenous people [foreigners; i.e. immigrant workers and their families, R.A.]? Reasonably, that can not be said. Indigenous people have been settled here for centuries, and have built their own culture and society, which may be protected against undesirable strange influences on the basis of the right of self determination." (Couwenberg, 1982b)

Couwenberg adds that the "inequality" should be diminished, but that complete equality is out of the question. De Jong (1982) and van Kemenade (1982) also argue for adjustment to the Dutch cultural system by immigrants, and especially immigrant workers' children (van Kemenade in his position as Minister of Education). They assume that immigrant workers' children will have more success in school if the school programme has a Dutch cultural orientation; minority language and culture teaching will have mainly negative effects on the educational achievement of the immigrant workers' children. Van Kemenade even states that integration in the Dutch educational system (with special attention to second language acquisition) will give better opportunities for the maintenance and development of a minority identity than attention to minority language and culture, especially when this is isolated in school. Van Kemenade feels that integration in the Dutch educational system is an essential condition for social-economic emancipation, which in its own turn is an essential condition for cultural emancipation.

The views of Couwenberg, in particular, were discussed at length. Important counter-arguments in this debate were:

— Couwenberg has a narrow-minded nationalist view of culture.

— Something like *the* Dutch culture does not exist; as in any other country or modern community culture is heterogeneous.

— Integration of immigrants in Dutch society is hindered mainly by the fact that too few measures are taken to give them a regular place in society; for example, the housing problem causes many social difficulties.

— Couwenberg's views give further support to discriminatory ideologies (the rise of a fascist party; see the first part of this section).

With regard to language education of immigrant children, the following conclusion can be drawn from these recent social-political trends. The opinions of Couwenberg, de Jong and van Kemenade about cultural adjustment imply that it would be better to forgo maintenance of immigrant minority languages. The acquisition of Dutch is emphasized, and it is expected that minority language education will have primarily a retarding effect. This could be a first step in the direction of the complete disappearance of minority language teaching for immigrant children.

Educational trends

Since about 1980, the call has been more frequently heard for *intercultural education*. The governmental *Policy Paper on Cultural Minorities in the Educational System* (*Beleidsplan*, 1981) also argues for the organization of intercultural education, which should promote the acculturation of indigenous and non-indigenous members of Dutch society. Acculturation implies a mutual process of learning to know, accepting and appreciating each other, and the adoption of a positive attitude towards each others' culture or cultural elements. From a progressive point of view, Miedema (1982) gives some further characteristics of intercultural education:

a. It is completely integrated in the curriculum, and it is meant for all children. It aims to break the isolation of immigrant children and the isolation of the school in the neighbourhood.

b. In intercultural education the children's personal experiences as social beings are recognized, and the creation of a unity in these experiences is pursued.

c. Parents should participate in school life.

d. The educational programme is centred mainly around themes which are connected with the children's experiences.

Van Esch (1982) adds to this:

e. Intercultural education fights against stereotypes and discrimination.

f. It tries to promote a positive self-concept for minority and majority children.
   According to Miedema, the educational system must change principally in an intercultural direction in order to contribute to the fight against social inequality.

Again, it is difficult to estimate the number (and the power) of the adherents to the intercultural education view, but my personal guess is that many people in educational circles are among these adherents. "Intercultural education" has become almost a kind of magic word: application of intercultural education will cure the problems of minority education.

Besides that, the term can be used for many types of curricula, masking the differences between them.

The concept of intercultural education contains many positive elements, but it also has some weak points. In the first place, a form of mutual acculturation is a marvellous objective; but in fact it requires some kind of equality from the outset, otherwise it can be feared that "the weakest culture" cannot have a real influence on "the strongest culture". Van Esch (1982:100) formulates a comparable objection:

"In our opinion, the view on society held by some advocates of intercultural education is too much a view of a harmonious society in which no specific group interests exist, in which there is no fight for scanty goods (work), in which there is for example no discrimination on the house and job market."

Furthermore, in proposals for intercultural education ethnic or racial contrasts seem to be reduced to "harmless" cultural differences (see also Mullard's chapter in this volume).

The second point concerns the educational achievement of minority children. It is also noticed by Miedema (1982), following Stone (1981):

"Intercultural education has respectable aims like the promotion of mutual solidarity, the analysis of minority and majority position in society, the fight against racism, but this should not hinder the striving for good educational achievement in subject matters. Minority students should enter the job market with good qualifications. The concept of intercultural education must not function as a pedagogical legitimation for an educational model which only gives immigrant children the opportunity to be tomorrow's immigrant workers."

The third point (and in the framework of this chapter, the most important) has to do with the position of minority languages. Miedema (1982), who supports intercultural education forcefully, already points to the fact that there is a tendency in intercultural education to throw minority language and culture teaching (and special courses in Dutch) out of the educational programme. According to van Esch (1982) it is possible to organize minority language and culture teaching in the context of intercultural education, but he does not point out how it will relate to something like mutual cultural adjustment or the often heard demand that Dutch and immigrant children should follow the same curriculum.

The problems and contradictions accompanying the concept of intercultural education become quite clear in an article of Haanen-Thijs, who describes the experimental educational programme in the school where she works; a school with about 30% immigrant workers' children and 30% Surinam children.

> "We ... have an emancipatory educational vision. That means a democratic educational vision. We pursue the optimal individual development of our children, and we want to educate them in such a way that they become verbally competent and self defensible citizens in a democratic society. A democratic society in which they can partici- pate completely. That means that implicitly we strive for intercultural education. ... We have respect for the culture, the language and the milieu of our children. We do not want to change or 'improve' them or their parents. We only want them to be nice and happy people who contribute actively to a better and more righteous society." (Haanen- Thijs, 1982:28)

After these in some ways rather utopian words (see van Esch's statements above) Haanen-Thijs describes the intercultural programme, and in this description *not one word* is said about minority language teaching. Therefore, the immigrant children's cultural and linguistic background is respected, but that does not imply that the educational programme provides for minority language teaching. Despite the fact that the concept of intercultural education contains many valuable elements, I want to stress its ambiguous character with regard to minority language teaching: on the one hand, the minority children's culture and language must be appreciated, but on the other hand minority language teaching is contrary to the starting- point of equality between Dutch and minority children. In fact, I think that intercultural education can be promoted by teachers, educational experts and politicians who are not very emancipation-oriented. In this way they legitimate educational practices in which there is no place for minority language and culture education; educational practices which might be essentially assimilative.

The minority perspective: language use and language attitude, and views on minority language teaching

In families of immigrant workers a clear shift can be seen: the children use more and more Dutch instead of their mother tongue. Haast & van Haastrecht (1982) interviewed Spanish children, and they all said that they used primarily Dutch among themselves. Lalleman carried out research on the Dutch language proficiency of Turkish children born in The Nether- lands (see Lalleman, 1983). In the context of this project, the Turkish parents were also interviewed (in Turkish). In 12 out of 20 families the children spoke mainly Dutch to each other, according to the parents; in four families alternately Dutch and Turkish, and in four other families primarily or only Turkish. Some of the parents pointed out that the school has an important influence on the diminishing use of Turkish; for example, when the children come home from school they speak Dutch.

Dosen, who has done exploratory research among Yugoslavian children, notes that the children lack motivation to use their mother tongue in communicating with Yugoslavian peers. From conversations with the parents she concludes "... that they have problems in selecting the language for communication with their children" (Dosen, 1981:125). She also supposes that the feeling of group identity will decrease and gradual assimilation will take place, when the mother tongue is not used consistently in the family (Dosen, 1982). In my view, the causality direction cannot be easily established (Dosen implies that language use is the causal factor), but certainly there is a positive relation between use of majority language in the home and assimilation.

Dutch is already partly replacing the respective minority languages as the language of daily family interaction. Immigrant workers' children often use only Dutch with their younger brothers and sisters; it should be noted that they are frequently in charge of bringing up these younger siblings, so this might have a large impact on their minority language proficiency (cf. also Kiers, 1982). Parents sometimes try to force their children to use the mother tongue, but it is difficult to fight the influence of the outside world. For example, Hülya, a 13-year-old Turkish girl, who had been in The Netherlands nearly four years, told me: "Father says: 'At home you must speak our own language'... We have tried, but did not succeed. My father says: 'You will get punished', but, he ... did not succeed!"

Haast & van Haastrecht (1982) provide direct empirical evidence about proficiency in the minority language of immigrant workers' children. They collected data on the Spanish of bilingual children in The Netherlands, but unfortunately they were not able to compare the Spanish proficiency of the immigrant children with the proficiency of monolingual children in Spain. The overall complexity of the Spanish of the immigrant children (measured by mean utterance length) seemed to be rather low, in comparison with the Dutch of Dutch children (but this could be due to structural differences between Dutch and Spanish).

Van de Wetering & El-Koundi (1983) studied the language proficiency of Moroccan children. Children aged about six years who were born in The Netherlands had higher scores on a Dutch comprehension test than on a comparable Moroccan-Arabic comprehension test. Furthermore, there is only indirect evidence on the minority language proficiency of immigrant children, i.e. evidence gained by interviews. In the above mentioned research project conducted by Lalleman, half of the Turkish parents were dissatisfied with the Turkish proficiency of their children. One mother feared "... that in the end it might fade away completely". In another project, Nelleke Altena and I had long talks with eight Turkish and Moroccan children who had been in The Netherlands nearly four years. All children said they had only a moderate or low command of their own language. Nadia, a ten-year-old Moroccan girl, said that she could count no further than ten in Moroccan-Arabic. Nearly all children seemed to have trouble in finding the right word. Youssef, for example, a 14-year-old Moroccan boy, said that he often used a mixture of Dutch and Moroccan with other Moroccan boys at school: "You have forgotten a few words, and you just say it in Dutch". Kiers (1982) reports the same phenomenon. Young Moroccan men had the idea that words from their mother tongue often "fly away", and they have to use Dutch expressions.

Generally, immigrant workers and their family members have a positive attitude towards the minority language: they set a high value on good proficiency. In Lalleman's study the Turkish parents were asked if they thought it important for their children to have a good command of Turkish, and in 18 out of 20 cases they considered it as (very) important. The young Moroccan men interviewed by Kiers unanimously held the opinion that speaking the minority language well is of great importance. The same attitude was expressed by the Moroccan and Turkish children in the research conducted by Nelleke Altena and myself. When asked for motivation, the following three types of answers were frequently given:

1. When we return (or have to return) to our country of origin the children must speak our language well;

2. A good command of the mother tongue is necessary for communication in the (extended) family;

3. When you are a member of a minority group, you must speak the language of that group (i.e. the minority language is considered as an important symbol for minority group identity).

Altena & de Haan (1984) interviewed representatives of 17 minority organizations (Moroccan, Turkish, Portuguese and Surinam organizations; local as well as national). For all organizations maintenance of the minority language seemed to be self-evident. Nearly half of the organizations did not have language maintenance as an explicit objective, because they held other priorities; nevertheless, they generally considered it to be an important aim. Nine of the 17 organizations said that language maintenance was one of their explicit objectives. Eight of these nine organizations actively tried to promote language maintenance (language courses, lectures on literature, theatre).

As can be expected, a positive attitude towards the minority language is connected with appreciation of minority language teaching. Various articles and publications contain pleas for minority language teaching. Triesschiejn (1983) summarizes a report of the Educational Inspectorate on minority language and culture teaching. This report states that the majority of immigrant parents have a strong desire for MLC teaching, which is inspired by emotional and nationalist feelings. They want more MLC teaching; preferably half of the curriculum should be in the minority language.

Nalbantoğlu (1982:41) says that minority language teaching is essential for immigrant children: "Only a considerable quantity of minority culture—absorbed by means of the mother tongue—helps the Turkish child to carry on, and it forms a base for a further development of personality in a new social context". Van de Wetering & El-Koundi (1983) look at MLC teaching from the perspective of Moroccan parents and teachers. The parents consider it important for their children to learn Arabic,

"... a language which is associated with Islam and the Arabic Islamitic civilization, their religion and their civilization. Arabic is a world language, to which the parents attach more prestige than to Dutch ... The language is also essential for the children, if they ever want to return to their country of origin." (p. 12)

Kaymak (1981), a member of the Society for Turkish Teachers in The Netherlands (H-TÖB), argues for integration of immigrants and immigrant children in Dutch society, which means for him that ethnic minorities enter into a larger structure and function within this structure, maintaining essential characteristics of minority identity. Kaymak chooses for a type of intercultural education with extended facilities for minority language teaching. He states that ethnic minorities must maintain their own identity, because this is the first condition for integration. In case of a loss of identity, integration cannot really be achieved. Kaymak associates identity strongly with language: "Identity is developed within a certain culture, and this culture is inseparably related to the minority language" (p. 5). The importance of minority language teaching is also stressed by the Society for Turkish Teachers in The Netherlands in its reaction to the Draft *Policy Paper on Cultural Minorities in the Dutch Educational System* by the Ministry of Education (H-TÖB, 1981). Many of the arguments in favour of minority language teaching given above are also presented in this reaction. In addition it is also noted that MLC teaching does not have to lead to isolation or segregation of minority groups.

Although the information on minority opinions is still rather limited, it can be concluded that immigrant workers and their families generally attach much importance to proficiency in the minority language and to minority language teaching. Because of their social position (which is marked by oppression, isolation and disadvantage), many parents will choose for a kind of segregative educational system which secures minority language teaching and strengthens minority identity; this can also be considered to be a reaction to the present situation of marginal minority language teaching. Progressive immigrants and immigrant teachers opt for education aimed at integration in Dutch society, but they also put a high value on minority language teaching.

Two educational experiments with minority language teaching

At the end of the first section of this chapter the educational situation of immigrant children in the early 1980s was described. This description shows that immigrant children generally receive no minority language teaching, or only a small amount of minority language teaching. In only a few cases educational experiments were organized in which minority language teaching played a much larger role. In the context of two experiments, research was conducted which will be summarized below.

The experiment in Leyden

Negative experience with the regular educational model caused the establishment of an experimental school for immigrant workers' children in the city of Leyden in October 1977. The school had the characteristics of a transitional bilingual school. The global structure of the educational programme was as follows: Moroccan and Turkish children (aged 6–12 years) who had arrived directly from their respective countries of origin attended classes which were specially organized for them. These classes were associated with a "regular" Dutch school. The children were instructed in all subjects in the native language by teachers from their country of origin. (It should be noted that about half of the Moroccan children did not have Moroccan-Arabic—which was used in the classroom—as their first language, but rather Berber. However, nearly all of them could speak and understand Moroccan-Arabic when they came to The Netherlands.) For about one hour every day, Dutch was the subject (as well as the medium) of instruction in lessons given by a Dutch teacher. As soon as the children were able to speak and understand some Dutch, they joined Dutch children for a few hours a week in activities which were meant to encourage their integration into Dutch school life. In the second year, school subjects were taught nearly half the time in the mother tongue of the children, and half the time in Dutch. After two years, the immigrant children went to "regular" schools in their neighbourhood.

The development and achievement of the children from the experimental school (the E-group) were compared with the development and achievement of Turkish and Moroccan children who attended "regular" schools (the C-group). The latter were at six different schools which did not share exactly the same programme for immigrant children, but they were similar because the programmes were dominant monolingual Dutch.

Table 3.1 contains information about the time spent on teaching in the minority language in three successive school years.

In the first year that comparisons were made, the E-group consisted of 25 children (11 Turkish and 14 Moroccan), and the C-group of 33 children (15 Turkish and 18 Moroccan); in later years some children were "lost". The length of stay in The Netherlands of the E-children and the C-children was nearly the same. In 1978 the mean age of the E-children was 9 years and 7 months and that of the C-children 9 years and 4 months. Interviews with the parents made clear that the socio-economic and educational backgrounds of the two groups of children were comparable.

The two groups were compared with respect to second language acquisition, social-cultural development, and arithmetic. Here I can give

TABLE 3.1 *Percentage of time that the mother tongue was used as the medium of instruction in the two school models (E and C)*

	E %	C %
1977–78	75	13
1978–79	40	17
1979–80	10	10
Mean over 3 years	41.7	13.3

only global information about the results. They are described more extensively in Appel, Everts & Teunissen (forthcoming), Altena & Appel (1982), and in Appel (1984). At the end of the first school year there were no striking differences between the E-children and the C-children with respect to tests and variables which measured oral *second language proficiency*. At the end of the second school year, the results for oral proficiency tended to be in favour of the children from the experimental school; the scores for written proficiency were nearly the same. At the end of the third year the E-children again outperformed the C-children; this time for oral as well as for written language proficiency. In general, it could be concluded that the amount of time spent in minority language teaching in the transitional bilingual school had no retarding effects on the second language acquisition of Turkish and Moroccan children; the children from the experimental, minority language school were even somewhat ahead.

With respect to the *social-cultural development* of the children the following conclusions were reached.

1. The reception of the Turkish and Moroccan children in the mother tongue classes gave them a feeling of security and safety; also in contacts with Dutch children and teachers the children's own group was a safe home base. This gave them the opportunity to determine the character and the frequency of contacts with Dutch children. In the first three school years the mean percentage of "problem children" in the C-group was nearly twice that in the E-group (24% vs. 13%). Social-emotional problems were exhibited in aggressive behaviour, apathy, isolation, strong fear of failure or a notable form of nationalism.

2. Initially there were no striking differences in cultural orientation between the two groups. At the end of the second school year 88% of the E-children and 71% of the C-children had a strong minority cultural orientation. At the end of the third year, the percentages were 72 and 76 respectively. A possible interpretation might be that for the experimental children a gradual cultural integration is attained; this is further supported by the fact that at the end of the third year 23% of the E-children and only 10% of the C-children had an "in-between" cultural orientation. Furthermore, many children from the C-group seemed to try more and more to express their own cultural background in the classroom. They developed a growing feeling of resistance towards the dominant (Dutch) school culture. The E-children were able to cope better with two cultures. The school did not affect the "hard kernel" of the cultural background of the children, but rather it affected the way in which cultural orientation was expressed in the classroom.

3. The transition to schools in the E-children's neighbourhood after two years had caused problems in only a few cases. If children experienced difficulties, they did not last very long. Generally, in the third school year the E-children had more social relations with other (Dutch and immigrant) children than did the C-children.

In *arithmetic* the E-group performed better than the C-group. Between the first and the second year, progress in arithmetic achievement was measured. Both groups made less progress than Dutch children, but the E-children generally did not lag behind as much as the C-children. In the second year the mathematical conceptualization abilities of the children were tested. On this test the children from the minority language classes also had higher scores than the children from the dominant Dutch schools.

The experiment in Enschede

Since 1978 bilingual/bicultural education for Turkish and Moroccan children has been organized in Enschede. In many respects, the educational model in Enschede is the same as the model applied in Leyden. However, an important difference is that children entering the minority language classes in Enschede have already been in The Netherlands for some time; in recent years many of the entering children have been born in The Netherlands and thus this situation is more relevant to the future situation in which hardly any "new" Turkish or Moroccan children of primary school age will come to The Netherlands. A further difference between the Enschede experiment and the Leyden experiment is that in Enschede the Turkish and Moroccan classes are attached to different schools and in Leyden to one school. Finally, integrational activities with immigrant children and Dutch children were organized in Enschede earlier and more often than in Leyden.

The experiment in Enschede is not yet completed, because new Turkish and Moroccan children are coming to the minority language classes every year. The evaluation of the experiment is also still in progress. This evaluation was not organized with a fairly stable experimental group and comparison group. The size and composition of the experimental group is continually changing (as a result of the continuation of the experiment); for some research objectives the achievements of the children from the minority language classes were compared with the achievements of children who attended schools with a regular programme, i.e. only a few hours of minority language teaching. Below I shall give some of the preliminary results, based on interim reports (Teunissen, 1983; van de Wetering & El-Koundi, 1983). It should be noted that the results point to tendencies; no hard predictive conclusions can be drawn.

— The Dutch language proficiency of the children from the experimental school surpassed the proficiency of Turkish and Moroccan children from regular schools. On a test for comprehensive reading the Turkish "experimental" children even attained almost the same level as Dutch children from parallel classes in the same school.

— Two years after leaving the minority language classes the language proficiency of the Turkish and Moroccan children was tested again. They approached the level of Dutch children. (There were no data on a comparison group of Turkish and Moroccan children.)

— Also, two years after leaving the minority language classes, the proficiency in arithmetic of Turkish children was compared with the proficiency of Dutch children (from the "former" parallel classes in the experimental school). The Turkish children even scored higher on one test than the Dutch children.

— The Moroccan children from the experimental school had a better command of Moroccan-Arabic than the children from regular schools (all children had Moroccan-Arabic as their first language).

— The Moroccan children from the experimental school scored low on a test for comprehensive Arabic reading, but they scored better than children from regular schools.

— One of the reasons for starting the experiment was that in schools there had often been conflicts between Dutch children on one side and immigrant children on the other. At the experimental schools these inter-ethnic conflicts occurred significantly less frequently. The teachers were of the opinion that this meant that an important aim of the minority language classes had already been reached.

— With regard to cultural orientation the children from the experimental schools seemed more "in balance" and less disturbed than the children from the regular schools. In investigating this cultural orientation it became clear that the "experimental" children were more used to dealing with two different cultural and ethnic domains.

Although at this moment nothing can be said with any certainty, the evaluation results of both the Leyden and the Enschede experiments give rise to the preliminary and tentative conclusion that minority language teaching for immigrant workers' children has no negative educational or social effects; it can even have positive results when compared with the regular educational situation in which the minority language is at best marginally used and taught. These results support the demands of immigrants for more provision of minority language teaching.

Notes to Chapter 3

1. The text contains many translations from Dutch sources. The translations in English are all mine.

   I wish to thank Moustafa El-Koundi, Henk Everts, Frans Teunissen, Joop Teunissen and Stella van de Wetering for providing information about research they are conducting, and Dawn Foor for her comments on an earlier version of this paper.

References

ALTENA, N. & APPEL, R. 1982, Mother-tongue teaching and the acquisition of Dutch by Turkish and Moroccan workers' children. *Journal of Multilingual and Multicultural Development* 3, 315–322.

ALTENA, N. & DE HAAN, D. 1984, Taalpolitiek en etnisch-kulturele migranten-groepen in Nederland. Unpublished paper, Instituut voor Ontwikkelingspsychologie, Utrecht.

APPEL, R. 1983, Minority languages in the Netherlands: Relations between socio-political conflicts and bilingual education. In B. BAIN (ed.), *The sociogenesis of language and human conduct*. New York, pp. 517–526.

—— 1984, *Immigrant children learning Dutch; Sociolinguistic and psycholinguistic aspects of second-language acquisition*. Dordrecht.

APPEL, R., EVERTS, H. & TEUNISSEN, J. (forthcoming), *Onderzoek naar een experimenteel onderwijsmodel voor Turkse en Marokkaanse kinderen in Leiden*.

BELEIDSPLAN, 1981. *Beleidsplan Culturele Minderheden in het Onderwijs*. 's-Gravenhage.

COUWENBERG, S. W. 1982a, Het vraagstuk der etnische minderheden— politieke en juridische aspecten. *Civis Mundi* 21, 169–174.

—— 1982b, Discussie over minderhedenvraagstuk moet worden ontdaan van demagogiek. *De Volkskrant*, 16.10.1982, p. 17.

DOSEN, R. 1981, Migrantenkinderen en hun moedertaal. *Samenwijs* 2, 125–133.

—— 1982, Migrantenkinderen en hun moedertaal II. *Samenwijs* 2, 214–228.

ESCH, W. VAN 1982, *Etnische groepen en het onderwijs*. 's-Gravenhage.

HAANEN-THIJS, M. 1982, Intercultureel onderwijs op de Lutherschool. *Moer* 1982, 2, 27–36.

HAAST, M. & VAN HAASTRECHT, T. 1982, Descripcion del Espanol de diecisiete ninos bilingues que se han educado en Holanda. Tesina doctoral, Rijks Universiteit Utrecht.

H-TÖB, 1981, Een alternatief; Reaktie op het Konseptbeleidsplan "Kulturele minderheden in het onderwijs".

JONG, M. J. DE 1982, Het onderwijs aan allochtonen; enkele feiten en visies. Civis Mundi 21, 196–203.

KAYMAK, A. 1981, 'Moedertaalonderwijs', Inleiding voor de bijeenkomst van de Vereniging van Turkse leerkrachten (H-TÖB) op 28 november 1981 te Utrecht.

KEMENADE, J. VAN 1982, Toespraak t.g.v. de opening van de vervolgconferentie over het onderwijs aan culturele minderheden (Ede, 19 april 1982), Uitleg-krant, vol. 4, nr. 168, 1–2.

KIERS, T. 1982, Taalvaardigheid en taalbehoefte van Marokkaanse jongens in Nederland. doctoraal scriptie, Instituut voor Algemene Taalwetenschap, Universiteit van Amsterdam.

KOOL, C., KONINGS-VAN DER SNOEK, M. & VAN PRAAG, C. S. 1980, Bevolkingsprognose allochtonen in Nederland, Dl. I Turken en Marokkanen (CSP-cahier 19), Rijswijk.

LALLEMAN, J. 1983, Turkse kinderen in Nederland: De relatie tussen hun taalvaardigheid en de sociaal-kulturele oriëntatie van hun ouders. Tijdschrift voor Taal-en Tehstwetenschap, 3, 134–151.

MIEDEMA, W. 1982, Intercultureel onderwijs. Moer 1982, 2, 3–15.

NALBANTOGLU, P. 1982, Turkse kinderen in het Nederlandse basisonderwijs. Moer 1982, 2, 37–46.

PENNINX, R. 1979, Naar een algemeen etnisch minderhedenbeleid? In Wetenschappelijke Raad voor het Regeringsbeleid, Etnische Minderheden. 's-Gravenhage, 1–174.

STONE, M. 1981, The education of the black child in Britain; The myth of multi-cultural education. London.

TEUNISSEN, F. 1983, Beknopt verslag van de externe evaluatie van het project moedertaalklassen te Enschede; Periode tot 1-8-1982. Vakgroep Onderwijskunde Rijks Universiteit Utrecht.

TRIESSCHEIJN, T. M. 1983, Het O.E.T.C. nader bekeken, Inspecteurs lichtten ruim vijftig lespunten door. Samenwijs 3:7, 207–211.

VALLEN, T., KERKHOFF, A. & MOLONY, C. 1982, Beheersing en ontwikkeling van het Nederlands van allochtone kinderen in het basisonderwijs, Deelrapport 1. Tilburg papers in language and literature.

WETERING, S. VAN DE & EL-KOUNDI, M. 1983, Evaluatie van het opvangklassen-experiment voor Marokkaanse kinderen in Enschede. Vakgroep Onderwijskunde Rijks Universiteit Utrecht.

4 The jewel in the crown of the Modern Prince

The new approach to bilingualism in multicultural education in England

ARTURO TOSI

Introduction

This chapter sets out to explore some controversial issues in the current education of linguistic minorities in England through the examination of a variety of approaches, from some early assimilationist policies through to the recent support for the teaching of mother tongues other than English. The broad purpose of the discussion is to relate the international debate about bilingualism to English policies and initiatives specifically concerned with the education of bilingual children. Particular attention will be directed, on the one hand, to the role of the professional debate as a mechanism for educational change and, on the other hand, to the efforts made by policy designers and implementors to re-shape conservative traditions in order to accommodate innovative recommendations. The purpose of the first two sections is to highlight the relevance of national politics to the study of curriculum development in general and the modern languages curriculum in particular. The last two sections propose a framework for discussion which may help to understand *whether* and *how* multicultural education can support the bilingualism of ethnic minority children and improve their educational opportunities.

The relation of national politics to social policies

The impact of immigration

It has been pointed out that the establishment of a significant ethnic minority population in Britain was neither planned nor anticipated by policy-makers (Layton-Henry, 1984). Apart from the nineteenth century's internal migration from Ireland and the settlements of Jews in the East End of London around the turn of the century, Britain's experience in dealing with immigrants before the 1970s was limited and inconsistent. A first Aliens Act was passed in 1905 only to control undesirable and destitute aliens. It was followed by a 1914 Act which was designed to regulate the residence of aliens without means of support or work permits, and was not applicable to British subjects from the overseas dominions and colonies of the Empire. With the end of World War II large numbers of colonial servicemen decided to settle in Britain, despite several efforts made to encourage them to return home (Cabinet Papers, 1950). In addition to them, a substantial group of Polish soldiers who were anti-Russian refused to return to Poland. For this group a special plan was designed in 1947 (the Polish Resettlement Act) to cope with housing, education and employment. That plan, which included the teaching of Polish as a mother tongue, is still considered nowadays "the most substantial coordinated attempt at integrating a large immigrant group in British society" (T. Rees, 1979).

For the reconstruction after the War Britain needed labour and started recruiting European political refugees (Lithuanians, Estonians, Latvians and Ukrainians) and unemployed peasants (especially Italians). The political refugee schemes (the Balt Scheme, the Westward Ho Scheme, the Blue Danube Scheme and the North Sea Scheme) were designed to meet labour shortages, especially in coal-mining, building and agriculture, whilst the Italian Volunteer Workers Scheme was expected to provide labour for under-staffed work in brickyards and in mental and tuberculosis hospitals (Political and Economic Planning, 1948). Neither group of aliens, however, benefited from the rights accorded to Commonwealth citizens nor from the favourable conditions of the early Polish Resettlement Act. Their work permits were for limited periods, they were not allowed to change jobs, they were discriminated against on matters of redundancy and promotion and they were not permitted to bring in their dependants for a number of years. Later in the 1950s, during the period of major reconstruction and new economic expansion, those areas of England which had developed industries experienced further labour shortages. This time some people were recruited from the West Indies, India and Pakistan through voluntary schemes and they were soon followed by substantial "chain" movements, based on sponsorship by friends and relatives, which made immigration grow rapidly throughout the 1960s.

Under the Immigration Act of 1971, the use of work permits ended virtually all primary immigration: the immigrants who had already succeeded in obtaining residence demonstrated the new composition of multi-ethnic British society. Commonwealth citizens were greatly over-represented in unskilled and semi-skilled manual occupations like ship-building, vehicle manufacture, textile manufacturing in general and transport. Political refugees were dispersed and found mainly in the service sectors of some major conurbations. Southern European peasants were still concentrated in certain districts which had textile and brick industries. The majority of professional people who had come with the immigrants from the colonies, and all the professionals from the groups of political refugees were forced to take manual jobs (Smith, 1977). Virtually no middle-class compatriots of the peasants from the rural areas of South Europe came to live in England, with the exception of a few diplomats and international company executives who are in permanent rotation.

The "race relations" problem

It has been argued that the politicization of immigration and "race relations" in Britain reveals popular hostility as well as a tendency, among political leaders, to see immigration as an added burden rather than a valuable asset (Simon, 1982). In the 1960s even the most progressive forces viewed immigration as a possible threat to the Labour movement or even to British society. In the 1970s the originally uncertain and exploratory debate became dominated in all the different political sectors by hardened positions of racist prejudice and outright racial hostility. The Conservative Party tried to dissociate itself from some extreme racist positions, such as those propounded by one of its leading members, Enoch Powell (1969). But the high electoral swings to the Conservative Party in parts of the country and constituencies with large settlements of Asian and Black minorities suggested that Powell's ideas were a major contribution to the Conservative victory in 1970. The more progressive forces were beginning to propose a positive programme of education, legislation and administrative action (Jenkins, 1967), but the political circles favourable to a less divisive and discriminatory approach were still recruiting fewer supporters. The balance of these different positions eventually settled around the common belief that immigration was posing unwelcome difficulties of social organization for the majority group and more problems of adjustment for the minorities (Patterson, 1969).

On the occasion of the Polish resettlement in 1947 the issue of cultural or racial threat did not arise. Though the main goal of the scheme was to anglicize the foreign settlers as much as possible, unique recognition was given to the importance of maintaining Polish language, culture and traditions (Zubrzycki, 1956; T. Rees, 1979). Fifteen years later, against a background of rising anxiety about "race relations" problems, the Commonwealth Immigrants Advisory Council (1964) proclaimed that "a national system cannot be expected to perpetuate the different values of immigrant groups". A different approach was introduced after 1965 by the political leaders of the liberal centre, which was based on the principle of social integration (Jenkins, 1971). However, in the construction of policies designed to meet this goal, there were two major obstacles to be overcome: the racial discrimination practised by the indigenous population, which was seen as a force that was preventing integration, and the conditions of deprivation developed by the concentration of immigrants themselves in certain areas (Ben-Tovim & Gabriel, 1982). The Urban Aid Programme (1968) was a response by the Labour government to racial discrimination, but in the scheme deprivation was still presented as a condition intrinsic to the minorities themselves: a "problem" which prevented their access to equal opportunities and one which needed to be approached with radical social measures, including education (Miles, 1982).

The ideology of racial disadvantage

Some educated people in Britain still believe that different biological characteristics hide diverse cultural attributes. Rex (1970) suggests that even more people would probably be willing to accept that the social tensions deriving from interaction between different linguistic and cultural groups are connected with questions of "race". In the 1970s social workers and other practitioners in the field of ethnic and social services were the first to point out the conditions of economic decline, physical decay and social disadvantage of the immigrant settlements. They identified them as institutional inadequacies, not characteristics of particular inadequate individuals or cultural groups. However, the notion of "deprivation" as used in official initiatives and in the speeches of political leaders (see, for example, Home Office, 1966) increasingly, though not always explicitly, referred to these conditions as expressions of groups' and individuals' cultural inadequacy, rather than descriptions of the structural conditions of inferiority in which they are forced to live.

Developing from the notion of cultural deprivation, the concept of immigrant children's special needs in education soon became the acceptable approach to cope with their alleged cultural and linguistic deficiencies. Gradually public attention was diverted away from the content of the curriculum and its dubious relevance to non-English children and directed towards seeking evidence for their presumed cultural limitations and linguistic handicaps. The assumption was that the discontinuity between these children and their school was the result of the malfunctioning of the children themselves, not of the school.

Language diversity and curriculum development

The relationship between the politics of "race relations" and changing approaches to the education of ethnic minorities is the focus of this section. My objective here is to underline the ideological continuity of some apparently diverse approaches. For this purpose three distinct sets of educational approaches will be distinguished and discussed: their respective philosophies rationalize diverse emphases in the educational debate and relate these emphases to the different organizational styles which are promoted by the central rather than the local authority.

Philosophy	*Emphasis*	*Organizational style*
Explicit assimilation	School problem	Dispersal
Implied assimilation	Special needs	Compensatory education
Concealed assimilation	Multiculturalism	Multicultural education

The dispersal approach to diversity

It is now widely recognized that in the early debate on the education of linguistically diverse children:

> "the official diagnosis of the educational problem posed by immigration was couched principally in terms of problems for the host community rather than for the immigrants themselves." (T. Rees, 1979)

Accordingly, dispersal measures were planned and the governmental Department of Education and Science (1965) issued a Circular on the Education of Immigrants which recommended on educational grounds that no school should have more than about 30% immigrant children. During the 1960s only a few teachers were reported (Townsend, 1971) to describe the dispersal measures as ethically wrong though educationally essential. All Education Authorities suddenly engaged in bussing immigrant and non-immigrant pupils as a means of dispersing them, though they never officially admitted it, as the policy was only to be used as a means of spreading pupils with linguistic difficulties. In these circumstances the various linguistic backgrounds of immigrant pupils were seen as further complications for the school and the Authority. Many schools in the major catchment areas reported that too many different tongues were represented and this generally reinforced the widespread argument that there would be no proper foundation for English language teaching other than the direct method. For the new arrivals there was neither assessment of linguistic proficiency nor clear guidance to encourage schools to refer pupils to special centres.

In those years the general climate of opinion was sympathetic to the dominant ideology that the linguistic diversity of these children was to be regarded as a factor capable of disrupting the education of indigenous children and of causing a decline in their standards of achievement. Accordingly the professional approach to the treatment of the children's diversity was explicitly addressed to helping the teachers rather than the child. This led quite a number of scholars to elaborate linguistic theories and teaching approaches which consolidated the educational credibility of that ideological standpoint. What used to be the most popular manual for teaching English to immigrant children would today leave quite a few ESL teachers with serious doubts about the professional acceptability of that approach:

> "If he can read and write his own mother tongue this might not always be very helpful, and his eye and hand movement may need to be completely retrained . . . Pupils who are completely illiterate may therefore be easier to teach except of course that there may be additional problems in rudimentary matters such as training them to hold a pencil or pen and to move it smoothly across the page." (Derrick, 1966).

The compensatory nature of multiracial education

By the early 1970s professional surveys, government enquiries and union reports (reported in Tomlinson, 1983) all agreed that schools were making little provision for linguistically diverse children and it was neither systematic nor effective. Several bodies were offered funds to conduct research into certain aspects of English as a second language, and yet there was no agreement as to why immigrant children did not achieve levels of literacy adequate to enable them to profit from the general education offered in the school. In the early 1970s ethnic minority communities became more vocal about their aspirations to retain their cultural and linguistic heritage and subsequently began to organize more radically their criticism of the quality of education offered to their children (see for example Coard, 1971, and *Race Today*, 1975).

After 1974 the Government seemed to adopt increasingly in its official statements the new notion of "multiracial harmony between different ethnic groups of which our society is now composed". Accordingly, education in multi-ethnic schools was identified as: "a potent instrument for increasing understanding and goodwill between the races" in order to achieve "harmony between the races in this country's multicultural and multiracial society" which was then believed to "be based on mutual understanding and respect". Despite these new declarations, however, the actual measures with which the Government wished to implement the new philosophy were still those designed to make immigrant pupils benefit from "special help given to all those suffering from educational disadvantage".

The construction of the concept of disadvantage in English education is well documented in the DES report *Educational disadvantage: Perspectives and Policies* (Department of Education and Science, 1975). The argument developed in the report, and finally agreed by the government's advisory Committee, was based on a compensatory approach to "the culture of poverty": i.e. that the knowledge and languages available to certain groups are not worth treating as educational knowledge and acceptable language, while those available to others are worth such treatment. In the formulation of the rationale for this philosophy the members of the government's advisory Committee devoted much of their work and discussions to establishing and defining what actually constitutes disadvantage in educational terms.

From the report of this enquiry (Department of Education and Science, 1975) it appears that only one member of the Committee strongly dissented from the new organization of the education of minority children, designed to compensate them for the disadvantage of being linguistically different from the indigenous child. Roy Truman, The Director of the ILEA Centre for Urban Eductational Studies, was then the first to indicate what later became widely recognized as the serious educational contradiction inherent in the new approach. In particular, he expressed concern for the concept of "disadvantage" and he pointed out that the new philosophy was based on a deficit concept. Such philosophy assumed that "poor educational attainment was the result of poor home environment and it ignored the possibility that disadvantage might be caused by inadequacies of the education system" (p. 13).

Since the publication of the Committee's report and throughout the 1970s, the implementation of the new compensatory approach has been variously interpreted by different Local Education Authorities and by different multi-ethnic schools. Progressive teachers increasingly argued that disadvantage is not a characteristic inherent in the children themselves, but is a condition foisted upon them when the school compares minority children's language with that of the indigenous child and subsequently treats their difference as a deficit. In the late 1970s, while classes of remedial education for non-native speakers of English proliferated in most authorities (Little & Willey, 1981; Willey, 1982) and some romantic discussions developed about the role of the mother tongue of the immigrant child (Brown, 1979), compensatory measures gradually abandoned their negative emphasis on special needs and adopted the more positive guise of "multiculturalism". Since the early 1980s the new multicultural philosophy, occasionally presented within a critical perspective (Brumfit, 1976, 1985), sometimes dismissed by radical theoreticians (Stone, 1981; Mullard, 1982, 1983), but more frequently celebrated by the rhetoric of politicians (Sir Keith Joseph, 1984), has invaded the debate on the education of minority children.

The majority's concern for the minorities' bilingualism

The debate about minorities' bilingualism began in the mid-1970s (see CILT, 1976) under the popular title of "mother tongue teaching" and it aimed to question the principles of monolingual English schooling and the effectiveness of compensatory education for children whose mother tongue was not English (Tosi, 1979; Saifullah Khan, 1980). A first governmental response (*Educational disadvantage and the educational needs of immigrants*, 1974) did not even mention the possibility of teaching ethnic minority children their mother tongue. Later, the report of another governmental Committee (*A language for life*, 1975) showed some sympathy ("no child should be expected to cast off the language and culture of the home as he crosses the school threshold"), but suggested neither the principles nor the practices for the teaching of mother tongues other than English.

Following those years of overwhelming dominance by a compensatory monolingual philosophy, professional resistance to a "mother tongue teaching" reform finds expression in the combination of two arguments, one ideological, the other educational: i.e. since English is the only acceptable language for education, anyone speaking another language must be disadvantaged. This position, which is still strong today, even in certain schools which are busy decorating their walls with symbols and pictures of ethnic cultures, provides the major popular and professional resistance against bilingual education. That is why in a country like Britain it is paradoxical, though quite normal, that bilingualism is discussed in schools and colleges as a subject of multicultural interest, but native fluency in languages other than English is still regarded as educationally undesirable. The argument is still that it might impair the bilingual child's learning of

English, but what is not always admitted is that it presents novel difficulties for monolingual schools.

The first steps in challenging the view that bilingualism simply implies a language deficit and an educational difficulty were taken in 1976: one came from the linguistic minorities themselves, the other from the European Community. The first move took place when many European and South Asian groups met and set up the Co-ordinating Committee for Mother Tongue Teaching (1980, now the National Council for Mother Tongue Teaching, 1985) with the intention of providing a professional channel for publicizing minorities' aspirations and demands, particularly in the area of minority community languages maintenance and education.

In the same year the European Community issued a Resolution (European Communities Commission, 1976), followed by a Directive which strongly supported the principle that the teaching of the mother tongue improves rather than impairs the linguistic and educational performance of bilingual children (European Communities Council, 1977). Subsequently, the Commission of the European Communities decided to take an important step and issued to four member states including Britain the invitation to set up projects designed to seek evidence of the educational benefit of teaching in schools the mother tongue of children of non-national origin. The Commission was obviously aware of the effect of the decentralization of the English system, and that is why it sought the collaboration of an interested Local Education Authority willing to establish a good model of administrative arrangements and pedagogical practices. Eventually, the responsibility for the new project, which was highly charged with political and educational significance, was allocated to Bedfordshire Education Authority (an account of the pilot project with a picture of the sociolinguistic situation of the Italian community in Bedford can be found in Tosi, 1984).

In 1980, four years later, Bedfordshire decided to terminate the programme when the EEC grant ran out. This raised many questions about the relationship between the pilot Authority and the Department of Education and Science on the one side, and the European Community on the other. Many of these questions are still being asked in international debate, even though it is now 10 years since the setting up of the project (Robinson, 1985; Cummins, 1985; Boos-Nunning et al., 1986; Simons, 1987). As for the national and international impact of the pilot bilingual programme, one of the main features of the EEC/Bedfordshire Project was that no research structure for the evaluation of the language competence and development of the bilingual children was ever built in. Bedfordshire insisted that such an investigative task was not expected from the project because no special resources had been granted by the EEC. The unfortunate consequence was that the impressive linguistic achievement (both in English with Punjabi and in English with Italian) registered in the bilingual programme could not be quantified and communicated to the professional world.

It is difficult to assess what effect that loss of political impact had on the EEC Commission, which sponsored the Mother Tongue and Culture Pilot Project with a view to promoting bilingualism ("not only as an important step towards the creation of school structures adapted to the real needs of migrants, but also as an important landmark to complete freedom of movement within the Community", as stated in European Communities Commission, 1977). Since its closure in 1980 the Bedford Project appears to have made a contribution to the new Conservative government's attempt to shift the focus of the debate on mother tongue teaching from educational responsibilities to financial implications. Significantly, this change of atmosphere was soon reflected by the national press, which reported the end of the project under the title of "Immigrant mother tongue 'costing too much'" (*Times Educational Supplement*, 1980).

Despite the Bedford experience, towards the end of the 1970s the integration of the ethnic minority and the academic sectors contributed to making a strong case that bilingual children's community languages should be developed and reinforced by the school. As a response to these arguments the Department of Education and Science set up two research projects. The Linguistic Minorities Project (1983 and 1985) was commissioned "to provide an account and analysis of changing patterns of bilingualism in a representative selection of areas in England" and was expected to assist new policy implementation. The Mother Tongue and English Teaching Project (Rees & Fitzpatrick, 1981) was set up in Bradford to provide quantified data on the linguistic benefit for pupils learning English after a transitional period of partial mother tongue education.

The aim of the bilingual education project commissioned by the Department of Education and Science, however, was not to evaluate the maintenance of the mother tongue and the development of bilingualism of ethnic minority children, but to speed up their acquisition of English and their induction into the English educational system (Fitzpatrick, 1984). As the principal aim of the Bradford project was to bridge the linguistic gap between the home and the school, competence in the mother tongue was not considered in the child's overall scholastic and academic development. The transitional bilingual arrangement was designed to support monolingual English education: this was clear from the project schedule—only one year—and eventually it was confirmed by the careful presentation of the findings. These were worded to sustain the thesis that bilingualism was not worth educational support because it does not help in the acquisition of English:

"subtle differences in performance of curriculum groups (i.e. English only and bilingually taught children) ... were not in our view such as to suggest that one curriculum was clearly more effective in respect of the acquisition of English, than the other overall." (O. Rees *et al.*, 1981).

The Bedford and Bradford projects (the only two projects set up to investigate bilingual education in England) produced contradictory con-clusions about the financial implications of using another language of education in addition to English. The Bedfordshire Authority's conclusion was that the cost of mother tongue teaching introduced for only 20% of the primary curriculum was excessive and intolerable for the county. The Bradford project succeeded in running the bilingual provision for as much as 50% of the timetable at no extra cost by employing ethnic minority teachers competent to teach bilingually.

Since the publication of these reports in the early 1980s, the argument about the relation of mother tongue teaching to the acquisition of English has been used in many official statements concerned with minorities' bilingualism. Their reference to the high cost of the provision (as in Bedford) and the neutral impact on the learning of English (as in Bradford) are still regularly used to overshadow other more important linguistic and educational facts. Since the official adoption of this new perspective, the bilingual conditions of minority children are no longer presented as a deficit but neither are they treated as an asset: this explains why the important findings of the Linguistic Minorities Project have never attracted much political or educational interest in the planning of a multicultural curriculum.

A framework for the analysis of majority—minority relations in education

In Britain there are still many schools with large numbers of non-English mother tongue speakers, where only English is used as a medium of instruction and European languages are taught as foreign languages. If one asks why multicultural education has not yet changed the language curriculum in these schools, the answer usually is that this is not a problem of national politics or central policies, since education operates within a decentralized system and school changes are made locally rather than centrally. Then the more relevant questions to ask are (1) whether there has been any change in the way in which the new multicultural approach treats competence in native languages other than English, and (2) what is the mechanism which, in a decentralized system, allows local pressure to introduce peripheral changes or, vice versa, allows central forces to prevent them? The discussion in this section suggests a framework for analysis which draws on the work of the Italian philosopher and historian Antonio Gramsci, and is followed by some explanatory hypotheses which may account for the recent multicultural approach to the bilingualism of ethnic minority children.

The "hegemony" theory

The crucial question about the relationship between the content of knowledge and the content of education was first posed in explicit terms by Gramsci (1926–1936) when he discussed how knowledge which is available to certain groups becomes "school knowledge" or "educational knowledge", and that which is available to others does not. Gramsci has exercised considerable influence on English sociologists of education, in particular since the cultural historian Raymond Williams (1961) adopted his approach in order to develop a framework for the study of the content of education.

Since the mid-1970s most of Gramsci's writings (1975, 1977) have been available in English translation and many of his ideas have thrown new light on the questions asked by sociologists of education, particularly in connection with the changing relationship between class, culture and schooling in contemporary British society. Recently more British scholars have been strongly influenced by the thoughts of the Italian philosopher (see, for example, Young, 1971, 1973; Entwistle, 1978, 1979; Stone, 1981; and Mullard, this volume, Chapter 17) and they have stressed the relevance of Gramsci's explanatory theory of the distribution of power and the mechanism of social control through the selection, transmission and evaluation of public knowledge. The major component of this theory is a framework for analysis which focuses on the changing power relations between groups: this is introduced by the key notion of *hegemony* which accounts for the mechanism of the reorganization of power.

The Gramscian concept of hegemony differs from the more familiar notion in international affairs, where one nation exercises political, cultural or economic influence over others. By extension, Gramsci analyses the relation of one class exercising influence over another within the same national context. Yet hegemony differs substantially from class dictatorship in that power is exercised by the dominant group through the monitoring of the balance between forces, rather than by means of force. Hegemony is the organization of consent through invisible cultural dominance rather than visible political power. Thus Gramsci's approach and the current concern of sociologists of education converge in their common attempt to interpret the role of educational changes in order to understand the mechanism of control which is exercised through social and cultural reorganization. The Italian philosopher indicates that in a modern society this process is one which provides the dominant class with a new form of control "which gives stability and bases power on wide-ranging consent and acquiescence" (Gramsci, 1926–36).

The reorganization of control

The concept of consent resulting from relation of forces is the key which distinguishes one dominant group's wielding of power in a democratic society from the use of force to control a subordinate group in a class dictatorship. Thus the hegemonic leadership of one group is still characterized by the exercise of power, but this is not founded on the overt use of the system to impose its interests on those of other groups. Instead, it relies on its covert ability to combine the interests of other classes or groups with its own interests. When this is achieved the hegemonic group has succeeded in extending its cultural control to include all state institutions and will therefore present itself as the sole authorized representative of all the different interests of a socially and culturally diverse society. Thus hegemony, through the establishment of alliances and balances of forces between diverse groups, can operate to neutralize forms of dissent, or to transform it into its own ideological network. This extraordinary political achievement was captured in Gramsci's eloquent comment (1957) that politics is an art as well as a science, for it needs to combine scientific analysis with imaginative persuasion.

Gramsci's theory contains the germs of the dichotomy currently inherent in much of the dilemma of progressive educationists. Some seek the enhancement in school of the status of all languages and cultures, including those characteristic of the pupils from lower social classes and minority groups. Others are more preoccupied with the persistent discrimination against minority and lower status cultures outside the school, and they would concentrate on making the mainstream language and culture more effectively available to the underprivileged. The conflict between these two positions well exemplifies the hegemonic control imposed by the dominant groups on the educational system: progressive educationalists may well agree about rejecting the current ideological principles governing the selection and transmission of knowledge, but they deeply disagree about the changes required to modify the system which perpetuates them.

The two positions described above are produced by the same ideological concern, and yet point towards opposite pedagogical conclusions, which are often identified with optimistic liberalism and pessimistic radicalism. Since the two positions involve, and encourage, two opposite approaches to the education of minority underprivileged groups, their conflict can be seen as the success of the majority privileged group: it has managed to establish new relations between forces capable of containing opposing interests, it has disorganized the opponents' alliance and shifted the balance of forces in its favour. In this way hegemony is achieved through a combination of persuasion and negotiation, as Gramsci envisaged when he drew on Machiavelli's description of the qualities of the Modern Prince (1974). From the pioneering work of the Renaissance political philosopher the Italian historian resorted to the abstraction of the Modern Prince, in an attempt to advance a theory of a conscious and controlled use of power. A similar attempt to develop an explicit theory of conflict to account for school policies, educational changes and the impact of research on education has already received considerable attention in England in connection with the education of the working class (Bernstein, 1971–3; Young, 1971; Entwistle, 1978, 1979) and in the USA in relation to the bilingual education of ethnic minorities (Spolsky, 1971; Kjolseth, 1971; Paulston, 1975; and Fishman, 1977).

It would seem that Gramsci's theory can be used also to account for some of the recent developments in the education of linguistic minorities in England. These developments have given rise to some remarkable controversies among progressive educators on crucial issues such as the bilingualism or semilingualism of minority children (see Martin-Jones & Romaine, 1986) and the multicultural or segregationist nature of their education (see Brook, 1980).

The treatment of bilingualism in multicultural education

Like other national educational systems, English education needs to be understood as a whole. Its decentralized nature stems from the discretion given to the heads of schools over the organization of teaching and the content of the curriculum, and the complex relationship between the schools, their local authorities and the central Inspectorate. Within this context, the establishment of a hegemonic approach must rest on activities of consultation and persuasion which operate in harmony with the mechanism of change. This is a mechanism which Bernstein (1971) described as one where:

> "weak central control does permit a series of changes which have, initially, limited consequences for the system as a whole [and where] on the other hand, there is much stronger central control over the organisational style of the school."

What is evident in England is that although the *formal* central control is weak, the *informal* system of central influence is strong, especially when Inspectorate and advisory channels are in synchrony with the central authority (the Department of Education and Science). The central control can exercise political pressure on the local authorities, and the Inspectorate and Advisory staff can bring financial pressure to bear on the individual school. Thus, when it comes to issues of national relevance, the explanation of mere coercion is, of course, too simplistic, but the whole mechanism of developing professional co-operation assumes ideological relevance. The discussion in this last section is intended to make explicit why in the field of the education of minorities in England there have been noticeable changes in the organizational style in schools, without there being any marked curricular changes in the recognition of and development of competence in languages other than English.

Reproduction of ideology and reorganization of education

In England multicultural education is still a depressingly vague and ambiguous notion. For example, there is no official indication which tells schools how the old educational principle of equal opportunities should now be translated into the new multicultural approach, nor is there a clear position about the role of non-English mother tongues in the curriculum. There are, instead, government directives and reports about English language education (Department of Education and Science, 1985)—but not about multicultural education—and these establish that the principle of equality of opportunity means equal treatment of children, rather than recognition of their native competence in a language other than English or their right to have it developed by the school.

This monolingual approach to the notion of equality of opportunity is hardly a new one in the English tradition of minorities' education, except that its formulations, in the past twenty years, have reflected diverse political concerns and these were implemented in schools with different organizational styles:

In 1964:   "A national system cannot be expected to perpetuate the different values of immigrant groups." (Commonwealth Immigrants Advisory Council, 1964).

In 1975:   "Educational disadvantage [is] a national problem . . . the needs of minority group children [are] specific and should receive special consideration." (Department of Education and Science, 1975).

In 1985:   "The problem facing the education system is not how to educate ethnic minorities but how to educate all children." (*Education for all*, 1985).

There is little doubt that today the multicultural debate equips many teachers to appreciate why bilingual minority children do not respond linguistically as does the majority monolingual child. What multicultural education still does not do is recognize the diverse linguistic competence of minority children as worthwhile educational knowledge in the curriculum. Despite the changing pressure from national politics and local communities, despite the new multicultural organization in schools, the education system has been quite consistent in reproducing this compensatory-monolingual approach to bilingualism throughout the years. In the past, the curriculum could afford to ignore any language competence which was not English. Today the current multicultural approach claims to provide ethnic minority children with the best educational opportunities. But these can hardly be found in those schools which teach only foreign languages. There are also schools which have begun to teach community languages (see Martin-Jones, 1984 and Reid, 1984), but their courses, too, are found to offer little support to bilingualism when they adopt a foreign language approach.

The explanation of the impotence of these minority language programmes and of their inclination to cling to the tradition of foreign language teaching cannot omit the ambiguous position of many English academics on the question of teaching mother tongues other than English. In the 1980s, this debate had already lost much of the political impact of the 1970s, without having achieved a solid agreement about educational objectives and their professional realization in the curriculum. For example, the question about minority children's bilingualism or semilingualism still divides educators (see the recent paper by Martin-Jones & Romaine, 1986), and their contributions tend to restore the unresolved dilemma about bidialectism in relation to the so-called "restricted" and "elaborated" codes, rather than to indicate new pedagogical directions. Hopelessly, when the dilemma about bilingualism in education is discussed at the level of theory, rather than practice, there are equally convincing arguments, put forward by expert linguists, who support totally opposite solutions. Some writers feel strongly that the ineffectiveness of the language education of bilingual children is primarily due to deficit notions associated with the ways we interpret and describe their bilingual competence. Others, who seem to be more preoccupied with the persistent discrimination outside schools, rather than with the status of minority language inside schools, argue that what bilingual pupils need is for the mainstream language to be more effectively available to them.

Gramsci would say that as long as this theoretical dilemma persists, and as long as the professionals are not in agreement about educational solutions, the system maintains the control of the ideological dispute and neutralizes its political opposition. This is certainly one way in which the hegemonic control of education in England succeeds in preserving the privileges of the monolingual majority. By constantly reviewing the arguments that explain why only the language competence available to the English majority is worthwhile educational knowledge, the system secures the consent of large sectors of society, including some people from the minority communities and others from the circles of educationalists.

From this hegemonic perspective, the report of the Swann Committee on the Education of Children of Ethnic Minorities (*Education for all*, 1985) has played a constructive role in the reorganization of public consent in connection with the issue of bilingualism in education. The impact of the Committee has been political as well as professional. On the one hand, the report has succeeded in prolonging the dispute about the effectiveness of multicultural education and this has increased divisions among its critics. On the other hand, the opposition to the persisting compensatory approach has either been dissolved through gradual transformations, which accommodate antagonism through professional co-operation, or it has been diverted into the sphere of politics.

This second option has recently developed the so-called anti-racist movement, whose basic philosophy involves using the school to combat the vehicles of discrimination and racism, instead of cultivating the myth of multicultural harmony. When this is the case one is inclined to agree with Pareck (1985, 1986) that multicultural and anti-racist education may ultimately have the same outcome. It is more difficult to agree with him, however, about the quality of that outcome: since it still concerns the school's organizational style, not the content of the curriculum, it has very little to offer to the improvement of the cognitive and academic performance of minority children. It would seem that the outcomes of compensatory, multicultural or anti-racist education vary very little when schools choose to remain monolingual, because they are politically or professionally impotent to cope with bilingualism. This impotence may take many organizational forms and theoretical justifications since so many different approaches can co-exist in a decentralized system. Thus the inadequacy to cope with bilingualism in England does not depend on an obstructive formal policy, but on informal directives which serve to inform the attitudes of the professional world. Some of these directives, which are presented within the new framework of multicultural education, are discussed below.

The ideological and professional challenges of bilingualism

As there is no such thing as a monocultural society, multiculturalism is an abstraction which can be educationally misleading. For example, the multicultural approach implies that it would be possible to educate all pupils multiculturally, whereas in reality it is extremely rare and complex to educate individuals even biculturally. When they live in an environment which mixes the affective and cognitive experiences of two or more distinct cultural groups, a very sophisticated curricular organization is required to train them to operate in two distinctive and independently rewarding cultural frames. Brumfit (1976, 1985), on the one hand, has repeatedly argued that it is naive to claim that the same can be done by the school with a multitude of cultures. Languages, on the other hand, unlike cultures, have a socially codified and agreed system of rules of how to acquire, to transform and to communicate ideas and emotions. Accordingly, most societies recognize their language as a relevant and useful kind of knowledge whose transmission to the next generation cannot be left to chance. But societies have rarely engaged in formal teaching of the functions, the roles and meanings of their own culture and yet they seem to be able to transmit them successfully, within the framework of their language.

The conclusion of this paper is that any multicultural approach which does not develop bilingualism within the curriculum is not in a position to provide better educational opportunities for bilingual children. This view is supported below by three arguments which concern (1) the cognitive, (2) the curricular, and (3) the professional dimensions of bilingual education.

1. It has been pointed out that one initial misconception of "multicultural education for all" is that there would be societies which are multicultural whilst others would be monocultural. According to this view British society would have recently moved from a state of monoculturalism to that of multiculturalism. This argument ignores the facts that it is impossible to

translate cultures lived by some into cultural competence to be acquired by others and that this is one of the limits of traditional foreign language education. The policy of teaching foreign languages to all children allows the cognitive resources of children from non-English backgrounds to remain ignored and neglected. Denying value to native competence in languages other than English, and excluding minority languages from education, removes from the curriculum the cognitive qualities and the communicable content of minority cultures.

2. The official argument used to justify the idea that bilingualism can best be developed when community languages are taught outside rather than inside the curriculum is that such languages could lose their "community" dimension if they were to be taken care of by curricular mainstream education (see Sir Keith Joseph, 1984; Department of Education and Science, 1984; and *Education for all*, 1985). This argument contains a fundamental contradiction. If it is true that minority children's under-achievement is caused by their cultural and cognitive diversity (see *Education for all*, 1985), why is it that language competence, the most quantifiable component of their diverse background in educational terms, is not recognized and developed in pupils who are academically at risk?

3. Some teaching of "mother tongues and community languages" other than English has been recently introduced by some authorities and schools under pressure from local minority communities. Other minority languages have been on offer for many years in courses outside schools run by the authorities of the country of origin. In both cases the central authority (Department of Education and Science, 1984) has made clear that certain conditions need to be satisfied before this provision can be offered inside the curriculum. These conditions suggest that the organization of the teaching should be patterned on the more established professionalism of foreign language teaching. This approach (see Tosi, 1986 and 1987) can be used to construct the "foreignness" of the community language course and this, in turn, affects the learnability of the language and the selection of competence in its speakers. It is interesting that the effect of this central directive to control the professionalism of community language education for bilingual pupils has once again had the effect of dividing progressive teachers. On the one side the suggestion has a certain appeal to those who hold an anti-racist position: they believe that in order to enhance the educational status of community languages, one needs to eliminate any existing dichotomy with traditional foreign languages. On the other side, those who are more interested in understanding the role of language teaching (i.e. whether it develops or selects competence) rather than its organizational style, point out that a foreign language approach to

community language education would only continue to penalize bilingual children for their "irregular" skills.

References

A language for life 1975, Report of the Committee of Inquiry into Reading and the Use of English, appointed by the Secretary of State for Education and Science under the Chairmanship of Sir Alan Bullock, FBA. London: HMSO.

BEN-TOVIM, G. S. & GABRIEL, J. G. 1982, *The politics of race in Britain 1962–73: A review of the major trends and recent debates*. In C. HUSBAND (ed.), 144–71.

BERNSTEIN, B. 1971, On the classification and framing of educational knowledge. In M. F. D. YOUNG (ed.), 47–69.

——1971–73, *Class, codes and control*, 3 vols. London: Routledge and Kegan Paul.

BOOS-NUNNING, V., HOHMANN, M., REICH, H. H. & WITTEK, F. 1986, *Towards intercultural education: a comparative study of the education of migrant children in Belgium, France and the Netherlands*. London: Centre for Information on Language Teaching and Research.

BROOK, M. 1980, The mother tongue issue in Britain: cultural diversity or control? *British Journal of Sociology of Education* 1:3, 239–56.

BROWN, D. M. 1979, *Mother tongue to English: The young child in the multicultural school*. Cambridge: Cambridge University Press.

BRUMFIT, C. 1976, The multicultural society. *Multiracial School* 5:1, 1–12.

——1985, Multicultural education, educational principles and second-language learning. In C. BRUMFIT, R. ELLIS & J. LAVINE (eds), *English as a second language in the United Kingdom: linguistic and educational contexts*. Oxford: Pergamon Press, pp. 175–80.

CABINET PAPERS 1950, *Coloured people from British colonial territories*. Cabinet memorandum by the Secretary of State for the Colonies, CP (50) 113, 18 May (Public Records Office).

CILT 1976, *Bilingualism and British education: The dimension of the diversity*. London: Centre for Information on Language Teaching and Research.

COARD, B. 1971, *How the West Indian child is made educationally subnormal in the British school system*. London: New Beacon Books Ltd.

Commonwealth Immigrants Advisory Council, 1963. Second Report: Education and Information. London: HMSO. Cmnd: 2268.

CO-ORDINATING COMMITTEE FOR MOTHER TONGUE TEACHING, 1980, *Newsletter 4.*

CUMMINS, J. 1985, Book Reviews: *Immigration and bilingual education* by Arturo Tosi. *Journal of Multilingual and Multicultural Development* 6:6, 515–19.

DEPARTMENT OF EDUCATION AND SCIENCE 1965, Circular on Education of Immigrants, Circular No. 7, June 1965.

—— 1975, *Educational disadvantage: Perspectives and Policies.* The Report of a conference convened by the Secretary of State for Education and Science, 16 April 1975.

—— 1984, *Mother-tongue teaching in school and community.* London: HMSO.

—— 1985, *The curriculum from 5 to 15.* Curriculum Matters 2. London: HMSO.

DERRICK, J. 1966, *Teaching English to immigrants.* London: Longman.

Education for all, 1985. The report of the Committee of Inquiry into the education of children from ethnic minority groups, chaired by Lord Swann. London: HMSO.

Educational disadvantage and the educational needs of immigrants, 1974. Observations on the report on education of the Select Committee on race relations and immigration. London: HMSO.

ENTWISTLE, H. 1978, *Class, culture and education.* London; Methuen.

—— 1979, *Antonio Gramsci: Conservative schooling for radical politics.* London: Routledge and Kegan Paul.

EUROPEAN COMMUNITIES COMMISSION 1976, An educational policy for the Community. Resolution of the Council of the Ministers of Education. Meeting within the Council of 9 February 1976. Background note published 26 March 1976.

—— 1977, *The children of migrant workers.* Collection Studies, Educational Series No. 1, Brussels.

EUROPEAN COMMUNITIES COUNCIL 1977, Council Directive on the education of children of migrant workers, 25 July 1977, 77/486/EEC.

FISHMAN, J. A. 1977, The social science perspective: Keynote. In J. A. FISHMAN (ed.), *Bilingual Education: Current perspectives.* Arlington, Virginia: Center for Applied Linguistics, pp. 1–49.

FITZPATRICK, B. 1984, The education of young bilingual children in England: a commentary on the Mother Tongue and English Teaching Project (1978–1981). Bradford College of Education. Unpublished manuscript.

GRAMSCI, A. 1926–1936, *Quaderni dal carcere*, 4 vols. Torino: Einaudi.

—— 1957, *The Modern Prince and other writings* (translation). New York: Monthly Review Press.

—— 1974, *Note sul Machiavelli*. Rome: Editori Riuniti.

—— 1975, *Letters from prisons* (translation). London: Jonathan Cape. Lawner Letters.

—— 1977, *Selections from political writings (1910–1920)*: Q. HOARE (ed.), J. MATHEWS (translation). New York: International Publishers.

HOME OFFICE, 1966, *Local Government Act 1966*, Section II.

HUSBAND, C. (ed.) 1982, *Race in Britain: continuity and change*. London: Hutchinson and Co. Ltd.

JENKINS, R. 1967, *Essay and speeches*. London: Collins.

—— 1971, *The production of knowledge at the Institute of Race Relations*. Independent Labour Party.

JOSEPH, Sir K. 1984, Address given by Sir Keith Joseph, Secretary of State, to the School Council Conference on Materials for Mother Tongue Teaching to children of migrants sponsored by the European Communities, 1984.

KJOLSETH, R. 1971, Bilingual education progress in the United States: for assimilation or pluralism? In B. SPOLSKY (ed.), *The language education of minority children*. Rowley, Mass.: Newbury House, pp. 94–121.

LAYTON-HENRY, Z. 1984, *The politics of race in Britain*. London: Allen and Unwin.

LINGUISTIC MINORITIES PROJECT 1983, Linguistic minorities in England. A report from the Linguistic Minorities Project. University of London, Institute of Education.

—— 1985, *The other languages of England*. London: Routledge and Kegan Paul.

LITTLE, A. & WILLEY, R. 1981, *Multi-ethnic education: the way forward*. Schools Council Pamphlet 18, Schools Council.

MARTIN-JONES, M. 1984, The newer minorities: literacy and educational issues. In P. TRUDGILL (ed.).

MARTIN-JONES, M. & ROMAINE, S. 1986, Semilingualism: A half-baked theory of communicative competence, *Applied Linguistics* 7:1, 26–38.

MILES, R. 1982, *Racism and nationalism in Britain*. In C. HUSBAND (ed.), pp. 279–300.

MULLARD, C. 1982, Multi-racial education in Britain: from assimilation to cultural pluralism. In J. TIERNEY (ed.), *Migration and Schooling*. Eastbourne, Sussex: Holt, Rinehart and Winston.

—— 1983, The social context and meaning of multicultural education. *Educational Analysis* 3:1.

NATIONAL COUNCIL FOR MOTHER TONGUE TEACHING 1985, The Swann Report: education for all? *Journal of Multilingual and Multicultural Development* 6, 6, 497–508.

PARECK, B. 1985, The gift of diversity, *Times Educational Supplement* 29 March 1985.

—— 1986, Bilingualism and educational investment. The IBM/North Westminster Lecture given at North Westminster Community School, 11 March 1986 (mimeo).

PATTERSON, S. 1969, *Immigration and race relation in Britain 1960–1967.* Oxford: Oxford University Press.

PAULSTON, C. B. 1975, Ethnic relations and bilingual education: accounting for contradictory data. *Working Papers on Bilingualism* 6, 1–44.

POLITICAL AND ECONOMIC PLANNING 1948, *Population policy in Great Britain.* London, April 1948.

POWELL, E. 1969, Text of speech delivered to the annual meeting in the West Midlands Area Conservative Political Centre. In B. SMITHIES & P. FIDDICK (eds), *Enoch Powell on Immigration.* Sphere, pp. 63–77.

Race Today, January 1975, Who is afraid of ghetto schools?

REES, O. & FITZPATRICK, F. 1981, *Mother Tongue and English teaching Project*, Vols. 1 and 2. University of Bradford (mimeo).

REES, O. A., FITZPATRICK, F., SHARMA, S. & NASSER, S. 1981, *Mother tongue and English teaching for young Asian children in Bradford.* Digest of a Report Vol. I and II to the Department of Education and Science.

REES, T. 1979, Immigration policies in the United Kingdom. In D. KUBAT (ed.), *The politics of migration policies.* New York: Center for Migration Studies, pp. 67–91. Reprinted in C. HUSBAND (ed.), pp. 75–96.

REID, E. (ed.), 1984, *Minority community languages in school.* National Council for Languages in Education (CILT Publications).

REX, J. 1970, *Race relations in sociological theory.* London: Weidenfeld and Nicolson.

ROBINSON, B. 1985, Bilingualism and mother-tongue maintenance in Britain. In C. BRUMFIT, R. ELLIS & J. LAVINE (eds), pp. 25–53.

SAIFULLAH KHAN 1980, The 'mother-tongue' of linguistic minorities in multicultural England. *Journal of Multilingual and Multicultural Development* 1:1, 71–88.

SIMON, R. 1982, *Gramsci's political thought: an introduction.* London: Lawrence and Wishart.

SIMONS, H. 1987, *Getting to know schools in a democracy: the politics and process of evaluation.* Lewes: Falmer Press.

SMITH, D. 1977, *Racial disadvantage in Britain.* Harmondsworth, Middlesex: Penguin.

SPOLSKY, B. 1971, The limits of language education. *Linguistic Reporter* 13:3, 1–5. Reprinted in B. SPOLSKY (ed.), 1972, *The Language Education of Minority Children.* Rowley, Mass.: Newbury House.

STONE, M. 1981, *The education of the black child in Britain*. London: Fontana.

Times Educational Supplement 1980, Immigrant mother tongue "costing too much". 8 March, 1980.

TOMLINSON, S. 1983, *Ethnic minorities in British schools: a Review of the literature, 1960–82*. London: Heinemann Educational.

TOSI, A. 1979, Mother-tongue teaching to the children of migrants. *Language Teaching and Linguistics: Abstracts* 12:4, 213–31.

—— 1984, *Immigration and bilingual education*. Oxford: Pergamon Press.

—— 1986, Home and community, language teaching for bilingual learners: Survey Article. *Language Teaching* 19:1.

—— 1987, First, second or foreign language learning: political and professional support for bilingualism in national and international education. Ph.D. Dissertation. University of London, Institute of Education.

TOWNSEND, H. E. R. 1971, *Immigrant pupils in Britain: the LEA Response*. National Foundation for Educational Research in England and Wales.

TRUDGILL, P. (ed.) 1984, *Language in the British Isles*. Cambridge: Cambridge University Press.

WILLEY, R. 1982, *Teaching in multicultural Britain*. Schools Council Programme 4, Schools Council.

WILLIAMS, R. 1961, *The long revolution*. London: Chatto and Windus.

YOUNG, M. F. D. 1971, An approach to the study of curricula as socially organised knowledge. In M. F. D. YOUNG (ed.), *Knowledge and control: New Directions for the sociology of education*. London: Collier MacMillan.

—— 1973, Taking sides against the probable. *Educational Review* 25:3.

ZUBRZYCKI, J. 1956, *Polish immigrants in Britain*. The Hague: Nijhoff.

5 Active bilingualism

The Swedish goal for immigrant children's language instruction

GUNNAR TINGBJÖRN

Immigration to Sweden

Few countries in the world have had such a linguistically and ethnically homogeneous population as Sweden. It is true that Finnish and Sami minorities have always lived in the northernmost part of the country, but they have been almost totally neglected by the Swedish authorities, both culturally and linguistically, until a few decades ago. A certain amount of immigration of specialists and people who have married Swedish citizens has taken place. Prior to World War II relatively few Swedes—except for those who emigrated to the USA during the 1800s—moved out of the country, permanently or temporarily. As a result, we had very little experience of immigration and multilingual and multicultural societies in Sweden when immigration on a large scale began during the second half of the 1960s. Within two decades this immigration has radically changed the population structure of the country.

Of Sweden's approximately 8 million inhabitants, about 1 million are immigrants and their descendants. The largest immigrant groups come from these countries:

Finland	337,000	Turkey	24,000
Denmark	60,000	Greece	20,000
Norway	60,000	Hungary	18,000
Germany	55,000	United States	15,000
Yugoslavia	55,000	Great Britain	14,000
Poland	34,000	Chile	12,000

The Scandinavians (i.e. Finns, Danes and Norwegians) and the Yugoslavs represent labour immigration. In the German group, the proportion of specialists and the number of persons who have immigrated due to marriage with Swedes is clearly greater than in the other groups. The Estonians arrived during World War II, so they have immigrated to entirely different circumstances (e.g. in terms of language instruction) from the groups which came during the last few decades. Even the Hungarians, the majority of whom came during the second half of the 1950s, have had a largely different reception in Sweden from that of the immigrants of the 1970s. In addition to the groups mentioned in the list above, we should add that during the last half of the 1970s there was a major immigration of political refugees from Latin America, and of an Assyrian group from Turkey. During the 1980s many Sino-Vietnamese refugees have come and in the last few years many refugees from Iran and Lebanon, among others. Free immigration ceased in 1967, apart from the immigration which takes place within the free Scandinavian labour market. Otherwise, immigration to Sweden consists mainly of refugees, members of the families of earlier immigrants and adopted children. The tendency at present is for a continued comprehensive migration *within* Scandinavia (we can even notice certain signs of "periodic commuting" between Sweden and neighbouring Scandinavian countries, particularly Finland) as well as immigration of small groups, from ever more distant countries, and as a result ever greater linguistic and cultural typological differences in comparison with Swedish language and culture.

Immigrants are unevenly distributed geographically in Sweden. There are major concentrations in the three urban areas: Stockholm, Gothenburg and Malmö, in the region around Stockholm, and in certain industrial areas in southern Sweden. Very few immigrants live in the northern part of the country. The age range is also uneven. The number of retired people is insignificant, while the majority of immigrants are at the age when they have children and build a family. Even if Sweden, contrary to all expectations, were not to receive any more immigrants, the number of children in nursery school and compulsory school from immigrant homes would rise significantly during the coming years.

This brings with it a revolutionary change for Swedish schools. Around 1960, about 1% of the pupils in the Swedish compulsory schools had a home language other than Swedish. In 1985, this figure had risen to about 10%, and all calculations show that in the year 2000, in less than 15 years, every third pupil in compulsory school will have a home language other than Swedish. At present, about 110,000 immigrant pupils attend Swedish schools. Of these, about half participate in some form of "home language" instruction, and about an equal number are judged by Swedish teachers to be in need of extra instruction in the Swedish language.

Stay in Sweden: involuntary, temporary, uncertain

The number of immigrants who come to Sweden with specialist jobs waiting for them is very limited. Neither is the number of people who move to Sweden to marry or join a Swedish partner particularly large, even if this number will presumably rise in the future, due to a rise in international contacts.

Most immigrants have not come to Sweden voluntarily. External force, in the form of political or religious persecution, has caused many to flee from their homelands. These refugee immigrants often end up in Sweden by chance; they could just as easily have come to another country with a liberal refugee policy. The majority of immigrants are, however, labour immigrants. They are temporary exiles from their countries. If there had been work and income possibilities in their native countries, they would have stayed there. Even for these, it is often a coincidence that Sweden is the country to which they have emigrated. The Scandinavian immigrants are, however, in this respect in a different situation considering the free labour market in Scandinavia, the geographical proximity and (for Danes and Norwegians) the intercomprehensibility of the Scandinavian languages.

Very few immigrant groups plan to stay in Sweden forever. The political refugees naturally hope to return to their homelands when the regime they despise, which has driven them into exile, has fallen. But dictatorial regimes, which depend on violence to remain in power, are unfortunately often successful in staying in power. Similarly, those who have fled to secure a job want to return home when new jobs are available in their home territories. But it often takes a very long time before an economic upswing takes place. It is unlikely that economic conditions in the home country will improve so much that the establishment of new industry in a depopulated countryside can take place.

Thus, many immigrants postpone the journey home they have looked forward to for one or two years at a time. When their stay tends to be longer than expected, it is difficult to raise their aspirations and to change erroneous linguistic habits. Among those who have continually expressed the hope of returning to their home countries, many will undoubtedly remain in Sweden forever. What is crucial to the attitude towards learning Swedish in these cases is not the increasingly definite permanent residence, but rather the feeling which is constantly kept alive, that the stay in Sweden is temporary, and will soon end. The insight that a return is an uncertain or futile hope leads to resignation, which is hardly an active stimulus to language learning.

Particularly for the immigrants from neighbouring countries, there is a clear tendency towards a return immigration to the country of origin even if conditions in the native country have not become noticeably better. Often these return immigrations lead to disappointment, and a new emigration, and the result even in these cases will be resignation.

For the adult immigrant, the involuntary exile existence, and its expected temporary nature, is certainly the most important factor explaining their lack of motivation to learn Swedish. This temporary exile must nevertheless be of great importance for the other members of the family as well—including the children—and their attitude towards Sweden, education in Sweden, and the Swedish language. As the Swedish educational system is built on the assumption that all pupils should receive their entire education in Swedish, and stay in the country to enter and work in the Swedish labour market, it is natural that immigrant pupils are caught in the middle of a situation with conflicting purposes, attitudes and values.

Are Swedish schools prepared to receive linguistic minorities?

Foreign language instruction in Swedish schools

In Swedish schools there has been a long tradition of instruction in modern foreign languages. During the past decades, English has been a required subject for all pupils, but otherwise foreign language instruction has been voluntary. Instruction has been culturally motivated (i.e. it has involved languages which are important for Swedes to know) and planned as traditional foreign language instruction (i.e. it has been an instruction closely controlled by Swedish teachers and textbook writers, with a relatively limited number of lessons each week). Swedish teachers have, during this time, built up a considerable fund of theoretical and methodological knowledge, on the one hand about how the Swedish language (primarily the Swedish written language) should be taught, and developed, for children who have grown up learning Swedish naturally in a Swedish-speaking environment, and on the other how pupils with Swedish as a first language should be taught certain foreign languages. In this way, instruction is based on the pupils' earlier linguistic skills, and is carried out in the foreign languages, with a "hidden" (in the best sense of the word) contrastivity, even though it is often to be taught using the direct method, i.e. without using Swedish, the language which is common to both pupils and teachers. The foreign languages which are taught in Swedish schools are the Germanic languages, English and German, the Romance languages,

French and Spanish, as well as Russian, a language from the Slavic group. All these languages belong to the Indo-European language family, and are closely, or relatively closely, related to Swedish.

On the other hand, several of the largest immigrant languages, such as Finnish, Turkish and Hungarian, belong to entirely different language families. The Swedes' own studies of closely-related languages have often given them the impression that all foreign languages have a structure similar to Swedish. This impression often results in their under-estimating the immigrants' difficulties in learning Swedish and developing bilingual skills in Swedish and in a language very different from it.

The goal of active bilingualism

The Swedish parliament decided in 1975, in total unanimity, that the goal for immigrant pupils' language learning should be *active bilingualism*. This implies that they should be able to use both their languages in all necessary and desired situations on the level of a first language, i.e. both those situations which arise as a result of the demands of the immigrants' surroundings, and also those in which they wish to participate. Their bilingualism should be a double-sided first language competence. They should acquire two first languages but the external conditions for reaching this goal are very unfavourable.

The goal of active bilingualism differs from the current instructional goal of immigrant minorities in other countries. It is a result of one of the goals of Sweden's immigrant policy, namely *freedom of choice*. If this promise of linguistic and cultural freedom of choice is to be anything other than empty words, it must be built on bilingualism on a level which does not exclude or restrict a return to the immigrant's own or to his/her parents' country of origin, when other conditions allow it. This demands first language competence and ability in the home language. The goal of freedom of choice also guarantees to immigrants the right to use their languages and develop their cultures within Swedish society as they choose.

Monolingual policies in other countries

Many countries have adopted a policy of assimilation, whose goal is that the immigrants should acquire the majority language as quickly as possible, while at the same time the majority society is uninterested in, or does nothing to make use of, immigrants' knowledge in the minority languages. For immigrant children, an assimilation into the majority society means losing linguistic and personal contact with their parents and with the parents' generation in the minority group, and in addition, with the native country and relatives there. Even if the parents are able to return to the country of origin this becomes impossible for the children as a result of their language loss. The immigrant country has taken the children as payment for the parents' exile. The time in school becomes impossibly difficult for many children, since it takes place in a language other than their mother tongue, and is planned and adapted for majority language children.

Countries that have adopted the guest worker philosophy can sometimes act in just the opposite way. They have a temporary need for foreign labour but have no ambitions to keep the immigrants in the country, much less their families, when they can manage with domestic workers. For the emigrant countries, it is understandably a source of national feelings of inferiority not to be able to employ their own residents; in these cases, they try to convince themselves that this is only a temporary measure, which will end as soon as possible, when a rapid industrial development gets under way. From diametrically opposed points of view, the authorities in the host countries involved can decide to establish minority language schools, in which instruction in large part can be directed from the home country, without consultation with the minorities involved. It is less expensive, and more peaceful, at least to begin with, for the immigrant country, and attractive to the emigrant country's sense of pride, to establish such a language and instructional policy. But naturally, it leads to all sorts of segregation and estrangement for the immigrants—particularly for the second generation—if they do not receive the best possible opportunities to learn the language of the majority society. This freedom of choice, which is laid down in Swedish immigrant policy, becomes totally illusory if it does not give the immigrants growing up in that society a chance to participate on equal terms with monolingual Swedes in education and to make relatively free choices when they enter the Swedish labour market.

It should be noted that it is not only in the traditional *Gaästarbeiter* situation that schooling takes place only in the minority language. If the stay in a foreign country is limited in time (e.g. contractual employment in international aid organizations or multinational companies), schools for the children of employees are arranged, if possible, with instruction in the children's first language, by teachers from the home country. An exception to this pattern is made when the temporary foreign employment is in an English- or French-speaking country. These languages' global status and opportunities for use make it attractive to allow one's children to receive their schooling in English or French. It is on the other hand never considered a possibility to put children in, for example, Arabic, Vietnamese or even Finnish schools. The parents who have such temporary foreign employment tend to be very language and instructionally conscious and can, on the basis of their own social and professionally secure positions, make definite demands concerning their children's schooling. They can almost always decide themselves to some extent about the length of their stay, and return to the home country, should the children not receive a satisfactory education, both in terms of language and other school subjects in the foreign school system. In almost all respects, these conditions which apply to foreign managers and professionals are different from those which apply to nearly all immigrant families in Sweden and in other countries.

Sweden's need for bilingual people

Unfortunately, little attention has thus far been given to the great interest Sweden ought to have in acquiring a number of bilingual and bicultural people at a very limited cost. These people can bring to Swedish society a revolutionary contribution of linguistic and cultural competence from a large number of languages and cultural areas, most of which were scarcely found in Sweden before. Society's needs are also the most meaningful motivation for the individual to become bilingual. While a person, or a group of people, is grateful for language and cultural support, as it improves the life situation of the individual, the family and the national group, what makes one's own language and cultural experiences really important is that they are sought after and of value for other people and for society.

Sweden's need for bilingual and bicultural people is not limited to or dependent on immigrants' continuing residence in this country for ever. It is actually of inestimable value for Sweden that there are people in other countries who can speak our language, who are acquainted with our culture, and perhaps have personal contact with Swedes and with their fellow-countrymen in Sweden, and who do not have too negative experiences of their stay and education in Sweden. Since there is an obvious— though, as already mentioned, too little recognized and noticed—social interest in immigrants' preserving and developing their first languages, the Swedish authorities ought to do all in their power to satisfy the common interest that immigrants themselves have in becoming bilingual.

Bilingualism—a necessary goal

The goal of bilingualism is very demanding, and difficult to attain, but it is necessary for a number of social and individual reasons. Since it is a unique goal, there are no directly comparable data available from other countries. It is not unusual that one meets people, both Swedes and foreigners, who question whether it is right or wise to establish this language instructional policy in Sweden, considering that the country is alone in its goal of active bilingualism. Naturally, one can and ought to question the present language policy. However, the fact that no other countries (including many larger, more powerful and richer ones) have decided to give their immigrants the possibility of acquiring a functioning bilingualism through the support of a bilingual education is not a crucial argument for Sweden to change its course with regard to this question.

One further point should be made with reference to the goal of active bilingualism. It is a goal which is desirable, both for the majority of immigrants and for society (both for the immigrant and emigrant countries, even though both Sweden and the immigrants' home countries have had a surprisingly difficult time realizing it). Like most goals, it is unfortunately impossible for all to reach. It is unrealistic to think that all the second-generation immigrants in Sweden can become totally bilingual. But this does not mean that we should abandon the goal. It would seem to be equally difficult to be totally monolingual as well, i.e. to be in command of all varieties (both oral and written) in all areas in all situations of life. Despite this impossibility of reaching perfection, nobody has, as far as we know, suggested that the monolinguals' only language should not be developed, or that we should establish limits that specify for which people, or to which levels, instruction in the mother tongue should be restricted, because it is not economically or pedagogically profitable to invest in language development at all. We should not set up bilingual perfection as a demand for arranging instruction in minority languages, either. Even when knowledge of a language is limited to certain domains, it is valuable. This is the motivation for the teaching of foreign languages in our schools. With second language instruction for minority students we are talking about far more advanced knowledge and skills, in any case within certain areas, as for example in control of the spoken language in everyday situations. That the languages to be learned are usually different from those taught as foreign languages ought rather to be viewed as an advantage, from the point of view of the majority society. The acceptance of the fact that not all immigrant pupils can attain complete first language competence in all subject areas during their school years leads to important organizational and pedagogical consequences, especially for small language groups. Despite the fact that for some groups the scope and results of mother tongue instruction may not lead directly and unproblematically to further education, or to a job in the home country, it nevertheless serves important immediate functions for individuals and for the societies in which they live.

The need to become bilingual in two languages with low prestige

The language abilities of Swedes are generally limited to the prestigious school languages, which are studied for cultural reasons (English, French, German and, to a limited extent, Spanish and Russian). Among these only Spanish (that is, its Latin American variety) is really important as an immigrant language. The vast bulk of the 140 languages has low prestige in Sweden, and can be used only within the language group itself. In addition, Swedish does not have a particularly high status outside Scandinavia.

For immigrants, learning Swedish seems to be motivated only by the fact that they are living in Sweden. Since most of them hope that their stay will be short, they do not see any reason to work long or hard on learning a language for which they do not think they will have any use after returning to their native countries. It is quite clear that the low prestige of the majority of immigrant languages is dependent on the fact that Swedish society has not understood the importance of, or the possibility for the immigrants to build up competence in, these languages. If the attitude of Swedish authorities and of Swedes in general towards language ability and bilingualism is changed, it would certainly lead to a marked improvement in language learning both in Swedish and in the first language ("the home language") and thus in bilingualism.

The most realistic way to raise the prestige of minority languages is to show that they are viable means of communication in Sweden. For schools, this means showing that these languages are effective means of instruction for minority students. At the same time, the *current* language status relationships in Sweden imply that the status relationships of the languages in other countries must be taken into account when comparing bilingual and second language instructional situations. The status of the languages involved is one of the most telling and important factors when judging the various effects and results which language instruction, language learning and bilingual environments can have or can be expected to lead to. Differences in language status make it impossible to transfer experiences from English-speaking countries like the USA and Canada directly to Sweden, or to equate without reservation the role of Finnish as a second language in Finland for the indigenous Swedish-speaking minority in that country with that of Swedish in Sweden for Finns who have come to Sweden during the past few decades, and who, as discussed above, in large measure wish to return to Finland.

In summary, the sociolinguistic factors, among them the current languages' status, are unfavourable for the development of active bilingualism among immigrants in Sweden. This should not, however, imply a passive acceptance of the present situation, but rather it presents us with a challenge to develop constructive ideas for what measures ought to be taken to improve immigrant pupils' language learning.

The situation of the minorities themselves

Differences between immigrant groups

Most of the bilingual societies described in the scientific and pedagogic literature on the subject deal with permanently resident indigenous minorities, who speak a different language from the majority. The extremely comprehensive Canadian research on bilingualism has thus primarily dealt with the official French–English bilingualism, and to a certain extent the native Canadian and Inuit (Eskimo) minorities in relation to the majorities. In contrast, immigrant minorities have so far not been given as much attention, despite the large number of European, and more recently the increasing number of Asian, immigrants in the country.

We should also point out that various language groups may draw very different conclusions from an identical view that their stay in Sweden is temporary. Some Finnish immigrants want to have a schooling with all instruction in Finnish and with instruction in Swedish only as a second language. The Latin American groups naturally hope to be able to return to South America, but many South Americans think that, once they have actually arrived there, the children can quickly pick up Spanish. In Sweden, they want to have exactly the same education for their children as the Swedish children receive. But the longer it takes for employment opportunities to increase in northern Finland, and the longer the South American military juntas remain in power, the more limited the freedom of choice of the Finnish and Latin American children becomes, if their education is largely monolingual. Under these conditions, Finnish pupils will have reduced chances of acquiring education in Swedish upper secondary schools or competing on the Swedish labour market except for a limited number of jobs. The Latin American children cannot accompany their parents back to South America, if they have not developed a bilingualism which makes it possible for them to continue their education or to find employment in their parents' native country.

The possibility of returning to the native country which must always be taken into account, on the one hand, and the freedom to choose to stay in Sweden, regardless of how social conditions may develop in Sweden and in the home country, on the other hand, make it very clear that the pupils must develop bilingualism. Naturally, the Finnish immigrant group can (in part) work politically for and carry out the establishment of a Finnish school. They have every right to do so, and a possible decision of this kind will depend on general political considerations between the two neighbouring Scandinavian countries, Finland and Sweden. But it would be wrong not to review in advance the likely consequences of such a schooling, both in terms of further education and future employment. It would also be wrong not to point out to Latin Americans and others who believe that it would be easy for children to recover a neglected first language in their own home country, that the difficulties in doing so are considerable, and often too much for them. In both cases, it is possible that the attitudes towards a bilingual education would be different if the minority groups had been confronted with educational alternatives (i.e. real bilingual education) other than those which are currently discussed in Sweden.

Only about 15% (mostly Finns) of the immigrants have the chance of acquiring an education in which their mother tongue is the medium of instruction, but this only in part of the lessons and in the first six years. This schooling has been organized according to transitional models, and a full bilingual education throughout schooling has so far not been tried.

Great differences between immigrant languages

Immigrants in Sweden differ from one another in almost every respect, apart from the definitional criterion, i.e. that they have come from another country. Their first languages are many, and different, both in relation to Swedish, and in relation to each other. There are currently about 140 different first languages represented in the Swedish educational system. A few (like Danish and Norwegian) are very closely related to Swedish. A few more belong to the same language group (e.g. Germanic languages like English, German, Icelandic and Dutch). Some languages belong to the same language family as Swedish, Indo-European (e.g. the Slavic languages, Greek, Albanian and Kurdish), but display great differences in comparison with the Swedish language. A great number are languages vastly different from Swedish, among them some which are spoken by large immigrant groups (Finnish, Turkish and Hungarian). Since these are languages of which Swedish teachers have hardly any prior instructional experience, and which very few Swedes can speak, it is rarely possible to apply a bilingual method in instruction in the second language, other than for teachers who happen to get pupils with just those languages which these teachers can speak. Except in home language classes and home language groups, this is something rare and usually a result of coincidence.

It is very rare, for example, that groups of adult immigrants learning

Swedish are made up of participants with the same first language. For the Swedish teachers, this extreme heterogeneity of their pupils' first languages and cultures implies above all that they must have knowledge they can generalize upon, which puts them in a position to be able to adapt their instruction to their pupils' background and previous knowledge in a most flexible way. Luckily, it is not the case that all 140 language groups have totally different problems from one another in learning Swedish. Because Swedish differs from all, or from most other, languages in a number of ways, some learning problems are common to all, or to almost all immigrants, regardless of their first language. Other problems in learning Swedish are shared with native speakers learning Swedish. Knowledge of language typology, language pedagogy and language psychology is necessary for these teachers.

Differences within each immigrant language

It ought to be mentioned, in connection with the large number of first language groups, that these groups are hardly monolithic units. Within these language groups there are differences and variations of all kinds. Linguistically speaking, "languages" are abstractions for, at times, significant dialectal and sociolectal variations. This becomes evident, for example, in the very great differences between the language of the home language teacher (often an educated urban middle-class person from the country's capital city) and that of the pupils (whose parents often come from an agrarian environment, or rural areas, with little or sporadic schooling). Regional and ethnic differences can be much greater for the immigrants (e.g. for Yugoslavians) than Scandinavians can imagine, based on experiences of comparable differences in our own countries. This means that many pupils do not feel at home with the language in instruction either in their first language, or in their second language. They constitute a "double linguistic minority", which implies great difficulties for them.

The major problems with linguistic heterogeneity, of course, stem from the fact that most of the languages are represented by only a very small number of individuals, who, in addition, vary in age and place of residence. It is only for the largest language groups in the communities and school districts with the largest proportion of immigrants that it is possible to organize instruction in a satisfactory way. Problems concerning instruction and teachers become difficult to solve for the vast majority of language groups. "The small group problem" is perhaps the most complicated and difficult factor within immigrant education.

Research findings: Confusion in the bilingual debate

Frequently research on immigrant pupils' language instruction is presented, both in newspaper articles and in research reports, as offering conflicting results. It is commonly said in Sweden that "researchers are not in agreement". This conclusion leads decision makers not infrequently to be hesitant and passive in making organizational decisions. The lack of agreement among researchers seems in any case to be the best known—in many cases the only known—"research result" among people outside the immigrant instructional sector. The reasons for this lack of consensus are many.

In comparison with the range and complexity of the field of research, very few researchers are involved, which means that individual investigations can make a disproportionately large impact. This has been the case particularly during the initial phase. Since immigrants and their education constitute a socially and politically sensitive area, of considerable interest to the general public, the mass media has devoted much attention to research and debate in this area. Items in the mass media have often been oversimplified in their descriptions of a complex reality. We can hardly place all the blame on the mass media, however.

The complexity of immigrant instruction is in itself a sufficient explanation for many of the differences in the investigations and observations made in totally different instructional conditions. At the same time, many articles, papers and books have been written by researchers whose direct experience of immigrant instruction in Sweden has been limited or non-existent. This has led to the transfer of arguments and possible implementations from other countries with different situations in relation to both bilingualism and instruction. Obviously, the need is great, in a country like Sweden, which has so little experience of immigration, bilingualism, etc., to gather experience, knowledge and theoretical developments from other countries and systems of education. Such a demand should not, however, imply an uncritical and oversimplified transfer of international findings to the Swedish situation. Neither should domestic theories and experiences, which are intended for totally different types and forms of language acquisition and education, be applied to the instruction of immigrant pupils in Swedish schools. Even if immigrants constitute an extremely heterogeneous category, and their language education must be judged in relation to a very large number of different factors, of which many display considerable variation, there are nevertheless certain factors in the Swedish immigrant situation which should be an obligatory basis for all standpoints, decisions and measures taken. The most important of these basic factors will be illuminated and discussed below.

Present organization of minority education

Remedial instruction instead of bilingual education

Immigrant instruction in the Swedish school system has gone through several phases since 1965. At first, only Swedish-medium instruction was offered, i.e. the pupils were placed directly in a Swedish class, which received instruction entirely in Swedish. Naturally, this proved to be an unfortunate solution. Then, remedial instruction in Swedish was begun, in small groups (3–4 pupils) or in preparatory classes (8–10 pupils). Remedial instruction (which still exists, and which is still obligatory for those pupils whom the Swedish teacher judges to need it) has reached enormous proportions. It is very clear that both the name "remedial instruction" and its arrangement are highly unfortunate. Constant interruptions in the classes, ordinary instruction in order to participate in remedial instruction are disturbing for the immigrant pupils' social, emotional and cognitive development together with their classmates. The pupils who (according to the teachers) achieve a good result in Swedish are "rewarded" by being able to go over to ordinary instruction in Swedish. In reality, they are punished, as they are thus unable to study Swedish on their own terms. Because the school system has not as yet faced up to the consequences of the fact that Swedish as a second language is a school subject in its own right, no established guidelines or requirements have yet (autumn 1986) been developed for teaching Swedish as a second language. Remedial Swedish, therefore, is not the instruction in Swedish it ought to be, i.e. the immigrant pupils' own school subject—Swedish as a Second Language; rather it is a sort of slow, repetitive elementary instruction in Swedish as a mother tongue, where the vast majority of teachers have no training whatever for their difficult and specialized task. In far too many cases, remedial instruction in Swedish is performed by teachers who are only temporarily employed for a few hours each week to teach immigrant pupils. Under these conditions it is an illusion to expect any methodological development to arise spontaneously in this area.

The increasing awareness of the importance of the first language for second language learning, and the still unsatisfactory results of the immigrant pupils' language learning, led to the passage of the so-called *Home Language Reform* in 1977. Through this act, pupils received the legal right to instruction in their own first language. Thus, instruction held in Swedish and in the home language, plus, for those who were judged to be in need of it, remedial instruction in Swedish were attained.

Mother tongue medium instruction

Very soon after the passage of the home language reform, many communities began organizing more and more "home language classes" and "composed classes" primarily in Finnish, but also in Turkish, Serbo-Croatian, Spanish and other major immigrant languages. The primary reason was that instruction in the home language (a voluntary 2–4 hours per week per pupil) has proved to be entirely insufficient if the immigrant pupils are to achieve active bilingualism. This is not so surprising. The limited interest on the part of Swedish society in knowledge of minority languages, the lack of language stimulation for the immigrant languages in Swedish society, the low prestige of the immigrant languages in Sweden, and the absence of instruction held in these languages are the major reasons the home language reform has proved to be insufficient to bring about bilingualism with the first language (the home language) as one of the components. There is not much to criticize in the political goal of active bilingualism and in the visions which have given rise to Swedish educational policy. However, there is often good reason to point out critically the differences between the goal and reality. The differences generally have been due to the fact that ideological and economic decisions have not been followed by appropriate administrative and pedagogical measures.

With the establishment of home language classes we have, however, taken two steps in the right direction. First, we now have instruction not only in the pupils' home languages as target languages, but we also have instruction in other subjects held in these languages. Second, instruction in Swedish in these classes must be carried out as Swedish as a Second Language, that is, on the pupils' own terms. Thus, in these classes, we have achieved instruction in both the first language and Swedish (as target languages) and instruction in other subjects carried out in both these languages.

Home language classes are bilingual classes in which the pupils' common home language heavily dominates during the early school years. Swedish increases gradually, to become the dominant language during the junior high school. Composed classes are classes which should ideally be composed of 50% immigrant pupils with a common language and 50% monolingual Swedish pupils. "Home language groups" would be a better name than "composed class". The best solution would be to speak of *bilingual* (Finnish/Greek etc.) *class* (= the present home language class) and *bilingual* (Finnish/Greek etc.) *group* (= composed class).

These two types of classes are set up primarily on the basis of the pupil population of the various school districts. If there are enough pupils from a particular language group, a "home language class" is established. If there is only about half this number, a "composed class" is established. The major barrier against starting a home language class is in many cases an insufficient number of pupils with a common first language other than Swedish. The major barrier against establishing a composed class in many cases is an insufficient number of Swedish-speaking pupils. Since immigrant groups come in periodic waves (e.g. due to crises and refugee situations around the world) they are usually given housing in newly-built areas (where relatively few Swedes with school-age children have yet moved).

The school authorities and teachers involved are in favour of class arrangements such as home language classes and composed classes and feel that they have found a defensible educational scheme for immigrant pupils from large language groups (at present about 15% of the immigrant pupils receive instruction in a home language or a composed class), even if many details can still be improved.

Despite the difference in terminology, both class models have a similar amount of instruction in each language, and both models appear to be getting more similar in terms of the content and allocation of instruction. A study carried out in 1980–82 of the special organizational models of instruction in 32 Swedish communities, 16 with many immigrants and 16 with only a few immigrants, showed that the communities generally had about the same proportion of instruction in the two languages in home language classes and composed classes. (SPRINS project 8-13, Department of Linguistics, University of Göteborg, 1981–82.) The terminological confusion is significant: what is called a home language class in one school district is called a composed class in another. Common to both is that the classes start with a considerable amount of instruction in the first language, and a limited amount in the second language, Swedish, and then they gradually increase the number of lessons held in Swedish. The point of intersection, where Swedish takes over the greater part of instruction, is in the fifth grade for home language classes, and in the fourth grade for composed classes.

The "home language"

In their first language in the strict sense, which within the Swedish school is called *the home language*, immigrant students are expected to reach first language level in a minority environment. In such a milieu language stimulation is considerably less than in a majority milieu. In particular, this is the case for an immigrant minority with low prestige and with an uncertain length of residence for many of its members, i.e. just those conditions which apply to most of the immigrants in Sweden. Sweden is far from being a bilingual country—it is a monolingual country with a large number of linguistic minorities. The limited opportunities for active and passive language stimulation apply even to the minority which is by far the largest, the Finns. The few hours of broadcasting time which are in Finnish on radio and TV, the columns in a few of the larger daily papers, and instruction in home language classes during a certain period in the school career are naturally in no way comparable to the presence of Finnish in Finland. With the possible exception of a few large work places, Finnish in Sweden is today limited to certain areas of organizational life and to the private sphere, i.e. interaction with family and friends.

The opportunity for using a minority language is far more limited for other language groups. Most minority language groups are very small. The majority of immigrants who speak these languages are limited to their own families—who may be the only speakers of the language in a community—for communication in their first language. The insignificant presence of minority languages in Swedish society places extremely difficult demands on the school, which has to compensate as fully as possible with directed learning (language instruction) for the inadequate so-called natural language learning.

Swedish

In the other language which is to be learned to the level of a first language, i.e. Swedish, there is, on the other hand, abundant opportunity for language stimulation in Sweden. We should not be led to believe, however, that opportunity is the same as use or even a real possibility for use. A number of invisible barriers of a social, psychological and emotional kind make many of the theoretically unlimited possibilities for language activities in Swedish difficult or impossible. A very strong psyche is necessary in order to play constantly on the other team's home field, so to speak.

The goal of Swedish as a first language must be reached in a language which, for the vast majority of immigrant pupils, is a second language. This makes the goal very difficult to achieve. To develop first language competence in the Swedish written language is not the least of the problems, for example. The learning of Swedish among immigrant children is certainly highly variable in quantity and quality during the pre-school period, but it always differs from the learning of Swedish which Swedish children achieve during the same time. Because most of the immigrant children live a large part of their lives in a language other than Swedish, their language development even during their school years is different from that of Swedish pupils.

Instruction in Swedish in the schools must therefore be planned in such a way as to take into account the differences which exist between those children who learn the language in a monolingual, majority milieu—i.e. Swedish children—and on the other hand those children who grow up in a bilingual environment, and with a language other than Swedish at home.

Very few pupils with a first language other than Swedish can participate in a natural way in Swedish instruction, which is planned and intended for Swedish pupils who have undergone a natural monolingual development in Swedish. In other words, all the pupils for whom Swedish is a second language should have the right to instruction in the language on their own terms, within their own school subject—Swedish as a Second Language.

Needed: An adequate instruction in both languages as targets and as the media of instruction

Traditional foreign language instruction is usually not sufficient to make the pupils bilingual. If that were the case, all the pupils in the compulsory school would be bilingual in Swedish and English, and many would even be multilingual, in French, German, etc. when they have finished high school. Intensive use of the language over a long period of time, in a variety of different meaningful situations is necessary, so that what might otherwise be called good language competence lives up to the label bilingualism. As far as the school is concerned, meaningful active language use consists of instruction using that language as the medium of instruction in various subject areas. But instruction *via* the language is also not sufficient for the development of bilingualism. Normal monolingual instruction in Swedish schools is, of course, designed for Swedish pupils who have developed their language over a long period of time. In order for the pupils to have a reasonable chance of attaining the goal of active bilingualism, they must receive instruction in their first language (both as a target language and as a partial medium of instruction) during their entire school career, i.e. even in junior and senior high school. On the latter level, it is reasonable that part of the instruction in the first language (as a target) follows students' course of study or specialization (i.e. that students can specialize in, for example, business Finnish, technical Spanish or social service Turkish) so that they thus attain linguistic competence which is adapted to their future employment prospects. This is the best way Swedish society can show its interest in the pupils' bilingualism and in both their own and society's need of their valuable abilities.

There is a clear tendency for instruction for the majority of immigrant pupils to be divided into at least three different parts, led by three different categories of teachers:

1. Instruction in the home language carried out by home language teachers;

2. Remedial instruction in Swedish (as a target language) carried out by teachers of various categories, often in the form of teaching hours to complete a teacher's teaching load;

3. Instruction in other subjects held in Swedish (or, in the case of home language and composed classes, also held in the first language) carried out by class- and subject-area teachers.

This means that it is up to the pupils to create a unified education out of many disparate elements. Such a task is difficult enough for monolingual pupils, but is often too much for minority language pupils, who really need the help of the school and teachers in co-ordinating the instruction in both languages, both as targets and as the media of instruction, in a way which is both well planned and thought through. The goal of gathering knowledge and of developing a social and emotional maturity comparable to that of monolingual children, and in addition of acquiring these in another language, otherwise becomes very difficult to achieve, and the outcome is left to chance. The only possibility for including bilingual learning within the school, in an instructional programme which is already overfull, is that instruction is co-ordinated, and that the various parts and the different languages can build on each other using a contrastive approach.

Aside from the obvious advantages of being able to carry out a feasible curriculum of study—without remedial instruction as a guiding principle—in which the pupils remain as a group throughout their educational career, it is clear that the social effects in terms of security and improved contact with the family are very important arguments in favour of home language classes and groups. But it is clear that the instruction and arrangements must be adapted to the size of the first language groups, to the linguistic and cultural distance from Swedish, and to the presence or absence of an orthography in the first language, etc. Consideration of the pupils' languages, teachers, parents, length of stay and arrival time in Sweden, make it imperative that we do not get locked into the view that all immigrant instruction must necessarily be planned according to one specific pattern.

Implementation of theoretical principles in the education of immigrant children

In the preceding sections, the basic conditions in the Swedish immigrant and educational situations have been discussed. These conditions naturally lead to demands for a number of follow-up decisions and measures for instruction of immigrant pupils in the school. Among the many serious consequences, four have been chosen here for a more thorough examination, as they have a general application regardless of linguistically and culturally specific circumstances.

Acquisition of basic reading and writing skills in the first language

The most important instruction which the school gives is the teaching of the basic skills of reading and writing. Practically all knowledge acquired later is built on these skills. Our ability to read and write makes us independent individuals who can acquire knowledge and communicate with other people on our own. Because of the pedagogically essential connection with earlier skills and knowledge it is only natural that pupils should be able to learn these basic skills in a language they know, and not in a foreign language. For the vast majority of immigrant children their first language is the language they know best and this is therefore the language in which they ought to learn to read and write.

In addition to the pedagogical advantages, we can argue that the security of the pupils demands that instruction at the primary level ought to be held in the pupils' first language. The pupils obviously feel more safe and secure starting school in a language they know, rather than in a language foreign to them. The home language teacher often becomes a person they can identify with, and this is something of which they have a great need. For the parents, the situation is radically different if the children's first instruction in school takes place in the parents' mother tongue. Contact between home and school is facilitated. This contact is particularly important, since many immigrant parents have had experiences in school systems in which teachers and principals rarely, if ever, take the parents' or pupils' opinions and viewpoints into account. When the Swedish school is concerned about, and gives instruction in, immigrants' mother tongue, then their language, culture, and parents and children attain higher status as well as the self-respect and self-confidence they need.

Even if, contrary to all expectations, it became clear that immigrant children's learning is not improved by their being given the opportunity to learn the basic skills of reading and writing in so-called bilingual classes, the social and status factors are so important that it would be justifiable to provide this type of instruction in order to make the children secure school pupils, without any concern about their language or their identity. This is a prerequisite for all future learning.

The right to learn Swedish as a subject on its own: Swedish as a Second Language

In the previous discussion, serious criticism has been levelled at the remedial philosophy as a basic principle for how instruction in Swedish for immigrant pupils should be designed. It ought to be natural for instruction in Swedish to be adapted to the pupils and not vice versa. Since the pupils have a first language other than Swedish, and/or grow up in a bilingual milieu, it is obvious that their acquisition of the Swedish language will be different from that of monolingual Swedish children. This is true for all immigrant children, even if the differences in terms of passive and active language stimulation in Swedish are very great. When many Swedish teachers determine that the children can speak Swedish "like Swedish children", it is almost always the result of a general impression of their pronunciation and perhaps of some other superficially observable component of their language competence. Pronunciation represents the greatest difficulty for adults in learning a language, while it is at the same time the language skill most easily acquired by children. It is therefore common for adults to over-estimate children's language ability based on their impressions of the children's pronunciation. The instruction of these pupils ought not to be organized on the basis of these uncertain judgements.

Since the pupils have a long period of development before school age, live in very different circumstances, and have extremely varied experiences outside school, it is odd that some claim that all pupils should have the same education for the sake of fairness. Such an education is very unfair to those who have grown up in a social and cultural milieu that differs significantly from that of the dominant group.

Functional and relevant instruction through the medium of both languages

It is not possible to achieve first language competence by means of traditional foreign language instruction. In order for the pupils to obtain as many active language skills as possible, they ought to be able to acquire knowledge through the medium of both languages. It is also necessary to take into account the very limited time available for learning two languages while the pupils are in school. If both languages are employed as media of instruction, language study will clearly become more relevant to the pupils. This would also seem to be the easiest way to give the home languages the higher prestige they need. When the instruction is led by teachers who have one of these languages as a first language—Swedish or the home language in question—the instruction will be functionally motivated for the pupils. It is functional to speak Swedish with a Swedish teacher and Finnish with a Finnish teacher. Many pupils certainly do not experience traditional language instruction as functional, but rather as a somewhat artificial situation where both teachers and pupils, who have a common, functional first language, attempt to perfect a technical skill in another, foreign code system. Teaching Swedish as a Second Language has a distinct advantage in comparison with teaching foreign languages. Instruction takes place in Sweden, a Swedish-speaking country, which gives the instruction a relevance for all both inside and outside the classroom.

Contrastively based instruction

The aim of education for immigrant pupils should be to provide for them a schooling which gives them knowledge *of* and *in* their two languages, and where all learning is built upon what has been learned in the past, in both languages (as media and targets of instruction). All the teachers in the school ought to have the responsibility of seeing that all Swedish pupils develop a language which can be used for a multitude of purposes. In the same way, it is the responsibility of all teachers to see that minority children become bilingual. This responsibility cannot be shifted on to the teachers in the home language and of Swedish as a Second Language.

Sometimes it is said that the target language must be kept "pure" in instruction, so that the pupils do not mix the different languages. This has also been given as an argument for postponing the introduction of the second language, i.e. Swedish, for a very long time. The danger of mixing, due to the fact that both languages are used in the same lesson, is certainly exaggerated, particularly if the pupils meet both languages in contexts which are realistic and meaningful. For minority children in a majority society, reality is bilingual. It cannot be methodologically incorrect for the school and its language instruction to take this fact into account. Rather than being a doubtful and harmful feature, language instruction which is based on the pupils' knowledge in both languages and cultures and which forms a basis for comparisons between different words, meanings, pronunciations, word orders and cultural patterns can clearly be a facilitating and time-saving method. It is probably only in this way that Swedish as a Second Language can gain the pupil-oriented individualization which is necessary if the lofty goal of competence on the level of a first language is to be reached.

The contrastive method can add many positive features to the instruction. The connection with the pupils' home languages and cultures means that occasions will arise when immigrant pupils will be able to use knowledge and experiences which their Swedish classmates and even the teachers generally lack. Instruction is enriched through the active participation of immigrant pupils, who thus gain confidence in their own knowledge.

Contrastively aware and adequately trained teachers

In order to carry out an ideal programme in bilingual education, all teachers involved ought to have expert knowledge of both languages and both cultures. Considering the fact that there are already about 140 different first languages in the Swedish school system, it would seem impossible to satisfy such a demand. Of course, it is highly desirable for as many teachers of Swedish as a Second Language as possible to learn one immigrant language. But for the vast majority, this goal of language competence would seem to be unattainable. We must nevertheless demand that all teachers be prepared with contrastive skills, in the form of excellent knowledge of the Swedish language, and good structural knowledge of the common immigrant languages. With the aid of these skills, the teacher should be able to compare and contrast the target language, Swedish, and the pupils' first language. Conversely it is an unavoidable requirement that home language teachers have not only excellent knowledge of their own language, but also have very good expertise in and about the Swedish language.

For both teacher groups, contrastive cultural knowledge is also necessary. If the immigrant pupils are to become functionally bilingual, and become active participants in two cultures, it is necessary that instructional time be used efficiently. This implies that new learning of knowledge and skills should build on old, and that both cultures should support one another.

In order to make a contrastive base for instruction possible, teacher training must be designed and adapted for the subject Swedish as a Second Language and the various home languages. Swedish as a Second Language is at least as important for the immigrant pupils as Swedish is for Swedish pupils. Because the pupils are expected to achieve first language competence in both their languages, they obviously need first language teachers—one with Swedish and one with their home language as a first language—in order to receive functional and relevant language instruction, and instruction which gives them totally adequate linguistic models.

6 From multicultural to anti-racist education

An analysis of programmes and policies in Ontario

JIM CUMMINS

Overview

Since the declaration of an official policy of multiculturalism in Canada by Prime Minister Trudeau in 1971, and the subsequent endorsement of this policy by provincial governments, Canadian educators have attempted to develop and implement "multicultural education" policies in classrooms across the country. Many of the larger urban boards of education set up workgroups in the mid-1970s to develop such policies and since that time teacher in-service activities have regularly focused on "multicultural education". However, to many observers it appears that by the time "multicultural education" policies filter down to the classroom, they amount to little more than recognition of holidays/festivals from a few cultures in addition to those observed by Anglo-Celtic Canadians, and the presence of some "visible minority" referents in textbooks and other curriculum materials. The advent of "multicultural education" has not given rise to dramatic changes in the interactions between educators and students. In most classrooms, the hidden curriculum still conforms largely to the ideology of "Anglo-conformity" (Troper, 1979).

In this chapter I examine some of the reasons why the rhetoric of "multicultural education" has failed to translate into reality and I illustrate the disjunction between rhetoric and reality with reference to policies and programmes in Ontario during the past decade. The argument presented is that the overt goals of multicultural education can be realized only when policy-makers, educators and communities acknowledge the subtle (and sometimes not so subtle) forms of institutionalized racism that permeate the structure of schools and mediate the interactions between educators and students. In other words, unless it becomes "anti-racist education", "multi-cultural education" may serve only to provide a veneer of change that in reality perpetuates discriminatory educational structures.

Clearly, a theoretical framework is required to document the ways in which institutionalized racism manifests itself in the educational system and the change processes required to combat this racism, i.e. to shift from an Anglo-conformity to an anti-racist orientation. A framework is presented that analyses the ways in which educators define their roles with respect to four overlapping dimensions of schooling: (1) incorporation of minority students' language and culture; (2) minority community participation; (3) orientation to pedagogy; and (4) assessment of minority students. These dimensions reflect the power relations in the society at large and thus the framework provides a means of analysing the extent to which educators challenge or accept the societal racism that is reflected in schools. The focus is on ways in which the structural power relations in society are realized within schools and manifested psychologically within individual educators. A central assumption is that implementation of anti-racist educational changes requires *personal redefinitions* of the way in which classroom teachers and other educators interact with the children and communities they serve. In other words, legislative and policy reforms may be necessary conditions for effective change, but they are not sufficient. Implementation of change is dependent on the extent to which educators, both collectively and individually, redefine their roles with respect to minority students and communities.

In the first section, a brief outline of the historical and social context of "multicultural education" in Canada is presented and this is followed by a discussion of the meaning of the term "institutionalized racism" and the ways it manifests itself in the interactions between educators and minority students. The theoretical framework outlined above for conceptualizing strategies for countering institutionalized racism in schools and empowering minority students is then discussed. The dynamics of the change processes required are illustrated with concrete examples from recent educational conflicts in Ontario. Finally, the broader context of planning and implementing change is considered with respect to the roles of ministries of education, universities, school board officials (i.e. administrators, principals, etc.) and ethnocultural communities.

Historical and social context of multicultural education

Harold Troper (1979) has argued cogently that multiculturalism has come to play a role in filling an "identity vacuum" among English

Canadians brought about by the gradual weakening of the bonds with Britain, partly as a result of large-scale immigration during the past 40 years. The prevailing attitude towards ethnic diversity in English Canada during the first part of the twentieth century was that ethnic groups should give up their own languages and cultures and become assimilated to the dominant British group. This Anglo-conformity orientation is well expressed by a speaker to the 1913 Presbyterian Pre-Assembly Congress in Toronto:

"The problem is simply this: take all the different nationalities, German, French, Italian, Russian and all the others that are sending their surplus into Canada: mix them with the Anglo-Saxon stock and produce a uniform race wherein the Anglo-Saxon peculiarities shall prevail." (Quoted by Harney & Troper, 1975:110)

The current endorsement of multiculturalism as national and provincial policy tends to obscure the strong assimilationist orientation of Canadian educators in the past and the racist character of much of our past public policy (e.g. immigration regulations). Despite recent reminders of the exclusion of Jews before and during World War II (Abella & Troper, 1984), the continuing saga of compensation for racism against Japanese-Canadians during the war, and the failure to alleviate the deplorable conditions of many Native Canadians, Canadians still tend to view themselves as having always been a tolerant and open society. As expressed by Troper (1979):

"Perhaps every country needs its myths and national clichés. For English speaking Canada one current and often repeated cliché is that Canada owes its distinctive character to a long fostered tolerance of cultural diversity—we are a mosaic while the Americans are a melting pot. ... If anything the opposite is closer to the truth. The survival of active and distinct ethnic communities in Canada ... occurred in spite of public policy and sentiment not because of them ... Ethnicity, if tolerated at all, was seen as a temporary stage through which one passed on the road to full assimilation. Prolonged ethnic identification ... was seen as a pathological condition to be overcome, not as a source of national enrichment and pride." (1979:9)

Given the recency of an official multiculturalism policy and the strong Anglo-conformity tradition that preceded it, it is hardly surprising that the orientations of many individuals within Canadian society (including educators) continue to reflect assimilationist assumptions. Nevertheless, serious attempts have been and continue to be made to change the assimilationist orientation in many schools. A recent statement by the Ontario Ministry of Education in a memorandum to Chairpersons of boards of education (announcing a province-wide conference on race relations and multiculturalism) can be taken as indicative of the desired reality towards which change is directed:

> "The philosophy of multiculturalism ... should permeate the school's curriculum, policies, teaching methods and materials, courses of study, and assessment and testing procedures, as well as the attitudes and expectations of its staff and all of its community." (December 1985:1)

Certain aspects of this statement are worth highlighting: first, the *role definitions* of educators are included as an important component of a multicultural orientation in schools. The statement implies that the attitudes and expectations of school staff should reflect a positive orientation towards the cultural and linguistic diversity of both students and communities. In addition, significant dimensions of programme delivery are highlighted; specifically, curriculum, which can be taken to include materials and courses of study, teaching methods and assessment/testing procedures.

Clearly, all of these are admirable objectives. However, up to this point the implementation of multicultural education policies appears to have lacked coherence and dynamism in many parts of Canada. With some noteworthy exceptions (e.g. the multicultural assessment system in the North York Board of Education) there has been little structural change either in the ways schools relate to minority communities or in the interactions students experience in schools. Following Appel (this volume) several reasons can be suggested for this: first, "multicultural education" focuses only on the educational system rather than on the power relations in the broader society. As societal institutions, schools tend to reflect the values and priorities of the dominant group and to reproduce the status and power differences between class and ethnic groups that are so evident in the wider society. No programme of "multicultural education" can be successful unless it takes account of the logic of its own rhetoric: namely, rather than reflecting the values and priorities of the dominant group in the wider society and reproducing the inequalities between class and ethnic groups, the rhetoric of multicultural education requires that schools actively challenge the societal power structure by empowering minority students. It is hardly surprising that few "multicultural education" initiatives have succeeded in even addressing this goal. Those that appear to challenge, even to a minor extent, the societal power structure and the priorities of the dominant group (e.g. heritage language initiatives,[1] bilingual assessment, etc.) tend to generate fierce opposition, a reaction which is entirely predictable (see below).

A second reason why "multicultural education" has often appeared to lack coherence is that there tends to be no clear position articulated with respect to minority languages and the extent to which schools (and taxpayers) have a role to play in encouraging their retention. For example, although official federal and provincial policies generally assert the close link between language and culture, many advocates of "multicultural education" are highly ambivalent about heritage language programmes which they see as being divisive and as erecting intercultural barriers rather than breaking them down. The ambivalence with respect to heritage language development reflects the lack of a coherent theoretical framework for analysing the multiple dimensions and goals of "multicultural education".

Related to this last point is the fact that multicultural education does not address, either theoretically or programmatically, the causes of minority students' academic difficulties nor explain the wide variation in achievement of different groups (see e.g. Cummins, 1984a; Ogbu, 1978; Wright & Tsuji, 1984).

In short, while the rhetoric of "multicultural education" articulates a variety of positive goals, it is necessary to examine critically the extent to which this rhetoric is symbolic, simply reflecting the "myth of multiculturalism" (Troper, 1979), or whether it reflects a real commitment to fully eradicating the racism that has characterized much of Canadian education in the past. As we shall see, the record in Ontario is mixed in that major changes have occurred in some areas while in other areas the institutionalized structure has made virtually no accommodation to students' cultural diversity.

Institutionalized racism and anti-racist education

Institutionalized racism can be defined as ideologies and structures which are systematically used to legitimize unequal division of power and resources (both material and non-material) between groups which are defined on the basis of race (see Mullard, this volume, Phillipson, this volume, and Skutnabb-Kangas, this volume (Ch. 1) for discussion of parallels between "racism", "linguicism", "ethnicism" and other "isms"). The term "racism" is being used here in a broad sense to include discrimination against both ethnic and racial minorities. The discrimination is brought about both by the ways particular institutions (e.g. schools) are organized or structured and by the (usually) implicit assumptions that legitimize that organization. For example, the over-representation of certain groups of minority students in vocational programmes at the secondary level in several Metropolitan Toronto boards of education (see e.g. Wright & Tsuji, 1984) can be analysed as a function of institutionalized racism in the educational system. There is usually no intent to discriminate on the part of educators; however, their interactions with minority students are mediated by a system of unquestioned assumptions that reflect the values and priorities of the dominant middle-class culture. It is in these interactions that minority students are educationally disabled. A concrete example will illustrate the subtle but devastating ways in which institutionalized racism can manifest itself in the well-intentioned interactions between educators and minority students.

An example of institutionalized racism in practice

The following psychological assessment was one of more than 400 assessments of ESL students carried out in a western Canadian city which were analysed by Cummins (1984a). It illustrates the assumptions that school psychologists and teachers frequently make about issues such as the appropriateness of standardized tests for minority students and the consequences of bilingualism for students' development.

Maria (not the child's real name) was referred for psychological assessment by her grade 1 teacher, who noted that she had difficulty in all aspects of learning. She was given both speech and hearing and psychological assessments. The former assessment found that all structures and functions pertaining to speech were within normal limits and hearing was also normal. The findings were summarized as follows: "Maria comes from an Italian home where Italian is spoken mainly. However, language skills appeared to be within normal limits for English."

The psychologist's conclusions, however, were very different. On the Wechsler Preschool and Primary Scale of Intelligence (WPPSI), Maria obtained a Verbal IQ of 89 and a Performance IQ of 99. In other words, non-verbal abilities were virtually at the average level while verbal abilities were 11 points below the mean, a surprisingly good score given the clear cultural biases of the test and the fact that the child had been learning English in a school context for little more than a year. The report to Maria's teacher read as follows:

> "Maria tended to be very slow to respond to questions, particularly if she were unsure of the answers. Her spoken English was a little hard to understand, which is probably due to poor English models at home (speech is within normal limits). Italian is spoken almost exclusively at home and this will be further complicated by the coming arrival of an aunt and grandmother from Italy.

There is little doubt that Maria is a child of low average ability whose school progress is impeded by lack of practice in English. Encourage Maria's oral participation as much as possible, and try to involve her in extra-curricular activities where she will be with her English-speaking peers."

Despite the fact that the speech assessment revealed no deficiencies in Maria's spoken English, the psychologist has no hesitation ("There is little doubt ...") in attributing Maria's academic problems to the use of Italian at home. The implicit message to the teacher (and parents) is clear: Maria's communication in L1 with parents and relatives detracts from her school performance, and the aim of the school programme should be to expose Maria to as much L2 as possible in order to compensate for these deficient linguistic and cultural background experiences.

How does this assessment (which was not atypical of the sample) represent institutional racism in action? First, the psychologist, despite being undoubtedly well-intentioned, lacks the knowledge base required to assess the child's academic potential. This is illustrated by the fact that an extremely culturally biased test, such as the verbal scale of the WPPSI, is administered and an IQ score reported, by the failure to distinguish between conversational and academic aspects of L2 proficiency among ESL students, and by the assumption that use of L1 in the home is contributing to the child's academic difficulties. A large body of research shows that this is not the case (see Cummins, 1984a).

Second, an implicit Anglo-conformity orientation is evident in the lack of sensitivity to the fact that the child's cultural background and linguistic talents differ significantly from those upon whom the test was normed; the institutionalized racism is manifested not only in the lack of knowledge but in the total lack of awareness on the part of the psychologist (and presumably the institutions that trained her or him) that there are any knowledge gaps. The psychologist is not conscious that the child's culturally specific experiences might have any implications for the administration or interpretation of the test; there is also no hesitation in drawing inferences about the negative effects of L1 use in the home nor in making recommendations about language use in school despite the fact that the psychologist has probably had no training whatsoever on issues related to bilingualism. In short, the institutional structure within which the psychological assessment takes place (e.g. with respect to policy/legal requirements and training/certification programmes) orients the psychologist to locate the cause of the academic problem within the minority child herself. This has the effect of screening from critical scrutiny a variety of other possible contributors to the child's difficulty, e.g. the educational experiences to which the child has been exposed (see Coles, 1978). Because the psychologist is equipped only with psycho-educational assessment tools, the child's difficulty is assumed to be psycho-educational in nature. The psychologists' training has resulted in a tunnel vision that is out of focus with respect to the experiential realities of the children being assessed.

A related way in which the example above illustrates institutional racism in practice relates to the fact that the psychologist's professional credibility depends on providing a satisfactory interpretation of the child's difficulty and making reasonable placement or intervention recommendations; to admit that the assessment reveals nothing about causes of the minority child's academic difficulties would jeopardize the status and credibility of the psychologist. Thus, at the level of both individuals and institutions (e.g. university departments that train teachers, psychologists and administrators) there tends to be a denial of any lack of expertise or need for significant change in training and/or certification programmes. This denial process is illustrated by the refusal of many psychologists even to try any alternative assessment procedures for minority students other than the culturally and linguistically biased tests which they have become "experts" in administering. Minority children become the victims of professional "credibility".

How do these subtle, unintentional forms of institutional racism victimize minority children? This issue is discussed in more detail later but the potential consequences can be illustrated with reference to the case of Maria. As a result of the assessment, there is an increased likelihood that Maria will be reprimanded for any use of Italian with other Italian students in school, thereby promoting feelings of shame in her own cultural background. It is also probable that the child's parents will be advised to use English rather than Italian at home.[2] If parents adhere to this advice, then they are likely not only to *really* expose the child to poor models of English, but also to reduce the quality and quantity of communication between adults and children in the home since they are likely to be much less comfortable in English than Italian. The importance of adult–child home interaction for future academic achievement has been demonstrated repeatedly (e.g. Wells, 1986) and thus, the advice to switch to English in the home has the potential to exert serious negative effects on children's development. Furthermore, it is likely to drive an emotional wedge between children and parents (including the recently arrived aunt and grandmother who will know no English) since parents may feel that communication of affection and warmth in Italian will reduce the child's future academic prospects.[3]

In summary, the example of Maria illustrates how students can become educationally disabled as a direct result of their interactions with well-intentioned educators. These interactions are mediated by the role definitions of educators which are moulded by a variety of influences; for example, the broader policy and legal structure within which they operate, the institutional structure within which they have been trained, and the school and school board structures (e.g. principal–teacher, administrator–principal relationships) that determine priorities for action on a day-to-day basis. All of these factors must be taken into account in analysing the operation and effects of institutionalized racism.

The dimensions of institutionalized racism in schools

A clear distinction exists between racism that is overt and intentional compared with the more subtle forms of institutionalized racism that are not associated with overtly racist attitudes. Within this latter category we can distinguish two major dimensions: first, the knowledge or informational dimension and second, the attitudinal dimension that reflects the extent of educators' acceptance of and openness to other cultural groups. Educators can be grouped along an "informed–misinformed" continuum with respect to the first dimension[4] and along an "intercultural–Anglo-conformity" dimension with respect to the second.

Thus, as illustrated in Figure 6.1, anti-racist education requires educators who are both informed with respect to the available research regarding minority students and who are also characterized by an intercultural orientation with respect to the desirability of promoting *all* students'

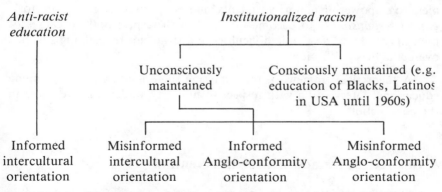

FIGURE 6.1   *Dimensions of anti-racist education and institutionalized racism*

linguistic and personal talents and reinforcing their cultural identity. An intercultural orientation also implies building on students' experiences in the classroom (or in the assessment situation) and sharing of these experiences among students from different cultural groups. Institutionalized racism is manifested in educator–student interactions that reflect either misinformation or an Anglo-conformity orientation or both. It is important to emphasize that an Anglo-conformity orientation is revealed in educators' actions (such as the psychological assessment of Maria above) rather than in their overtly expressed attitudes.

The informational and attitudinal dimensions are clearly not independent since educators with an intercultural orientation will tend to seek out the information required to promote minority students' personal and academic development fully while those with an Anglo-conformity orientation will tend to deny that their knowledge base is in any way inadequate and reject any information that challenges their sociopolitical attitudes.

However, some educators may accept research information (e.g. regarding the benefits of bilingualism) but override the programmatic (and interactional) implications of this information because of their strong Anglo-conformity orientation.[5] Others may be genuinely intercultural in their orientation but lack important information; for example, they may truly believe that using two languages in the home "confuses" bilingual children and consequently advise parents to switch to English. In other words, the resulting interactions are still disabling for minority students (and are manifestations of institutionalized racism) despite the educator's genuine intercultural orientation. However, if this misinformation persists despite ample opportunity to correct it, then one might suspect that the apparent intercultural orientation is simply a façade. A genuine commitment to empowering minority students implies acceptance of the educator's *ethical responsibility* to become informed with respect both to causes of minority students' academic difficulties and strategies for helping students overcome these difficulties.

A theoretical framework for analysing these issues and for planning educational intervention with respect to minority students is presented in the next section.

A theoretical framework for intervention

The framework presented in Figure 6.2 is adapted from Cummins (1986) in order to reflect issues that are particularly relevant to implementa-

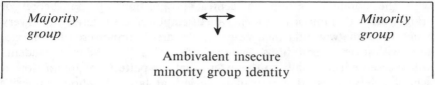

(1) SOCIETAL CONTEXT

Majority
group

Minority
group

Ambivalent insecure
minority group identity

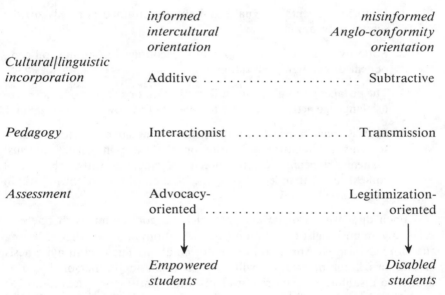

(2) EDUCATIONAL CONTEXT

Educator Role Definitions

	informed *intercultural* *orientation*	*misinformed* *Anglo-conformity* *orientation*
Cultural/linguistic *incorporation*	Additive	Subtractive
Pedagogy	Interactionist	Transmission
Assessment	Advocacy- oriented	Legitimization- oriented

Empowered
students

Disabled
students

FIGURE 6.2. *Empowerment of minority students: a framework for intervention*

tion of anti-racist education policies in the Canadian context. A considerable amount of data shows that power and status relations between minority and majority groups exert a major influence on school performance (Cummins, 1984a; Ogbu, 1978). Minority groups that tend to experience academic difficulty (e.g. Finns in Sweden, Hispanic, Black, and Native American groups in the USA, Franco-Ontarian, Black and Native groups in Canada) appear to have developed an insecurity and ambivalence about the value of their own cultural identity as a result of their interactions with the dominant group. A central proposition of the theoretical framework is that minority students are disempowered educationally in very much the same way that their communities are disempowered by interactions with societal institutions. The converse of this is that minority students will succeed educationally to the extent that the patterns of interaction in school reverse those that prevail in society at large. In short, minority students are "empowered" or "disabled" as a direct result of their interactions with educators in schools. These interactions are mediated by the implicit or explicit role definitions that educators assume in relation to four institutional characteristics of schools. These characteristics reflect the extent to which:

1. Minority students' language and culture are incorporated into the school programme.

2. Minority community participation is encouraged as an integral component of children's education;

3. The pedagogy promotes intrinsic motivation on the part of students to use language actively in order to generate their own knowledge; and

4. Professionals involved in assessment become advocates for minority students by focusing primarily on the ways in which students' academic difficulty is a function of interactions within the school context rather than legitimizing the location of the "problem" within students.

Each dimension can be analysed along a continuum, with one end reflecting an anti-racist orientation (role definition) and the other reflecting the more traditional Anglo-conformity orientation. The overall hypothesis is that this latter orientation will tend to result in the personal and/or academic disabling of minority students while anti-racist orientations (as operationally defined with respect to the framework) will result in minority student empowerment, a concept that, in the present context, implies the development of the ability, confidence and motivation to succeed academically.[6]

At least three of the dimensions analysed (cultural/linguistic incorporation, community participation, and assessment) are integral to most statements of "multicultural education" policy. Although policy with respect to linguistic (as compared with cultural) incorporation has tended to be vague and ambivalent, the linguistic component is regarded as central to the present framework on the grounds that a multicultural education policy which ignores linguistic diversity is vacuous and there is considerable research evidence showing the importance of the linguistic component for minority students' academic achievement. The inclusion of "pedagogy" as a central dimension of a framework for analysing anti-racist education may appear unusual; its relevance, however, derives from the fact that genuine incorporation of students' experiences (cultures) into the school programme requires that educators abandon pedagogical assumptions which focus primarily on transmission of pre-determined knowledge and skills.

The question to be posed in considering these dimensions is to what extent educational policy-makers, administrators, psychologists, principals and classroom teachers in Ontario have actually adopted anti-racist as opposed to Anglo-conformity role definitions.

Cultural/linguistic incorporation

Considerable research data suggest that for minority groups who experience disproportionate levels of academic failure, the extent to which students' language and culture are incorporated into the school programme constitutes a significant predictor of academic success (for example, Campos and Keatinge, this volume; Cummins, 1983). In programmes where minority students' L1 skills are strongly reinforced, their school success appears to reflect both the more solid cognitive/academic foundation developed through intensive L1 instruction and also the reinforcement of their cultural identity (see Skutnabb-Kangas, 1984).

With respect to the incorporation of minority students' language and culture, educators' role definitions can be characterized along an "additive–subtractive" dimension (see Lambert, 1975 for a discussion of additive and subtractive bilingualism). Educators who see their role as adding a second language and cultural affiliation to students' repertoire are likely to empower students more than those who see their role as replacing or subtracting students' primary language and culture in the process of assimilating them to the dominant culture. In addition to the personal and future employment advantages of proficiency in two or more languages, there is considerable evidence that subtle educational advantages result from continued development of both languages among bilingual students. Enhanced metalinguistic development, for example, is frequently found in association with additive bilingualism (e.g. Hakuta & Diaz, 1985).

When we examine the Ontario situation, we find considerable evidence of ambivalence at a policy level towards full educational incorporation of minority languages and cultures. More than 90,000 students receive heritage language instruction through the provincial government's heritage language programme (two and a half hours per week of instruction outside the regular five-hour school day), and the rhetoric which rationalizes this programme clearly acknowledges the validity of an additive orientation. However, one can question the adequacy of two and a half hours of instruction to achieve the goal of active bilingualism. The ambivalence of policy-makers with respect to promotion of minority languages is also evident in the marginal status which the heritage languages programme has had during the first decade of its existence (1977–87). The programme has not been legitimized as an important component of children's education in that it can only be offered outside the normal five-hour school day. Also, in contrast to western Canada, it is still illegal to offer bilingual programmes (e.g. 50% heritage language, 50% English) in Ontario schools.[7]

When we move to the level of school boards we find most boards responding to community requests for the heritage language programme; however, in at least one case (Scarborough) the board has refused to implement the programme despite strong and prolonged community pressure.

At the level of the school itself, we find generally little enthusiasm among principals and regular programme teachers for incorporation of heritage language programmes within an extended school day. In the Metropolitan Separate School Board (MSSB), the programme for Italian, Portuguese and Ukrainian has been integrated for almost a decade with relatively little controversy (but see Berryman, 1986) but in the Toronto Board the attempt to integrate the programme into an extended school day was strongly resisted by regular school staff. Much of the resistance was fuelled by the perception among teachers that they had not been adequately consulted by the board, but there was also a strong feeling among many teachers that the heritage language programme had little educational merit and would disrupt the teaching of the core curriculum. In some situations, ethnocultural community groups reported that teachers had explicitly communicated these beliefs to students in class. Parents still frequently report that teachers and other educators advise them to use English rather than their mother tongue in the home on the grounds that children's school progress is impeded by lack of exposure to English.

In short, with respect to cultural/linguistic incorporation, an institutional structure has been created in the province whose aim is to further students' appreciation of diverse cultures and to provide opportunities for language maintenance and acquisition. However, this structure falls short of recognizing heritage language learning as fully educationally legitimate and there is little evidence that a "philosophy of multiculturalism" does actually permeate the curriculum and policies of most schools in the province. The evidence that exists (e.g. Samuda, 1979) suggests that the rhetoric of "multicultural education" at a policy level is reflected to a much lesser extent in the actual interactions between educators and students. These interactions appear as likely to convey "subtractive" messages to minority students with respect to their language and culture as they are to encourage language development and cultural reinforcement. In other word, Anglo-conformity is alive and well at a classroom level in many schools despite the lip-service paid to vague principles of multicultural education.

It is also worth noting that, in contrast to the United States, there has been very little discussion of the relevance of bilingual education programmes to promoting the academic achievement of minority students who are "at risk" educationally. The heritage language programme is seen as an "enrichment" opportunity rather than as an intervention designed to reinforce students' conceptual foundation (see Cummins, 1983). There are some exceptions, for example the L1 tutoring programme implemented for Spanish-speaking students in North York, but generally intervention for minority students "at risk" does not go beyond the regular English language remediation programmes. There has been virtually no use made of heritage language instructors for either L1 assessment or remediation for minority students.

Community participation

It has been argued (Cummins, 1986) that minority students will be empowered in the school context to the extent that the communities themselves are empowered through their interactions with the school. When educators involve minority parents as partners in their children's education, parents appear to develop a sense of efficacy that communicates itself to children with positive academic consequences (see for example the "Haringey Project" in Britain (Tizard, Schofield & Hewison, 1982) and Ada, this volume, Chapter 9).

The teacher role definitions associated with community participation can be characterized along a *collaborative–exclusionary* dimension. Teachers operating at the collaborative end of the continuum actively encourage minority parents to participate in promoting their children's academic progress both in the home and through involvement in classroom activities (see Ada, this volume). A collaborative orientation may require a willingness on the part of the teacher to work closely with mother tongue teachers or aides in order to communicate effectively and in a non-condescending way with minority parents. Teachers with an exclusionary orientation, on the other hand, tend to regard teaching as *their* job and are likely to view collaboration with minority parents as either irrelevant or actually detrimental to children's progress. Often parents are viewed as part of the problem since they interact through their L1 with their children at home. From the perspective of many teachers, parents' demands to have their languages taught within the school system further illustrates how misguided parents are with respect to what is good educationally for their children. From the parents' perspective, teachers' resistance to heritage languages represents an attempt to exclude the community's values and priorities from the educational system and suggests to them that the rhetoric about the importance of community participation refers only to participation by the Anglo-Celtic community.

A number of larger school boards employ school–community liaison officers to increase the participation of minority communities in the education of their children. However, there is a potential conflict of interest for employees of school systems if they attempt to become advocates for ethnocultural communities. This conflict of interest derives from the fact that school–community liaison officers are still expected to represent the interests of the school system which may not be willing to acknowledge problems that exist and may have a vested interest in maintaining the status quo. Thus, alerting communities to their rights and/or interests may be regarded as stirring up trouble.

This can be illustrated with reference to the 1984–86 heritage language controversy in the Toronto Board of Education[8] where the School–Community Relations (SCR) department was active in attempting to communicate research results to ethnocultural communities about the value of heritage language development, and also played a role in encouraging community participation at consultation meetings held to discuss integration of the programme in particular schools. In many cases the message they were conveying to communities was the opposite to that which regular programme teachers were attempting to convey.[9] As a consequence, many trustees and teachers opposed to integration of heritage language teaching did not view the activities of the SCR department favourably. These trustees gained control of the Board in the autumn 1985 elections; the SCR department was subsequently disbanded and, in August 1986, the co-ordinator was relieved of his duties "because of the unavailability of work" (*Role Call*, Volume 9, no. 1, November 1986, p. 8).

The policy issue that arises with respect to community participation is whether employees of school boards are the appropriate people to represent the educational interests of minority communities, since one cannot assume that the interests of communities will match the interests of the boards. For school board employees to support the interests of communities against those of the status quo is to risk job security and/or advancement.[10]

Pedagogy

Several investigators have suggested that the learning difficulties of minority students are often pedagogically induced in that children designated "at risk" frequently receive intensive instruction that confines them to a passive role and induces a form of "learned helplessness" (e.g. Beers & Beers, 1980; Coles, 1978; Cummins, 1984a). Instruction that empowers students, on the other hand, will aim to liberate students from dependence on instruction in the sense of encouraging them to become active generators of their own knowledge.

Two major orientations can be distinguished with respect to pedagogy. These differ in the extent to which the teacher retains exclusive control over classroom interaction as opposed to sharing some of this control with students. The dominant instructional model in most Western industrial societies has been termed a "transmission" model (Barnes, 1976; Wells, 1982); this can be contrasted with a "reciprocal interaction" model of pedagogy.

The basic premise of the transmission model is that the teacher's task is to impart knowledge or skills that s/he possesses to students who do not yet have these skills. This implies that the teacher initiates and controls the interaction, constantly orienting it towards the achievement of instructional objectives.

It has been argued that a transmission model of teaching contravenes central principles of language and literacy acquisition and that a model allowing for reciprocal interaction between teachers and students represents a more appropriate alternative (Cummins, 1984a; Wells, 1982). This "reciprocal interaction" model incorporates proposals about the relation between language and learning made by a variety of investigators, most notably, in recent years, in the Bullock Report (1975), and by Barnes (1976), Lindfors (1980) and Wells (1982). Its applications with respect to the promotion of literacy conform closely to psycholinguistic approaches to reading (e.g. Goodman & Goodman, 1977; Holdaway, 1979; Smith, 1978) and to the recent emphasis on encouraging expressive writing from the earliest grades (e.g. Chomsky, 1981; Graves, 1983).

The Ministry of Education and most boards of education in Ontario endorse an interactionist emphasis at a policy level but in many programmes (particularly second language programmes such as core FSL, immersion, heritage language programmes) the actual practice is still very much transmission-oriented.

A central tenet of the reciprocal interaction model is that "talking and writing are means to learning" (Bullock Report, 1975:50). Its major characteristics in comparison with a transmission model are as follows:

— genuine dialogue between student and teacher in both oral and written modalities;

— guidance and facilitation rather than control of student learning by the teacher;

— encouragement of student–student talk in a collaborative learning context;

— encouragement of meaningful language use by students rather than correctness of surface forms;

— conscious integration of language use and development with all curricular content rather than teaching language and other content as isolated subjects;

— a focus on developing higher level cognitive skills rather than factual recall;

— task presentation that generates intrinsic rather than extrinsic motivation.

In short, pedagogical approaches that empower students encourage them to assume greater control over setting their own learning goals and to collaborate actively with each other in achieving these goals. The approaches reflect what cognitive psychologists such as Piaget and Vygotsky have emphasized about children's learning for more than half a century. Learning is viewed as an *active* process that is enhanced through *interaction*. The stress on action (Piaget) and interaction (Vygotsky) contrasts with behaviouristic pedagogical models that focus on passive and isolated reception of knowledge.

The relevance of these two pedagogical models for multicultural education derives from the fact that a genuine multicultural orientation is impossible within a transmission model of pedagogy. To be sure, content about other cultural groups can be transmitted but appreciation of other cultural groups can come about only through interaction where experiences are being shared. Transmission models entail the suppression of students' experiences and consequently do not allow for validation of minority students' experiences in the classroom. Ontario (particularly Metropolitan Toronto) has potentially the perfect learning environment for genuine multicultural education given the diversity of human resources in most classrooms and communities. However, these resources can be utilized only when educators have

— an additive orientation to students' culture and language such that these can be shared rather than suppressed in the classroom;

— an openness to collaborate with community resource persons who can provide insight to students about different cultural, religious and linguistic traditions; and

— a willingness to permit active use of written and oral language by students so that students can develop their literacy and other language skills in the process of sharing their experiences with peers and adults.

Assessment

Historically, in both Canada and the United States, psychological assessment has served to legitimize the educational disabling of minority students by locating the academic "problem" within the student herself. This has had the effect of screening from critical scrutiny the subtractive nature of the school programme, the exclusionary orientation of teachers towards minority communities, and transmission models of teaching that inhibit students from active participation in learning.

This process is virtually inevitable when the conceptual base for the assessment process is purely psycho-educational. If the psychologist's task (or role definition) is to discover the causes of a minority student's academic difficulties and the only tools at her disposal are psychological tests (in either L1 or L2), then it is hardly surprising that the child's difficulties are attributed to psychological dysfunctions.

To what extent have multicultural education policies influenced assessment and placement of minority students in Ontario? Very little, it appears. The Ministry of Education commissioned a survey of policies and programmes with respect to testing, assessment, counselling and placement of minority students in the late 1970s (Samuda & Crawford, 1980). This report documented the fact that a large majority of school boards had no policies or special provision for assessment and placement of minority students.

It is disturbing to contrast the concern for issues of discriminatory assessment in the United States with the virtual absence of any sustained consideration of these issues in Ontario, with the exception of a few boards of education. One might have expected that the endorsement of multicultural education policies in Ontario would make policy-makers and psychologists highly sensitive to issues of educational equity but there is little evidence that this has been the case. Even in the larger urban school boards where assessment policies do exist, these policies frequently bear little relationship to the research data that exist on minority assessment issues.

Ethnocultural community groups have expressed concern about discriminatory assessment and streaming of minority students into vocational programmes since the early 1970s. First, the Dante Aligheri Society raised these issues with the Toronto Board on behalf of Italian students and more recently Portuguese, Greek and Black parents have expressed similar concerns. In the late 1970s, several Boards of Education adopted policies of delaying formal educational and psychological assessment of minority students until they had been in Canada for at least two years. However, the figure of two years was based on *assumptions* about how long it took children to learn English rather than on any empirical data. The empirical data, in fact, suggest that a much longer period (at least five years on average) is required for immigrant students to catch up with native speakers in academic aspects of English, although they may acquire relatively fluent conversational skills in English within about two years (Cummins, 1984a).

During the late 1970s and early 1980s, Ontario phased in its special education bill (Bill 82), modelled on the US special education bill (Public Law 94-142) which required school boards to identify all exceptional students (e.g. gifted, learning disabled, etc.) and provide them with an education appropriate to their needs. In the United States, many studies had documented the effects of discriminatory assessment of minority students as illustrated by the massive over-representation of Hispanic and Black students in classes for the retarded. Litigation in the early 1970s required school districts to take steps to correct these abuses and relatively strong non-discriminatory assessment provisions were built into special education legislation (Public Law 94-142). Specifically, students were required to be assessed in their primary language unless it was clearly not feasible to do so. Throughout the 1970s and 1980s, psychological and special education journals in the United States have printed numerous articles on issues related to assessment of minority students, and the new field of "bilingual special education" was born.

In Canada, by contrast, there has been minimal discussion of issues concerned with discriminatory assessment among academics and policy-makers involved in special education, and the issue of non-discriminatory assessment has been virtually ignored in special education legislation (Bill 82) and in subsequent documentation.[11] Similarly, the issue of non-discriminatory assessment has scarcely been raised in mainstream Canadian academic journals during the past decade. No courses on issues such as bilingualism, cultural diversity, non-discriminatory assessment are required or even offered in university departments which train school psychologists and special educators. Certification examinations for psychologists similarly ignore the issue despite the fact that in cities such as Metropolitan Toronto, with close to half the school population coming from non-English-speaking backgrounds, as many as 75% of the students being assessed are likely to have been exposed in the home to a language or dialect other than standard English.

Discussion of questions dealing with non-discriminatory assessment in support documents dealing with Bill 82 is limited to vague cautions such as the following:

"Where a child's language is other than English or French, a reasonable delay in the language-based aspects of assessment should be considered." (1980:5)

A more recent memorandum to school boards gives somewhat greater recognition to potential problems in assessing minority students:

"If the pupil's first language is other than English or French and/or the pupil lacks facility in either of these languages, consideration should be given to postponing the assessment, or, where possible, conducting the assessment in the child's first language." (Policy/Program Memorandum No. 59, p.2)

However, no suggestions are given as to what constitutes a "reasonable" delay, nor are pitfalls associated with L1 assessment considered. There appears to have been no obvious response at a policy level to the findings of the Samuda & Crawford (1980) report showing that many school boards across the province fail to pay even lip-service to Ministry guidelines regarding the testing of minority students. Apart from a handful of school boards, there is little evidence of minority students' cultural and/or linguistic backgrounds being systematically taken into account in the identification and placement process. Similarly, although Bill 82 mandates parental participation in Identification, Placement and Review Committee (IPRC) meetings, there is little evidence of sustained consideration of how to ensure meaningful parental participation when parents do not speak fluent English and/or do not understand the purpose or consequences of placement decisions that are being made.[12]

In short, academics, policy-makers and, to some extent, administrators in school boards have tended to show little sensitivity to issues concerned with non-discriminatory assessment despite the evidence from the United States and Canada that typical psychological assessment procedures significantly underestimate the academic potential of minority students. No specific training has been or is currently being provided for psychologists on issues related to bilingualism and minority language development despite considerable evidence that misconceptions about the effects of bilingual language use in the home and the learning of heritage languages at school are common among both psychologists and other educators (Cummins, 1984a). Institutionalized racism with respect to the assessment of minority students has remained virtually unchallenged at the levels of policy and legal provision, professional training and certification, and (with one or two exceptions) school board programmes.

The alternative role definition that is required to reverse the traditional "legitimizing" function of assessment can be termed an "advocacy" or "delegitimization" role (see Mullard, 1985 for discussion of delegitimization strategies in anti-racist education). The psychologist's or special educator's task must be to "delegitimize" the traditional function of psychological assessment in the educational disabling of minority students; in other words, they must be prepared to become advocates for the child in scrutinizing critically the social and educational context within which the child has developed.[13]

Implementation of strategies to reverse discriminatory assessment policies is likely to be complex since these policies are rooted in the very organization of school systems and in the conceptualization of entire fields, such as special education and school psychology, where the normative "medical" model of scholastic dysfunction still predominates. Ortiz & Yates (1983), for example, reported that Hispanic students in Texas were over-represented in the "learning disabilities" (LD) category by a factor of 300%. In other words, despite non-discriminatory assessment provisions, the structure preserved itself by a simple shift from an Educable Mentally Retarded (EMR) classification to a LD classification. In short, the data suggest that the structure within which psychological assessment takes place orients the psychologist to locate the cause of the academic problem within the minority student herself and policy changes alone are unlikely to alter this structure significantly.

Samuda (1979) reports a similar disjunction between policy and school practice in Ontario with respect to the educational assessment of minority students. A strong assimilationist element was evident among school principals, teachers and resource people, especially in Metropolitan Toronto:

> "Statements by Chairpersons of school boards, the various Work Groups on Multiculturalism within Metro Toronto, all illustrate the fact that the thrust for reform has developed outside and apart from the schools. And, significantly, there exists a lag between the words of the politicians and the attitudes and practices of the teachers who are the principal instruments in the assessment, placement, and educational treatment of the new Canadian. The one recurring and persistent need is for the re-education—the inservice training—of teachers, administrators, and consultants, to move from an ethnocentric stance to a clearer understanding of the basic intent and meaning of the Province's multicultural policy and what it means in terms of educational policy and practice. The central feature for change must be the teacher's attitude, the teacher's understanding and acceptance which can only come by implementing preservice and inservice teacher education programs..."(1979:49)

Samuda goes on to emphasize the need "to make drastic changes in the kind of training that takes place in the faculties of education throughout the province where there is scant evidence of any real change in perspective from that of the ethnocentric WASP middle-class pattern" (p. 49).

The types of change process that should operate at different levels of the educational hierarchy are examined in the next section.

Conceptualizing the change process in anti-racist education

In conceptualizing the change process in anti-racist education, it is necessary to specify: first, the levels or constituencies involved in effecting change; second, the specific areas where change is required; and third, the practical strategies for implementing change. The levels involved in effecting change are outlined in Figure 6.3.

As discussed above, the most direct determinant of minority student outcomes is the type of interaction students experience with educators and their parents (or other significant adults). The role definitions of educators with respect to the dimensions discussed in Figure 6.2 (cultural/linguistic incorporation, community participation, pedagogy, and assessment) mediate their interactions with minority students and play a major role in empowering or, alternatively, disabling students. Thus, major changes in interactional structures that challenge the broader institutionalized racism

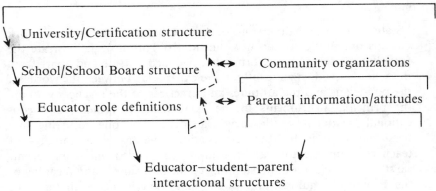

Policy/Legal Structure

University/Certification structure

School/School Board structure ↔ Community organizations

Educator role definitions ↔ Parental information/attitudes

Educator–student–parent
interactional structures

FIGURE 6.3   *Change processes in anti-racist education*

can be effected by individual educators. However, the actions of individual educators are clearly influenced and constrained by the immediate school and school board context within which they operate as well as by both their training and the policy/legal context that exists within the society. For example, a teacher of Latino students in the United States may attempt to implement interactional pedagogy and strongly promote students' L1 academic skills but be reprimanded by the school principal who is concerned that the class is noisy (because there is a lot of language going on) and that there is too much Spanish being spoken. Similarly, change is less likely when there is no recognition of the need for change at the levels of policy and university training. The case of Bill 82 in Ontario, considered above, is a good example of how inadvertent institutionalized racism with respect to assessment of minority students was perpetuated by the failure of policy-makers and academics to acknowledge that there is even an issue here for educators to consider.

The relationships outlined in Figure 6.3 are two-way relationships; in other words, influence can be exerted upwards (e.g. from individual teachers to school/school board policy) as well as downwards. Also, no rigid hierarchy of influence is intended. For example, policy provisions can (and usually do) affect schools without going through the university structure. Also, individual teachers can take advantage of legal provisions to effect changes in school board policy, as described by Curtis (this volume). Parents and communities can also directly impact various levels of the educational hierarchy (see Honkala *et al.*, this volume, Chapter 10).

According to the framework developed above, change towards anti-racist education must focus on the ways in which structural economic/ political factors are manifested both in the knowledge base and in the mind set or orientation of educators. These two are closely linked since information will frequently be ignored or denied by educators who are characterized by an Anglo-conformity orientation. These educators also tend to be reluctant to acknowledge that they hold Anglo-conformist views and may claim that they believe strongly in "multiculturalism".

Among the issues that educators and policy-makers should internalize as part of their knowledge base are the following:

— limitations of standardized tests;

— language/academic development among minority students;

— bilingualism in the home;

— bilingual/heritage language programmes;

— dialect differences;

— cognitive/cultural styles;

— parental involvement.

There is an ethical responsibility for educators at all levels of the educational hierarchy to ensure that *all* those interacting with or setting policy for minority students have internalized and are acting in ways consistent with this knowledge base. This applies not just to teachers but to principals, resource persons and administrators also.

However, although acquisition of the knowledge base is a necessary condition for anti-racist educational practice, it is not a sufficient condition. Also required is an intercultural orientation on the part of educators.

The task of changing basic attitudinal orientations is formidable and experience suggests that strong policy/legal provisions and incentives at the levels of Ministries of Education, universities and school boards are necessary. In addition, principals should make it clear that teachers with an Anglo-conformity orientation are out of place in their schools, and teachers should also communicate to other teachers that behavioural or attitudinal manifestations of institutionalized racism are unacceptable to them.

It would also be advisable to create an independent structure outside the school boards and the Ministry of Education to monitor the progress that boards are making towards implementation of anti-racist education. At a federal level in Canada, the auditor general and the Commissioner of Official Languages play such monitoring roles in the areas of government spending and national official language provisions.

Provision should also be made for "community advocates", again independent of school boards, to provide input to parents (in their own languages) about their rights and to represent parents at times when crucial decisions are being made about their children's future (e.g. at student placement meetings following formal psychological assessment). It is essential that these community advocates be independent of school boards, since there is otherwise a conflict of interest when an employee of a school board potentially opposes school board policy or practice in advocating minority students' and parents' rights. The recent demise of the Toronto Board's School–Community Relations department discussed above illustrates the potential consequences of promoting informed parental participation in opposition to the wishes of some politicians and educators.

In conclusion, anti-racist educational initiatives are possible at all levels of the educational hierarchy, from the individual teacher or parent to government policy-makers. However, these initiatives are likely to be successful only when they represent a challenge to the societal power structure. Given the commitment by many people in society to maintain the dominant–dominated power relationships, we can predict that educational changes which threaten this power structure will be fiercely resisted. The fact that, in Ontario, up to this point multicultural education initiatives (with the exception of heritage language programmes which are outside the "mainstream" of multicultural education) have met with little or no resistance is an indication of how little they threatened the educational basis of Anglo-conformity and, by the same token, how little they are likely to have empowered minority students. It remains to be seen to what extent the current anti-racist education initiatives being undertaken by the provincial government will challenge the roots of institutionalized racism in Ontario education.

Notes to Chapter 6

1. "Heritage language" is the most commonly used term in Canada to refer to mother tongue programmes. However, a variety of other terms (e.g. ancestral, ethnic, ethnic minority, modern, "third" (after English and French), non-official (in contrast to the official languages)) have also been used, reflecting the confused status of the entire enterprise in many parts of Canada. See Skutnabb-Kangas, this volume, Ch. 1, for a detailed discussion of the various ways in which the term "mother tongue" has been used.

2. This is still an extremely common practice in North American schools.

3. See Rodriguez, 1982 for an autobiographical account of the emotional schism brought about by teachers' advice to parents to switch from Spanish to English in the home.

4. In some cases "disinformed" would be more accurate since the misinformation is promoted by political or social forces that are attempting to maintain the status quo with respect to dominant-dominated group relations.

5. This appears to characterize many of those associated with the "US English" movement in the United States who strongly promote better "foreign" language programmes while arguing for the eradication of minority students' home languages.

6. Galtung's work, as discussed by Skutnabb-Kangas, this volume, Ch. 11, is relevant to the analysis of minority student and community empowerment.

7. At the time of writing (February 1987) it appears possible that these restrictions may be lifted and heritage language instruction may be incorporated within the regular school day. A private member's bill (Bill 80) proposing incorporation of heritage language instruction within the regular school day has been endorsed by all three political parties. However, as in past debates on heritage language teaching in Ontario (see Cummins, 1984b), a strong backlash is likely. The tone of this backlash can be seen from the comments of one columnist (Judi McLeod, an ardent critic of heritage language programmes) who writes in a column entitled "All Aboard for More Hogwash": "... I call the bill hogwash. The nauseating strategy of the lib-left will undoubtedly see any who speak against the heritage-language bill branded as racists and bigots. Yet educators keep telling us that one of the most pressing educational problems is the number of students graduating from high schools without an adequate grasp of English" (*Toronto Sun*, January 19, 1987, p.18).

8. This controversy centred on the attempt by the Toronto Board to integrate the teaching of heritage languages within a school day extended by half an hour rather than outside regular school hours (e.g. after school or on Saturday). Regular programme teachers worked to rule for several months (e.g. refusing to participate in all extracurricular activities such as sports) and threatened full strike action to protest at what they saw as a decline in the quality of education and in their working conditions caused by the teaching of heritage languages during the extended day.

9. In an interview published in *Role Call* (Volume 8, no. 3, April 1986), the Toronto Teachers' Federation monthly newspaper, Charlie Novo-grodsky, the co-ordinator of the SCR Department, described the conflict between the SCR Department and the teachers in terms of "a classic confrontation between, on the one hand, a heartfelt community desire (in many hearts) to have their culture and language recognized as part of their regular school curriculum through an integrated program: that desire coming up against an equal desire, on the other hand, on the part of people who are closest to the work—teachers—to control the condition, including the time and scheduling under which they deliver their work. It is a classic community control versus professional control issue."

10. The strike by Finnish parents in Rinkeby, Sweden (see Honkala, Leporanta-Morley, Liukka and Rougle, this volume) illustrates the importance of informed minority community groups to monitor actions by schools or school boards that might jeopardize their children's academic development.

11. This raises some disturbing questions; for example, was the issue of non-discriminatory assessment ignored because those who drafted Bill 82 were genuinely ignorant of the issue or because they considered it to be an unimportant or marginal issue? The first supposition is hardly credible since the issue was highlighted in most of the major academic journals in special education and school psychology during the previous decade; thus, it may be that the issue was simply an awkward question that was more convenient to ignore than to deal with. The lack of sensitivity among ethnocultural groups and opposition parties to the implications of the legislation for minority groups certainly facilitated this strategy. The Bill constitutes a prime example of how institutionalized racism can be perpetuated at a policy/legal level.

12. At the time of writing (February 1987) a comprehensive review of race relations policy in education is being conducted by the Ministry of Education in which serious consideration is being given to the manifestations of institutionalized racism in the educational system and strategies for eliminating it. Assessment of minority students is a major focus of this review.

13. It is worth noting that assessment and pedagogy are closely linked in that classroom teachers have considerable opportunities to observe children undertaking a variety of cognitive and academic tasks when the instruction is individualized and interactional. This information can

and should play an important role in assessment/placement decisions. Within a transmission model, when the instructional tasks are teacher-imposed rather than expressive of children's own experience, then the instruction tends to mirror the biases of standardized tests and consequently provides much less opportunity for observation of children's capacities.

References

ABELLA, I. & TROPER, H. 1983, *None is too many.* Toronto: Lester & Orpen Dennys.

ANDERSON, S.E. & FULLAN, M. 1984, *Policy implementation issues for multicultural education at the school board level.* Ottawa: Multiculturalism Canada.

BARNES, D. 1976, *From communication to curriculum.* Harmondsworth, Middlesex: Penguin.

BEERS, C. S. & BEERS, J. W. 1980, Early identification of learning disabilities: Facts and fallacies. *The Elementary School Journal* 81, 67–76.

BERRYMAN, J. 1986, *Implementation of Ontario's Heritage Languages Program: A case study of the extended school day model.* Unpublished Doctoral Dissertation, O.I.S.E.

BULLOCK REPORT. 1975, *A language for life.* Report of the committee of inquiry appointed by the Secretary of State for Education and Science under the chairmanship of SIR ALAN BULLOCK. London: HMSO.

CHOMSKY, C. 1981, Write now, read later. In C. CAZDEN (ed.), *Language in early childhood education.* 2nd edition. Washington, DC: National Association for the Education of Young Children.

COLES, G. S. 1978, The learning disabilities test battery: Empirical and social issues. *Harvard Educational Review* 48, 313–340.

CUMMINS, J. 1983, *Heritage language education: A literature review.* Toronto: Ministry of Education, Ontario.

—— 1984a, *Bilingualism and special education: Issues in assessment and pedagogy.* Clevedon, England: Multilingual Matters. Co-published in the United States by College Hill Press, San Diego.

—— 1984b, Linguistic minorities and multicultural policy in Canada. In J. EDWARDS (ed.), *Linguistic minorities, policies and pluralism.* London: Academic Press.

—— 1986, Empowering minority students: A framework for intervention. *Harvard Educational Review* 56, 18–36.

GOODMAN, K. S. & GOODMAN, Y. M. 1977, Learning about psycholinguistic processes by analysing oral reading. *Harvard Educational Review* 47, 317–333.

GRAVES, D. 1983, *Writing: Children and teachers at work*. Exeter, NH: Heinemann.

HAKUTA, K. & DIAZ, R. M. 1985, The relationship between degree of bilingualism and cognitive ability: A critical discussion and some new longitudinal data. In K. E. NELSON (ed.), *Children's Language, vol. 5*. Hillsdale, NJ: Erlbaum.

HARNEY, R. & TROPER, H. 1975, *Immigrants: A portrait of urban experience, 1890–1930*. Toronto: Van Nostrand Reinhold.

HOLDAWAY, D. 1979, *Foundations of literacy*. New York: Ashton Scholastic.

LAMBERT, W. E. 1975, Culture and language as factors in learning and education. In A. WOLFGANG (ed.), *Education of immigrant students*. Toronto: O.I.S.E.

LINDFORS, J. W. 1980, *Children's Language and Learning*. Englewood Cliffs, NJ: Prentice Hall.

MULLARD, C. 1985, The social dynamic of migrant groups: From progressive to transformative policy in education. Paper presented at the OECD Conference on Educational Policies and the Minority Social Groups, Paris, January.

OGBU, J. U. 1978, *Minority education and caste*. New York: Academic Press.

ORTIZ, A. A. & YATES, J. R. 1983, Incidence of exceptionality among Hispanics: Implications for manpower planning. *NABE Journal* 7, 41–54.

RODRIGUEZ, R. 1982, *Hunger of memory*. Boston: David R. Godine.

SAMUDA, R. J. 1979, How are the schools of Ontario coping with a New Canadian population: A report of recent research findings. *TESL Talk* 11, 44–51.

SAMUDA, R. J. & CRAWFORD, D. H. 1980, *Testing, assessment, counselling, and placement of ethnic minority students*. Toronto: Ministry of Education, Ontario.

SKUTNABB-KANGAS, T. 1984, *Bilingualism or not: The education of minorities*. Clevedon, England: Multilingual Matters.

SMITH, F. 1978, *Understanding reading*. 2nd edition. New York: Holt, Rinehart & Winston.

TIZARD, J., SCHOFIELD, W. N. & HEWISON, J. 1982, Collaboration between teachers and parents in assisting children's reading. *British Journal of Educational Psychology* 52, 1–15.

TROPER, H. 1979, An uncertain past: Reflections on the history of multiculturalism. *TESL Talk* 10, 7–15.

WELLS, G. 1982, Language, learning and the curriculum. In G. WELLS, *Language, learning and education*. Bristol: Centre for the Study of Language and Communication, University of Bristol.

—— 1986, *The meaning makers: Children learning language and using language to learn*. Portsmouth, NH: Heinemann.

WRIGHT, E. N. & TSUJI, G. K. 1984, *The grade nine student survey: Fall 1983*. Toronto Board of Education, Research Report No. 174.

Section II: Experiential perspectives

Section II, *Experiential perspectives*, adds depth to the more research-oriented descriptions of minority education. A group of immigrants living in Sweden, one American (Kristal-Andersson), one Brazilian (da Silva), one Greek (Kallifatides) and three Finns (Jalava, Kalasniemi, Leporanta-Morley) portray the immigrant experience in a country which poses as the conscience of the world and a champion of human rights outside its borders. Two Sami, living respectively in Norway (Lukkari) and Sweden (Marainen), show that the indigenous experience and search for identity have close affinities with those of the immigrant. The Zulu poem (Kunene) summarizes the centrality of language as a cultural core value for all these multilingual groups.

7 Mother tongue and identity

Nobody could see that I was a Finn

ANTTI JALAVA

My first impressions of Stockholm were dazzling. In the eyes of a nine-year-old kid, who had only seen little country towns, the Big City seemed like a vast amusement park, full of breathtaking activity and people swiftly on the go. Green serpents lunging out of black tunnels, roaring traffic carousels, houses taller than church steeples and shop windows overflowing with all kinds of merchandise. The people looked healthy and prosperous, and everybody wore good clothes. You could not see old ladies dressed in black, or disabled war veterans sitting on park benches with a sleeve or pants leg hanging limp and empty. Wonder-struck by the things we saw, we would point and gasp. As I took in my new surroundings with eyes as round as saucers, I thought pityingly about the folks back home, who could not behold all these wonders and who had to buy their liquorice from Leppänen's little country store, unaware of the existence of department stores bigger than ten cowsheds put together.

Our apartment was located in an old suburb. There the people knew each other; there a true community spirit prevailed, a sense of belonging together. It was like a village encircled by a noisy and nameless metropolis.

We lived in a condemned house; but with the help of a few cans of paint, new wallpaper, some cement and a few days' carpentry, we got our rooms to look like new. Everything seemed to be falling into place.

I went into our back-yard, where some boys were kicking a ball around. The boys stopped to stare at me for a while; then I said something in Finnish, and the next second I had to flee into the hallway to escape a hail of stones and loud abuse. My father said it would take some time before I would be accepted. He was right.

My parents were workers, and because there was a shortage of labour they were welcome. They had, so to speak, been awaited. When I would go to meet them in the afternoon at the telephone factory, which was located within walking distance of our home, they looked both tired and glad. Often they were accompanied by other Finnish workers. They said there was plenty of work, as much as anybody would want to do; the going was hard but the pay was pretty good—which was something you couldn't say for unemployment-ridden Finland. Yes, everything seemed to be turning out all right.

My parents were welcome, sure enough, but as far as we kids were concerned, matters were altogether different. After all, we were not useful, productive, and on top of everything else we couldn't even speak Swedish. The principal of my new school did not really know what to do with me when I was admitted; she was just as embarrassed and at a loss as I was, and when she escorted me to the elementary third-grade classroom we walked hand in hand. Holding hands was the only language we had in common. There was a vacant seat in the rear of the classroom. The boy I was placed next to protested vehemently, but I was ordered to stay put, anyhow. The flush-faced fellow whose bench I had to share was named Osmo. It was a Finnish name and he came from Finland, but even so for some reason he refused to speak a word of Finnish. Later I came to understand why he behaved as he did; and if I had only guessed that his fate would also be mine, I would have taken to my heels and run for my life.

My new classmates were curious: they watched my every movement closely, they walked in circles around me, they sniffed in my presence, and they felt the muscles on my arms. After that, they began to call me Finnbiscuit, and that was my nickname until I learned to speak Swedish as well as Osmo did ... or, more precisely, until I had adjusted to their ways to the extent of my passing in their eyes for a real Swede.

Adjusting was not, however, at all simple. To what did one have to adjust and how? There was nobody to explain things, there were no interpreters, no Finnish teachers and no kind of teaching of the Swedish language. And I was no chameleon, either, for I only wanted to be myself, out of habit and instinct. When the others wrote in Swedish, I wrote in Finnish. But that was something that just couldn't be done. The teacher grabbed my pencil and angrily shook his finger at me. In spite of everything, I continued to fall back on my mother tongue. From the time I had learned to spell, it had given me pleasure to put together sentences on paper.

There was a row at my desk. The teacher tore up my paper and stamped on my words that he had thrown on the floor. He scolded me loudly. I pulled a wry face and muttered, "Damn fool!" Osmo pulled at my sleeve and shook his head in warning. But I felt indignant and hurt, and I threw a tantrum. In the principal's office, I got my hair pulled and a Finnish boy from an upper grade was brought in to tell me writing compositions in Finnish was prohibited. I asked him why and he whispered in my ear in his Savoian dialect that he didn't know.

That night I threw a stone through the window of the principal's office. I never again wrote in Finnish. I just sat idly at my desk, silent and bewildered. What the dickens was this all about? Where had I ended up? Had everybody gone crazy? If grandma heard that I'd stopped writing Finnish, she'd die.

Blood was spilled and teeth knocked loose in the school yard. I was a pretty hot-headed rascal and soon I learned to hold my own as a scrapper. Mostly, I was forced to defend myself against boys in the intermediate grades. This often proved hard because they always ganged up on me and used mean tricks. Somebody had told them Finns were shits, so it was all right to give them their lumps. The taste of blood in my mouth every day made me wary, and I tried to avoid the school. To reach the school yard, everybody had to walk through a tunnel, and soon I was having nightmares about the tunnel. There my tormentors would often stand in the morning waiting for me, but instead of turning tail I'd head straight for them and put up a fight until I was knocked out.

After dark, however, came the time for revenge. There were quite a few of us brothers and the streets in our neighbourhood were dimly lit. As soon as we'd recognize any of our tormentors, we'd step out of the shadows and dish out blows that must have made their ears ring. It was violence coming and going, it was the only language understood by all. But violence brutalizes, makes one unscrupulous; it covers one's face with a cold mask. Therefore, in truth, I did not grow up as any Sunday school child or angel of the Lord. That I freely admit. But the alternative would literally have been to crawl in the gutter, and that was something I could not accept.

By the time I was promoted to the junior grade I had picked up quite a lot of the Stockholm slang. The language of my textbooks and teachers, on the other hand, was middle-class Swedish, to me quite incomprehensible and hard even for my classmates to understand, for most of them belonged to the working class and were accustomed to a totally different way of speaking. Their parents, just like my own, knew a lot, but the bourgeois school system despised that kind of knowledge. As time passed, I fell more and more behind my class; school seemed totally meaningless. Somehow I felt as though I didn't exist and the teacher's eyes would always look away over my head. I started to daydream and to play hookey.

My homesickness was fierce and seared my mind. I went frequently down to the terminal for Finnish boats, I wept secretly, recollected faces and voices, and in my imagination I was back home. In my sleep, too, I dreamed of familiar faces and voices, of tall pines with trunks a rusty red and the shimmering waters of great Lake Saimaa; and every morning without fail I felt compelled to curse reality and to confront it in a rage or with sobs.

When the idea had eaten itself deeply enough into my soul that it was despicable to be a Finn, I began to feel ashamed of my origins. Since going back was out of the question—and the thought of going back was what had sustained me—there was nothing else for me but to surrender. To survive, I had to change my stripes. Thus: to hell with Finland and the Finns! All of a sudden, I was overwhelmed by a desire to shed my skin and smash my face. That which could not be accepted had to be denied, hidden, crushed and thrown away. A Swede was what I had to become, and that meant I could not continue to be a Finn. Everything I had held dear and self-evident had to be destroyed. An inner struggle began, a state of crisis of long duration. I had trouble sleeping, I could not look people in the eye, my voice broke down into a whisper, I could no longer trust anybody. My mother tongue was worthless—this I realized at last; on the contrary, it made me the butt of abuse and ridicule. So down with the Finnish language! I spat on myself, gradually committed internal suicide. I rambled by myself through the woods of Årsta and talked to myself aloud in Swedish. I practised pronouncing words to make them sound exactly like the ones that came out of the mouths of Swedes. I resolved to learn Swedish letter perfect so nobody could guess who I was or where I came from. They still laughed at my Finnish accent—but after a while, never again!

My tongue was still limber and flexible. At the age of thirteen, I was just about ready. As long as I was a bit careful, nobody could tell I was a Finn, neither by my speech nor by my ways. The only thing that betrayed me was my name. But, for some reason, I did not dare to change my name. I kept it.

I spoke Finnish only when it was absolutely unavoidable. "Why are you always so quiet?" my parents would ask me at meal-times. "Why don't you talk to us any more?" For an answer they would get an evasive glance. I was incapable of anything else; my tongue had run dry, its power of speech gone.

When word came from Finland that grandmother was dead, I merely shrugged my shoulders in indifference and went over to see Åke. He was one of my bitterly won-over buddies. I did not want to remember, I would not allow myself to think of grandma, who had existed once upon a time, long ago, when I used to live in another world. But that night I dreamed about grandma: she was out on the pier washing clothes and she called out my name. In the morning I woke up feeling a treacher and filled with longing. I did not go to school but lay in bed all day, staring at the ceiling and remembering, as if in secrecy, what I did not otherwise dare to remember. Then the act continued, that of self-denial, that of pretending ever more completely. In short, in order to live in harmony with my surroundings, I had to live in perpetual conflict with myself.

I never told anybody about the old times in Finland, not even by a slip of the tongue. I had cut off part of my life, and this caused me inexplicable distress, which later developed into a sense of alienation. My distress then turned into a longing for sincerity and spontaneity.

In the upper grades, one had to apply oneself to one's studies in earnest and compete for the best marks. Others were way ahead of me in knowledge, so I had to study as hard as I possibly could. But it was no use, no matter how hard I tried the meaning of words eluded me; I had to read lines over and over again and still could not understand. My examinations turned out badly; I always got the worst marks. This, again, put me in low spirits, and made me think I was stupid. Paradoxically, however, deep down inside me I had a feeling that I had a head for books. But words mocked me, refused to open up for me; they gave off no odour and seemed to be totally barren; I recognized words but failed to grasp their sense. The depth and diversity of language were lost; this matched the loss of my mother tongue, my Finnish.

Continuous failure at school forced me to search for something else. Those sliding downhill could always find pot down around the subway station, or they might seek diversion in pilfering or acts of mischief. For my part, I was attracted to sports. At least on the athletic field, I had a chance to engage in honest competition; the stop-watch ticked away at the same rate for everybody, all you had to do was to run like hell and stay in your own lane. I trained and entered races and I began to win plaques and trophies. People slapped me on the back and said I was a chap worth my salt. It helped a bit to salve my wounds and restore my self-respect. Besides, it gave me a chance to travel and see the world, to live in hotels and meet celebrities whose pictures appeared on the front page of the *Dagens Nyheter*.

Athletics called for trained muscles and strong lungs. What it did not give was a healthy soul, and a healthy soul was my deepest desire, for my mind was in a chaotic state, on the verge of a breakdown. I was troubled by a growing sense of emptiness and alienation. I was conscious of never—hardly ever—using the words "our country" or "us Swedes". It never crossed my mind to speak of "us Finns" or, with reference to Finland, "my country". I was without a people, without ties. Perhaps this is what made me feel empty. Or perhaps the reason could be found in the dismal faces flitting in the mirror of my soul.

I was sixteen years old when one June day I stood in the sun-drenched school yard and looked at my graduation diploma. My ears burned red with shame. Then I let out a hysterical laugh and headed for home. At the foot of the stairs little Timo was sitting and playing marbles. He had come from Joensuu, Finland, three weeks before but could already say, "Låt bli" ("Don't"). I folded up my diploma to make a paper swallow and lured Timo to accompany me up to the attic. There I lifted him up to the window and let him fling my swallow into the air. Timo shrieked in delight as the paper swallow spun down towards the ground. As for myself, I was no longer capable of yelling in Finnish—even though, down in my heart, I might have had the desire.

Poems

THEODOR KALLIFATIDES

My language and I

Every time I say stone
I think of other stones
and sea only partly
means sea

I have lost my language
things have no taste any more
in my mouth
there is always an infinite
silent moment
between me and the new words
a silence which I fill
with grey leaves
no there are no grey leaves

The new words are like *dolmas*[1]
stored in the freezer
too long
I can't fill this mute moment
which has frozen like a drop of water
over an unintended defeat
and to speak has become
a craft
with masses of sweat and tired muscles

But if I can't walk with the new words
I can at least crush them

(From *Tiden är inte oskyldig* (*Time is not innocent*). Translation by
Tove Skutnabb-Kangas)

1. *Dolmas* are prepared by stuffing blanched vine-leaves with minced lamb
and cooked rice, or vegetables. The leaves are rolled into balls and
braised in very little stock with oil and lemon juice added. They can also
be made with fig or hazel-nut tree leaves, or cabbage leaves (as in
Sweden). The Turkish word "dolma" is used in many languages
throughout the Middle East and North Africa, and also in Scandinavia
(Swedish "kåldomar", cabbage dolmas) (Editor's note)

BINNIE KRISTAL-ANDERSSON

Till min svenska pojke
(*To my Swedish son*)

Yesterday
we sat
in the grass
The sun was shining
The birds were singing
so different
from the city
which was
your only
reality
until now
the country
Swedish landscape
which you, my son
belong to, so new
for me
which I slowly
learn to love
never belong to, as you,
but love.

You said
excitedly
"Mamma, look a paperbird ..."
Paperbird
so beautiful
but as mother
I tried to find
the right word.
It was "fjäril".
But I couldn't
remember
"fjäril"
in Swedish.
So it became
butterfly.
But it wasn't the same
for you.

"Can you say butterfly?" I said
and you answered angrily, as only a three year old can,
"No! I can't!"
and went to your
Swedish father
to find
the "right"
word.

That hurt.
You who are only three,
and your world
so important
a Swedish world
I try to share with you
be part of.

It goes sometimes
...until I can't
     say the word
     you want to learn
...until I can't
     caress you
     in Swedish
...until I see you
     slowly walk
     from me
     towards
     the others
     who can
     your world.

(From *Svenska för invandrare*, Immigrant-Institutet, Borås, 1975, pp.
47–49. Translation by Tove Skutnabb-Kangas, Robert Phillipson and
Binnie Kristal-Andersson)

Matti och hans bror
(*Matti and his brother*)

I was sitting by the sandbox
in a playground
in Eskilstuna

watching
the children.
It was a sunny day
a holiday
and the park
was filled
with children.
Four boys
played by the swings
two were Swedish
two Finnish
The Finns were brothers.

"What's your name?" asked the ten year old
the Finn about the same age
"My name is Matti."
"Matti ... Is that a name?" he said and
turned
laughing to his Swedish friend.
"Matti ... that's not Swedish. That's no name!"
The Finnish boy looked hurt, but
didn't answer—
obviously used to that
"Can you speak Swedish?" asked
the other boy
"Yes I can", the Finn answered proudly
"But your little brother, he can't."
"He is just a little boy", answered the Finn
The Swedes laughed
"He is just a little boy", swinging and mocking
his Finnish accent
"How old is he?"
"Eight" he answered suspiciously
"Then he goes to school, and can't speak
SWEDISH!"
The Finnish
boys continued
swinging
but not with
the joy
of swinging
but thoughtfully

slowly
waiting
for the next
jeering
word.

(From *Svenska för invandrare*, Immigrant-Institutet, Borås, 1975, pp.
29–31. Translation by Tove Skutnabb-Kangas, Robert Phillipson and
Binnie Kristal-Andersson)

Den svenska negern
(*The Swedish Negro*)

I met him
one day
at Slussen.
He was alone
With his drunk and silent eyes
he sought
escape from
the loneliness
forced on him.
He was small,
dark, with black eyes
looking
stupid
if one wanted
to compare them
to the light blue Swedish gaze
I was a foreigner
also
but it didn't show.
He said angrily
"Damn Swedish bitch!"
I knew
from my
childhood upbringing
that I shouldn't
talk to
drunkards
But I did.

"I'm not Swedish" I said.
He stared at me
and tried to look sober.
He said "Hello"
I said "Hello"
and left.

(From *Svenska för invandrare*, Immigrant-Institutet, Borås, 1975, pp. 55–56. Translation by Tove Skutnabb-Kangas, Robert Philipson and Binnie Kristal-Andersson)

PIRKKO LEPORANTA-MORLEY

My language is my home

In my mother tongue
my hatred is sanguineous
my love soft.

My innermost soul
is in balance
with my language.
The closeness of it
caresses my hair.

It has grown
together with me,
has taken root in me.

My language
can be painted over
but not detached
without tearing
the structure of my cells.

If you paint
a foreign language
on my skin
my innermost soul
cannot breath

The glow of my feelings
will not get through
the blocked pores.

There will be
a burning fever
rising in me
looking for a way
to express itself.

GUILEM RODRIGUES DA SILVA

About the importance of having a language

(to Tove Skutnabb-Kangas)

I love people's birdquick gestures
when they do not see me
when I look at them
like at birds
outside my window
If I waved at them
they would fly away
for ever frightened
by my black hair
and my brown dreamer's eyes

There are days when I
cannot speak any language
without an accent
not even my own
Then I would like to be
like Picolino, the clown in Rio Grande,
advance and say words of love
without being accused
of offensive behaviour
That would be like owning the world
without having a name
without having a face.

Darkness

Suddenly but not unexpected
they came over me, white kisses
cold caresses with velvet skin

and shook away my everyday
Where am I?
Why is it snowing?
Who has planted me here?
When did I contemplate dying so far away
from my roots?
And if I die in a hard winter like this
how will the grave-digger
be able to make the earth
receive me?

My language

(*Mitt språk*, dedicated to Sten Soler)

When I say earth in Portuguese
TERRA
the double "rr" crunches between my teeth
like particles of earth
FLOR
flowers on my lips
Moon is perhaps more beautiful than LUA
but never sea than MAR
with never ending beaches
where every ray of sunlight
converts the grains of sand to diamonds
My language is the guarantee for my life
a constant reminder
of sorrow
of joy
of rage
Here I have mostly been at the receiving end
I express thanks for what is obvious
I say "How are you?"
and it is difficult not to mean it.
Non-alcoholic
no smoking
the silence
the discrete sighs
Oh I know I have what it takes
to thrive here

in spite of the prepositions
which still complain of rape
But my language
which is vital for me
like most things from my underdeveloped country
is suffocated by the foreign and well known
There is a daily fight
with monologues in front of the mirror
with reading aloud
to keep my language alive
Every time I look up a word in a dictionary
for the spelling
I am further removed from my roots
Soon I shall stand wordless and naked
in the cold north wind

(All three from *Innan natten kommer*,
Invandrarförlaget, Borås, Sweden, 1982. Translation by Tove
Skutnabb-Kangas and Robert Phillipson)

RAUNI MAGGA LUKKARI

I row across my river[1]
my father's river
my grandfather's river
Row alternately to the Norwegian side
the Finnish side
I row across my river
to my mother's side
my father's side
Wondering
where do homeless children belong

(from *Losses Beaivegirji*, 1986. Translation by Tove Skutnabb-Kangas
and Robert Phillipson)

1. The Teno/Tana river marks the border between Finland and Norway, and
   Rauni's parents came from different sides of the river. The Sami have never
   accepted the state borders as a dividing line: Samiland cuts across these
   borders, and most Sami claim the right to cross wherever they wish.
   (Editor's note)

MAZISI KUNENE

On the Nature of Truth
"People do not follow the same direction, like water" (*Zulu saying*)

Those who claim the monopoly of truth
Blinded by their own discoveries of power,
Curb the thrust of their own fierce vision.
For there is not one eye over the universe
But a seething nest of rays ever dividing and ever linking
The multiple creations do not invite disorder,
Nor are the many languages the enemies of humankind
But the little tyrant must mould things into one body
To control them and give them his single vision.
Yet those who are truly great
On whom time has bequeathed the gift of wisdom
Know all truth must be born of seeing
And all the various dances of humankind are beautiful
They are enriched by the great songs of our planet.

(First published in *The Ancestors and the Sacred Mountain*:
Heinemann Educational Books)

Living with two languages

JUKKA KALASNIEMI

As the name above indicates very clearly, I am personally of Finnish ancestry. It may therefore be appropriate to try to address this particular, somewhat special topic.

The memory slips, but I myself must have come to Sweden when I was approximately two years old. Therefore I have, right from the start, enjoyed the privilege of growing up with two quite different languages.

I have always had both Swedish and Finnish companions, and in my own view my proficiency in both languages is not inconsiderable. Nonetheless all this has naturally not come about through my own brilliance. No, it is highly probable that the foundation of my bilingualism was laid by attendance in a Finnish-medium class for the first nine years of schooling.

I very well recall that many Finnish parents were speculative about whether attending a Finnish-medium class was good for the children's future development. They thought that the teaching was conducted excessively in Finnish, that the youngsters were being isolated from their Swedish peers, as they were placed in separate classes. The children did not have enough time to learn to master the Swedish language to such an extent that they would be able to manage in Swedish society painlessly later on.

There was a lot of such "talk" at that time. Far too much, in my personal view. Why complain? Some immigrant parents (meaning Finnish parents) went as far as to place their children in completely normal Swedish classes, without the children being able to understand a word of what was said, recent arrivals that they were. That is what I call giving the children a bad start in life.

What it is really all about is being able, by means of language, to find one's own identity. Or, as Marianne Alopeus writes in her article "Thank you for my language", in *Svenska Dagbladet* of 20 January 1978: "If we do not belong completely anywhere, at least we do in our mother tongue. That is where our identity is."

I repeat my question: "Why complain?" If opportunities for immigrant education are provided, the children have a better chance of "finding their own selves" and becoming accepted by the environment. One must now throw away one's background and one's language, and believe that one becomes a Swede by doing so.

You still have your name and in many cases also your appearance against you. It is much easier to become accepted and appreciated for what you are than for what you pretend to be.

That is why immigrant education is so good. Even if one has not planned to return to the home country, one has at least learned something of one's "own" language and one's "own" culture. There is security in knowing where one belongs, and what one's roots are.

(Translation by Robert Phillipson and Tove Skutnabb-Kangas)

Returning to Sami identity

JOHANNES MARAINEN

I grew up in Saarivuoma, one of the Sami villages within Kiruna, in northernmost Sweden. It is no use looking for this village on the maps, it isn't there. Sami villages are of no interest to the Swedes, they exist in reality only for us Sami. Actually they are not villages but large areas within which groups of Sami move with their reindeer.

In my childhood the families followed the reindeer, and thus we stayed in different areas within the "village", depending on where the herds went during the various seasons. In addition, we had an area in Norway that we could use during the summer months.

As a child I had the opportunity to live and grow in an intact Sami environment. All of us in my village depended solely on our herds of reindeer, and our way of living was still fairly uninfluenced by Swedish society. We had our own language and our own culture and lived our own lives.

When I started school I took my first step away from my Sami environment. In those days I considered school an insignificant episode, however. I was absolutely certain that when I had fought myself through six years of school, I would return to Sami life again.

I went to first grade in a summer- or tent-school. The school looked exactly like my own home. It was a tent, made of canvas, stretched over tall, slender birch poles with an opening for the smoke in the middle. We sat on boughs around the open fire with a slate or a book on our outstretched legs.

The next summer the school was several kilometres from where we were living, and I used to run over a mountain every day on my way to and from school. The school was placed in different areas each year. The third summer the school was a long distance from where my family was living, so I boarded with another Sami family near the school.

The fourth year came, and in August I had to go to a boarding school near our winter area. I would not be able to see my parents and sisters and brothers until they came down from the mountains, which would be around Christmastime. The younger children, who had been going to summer school, moved into the boarding school after Christmas. We were released from school just in time for the spring herding, in April, and could leave with our parents for the summer area.

Thus our schooling was suited to Sami life, but I am sorry to say that it was only the organized part that was suitable. Culturally and linguistically the school was a shock to me. "Mother tongue" was the dominant subject during the early school years, but I did not understand until much later that "tongue" means language. The term "mother tongue" did not mean anything to me, I just accepted that it meant Swedish. *Eatnangiella*, my mother's language, it definitely was not.

Like all the other beginners I did not understand a single word of the "mother tongue" and it would take many years before I was able to speak it. During school time we were not allowed to use our own language, not even during recess. We were supposed to become "mother tongued" as soon as possible.

Life in school seemed strange in all respects and staying there seemed so unnecessary to me. What we learned in school were things which we did not need in our way of life. Due to the lack of connection between what we learned in school and my own culture, I did not take anything seriously. I accepted and learned what I had to, but at the same time I felt that it had nothing to do with me. When school was over, what I had learned there would no longer be a reality to me. It was something which would not be necessary in my future life, outside school. If I wanted to talk to the people who lived outside my Sami village, I would not be able to speak to them, either in my own language or in the Swedish language I had learned in school, because these people spoke only Finnish! Nor could I use the "mother tongue" to make myself understood during my summers in Norway.

Before long, however, I became interested in reading. The school library was soon exhausted, and my happiness knew no bounds when I was entrusted with the housemother's own collection of Hans Christian Andersen's fairy tales.

I still remember how proud I was when I got my very first own book. I received it one spring from my teacher just before I went with my family into the mountains. I am sure that that book is one of the most read books in the world, at least in the number of times it was read by the same person! I read it time and again, and was scolded when I could not put it away, even when it was time to take the canvas off the tent poles for our move to another area.

But still, just like my friends, I looked forward to the day I would be *free*. I had no thought of leaving my Sami life, and it was not common that anybody moved away from the Sami village. None of my friends had continued their studies, but my teacher in the sixth grade suggested that I should go to Middle School in Kiruna. My parents were of no help to him. In accordance with the free Sami upbringing, my parents considered that this was something I had to decide by myself.

Kiruna did not tempt me, instead it frightened me. Of course, it had been rather exciting to go to the dentist in Kiruna, and those visits had been highlights of the year. But actually to *move* there was quite another matter.

In spite of everything, my teacher succeeded in making me move, and I started middle school in Kiruna. After a few months, however, I had had enough. I felt, in all respects, very small and very unimportant in the big city. In school it was better. I had nice and pleasant friends. But in certain subjects I was handicapped. For instance, English was not a new language for my classmates, but it was for me. The principal suggested that he, personally, should help me with my studies privately, but I stood stubbornly by my decision to get out of school. The principal, however, did not agree, but suggested that I take one year off, something I accepted right away. "You will never see me in this school again!" I thought when I walked away.

The spring and summer turned out to be exactly the way I had imagined Sami life would be. I felt wonderfully free. There were no hours to keep. Sometimes I had to work hard, of course, but I felt that I could decide myself how much work and how much time I wanted to put in, although, sometimes, the work decided that for me.

I had never before taken part in the fall herding and had not imagined the hardships of moving the reindeer in darkness over ice and snow, on ground that was fit for neither skiing nor walking. As a result I reconsidered, and called the principal as soon as we reached our winter quarters.

Again I got nice schoolmates who were not prejudiced, but they did share with many other Kiruna dwellers the common misunderstanding that: "Sami have all the rights and no obligations".

Aside from that, school was the one place in town where I felt secure and safe. I soon learned that outside school it was better for me to demonstrate my Sami roots as little as possible. Despite that, I was called "Sami devil" every day. I tried to pretend that I did not hear, but each time a thorn stuck into my heart, and eventually I carried inside me a whole forest of thorns. I tried to suppress my feelings and wrapped all the thorns into all kinds of excuses, so they wouldn't hurt anymore. The worst of it was that all this Sami hatred was concealed, nobody wanted to show their contempt openly. There were lots of Kiruna dwellers who were unaware that it existed and who would have been hurt if someone had mentioned that there was Sami hatred in Kiruna.

I had several very nice Swedish friends, but the attitude in the rest of the community made me feel insecure in Swedish company. First, I felt insecure about myself, and second, I always felt that I had to be ready to defend my people. As a result I spent most of my time outside school with Sami friends. The same kind of children play best together...

As time went by more and more Sami youths came to town and it was natural that each sought the others out, even if we had not known each other earlier. The "mother tongue" became our language when we were together in town. Our own language was used only in our boarding rooms and in the Lapp Inn, the only hotel in those days which accepted Sami, and the Lapp café.

Thus I felt like a stranger among the Swedes and, unfortunately, felt a little bit like a stranger with my people who remained in the Sami village.

It was mostly children my age, especially boys, who showed a changed attitude. It became harder to talk to each other and I felt extremely sad. Now I realize that we were just feeling insecure, all of us. Our new experiences were different. I was no longer sharing their lives as active reindeer herders. They, on their side, were ignorant of my experiences in my new school.

We Sami in town learned fast that the best, and certainly the easiest, way to cope was to adapt, and as far as possible become Swedish. Unfortunately this drove many of us to self-denial. Once I saw some Sami youths purposely avoiding their parents in order not to demonstrate their Sami origin. It hurt me unbelievably and filled me with feelings of shame. To be absolutely honest, it could have been me, who felt forced to act the same way! It is painful to remember that it was quite often necessary for me to force myself not to deny myself, which to me felt extremely humiliating.

I continued my studies and accepted myself as more or less Swedish. For a Sami it is not difficult at all to live as a Swede in Swedish society outside the Sami area. In the end it was even possible to overlook the occasional Sami Devil invectives which were unavoidable. After all, there are quite a few good-natured, jolly fellows who, because they are registered jokers, have a right to give others less flattering names. But, of course, it is just jokingly. Or is it?

In time I became a teacher of the "mother tongue" in a high school in Gothenburg, and I felt quite content with my life. I had not been discriminated against. I had received the same good education as other Swedes. I had a job which I liked. Did I have anything to complain about?

I soon realized that as a Sami I was considered an exotic being in Gothenburg. There were requests that I give lectures on Sami. I hesitated long before I dared to stand up and talk, because in reality I knew nothing about Samis, nothing about my people. All I knew about were my own experiences.

At last I agreed to give a lecture, and in order to remedy my ignorance I went to a library and borrowed a book about the Sami. As I was reading the book I realized for the first time that we Sami indeed had our own history! I had not been allowed to read my history in nomad school. I had learned about King Karl, the young hero, and other brave Swedish kings, who had made the Swedish name fly in honour over the earth. For my history, it might possibly even have been favourable if the tyrant Danish King Christian had kept Sweden.

Well, my father happened to be visiting when I gave my first lecture on Sami in Gothenburg. As we were returning home, I asked him what he thought of my speech. He answered: "Well, I did not understand much of what you said, but they did applaud, so I assume that it was good." The answer did not surprise me, and I decided to translate my speech into the Sami language for him. It was then that I got my life's greatest shock! I realized that "mother tongue" had taken over my *eatnangiella*. I realized in horror that *I could no longer relate the most common and everyday matters in my own language*!

That was the first time since I grew up that I realized the negative sides of my becoming Swedish. I started to comprehend that the Swedish educational system had robbed me of something valuable, yes, perhaps the most valuable thing I had owned—my language. I could no longer talk to Father! This fact made me shiver. I became desperate, despondent. And then I became angry.

I had imagined that I still knew the Sami language, but due to the broken contact with my Sami environment and culture, my language had not developed in a natural way. I realized that I stood on a level comparable with a seven-year-old's linguistic capabilities. I could still talk about certain matters in Sami, but I was not able to keep a conversation or a discussion going.

As I was unable to develop my language in natural daily contact with other Sami, the school should have given me a chance to study my language. But what had it done instead? It had forced a new "mother tongue" upon me. I had been robbed of my own language, my own history and my own culture. The school had substituted something that was now well known to me. What was foreign to me was I, myself. I felt cheated!

I realized that the first thing to do was to study my own language. I asked for leave of absence in order to study Sami, but that was not granted. A "mother tongue" teacher asking for time off in order to study his mother tongue! Unthinkable. So, instead, I studied my language at night as I continued working and teaching. Later I was granted a leave of absence to study history because I was considered overqualified for "mother tongue" studies.

But I was certainly not overqualified to study my mother's language. I sat there with big dictionaries and began the painfully slow struggle to learn my own language. I was like a beginner, starting off with the vocabulary.

The most difficult part of my journey to my roots remained. I had to find my way to my Sami identity. I felt obliged to go back and analyse my development. I had to understand how the transformation from Sami to Swede had happened. I forced myself to remember all the bitter experiences which had made me choose the easiest road, accepting myself as Swedish and living like other Swedes. I went through all the painful memories as I tried to understand and realize what had happened. I no longer tried to erase, forget and hide, nor did I pretend not to hear anymore.

It was hard enough to accept myself, but it was harder still to explain myself to others. I felt shame and guilt because I had betrayed my people. My people and myself. It hurt to remember and it was painful to tell others. I did it because I felt it was necessary for me, and perhaps I could help others who were looking for *their* identity.

Today I am not ashamed anymore and I hope that other Samis do not feel shame that they have, through pressure from their peers, been forced to self-denial.

Today I accuse not all those who voluntarily hurt me and made me choose "Swedish", but those who are responsible for the cultural development. I accuse those who taught us to dislike our language, our culture and even ourselves. We were given an inferiority complex in school. Our language was not good enough. We were given a new "mother tongue". Our history was not worth studying.

How has all this new insight changed my life? Outwardly not much. I haven't moved back to my family, but still I feel that I am with them again. I have found my identity. I know now that I have a culture of my own, and my own history which, in itself, is worth knowing.

I am a Sami among Swedes. I do not feel that I belong with them the way I feel with Sami from Norway or Finland. Our Samiland is divided by national borders, yet *Samieatnam*/Samiland does not know of any borders between all of us Sami in the North. There are no borders on our maps.

In my warm, mild mother tongue foreign words intertwine.
Become a memory you trampled earth
where my tent stood and I played.
The sound of the bells hanging around the necks of my Father's
    reindeer
has remained in the bottom of my soul.
Grown into my retina is our reindeer mark.
Everything I felt is part of my heart.
Remain in my memory; Father's staff,
lasso of sinews, loop in the edge of the sleigh,
the round-up and moving of the deer, the sled with the fare
Down by the river is the half load waiting for the baby.
Still moving up the valley,
remember the slender bow above the neck of the pack reindeer
Hold on to the land you inherited with all your heart!

But the right to the land, you have lost.

PAULUS UTSI

Section III: Community struggles for educational rights

Section III, *Community struggles for educational rights*, shows both the richness and the similarity of struggles for appropriate education for minorities, and the importance of the communities' own action. Jordan and Stairs describe indigenous groups (Aborigines, Canadian Native and Inuit, Sami), while the rest of the articles are about two of the (potentially?) strongest groups in the world, representing a group part of which was colonized earlier, but mostly consisting of more recent immigrants: Spanish speakers in the United States (Ada, Curtis) and Finns in Sweden (Honkala *et al.*, Hagman and Lahdenperä).

8 Rights and claims of indigenous people: Education and the reclaiming of identity

The case of the Canadian Natives, the Sami and Australian Aborigines[1]

DEIRDRE F. JORDAN

Identity and claims to rights

An examination of the claims of aboriginal peoples for the recognition of land rights reveals that they do not pursue these claims as if this were merely a question of disputed ownership, or an assertion of the injustice of a powerful group taking land from a less powerful group. Claims to land rights are part of a complex of intertwined issues, having at their core one all-embracing claim: the right to identity as an indigenous people, the right to self-determination as a people.

Berger (1977:95) in his exhaustive inquiries relating to possible economic, social and cultural effects of the development of the northwest of Canada became quite convinced of the link between identity and land:

"The native peoples' identity, pride, self-respect and independence are inseparably linked to the land and a way of life that has the land at the centre."

Paine (1982), when summarizing the cultural consequences of the building of a hydro-scheme in the land of the Sami people, makes the same point as Berger, namely that certain forms of development act to destroy the culture of the people:

"The proposed Alta/Kautokeino hydro-scheme brings the Saami world in Norway very close indeed to its 'to be or not to be'. The likely consequences are so encompassing, they affect sedentary as well as pastoralist Saami: their ecology, economy, demography and hence *their own sense of self as Saami.*" (Emphasis added)

The forces of economic expansionism of the dominant group (invest-igated by Berger and Paine) have long been at work, destroying the culture of indigenous peoples with few voices raised in protest. The assumption made, almost universally, in contemporary societies which have both indigenous and colonizing populations, is that conflicts between the social/cultural interests of indigenous people on the one hand, and the material interests of the dominant group on the other, are judged to be legitimately resolved by reference to economic indices.

Schooling and identity

It must be pointed out, however, that history shows that it was not only forces springing from economic bases, and the exploitation of material resources, which, breaking the nexus of indigenous people with their land, acted to destroy their culture and substitute for a positive identity the negative traits with which indigenous people have come to be stereotyped. One of the crucial forces which has acted to destroy the identity and the culture of indigenous people has been that of schooling.

Berger (op. cit.:90) asserts: "The schools and what was taught in them offered a challenge to the culture of the Dene and the Inuit, *to their very identity as a people*" (emphasis added). Dianne Longboat (1984:1) asserts:

"The education provided to Indians by the Government of Canada and its colonial predecessor governments has been an important element of an overall policy of assimilation. It has been a means of seeking to replace traditional languages, religions, history and cultural traditions, values and world views with those of the European settler nations, and to modify the values of the Indian nations through those who are weakest and can offer least resistance ... the children. *Education has worked with the long-term objective of weakening Indian nations through causing the children to lose sight of their identities, history and spiritual knowledge.*" (Emphasis added)

In the case of all three peoples under consideration, it was missionaries who brought literacy to the indigenous people. Intent on saving souls, they studied the vernacular in order to translate the Bible.[2] Nevertheless, while early missionaries in many cases preserved the language of the indigenous people, they actively set out to destroy their "pagan" religious practices, and hence their culture, which in practice also meant the breaking down of the authority structures of the family and the group. The destruction was hastened by the establishment of residential schools. In Canada, the period 1850–1950 was marked by the rise of residential school programmes beginning with a small number of religious boarding schools (Indian and Inuit Affairs, 1982: Annex C). These schools were instituted to centralize educational activities. The Sami school was "reformed" in 1913 to be a school that would migrate with the people. The children were accommodated in Kator, intended to replicate the nomadic dwellings, but which were in practice insanitary hovels, condemned by the people. The school was deliberately of a lower standard than that of the majority population (Ruong, 1983:45). In the case of Australian Aborigines, residential schools were unashamedly seen as the best means of removing children from the influence of their parents. Many children, taken from their parents, completely lost touch with them, and in middle age set out on the traumatic search for their families.

For many, if not most of these people, schooling away from home is remembered as a searing experience, the designation in conversation most often used being "cruel". This is often remembered as physical cruelty; the striking of children as a disciplinary measure is not part of the socialization of indigenous peoples. However, it was the psychological cruelty of removal from family and immersion into an alien way of life which was perceived as equally destructive, so that generations of indigenous people internalized negative attitudes to the "whitening" processes employed in the schools.[3]

As assimilation became official policy in Canada and Australia (about 1950–70) the attack on the culture of the indigenous peoples was spearheaded in the schools, and focused on language.

"Every Friday evening ... it was time for us to report whether we spoke our language, Cree, during the week. If we confessed to using our own language, we were denied the visit with our parents and younger brothers and sisters which was the only privilege we had. In other words, we had to lie to the ministry in order to visit with our parents and relatives." (Gilbert Faries, Moose Factory; The Royal Commission on the Northern Environment, 1978:207).

In the case of the Sami, a "rigorous Norwegianization policy" was adopted from about 1880 (Eriksen & Niemi, 1981:361). The term *fornorskings-politikk* (Norwegianization) was primarily associated with language and school policy (ibid.: 354; Hoem, 1983:7, 8). Eidheim (1971:57) states that the school aims exclusively at communicating those values which are current in an idealized Norwegian society, and for generations it has had the implicit goal (at times explicit) to Norwegianize

the Lappish communities. The policy of assimilation required not only that
the children were forbidden to speak their language at school, but it was
assumed that everyone was able to speak the dominant language. The
children were not, for example, taught Norwegian. Yet the students were
expected to understand that language and the content of the
curriculum—all presented in a foreign language. Adults, today in their
forties, describe the humiliation of being treated as unteachable in school,
when in fact they had no understanding of the content presented in another
language. One person attested that a teacher friendly to the Samis, who had
some understanding of their language, was forbidden to speak to them in
Sami. Eidheim (1971:60) asserts that, "The Norwegians not only regard
Lappish as an inferior language in a general sense, but also judge it highly
improper and challenging if it is used in their presence". In general the
school *created* negative stereotypes. For the Sami people, schools were
places where their lack of knowledge of the majority tongue was used to
create typifications of "stupidity".

Co-existent with, but contradicting, the "theorizing" and practices
directed towards assimilation, was the theorizing that indigenous people are
not-quite-human, and therefore *not able* to be assimilated, and not able to
benefit from the same education as "white" people. Pseudo-scientists in the
wake of Darwin decided that Australian Aborigines were the missing link
between apes and men. Ruong (1983:38) points out that "social Darwinism" legitimated the treatment of the Sami as an inferior race.

In the case of many Australians for whom history has been silent about
Aborigines, negative stereotypes of the people were accepted and the low
level of schooling of adults, as well as the lack of achievement by students in
the schooling situation, was seen in terms of a social pathology model: the
people are of low intelligence, unteachable, good at sport, not at academic
work, and so on. Rowley (1971:8, 20), however, in tracing policy back to
the early 1900s, saw the "native problem" as one caused by white prejudice
against skin colour; mainstream society did not want Aboriginal people in
the towns or in the schools.

> "The official fuss about a few thousand persons of unsuitable com-
> plexion and the concurrence by the West Australian government in the
> prejudice of country town people, which was forcing these people out
> of the schools and even out of the towns is an excellent illustration of
> how prejudice creates its own special problems ... the transfer of these
> prejudices to all offspring of Aborigines who have the Aboriginal
> stigma had been almost universal and automatic in the past."

West Australia was not the only state to force Aboriginal people out of
schools and out of towns. In Rowley (1971:48ff.) may be found a detailed

account of restrictions placed on the movement of part-Aboriginal people in all states which in turn led to restrictions being placed on their access to education. The 1936 Act of New South Wales, the 1939 Acts of Queensland and South Australia, and the Amendment Act of 1936 in West Australia all provided for part-Aboriginal people to be removed from towns to reserves. On reserves, the highest level of education considered appropriate for Aborigines was fourth grade of primary school, often taught by untrained people. In the towns, Aboriginal children were not free to enter ordinary state schools in New South Wales until 1949 (Gale, 1972:245), and "well in the 1950s, each time there was a protest by white parents concerning Aboriginal children being admitted to a school the education authorities took heed of the complainants and sent the black children home" (Lippmann, 1981:139). Fitzgerald (1976:185) makes the observation that "From the child's viewpoint, 'dropping-out' is often the most sensible thing he can do when the school is inimical to self-esteem and the development of personality."

Thus in each of the countries under consideration, though the expressed, manifest aim of schooling was assimilation, the organization of the schooling often assumed that the indigenous peoples were considered incapable of learning: in each case, lower standards were expected in schools and fewer years of schooling were judged appropriate. The destruction of the culture and identity of indigenous people through the structures of schooling, the low expectations of teachers and lack of opportunity have left a legacy of memories of rejection, of internalization, of negative stereotyping and of the creation of a negative identity. It has also left a legacy of distrust of the "white" school system as an agency of assimilation, and the conviction that the structures of "white" schooling are ill-adapted for indigenous peoples.

The Royal Commission on the Northern Environment (1978:207) heard evidence from one area that:

"Within those 25 years [during which formal education had been available] the education system had produced in our area only two university graduates,[4] countless elementary secondary and post-secondary dropouts, a large absenteeism record and indifference to education as a whole by community members."

Indigenous people see two great problems connected with schooling—the loss of identity of their youth, and the massive drop-out from schools and educational institutions caused by the alienation of students from their ethnic identity. In every case, they see the faults lying in a white system unadapted to the needs of indigenous people.

The post-war period—the construction of policy

The events of World War II and its aftermath caused a profound shift in the conceptualization of the place of indigenous peoples within dominant societies. Indigenous people from each of the countries discussed, who had for so long been regarded as second class citizens, stereotyped as dependent, lazy and lacking in initiative, fought in the war with distinction. Their contribution (and the recognition of their positive characteristics) could not be denied. Furthermore, the dominant groups had experienced the apprehension, and in some cases, the reality of loss of freedom. The Norwegians, for example, suffered the trauma of Nazi occupation, the loss of democratic procedures, the curtailment of their own freedom and the humiliations of being a subject group. It was no longer possible for them to continue to advocate human rights in the public forum of the United Nations (as they had done forcefully within the League of Nations) without concerning themselves with the rights of the Sami.

The waves of immigration following World War II also led to the need to formulate national policies about new minority groups—assimilation gave way to new policies of pluralism and multiculturalism. As Labour Parties came to power in each of the countries under consideration, ideologies of equality of opportunity set parameters which included social, cultural and economic equality for minority groups. These ideologies of equality meant that the stigma associated with native identity could no longer be tolerated. Furthermore, as welfare policies were implemented, the poverty and powerlessness of the indigenous people became apparent.

The disjunction in the social fabric of the entire western world permitted new ways of looking at reality, and the construction of new sets of values, of ideologies that differed in fundamental ways from the pre-war period. New conceptualizations concerning indigenous peoples were codified in all three countries in the late 1960s and early 1970s in the forms which reflected the push of indigenous people towards self-determination and, in turn, led to further crystallization of the claims to rights as indigenous people.

In describing these movements, a fundamental difference must be recognized between the Sami, on one hand, and the aboriginal people of Australia and Canada on the other. In the case of Canadian Indians, the problem was to *preserve* their status as aboriginal peoples, the first nations of Canada. The Sami, on the other hand, had been subjected to policies of assimilation for over one hundred years. Their status as an *ethnic* group was not, and still is not, recognized.[5] Their problem has been to *gain* recognition of status as aboriginal people. Furthermore, the Sami differ fundamentally from aboriginal Canadians and Australians in that they are one people with a common language separated by the boundaries of the dominant nations (Norway/Sweden; Finland/Russia),[6] by the different orthographies authorized in each country and by different census definitions of Sami. The identification-from-without by governments has acted to fragment the group. The Swedish government, for example, recognized Sami not as an ethnic group, but as an occupational group concerned with reindeer herding. In Canada and Australia the "identification-from-without" acted in the opposite way. In both countries, groups not sharing the same language have been *united* by government policy which has failed in the past to recognize differences; "The Aborigines", "The Indians" were treated in legislation having reference to education as if they were a monolithic group, which, patently, they are not.

Contemporary claims to rights of identity in all three countries have arisen from a reaction to assimilationist policies; hence it is understandable that the Sami, subject to policies of "Norwegianization" for over one hundred years, should have begun to lay claim much earlier than did Indians and Aborigines to their right to control education *so that they could reclaim their ethnic identity*.

The Sami

Since many of the Sami had internalized the negative identity[7] offered to them by the Norwegians, and had actively espoused the notion of assimilation (Eidheim, 1971:50–67), the early protests were, on the whole, individual, and the first Sami Association founded in 1904 did not have a strong basis of support. However, as in the case of other indigenous peoples, the revival took on a great momentum after the war and in 1953 Sami Associations founded separately in Sweden, Finland and Norway collaborated to call together a conference. Ruong (1983:51) sees this as a milestone, both in the crystallization of a "Lappish" national consciousness in the three Scandinavian countries, and the demonstration of this sense of reclaimed identity to the majority populations.

In 1956 the Scandinavian Lapp Council was formed. Its initial concerns were with education for a changing world—but an education that preserved identity. Children should learn to read and write Sami as a first tongue; they should be instructed in the language and history of their people. A series of conferences followed. Always central to the issues discussed were the twin claims to rights—the right to land and the right to identity, the latter always including the right to control educational policy.

The notion of a research institute had been nurtured from as far back as the 1920s when the idea was first put forward by the Sami teacher, Per Fokstad. The dream became a reality when the Sami *Institut'ta* was established in 1973 in Kautokeino, a Sami village far to the north of the Arctic circle. Ruong (himself a Sami) highlighted the connection between self-determination/identity/education: "Its construction and the development of its activities sharpen and refine the tools for the assertion of identity, the culture and the belief in autonomy"[8] (Ruong, 1983:99).

The acceptance of the Institute and its policies, as evidenced by the financial support given to the Institute by the Nordic Council of Ministers (Denmark, Norway, Finland, Sweden, Iceland) may be taken as equivalent to the acceptance, also in 1973, by the Canadian Government of the policy proposals of the National Indian Brotherhood.

Canada

The impulse which triggered off the mobilization of the Canadian Natives to press for the recognition of their special status, their special claims to identity, and their rights to self-determination in education came in a paradoxical way, from the circulation of a policy statement on Indian Affairs by the Canadian Government.

In the late 1960s, the Hawthorn Committee summarized its findings in the following way:

"... The atmosphere of the school, the routines, the rewards, and the expectations provide a critically different experience for the Indian child than for the non-Indian. Discontinuity of socialisation, repeated failure, discrimination and lack of significance of the educational process in the life of the Indian child result in diminishing motivation, increased negativism, poor self-image and low levels of aspiration" (Hawthorn & Tremblay, 1967:130)

The low standards of Federal schooling for Natives had caused the people to push for an end to segregation in schooling. In 1969 a Government White Paper was circulated. It sought to resolve the problems caused by the lower status education offered by Federal services, by relinquishing this to the more esteemed provincial education bodies. The Native people, however, saw this as removing their claims to special status as the original people of Canada. In other words, their claim to identity was at stake. Self-determination became the "catchword" of the people, and both the Department of Indian Affairs and the Native people saw that self-determination was inextricably allied to, and based in, education.

"The discussion of jurisdictional matters served to raise further *Indian consciousness of the need for self-determination, for active Indian participation in the remaking of an Indian education system.*" (Indian Affairs, 1982, Annex C:8; emphasis added)

The Government White Paper

"caused the reawakening of political consciousness, and the emergence of provincial and territorial Indian political organisations designed to protect the rights of the first nations ... *education was an issue of primary concern, a pivotal developmental issue in refuting the assimilationist policies of the Government of Canada* ... In 1972, the National Indian Brotherhood produced a landmark policy statement: 'Indian Control of Indian Education'. The significant feature of all these policy statements since the White paper is the call for Indian control of, and input into, all facets of education affecting Indian people." (Longboat, 1984:3; emphasis added)

It was not only Indians whose theorizing was directed towards self-determination. Jean Chrétien, Minister of Indian Affairs and Northern development, in exploring the problems of drop-outs/push-outs, identified as problems the alienating structures of the philosophy of the schools, of white-centred curriculum which did not recognize language differences and cultural differences, of history which made no mention of the Indian, of the lack of training and lack of sensitivity of teachers to cultures other than their own, and of the lack of representation and participation of Indian parents on school boards.

Berger (1977:181), five years later, made much the same points. He summarizes the views of the Native people:

"They insist that they must control the education of their children, if it is to transmit their culture as opposed to ours. They say that the curriculum must include such subjects as native history, native skills, native lore and native rights: that they must determine the languages of instruction; and they insist that they must have the power to hire and fire teachers and to arrange the school year so that it accommodates the social and economic life of each community."

The claims of native people, commented Berger, did not reject what was held as knowledge by the dominant group. Rather, they made it clear that they sought a balance between the two cultures, but a balance of their own making.

The Indian Brotherhood (1972) were equally clear in what they wanted of education.

"What we want for our children can be summarized very briefly:
... to reinforce their Indian identity.
... to provide the training necessary for making a good living in
modern society.
*We want education to give our children a strong sense of identity with
confidence in their personal worth and ability.*" (Emphasis added)

Australia

The early policies towards Aboriginal people in Australia were a denial
of the existence of the people. The Foundation Act of South Australia in
1834, for example, declared the land unoccupied. Pseudo-scientists warped
Darwin's theories to proclaim the Aboriginal people as the missing link
between apes and men—a "theory" which exonerated those involved in
shootings, massacres and exploitation of the people. By the 1860s the
official policy had become one of segregation.

It was not until the 1940s that, in the belief that the Aboriginal people
were a "dying race", the "problem" of part-Aborigines was dealt with by a
policy of *dispersal*, the forerunner of assimilation.

"It would appear that the more ready means of bringing about a
process of physical and social assimilation of the Australian mixed
bloods into the community would be by the simple device of ensuring
that a maximum dispersal or spread of the minority group will take
place." (Tindale, 1941:119).

By the 1950s, assimilation had become official policy. In 1951
Hasluck, the then Minister for Territories, reported to Parliament that the
Native Welfare Conference held in Canberra

". . . agreed that assimilation is the objective of native welfare
measures. Assimilation means, in practical terms, that, in the course of
time, it is expected that all persons of Aboriginal blood or mixed blood
in Australia will live like white Australians do." (Hasluck, 1953:13)

In the mid-1960s, one State, South Australia, following the election of
a Labour government, turned its back on previous policy. Laws were passed
regarding land rights for Aborigines.[9] Anti-discrimination laws were aimed
at changing the practices, if not the attitudes, of the white population
towards Aborigines.[10] For the first time, there was a move away from
policies aimed at the control and containment of the Aboriginal people
towards policies requiring consultation and negotiation. A new era had
begun wherein Aboriginal people were seen as adults who had opinions
worth consulting, who had a right to autonomy over their lives. For the first

time, theorizing about a positive Aboriginal identity was offered by government.

King, the South Australian Minister for Aboriginal Affairs in the Labour government, issued a statement in 1971 entitled *The Shaping of a New Aboriginal Policy in South Australia*. He repudiated the official policies of assimilation held by the previous Liberal governments and maintained that

"The final wrong would be to attempt to destroy the Aborigine's racial and cultural identity and to turn him into a pseudo-white man. A most encouraging sign is the development among Aborigines of the desire to identify with their own people and to be proud of their race and its culture.

This desire of educated Aborigines to be with their own people, rather than escape from their environment into the white community, is a most hopeful indication of the rapid recovery of self-respect of the Aboriginal people." (Hansard, 1971–1972:756–759)

To make it possible for the Aborigines to "identify with their own people",[11] but yet remain within white society, King proposed a policy radically different from that operating at the Federal level. Assimilation was to give way to *integration*. He defined the policy of integration as

"... the right of the Aboriginal people to live in our community on fully equal terms but retaining, if they so desire, a separate and identifiable Aboriginal heritage and culture." (op. cit.:756)

The policy of integration put forward by King was one that provided the possibility for the recognition of an *alternative* Aboriginal identity located *within* mainstream society.

The policy made a major impact on "official" theorizing about Aborigines; for the first time mainstream society projected a *positive* psychological world with which Aboriginal people could interact and which they could appropriate. They now had the possibility of locating themselves, and being located by the white world, within a positive Aboriginal identity. In Australia it was thus not so much Governmental action in response to Aboriginal demands (as was the case in Canada and Norway) but rather a new social awareness on the part of legislators that brought about change.

Into the 1970s—the Federal level

When the Labour Party came into power at the Federal level in 1973, policies which had been developed in South Australia concerning

Aboriginal affairs became official party policy. The platform statement of the Federal Labour Party proposed legislation against all forms of discrimination and the promotion of the rights of Aborigines with regard to social services, land rights and health—all new policies. It also recognized the need for *positive discrimination*:

— Aboriginal people were to receive the *standard rate of pay* for employment and the same industrial protection as other Australians, a dramatic departure from practice.

— *Educational opportunities* were to be provided that were in no way inferior to those of the general community. Preschool and adult education were to be provided as broadly as possible.

— The philosophy underlying these programmes was that of *self-determination* for the Aboriginal people, and the exercise of a *greater autonomy* in all areas of their lives.

The policy of self-determination initiated by the Labour Party was modified by the Liberal/National Country Party Coalition to one of self-management. There was no emphasis in this policy, as there was in the South Australian policy, on the active encouragement of the politicization of Aboriginal groups. The possibility of structural differentiation was not entertained. Nevertheless, there was a theorizing that recognized differences in the life style of different groups of Aboriginal people.

The preamble of the 1975 Platform Policy of the Liberal Party noted that:

"... the life styles of Aborigines will, of necessity, vary between those living a more tribalized state in or near their traditional lands and those living in or near towns or cities. Policies must therefore reflect this fact." (Guidelines, Liberal/National Party policy, 1975)

As in the case of the Labour Government, there was positive support for the retention of Aboriginal values and Aboriginal culture.

"Aboriginal values are an intrinsic part of Australia's culture and heritage. We are part of each other. Without mutual respect and support for each other's cultural integrity, we cannot secure our personal identities." (Ibid.)

The policy statements of both political parties in the 1970s represented a new era for Aboriginal people in so far as government policy and legislation was concerned. Aboriginal people seized the concept of self-determination and interacted with it to build a new, positive world of meaning for themselves. The tradition-oriented people expressed this by saying "The *marrngu* (the people) are the boss!" This was used both as a rallying cry and as a firm basis for building a world of meaning in which Aboriginal people might exert autonomy. On all sides, Aboriginal people at every level in society, and in every sphere of action, health care, legal rights, educational policy-making, asserted, "We will do it ourselves". It was no longer accepted without question that white people would work on behalf of Aboriginal people. The meaning of working *for* Aboriginal people changed. Aboriginal people *employ* white staff to "work for" them—in Aboriginal independent schools, in legal services, in health care. The role of the non-Aboriginal is to implement the policy of the Aboriginal people; white people work for Aboriginal people, or with Aboriginal people to further the aims of the latter.

In sum, while Aboriginal people are physically located within a multicultural society, more and more they are entering into situations which are structurally alternative, and within which they have greater control of their futures. While originally this was not by choice, social interactions have produced a situation where the Aboriginal voice, expressing their political, cultural, physical and educational needs, is heard.

The positive theorizing of the governments in the 1970s has borne fruit in the 1980s as the Aboriginal people have been given, and have taken, responsibility for their own development, and incipient, rudimentary theorizing—"We will do it ourselves"—has been realized in the educational sphere through the activities of the National Aboriginal Education Committee established in 1977 to give advice to the Department of Education on Aboriginal needs, and ways of meeting these needs, and to advise the Department of Aboriginal Affairs and indeed all instrumentalities concerned with education. The Committee was to assist the Department in monitoring existing programmes and researching and proposing new programmes.

Self-determination and education—the contemporary situation in Canada

The acceptance of the Policy of the National Indian Brotherhood in 1973 has resulted in Native people becoming significantly involved in the control of education. Before this there were some 200 Indian school committees, with the people having some more or less "token" input. By 1980, 77% of the bands (450 out of 573) were administering all or part of their programmes; there were 137 band-operated, on-Reserve schools

(Indian Affairs, 1982:14) and three Native or Inuit school boards exercising the same control as Provincial boards had been created under Provincial Law—the Nishgas of British Columbia and the Cree and Kativik School Boards of Northern Quebec.

The Indian Affairs Document, *Indian Education Paper*, Phase I, while documenting the indicators of progress in Indian involvement in education, (greater control, greater participation in terms of enrolments, support for the teaching of language as part of the curriculum, the establishment of cultural/educational centres) nevertheless acknowledges the deficiencies in the implementation of policy:

> "Although bi-lateral agreement was achieved in the adoption of the 1973 policy, adequate policy definition, devolution preparation and procedures were not developed. As a result, *a considerable gap was formed between expectations and reality.*" (Indian Affairs, 1982:6; emphasis added) In particular, "The basic problem with local control of Indian education is that the concept has been implemented without the federal/Indian relationship involved having been defined and without the necessary structures having been developed" (p. 31).

The document highlights problematic areas: the differing perceptions of the respective rights and obligations of the Department of Indian Affairs, Indian Education authorities and provincial jurisdictions; the time lag between change in Indian society and changes in their educational services (p. 16); the disparities which have developed between Departmental statements of intent and actions which have, or have not, been initiated to achieve these goals (p. 17); the lack of ability of the Department of Indian Affairs to support adequately the curricula function ("activities are largely unco-ordinated, and there is great duplication of effort, because the Department does not have the capacity, either at headquarters or in the regions, to support a professional curriculum development program. Budgets do not offer the alternative of having this function performed under contract") (p. 26). There has been little, if any, research into the reasons for low achievement by students and the high drop-out rate (p. 21); the construction and maintenance of buildings is a problem (p. 22); staffing is characterized by high rates of turnover, inadequate training for transcultural education and low morale (p. 23).

The Native people provide a parallel analysis:

> "Roles, relations and obligations have never been clearly defined as between the Department and the First Nations in any scheme for the implementation of Indian control of education programs. Differing

concepts of control, jurisdiction, funding requirements and standards have obstructed the movement of real Indian control from a mere idea to an implemented reality." (Longboat, 1984:20).

There are intractable structural problems obstructing the satisfactory implementation of local control of education for the Native people; the policy is being implemented under archaic legislation which did not foresee the possibility of Native intervention in their own affairs: the legal right of the band-councils to employ teachers, for example, has been challenged in the courts. The Department of Indian and Northern Affairs, like the Department of Aboriginal Affairs in Australia, was never constituted to administer educational programmes: the budget is out of phase with the school year, support for curriculum development is lacking, and so on.

On the side of the Native peoples there are also enormous problems to be overcome. There is the lack of experience of involvement in educational policy making and implementation. In some cases, the urgency of the need for local controls impels action at a pace greater than that which can be absorbed and consolidated by the communities. There is need of education of the people to facilitate the management of their new responsibilities, and to test the long-term commitment needed to solve the burdensome practicalities of developing new structures. While the National Indian Brotherhood exists as a policy body, the agreed policy, of necessity, is fragmented and given different directions at the local level where there is the question of implementation. Different histories, different community composition, different local leadership styles all act to produce different conceptualizations of Indian identity, and hence of the "Indianization" of education appropriate to a particular group. The formulation and implementation of policy suited to local conditions needs great perception and time from people whose energies are already highly committed to the activities furthering the advancement of the group in a multitude of areas, of which the school (though extremely important and valued) is only one. Thus local control, in practice, may be reduced to the management of a "white" curriculum, "white" organization and methodologies.

The Department of Indian Affairs states quite clearly that "Indian local government is not a service agency for the delivery of federally conceived and planned programs" (Indian Affairs, 1982:28). However, the reality is that, without personal experience in the "world" of education, it is difficult at the level of implementation to evolve a system that is fundamentally different from "white" education.

Nevertheless, despite all the problematic issues outlined above, very real progress has been made. The Inuit and Indian school boards established under the James Bay Agreement (1975) in Quebec Province, do, in fact, control education with the power to decide on the language of instruction, the curriculum, the hiring of teachers and the structuring of the school year. They may well provide models for other situations, as their initiatives develop. There are numbers of schools controlled by boards on reserves which are "Indianizing" their philosophy, the content and the structures of courses and staffing. Where these are successful, they serve in turn as models for other bands to adapt. At a still more individual level, there are people who have supported the notion of "survival" schools, which are aimed both at the "survival" of Indian culture and the survival of individual students who are "push-outs" from mainstream schooling.

Non-indigenous support has been an element in the early stirrings of independence for indigenous people in each of the countries discussed. While the need and desire for this support has decreased, it plays an important part in the interaction between government personnel and the bands. The support of non-indigenous people will continue to play an important role in one particular area, that of increasing the access of Native people to, and their participation in, higher education, so that eventually Native people themselves will be in positions of power within educational structures. The Native Indian Teacher Education Programmes (NITEP) established across the country support students both within the Universities and with outreach programmes, chiefly in the area of teacher-training. Brandon University offers a number of off-campus courses, designed for Native people who would experience difficulty in being on-campus. One of its programmes established in 1974 serves students in isolated northern reservations; a second programme (1970) provides courses for teacher aides; the Winnipeg Centre Programme serves the disadvantaged in the urban community of Winnipeg—both Native and immigrant students are eligible for enrolment. Universities are developing special entry programmes (for example, the University of Manitoba with its special emphasis on entry for medical students) and programmes in Native studies designed for Natives and non-Natives. Native people themselves, who already have a significant input in the programmes mentioned, have initiated and control two major institutions (the Federated Indian College and the Gabriel Dumont Institute) and a research Institute, Mokakit (established in 1984). All these programmes are making a significant contribution to furthering the higher education and preparation of people needed to formulate and implement policy for the "Indianization" of education.

The one common denominator reflected from all these multi-faceted activities is clear: it is the concern for identity—the reclaiming of *pride* in identity, the reclaiming of autonomy.

The Sami

In Norway, since the Sami are not officially recognized as an ethnic group, but merely as "those who speak Sami", contemporary efforts are directed to gaining legal status. Ruong (1983:75) analyses the effects of current law on Sami identity.

"The attitude of the greater societies may be expressed politically within the governing bodies, administratively in the bureaucracy and judicially in the legislation. The last is very important. For the attitude of the society is crystallised in its laws. In my opinion, legislation on reindeer pastures and reindeer breeding creates an unfortunate dividing line between reindeer breeders and other Lapps. Indeed it cuts across the Lappish nation and complicates, and in a sense prevents, a real community of interests, i.e. a deeper communication and contact between Lapps who are reindeer breeders and Lapps who are not."

Theorizing about group identity has come to rely on the issues of a common history and a common language. The latter has come to assume a pivotal role in Sami identification of themselves as a group and in the claims for autonomy made by the Sami on the Norwegian government. Their claim to civil rights is two-pronged: the policy presses for the right to protection of land/livelihood and language. They seek that the latter should be given full recognition both in those areas in which Sami comprise a majority, and areas in which they have come to be a minority due to a change in proportion of population after Norwegian colonization. In these Sami areas, they seek that regulations by law should ensure

—that the Sami language is established as an official language

—that Sami language is taught in schools as both a native and foreign language, and that Sami language *is used as a language of instruction and a medium of information*

—that teaching materials and instructions in the schools are grounded in Sami culture and traditions, in accord with the wishes of parents

—that Sami language is used in public instructions and official transactions. (Samiraddi, Sami Political Program, 1981; emphasis added)

In order to make these policies effective a pre-eminent degree of support is given to research, particularly as it is integrated into supporting the rights claimed, and making their implementation possible. The vocabulary of the language, for example, is being extended and stabilized across the geographical borders so that it can become the medium of instruction[12] and a history of the Sami has been written.

In the school curriculum, changes are taking place which recognize the Sami movement. The first of these was seen by Ruong (1983:138) as happening in Norway in the immediate post-war era following a recommendation to the Minister of Education in 1947, suggesting co-operation with Sweden regarding the publication of Sami textbooks. A step of crucial importance for Sami solidarity was taken when Norway and Sweden adopted a common orthography.

Following the 1963 debate in the *Storting* a Sami upper secondary school opened at Karasjok in 1969, and small grants were allocated by the Government for a library established at Karasjok with the largest holding of Sami literature in Scandinavia, and the establishment of museums at Karasjok and Tromso.

The formulation and implementation of policy with regard to schooling is carried out by the Sami Education Council (established in 1975). The Council is responsible for educational planning (and negotiation with Norwegian education authorities) and for developmental work (e.g. language material, new curricular material adapted to Sami needs). It engages a combination of experts and practising teachers to carry out this work.

The two basic principles enunciated by the Council (Keskitalo, 1985:10) are that

—the school must give the new generation of Sami the possibility to interact with the wider society

—at the same time, and as part of this, the school must give the Sami the possibility both to conserve and further create their ethnic and cultural identity.

While language was the criterion of identity emphasized above all others in policy statements to government, a scanning of issues raised at successive Lapp conferences shows that growing importance is being placed on the cultivation of objective distinguishing characteristics, which mark off the Sami as an ethnic group different from Norwegians, and hence substantiate their claims to autonomy. The conferences have promoted research into and study of traditional Sami handicrafts associated with activities previously essential to everyday living; there is a reclaiming of a particular form of folk music, unique to the Sami, the Yoik, and the development of Sami art, poetry and literature. "The re-claiming of identity can more and more be seen as cultural and spiritual" (Per Fokstad, 1953, Scandinavian Lapp Conference).

These preoccupations of the policy-makers are reflected in the structures of educational institutions. In the vocational school at Kautokeino, for example, there is an emphasis on the study of traditional handicrafts, as well as the "modernization" of traditional occupations—the breeding and marketing of reindeer. Other subjects are selected for their relevance to contemporary employment opportunities in local communities.

The current efforts of the Sami Educational Council to bring about innovations are facilitated at the primary level by the fact that there is a widespread liberalization of curriculum taking place at the national level which permits the possibility of adaptation to local conditions within general guidelines (Keskitalo, 1985:9). For the Sami (as for Norwegians) the opportunity of adapting the curriculum to their particular circumstances is dependent largely upon how creative the local school board and the local school are in taking advantage of these possibilities, since Government policy commits it to support, however reluctantly (Eidheim, 1982:76), the establishment of bilingual, bicultural schools for the Sami.

The establishment of a Teachers' College at Alta, providing courses in Sami language and culture for both Sami and non-Sami, should provide a pool of teachers sensitive to Sami policy, and qualified to develop initiatives.[13] It has been pointed out above that Sami people have had negative experiences in the schooling offered them. In addition, it would appear that there are certain cultural obstacles to be overcome with regard to cultivating positive attitudes to education. There has always been an uneasy relationship between the Sami people and formal education. While, on the other hand, those members of the society who have opted for an academic career have been singularly successful, many Sami parents (just like many Aborigines—see Chief Saul Fiddler in The Royal Commission on the Northern Environment, 1978:207) have been reluctant to expose their children to the same situations they experienced by sending them to urban centres for education. Moreover, the knowledge and skills necessary for traditional Sami occupations have always been passed on within the group. It is only as the traditional occupations become more integrated into the total economy (and involve more book-keeping, the study of better breeding methods for reindeer, of marketing of primary products and handicrafts) and as young people move into the professions, that the Sami people are experiencing the need to look outside the traditional practical education found within the group and seek the benefits of formal education at the secondary and tertiary level.

In addition to the secondary education available at Karasjok, plans are in preparation for the extension of the secondary school and the further adaptation of the vocational school at Kautokeino to local needs; teacher education is available at Alta, and the University of Tromso is a stronghold for the preservation of Sami culture and research into Sami culture and language. [14] The location of Sami institutions and high schools, and Sami individuals doing research, in Sami villages rather than in "Norwegian" urban situations, is seen as a particularly important strategy. In the case of the siting of the school, the aim is the retention of students who would otherwise drop out; in the case of teacher training institutions and of individuals carrying out research there is an attempt to prevent a separation from the "real" village situation. In each case, however, the siting is seen as a means of building and proclaiming Sami identity and autonomy.

The major Sami thrust in terms of autonomy and control, however, has been through the Sami *Institut'ta*. [15] Essential research activities are carried out there; its importance, however, lies in its symbolic function. It stands as a sign of unity for *all* Sami across geographical boundaries, it produces unity of policy on vital issues, it provides a single organization which puts pressure on *governments* to unite in their policy towards the Sami, and above all, it proclaims to the world a *positive* identity for the Sami people.

> "The establishment of the Sami *Institut'ta* in a Lapp village is a great event in the present situation, and the history of the Lapp people. Its construction and the development of its activities sharpen and refine the tools for the assertion of identity, the culture and the belief in autonomy." (Ruong, 1983:97)

These changes have all taken place *within* a Norwegian framework. In 1985 a submission was presented to the Norwegian Parliament seeking the establishment of a Sami Committee to advise the Norwegian Parliament on Sami issues, similar to the so-called Sami Parliament in Finland that was approved. Its activities will be crucial to further developments in education.

Australia

A major difference between the situation in Australia and in Canada and Samiland is that there is no one body embracing all Aboriginal organizations. The National Aboriginal Education Committee (established in 1977) co-exists with other organizations, each concerned with separate issues, such as land claims, the Arts, the development of economic ventures, legal aid services and health services. The National Aboriginal Education Committee and the Aboriginal State Education Committees are policy-making bodies, *consulted* by government. They lack the power fundamental to self-determination. The National Committee has, therefore, as one of its objectives, the establishment of a National Aboriginal Education *Commission* which would be a statutory body established by an Act of Parliament. The Aboriginal people believe (and they were supported in this by the Australian Schools Commission) that self-determination in decision-making relating to Aboriginal education cannot become a reality until the responsibility for funding programmes for Aboriginal people belongs to the Aboriginal people themselves.

Nevertheless, despite these qualifications, the National Aboriginal Education Committee (NAEC) has more than fulfilled the expectations held out for it; it has carried out a series of evaluations on existing projects (e.g. the Black community school in Townsville, the Aboriginal Community College in Adelaide, etc.). In 1979 it researched the need for Aboriginal teachers and the opportunity for teacher training for Aboriginal people in response to a National Inquiry into Education; it articulated and disseminated NAEC policy in this area, policy which was accepted and implemented by the government and by institutions of higher education resulting in a significant increase in the number of Aboriginal people graduating as teachers. The acceptance of this policy was re-affirmed by the Minister of Education, Senator S. Ryan, in allocating funding in 1984. In 1985, the NAEC produced a comprehensive document to guide the government in the allocation of funds for the 1985–87 triennium (*Aborigines and Tertiary Education—A framework for the 1985–87 triennium*). Together with the Commonwealth Tertiary Education Commission it mounted a review of support systems for Aboriginal students in higher education (Jordan, 1984).

At the "grass roots" level, differences in history and development such as those found amongst the peoples of Canada are equally evident among the people of Australia. There are urban dwellers whose language has long ceased to be used, whose "mother tongue" is now English; there are tradition-oriented people who speak only their own language; there are people who have had contact with the white world who are able to speak a species of English (Aboriginal English) but who continue to use their own language in social interaction. The outcome of the policy of self-determination in the sphere of education has therefore taken on different forms depending on the history, ideology, geography, economic base and social interaction of various groups. In some cases, in the far north, where the Aboriginal people are in the majority, the response has been in the form of the out-station movement. The people have moved back to their homelands, away from cattle stations, away from white contact in general, to reconstruct a tradition-oriented identity. Schooling, however, and in particular the learning of English, is highly valued, and the people make the request for white teachers to follow them as they move away into isolated areas. For other tradition-oriented groups in much the same areas, there has been a movement towards "community" schools whose organizational patterns may, to some extent, be seen as micro-versions of the Kativik and Cree Schools Boards of Quebec Province, and the Nishgas of British Columbia. The (Aboriginal) boards most often have only one school for which they are responsible, or, in some cases, where missionary and government activities in the past have brought about an agglomeration of different language-speaking groups, the social structure imposed from outside breaks down naturally into language-speaking groups, and the people move off into separate "camps" again, after they have secured the services of teachers. The responsibility of the Aboriginal School Boards of these "community schools" extends to the structuring of curriculum, the hiring of teachers (who are required to respect the philosophy of the group), the structuring of the school year, approval of the subjects taught and their content (carefully scrutinized for anything contrary to the philosophy of the group) and the methodologies used. White teachers are responsible for "white stuff" (necessary for interaction with the white world); education/ socialization is the province of the Aboriginal people. In the urban situation, too, there are examples of the development of independent schools. While the issue which triggers off the founding of such a school is often the problem of combatting the drop-out of indigenous people from white schools (the problem common to all three countries), the aim is one of fostering a positive Aboriginal identity.

As in the case of Canada, efforts have been made since the early 1970s on the part of Colleges of Advanced Education to provide for Aboriginal people entering teacher training programmes through mature age entry schemes, with systems within institutions providing academic and social support for the students. In the 1980s, these programmes have been broadened in scope to include courses in Social Welfare, Medicine and Law with projected support systems in the field of nursing. This is seen as a major thrust in self-determination. The Public Service has identified posts to be appropriately filled by Aboriginal people. The provision of greater access to, and participation in, education will enable the "Aboriginalization" of these services, and will provide a pool of people not only equipped by their own background to formulate policy, but having had experience within the academic world, and the world of schooling, which permits them to identify strategies for achieving a major input in those areas where decision-making takes place.

Australia lags sadly behind both Canada and Samiland in its representation in the academic world. The first Aboriginal University Professor was appointed in 1985; other academic appointments of Aboriginal people could be counted as less than a dozen. The thrust of the 1970s into higher education must be followed in the second half of the 1980s by an emphasis on entry into higher degrees, so that not only will Aboriginal academics influence the policy-making bodies of autonomous institutions such as Universities and Colleges of Education, but also, as in the case of the Sami and the Canadian Indians, there will be self-determination, an "Aboriginalization" of research being carried out on Aboriginal issues. [16]

The future—the claim to identity

In the past, the identities offered to indigenous people by the dominant society have been negative; assimilationist policies *made* the people dependent economically and culturally. Their claims today are not to *new* rights; they *re*-claim prior rights of a positive identity, rights to ethnicity distinct from (but not necessarily separate from) mainstream society, and the right to the same degree of self-determination enjoyed by members of the majority group.

Dominant groups speak of "the Sami problem", the "Indian problem", the "Aboriginal problem"—concepts reflecting the ethnocentrism of people who have *caused* problems by breaking the nexus of the indigenous people with their spirituality, their culture, their language, their land and their means of livelihood. The "problem" they conceptualize is a "white" problem.

The real problem of the indigenous people is one of constructing anew an ethnic identity. They cannot return to the past, but they must establish whether there are aspects of the life style from the past which can still be credibly integrated into their contemporary "theorizing" about identity in order to give coherence to the group.

For many indigenous people, the fact that they have been marginalized has preserved a *feeling* of ethnic identity even when all the practices of the colonizing societies worked towards assimilation, and where the language and the customs of the native people have been destroyed.

Current theorizing of the dominant groups had projected a conceptualization of *a positive identity* and of *self-determination* as a strategy in structuring their societies. The three indigenous groups under consideration have interacted with enthusiasm, to create a new reality. What are the problems they find in doing this? What are the solutions which they are developing to make self-determination a reality? What place does education/schooling play in the construction of identity? What, if any, are the common threads across the groups?

Problems

Dependence—financial/legal

The Canadian Natives question the power of the Government to impose restrictive legislation on them. They complain:

"... Canada has used its powers in the British North America Act of 1867 to make laws governing all manner of things internal to Indian Communities: *who their people are*, what titles they hold to their lands, how their governments are formed, what powers they have ... *and what kind of schooling their children will receive.*" [17] (Longboat, 1984:7; emphasis added)

The assertion of identity and the allied issue of the control of education is thus contexted into legal considerations concerning the recognition of rights of indigenous groups. Legal bases for self-determination must be decided before fiscal control, essential for self-determination, can be a reality. Indeed, financial support is necessary for the initial fight for justice—since the fight will always be on the terms of the dominant group.

The Sami people identify the problem:

"The arsenal and the material which the States as parties in a trial possess against individuals or helpless folk groups is tremendous, still the judgement will be reached according to the laws prevailing in the greater societies." (Ruong, 1983:132)

Thomas Cramer, the Lapp Ombudsman in Sweden, analysed the problem from the Sami point of view in the Sixth Lapp Conference held in Finland in 1968: "At trials, the Crown stands as both plaintiff (exploiter) and defendant (for the Lapps) at the same time in the same case."

In the case of Australia, endeavours have been made from time to time to recognize Aboriginal law by identifying crimes which are, basically, against Aboriginal tribal law and should therefore be tried by Aboriginal Courts. There is no recognition of aboriginal law, however, in any of the countries concerned when there is a clash between the interests of the dominant group and indigenous groups. In confrontation between the two, it is not only the *law* of the former which is invoked; opinions are formulated and judgements handed down from within a framework which is totally that of the "white" society.

Where Canadian Natives gained full control over education in 1975 under the conditions of the James Bay Agreement, this would seem to have occurred partly because of the financial aid given them to assemble their case. [18] Under the agreement reached, "The Cree School Board has special powers, unequalled in other school boards across the land and certainly beyond comparison with powers related to the administration of other Indian boards in Canada" (House of Commons, 1983:30).

Self-determination, even when it *appears* real, rests on a fragile base when communities remain dependent on funding from the dominant group, whether for preparing documentation for legal battles, appointing consultants for curriculum development, or hiring teachers.

Size of the group

The nexus between self-determination and identity is based in a critical way on the size of the group. Schooling, whether carried out on reserves or in cities, must lead to some employment opportunity for students if they are to continue to be motivated at upper levels. If there is no connection between schooling and employment (either within the group or within the wider society), then one may expect high drop-out rates. In each situation examined, there are continuing attempts within the local communities to identify job opportunities and structure education accordingly. Nevertheless, the size of a particular group will be of paramount importance. If it is not sufficiently large to accommodate the youth, then they are forced either into depending on Social Welfare benefits, or they are under pressure to leave the group, thus further reducing its viability. The connection between the size and viability of the group also has implications for language. If the Aborigines, or the Sami, or the Canadian Natives and Inuit must "immigrate" to the urban situation for employment, not only is the economic viability of the community affected, but also the cultural viability, as the preferred language for employment will have to become that of the dominant group. Thus economic and cultural viability, and self-determination are interwoven threads of a total fabric.

Indeed, the question must be asked whether autonomy can *ever* be real, when the finances of the group are controlled from outside. If the group is not economically viable, then the more realistic conceptualization of their political status might be one of self-management, rather than self-determination.

Membership of a pluralistic society

The contemporary granting of positive status to indigenous people is not an issue existing in isolation; it must be seen as situated within a general theorizing about pluralism in society, a theorizing about multicultural societies.

In Canada, the reconceptualization of society to recognize the claims of the French brought immediate reactions from immigrant groups for recognition as part of the multicultural society. In Samiland, the influx of post-war immigration caused a reconceptualization of Scandinavian society in pluralistic terms. There was some effort on the part of the immigrants to establish contact with the Sami in order to establish their common interests and strategies. In Australia, policies of integration, replacing "assimilation", were enunciated.

In each country, the conceptualization of a multicultural pluralistic society has excluded indigenous people. The latter have also acted to exclude themselves on the grounds of their unique status—they are *not* immigrants, they are the original, indigenous people. The reality of history is that their "uniqueness" has not been recognized. All their actions took place "within the framework of the dominant majority groups' statuses and institutions where identity as a minority group gave no basis for action" (Eidheim, 1971:Preface).

If self-determination in education is to have any meaning, it is of the utmost importance that indigenous people can construct from their own organizations their own institutions, from within which they can create a status that permits positive interaction with the *majority* group and at the same time calls forth a positive assessment from the *minority* group as a whole—that is, ethnic identity must be seen in positive terms by the dominant group and the minority group alike.

If the people themselves cannot perceive their institutions, and in particular their educational institutions, as offering positive opportunities and reinforcing identity, then, where command of language and physical characteristics permit people to "pass" into the dominant society, voluntary "migration" into the dominant group will be the most compelling option open to people. That is, "pluralism" in a society offers real choices only when parallel groups receive parallel esteem (cf. Eidheim, 1971:50ff.). Ethnic groups then must build societies in which they have equality of esteem with the dominant group. At the same time, due to the diversity of history and development already mentioned, further inter-related problems of pluralism face minority ethnic groups. The first is that they themselves must provide for pluralism within their own theorizing to allow for (1) different formulations of identity in different circumstances (for example, in the case of tribal and urban Aborigines), (2) different modes of interaction within and between different sections of the ethnic group (for example, within and between groups of coastal Sami and reindeer Sami), and (3) different strategies being exercised between sections of an ethnic group and the dominant society. Theorizing about identity must allow for differences in occupation, religion and, indeed, even political loyalties.

The paradox exists that it is not expected that the dominant group should have an agreed view on any and every subject (witness the violent disagreements about entry to the Common Market, nuclear power, etc.) yet the dominant group, and sometimes leaders within ethnic groups, grow impatient when ethnic groups do not share a single, coherent view on a particular topic. Nevertheless, despite the unreasonableness of expecting people to have one view, ethnic groups must be able to promulgate theorizing that is sufficiently coherent to enable the governments of dominant groups to respond to the voice of the minority group, yet broad enough to allow for different modes of interpretation in local situations.

It is not only to outsiders that this coherent view must be projected. If the next generation is to be socialized into the customs and language of the authority group as its preferred group, then a "world-of-meaning" must be projected which is plausible not only to contemporary adult members of the group but also to the neophytes, the youth. Certain cultural attributes from the past, which can still have currency today, must be selected and emphasized as distinctive of the group. The appreciation and dissemination of the art, literature, music and dancing of ethnic groups revive cultural values. Per Fokstad put to the Pan Lappish Conference of 1953 the notion that through art and through literature cultural values are created. Ruong (1983:57) commented wryly:

> "Fokstad's lecture was not comprehended on its delivery at the conference. Only after later perusing does the reader realize that he was trying to describe the heart of the complex of themes discussed at the conference."

Undoubtedly, Fokstad had alerted the people to new areas as subjects of mythology/theorizing which would give a sense of pride and cohesion. In subsequent years, the songs and poems of the Sami were brought back into the general orbit of "culture", and there was a reinstatement of the Yoik, a traditional, primitive form of folk music.[19] For this reason these were banned by Church authorities; they were also banned by Norwegian authorities because of their association with merry-making.

The problem, however, is to find a way of theorizing which, while it is firmly contexted into the past history of the group, does not mythologize in a way that prevents contemporary development.

Theorizing that has proved most fruitful in the past has often come from individuals—the "dream" of a Sami research Institute, for example, came from one individual. It was supported over time (in this case, 50 years) by other individuals, until it became a group "dream", and eventually a group reality. Once established, however, this particular institution has taken on a life of its own and has become a symbol of coherence and power. This symbol in itself then generates further theorizing. Similarly, the holding of Pan-Sami conferences, the assembling of the diverse groups of Canada's first Nations, of the members of the National Aboriginal Education Committee, representing Aboriginal people differing greatly in their world views—these organizations are symbolic in that they provide a rationale for proclaiming, "We are one people with a common history: we have a strong feeling of solidarity". This feeling has been confirmed by joining with other groups in the World Council of Indigenous People; within this organization there is a further sense of the common histories of oppressed peoples.

Often those attending the conferences of such organizations do have a strong feeling of solidarity. Their problem is to communicate this to the rest of the group. It is in this area that the claim to the right to ethnic mass media assumes importance. Radio, newspapers and television programmes, like organizations, create and nurture a feeling of solidarity, and a belief in the recognition by others of a positive status in society. The Sami recognize the symbolic importance of the official public use of a hitherto despised language.

However, for ethnic groups the pre-eminent site of communication of values remains educational institutions. Sociologists have held that one of the functions of the school is to reproduce society and transmit its cultural values at the same time that it concerns itself with knowledge. It is therefore inescapable that each of the indigenous groups discussed has seen schools as the major site where the battle for ethnic identity is lost or won, where their theorizing will be implemented and cohesive values formed.

Notes to Chapter 8

This chapter is a revised version of an article previously published in J. Rick Ponting (ed.) (1987) *Arduous Journey*, Toronto: McClelland & Stewart.

1. As part of the movement to reclaim their ethnic identity, indigenous people throughout the world are claiming the right to *name* themselves. The preferred form in Canada is Native (Indian), Inuit (Eskimo); in Scandinavia, Sami (Lapps); in Australia, Aborigines. The preferred forms of naming will be used throughout except in quotations. The Sami of Norway make up the largest group in Scandinavia; for this reason that particular section of the Sami will be referred to in the discussion.

2. Initially the missionaries to the Sami used the Sami language and some of the teachers were recruited among the Sami (Hoem, 1982:10). Similarly, in Canada, the early missionaries (1600–1750) presented "programs concentrated, naturally, on religious matters. Basic formal instruction was also given in Indian languages ... From 1750 to 1850 the use of the native languages by missionary educators remained a prominent feature; in 1833 ... Father Belcourt at St. Eustache was credited with having developed a Chippewa language grammar for use in his work; in 1836 the Reverend James Evans, having developed a Cree syllabic orthography, produced the first Cree grammars and primers" (Indian Affairs, 1982:Annex C). School and Biblical tracts were printed in South Australia in the Ngarrindjeri language in 1862 by the missionary George Taplin (Jenkin, 1979:108).

3. Kleinfeld (1973:Preface) noted the destructive forces located within the structures of the Alaskan education system, at that time based on residential schools.

> "In all of these programs, the majority of village children were developing serious social and emotional problems as a result of their high school experiences. Our follow-up study of graduates from these school programs suggested that in many cases, the school experience had left these students with a set of self-defeating ways for dealing with the world.
>
> The problems of rural secondary education cannot be blamed on particular individuals or on particular inadequacies such as irrelevant curriculum or insufficient staff. The problems of rural secondary education are caused by the structure of the educational system as a whole ... the damage is primarily done through a total system which separates children from their families at a critical development period and places them in unhealthy environments for growing up."

4. University graduates for the *whole* of Australia are set out below:

Aboriginal graduates from Universities throughout Australia

1970	1971	1972	1973	1974	1975	1976	1977	1978	1979	1980	1981	1982
1	—	2	4	1	4	5	9	6	5	7	7	16*

* includes 8 Dip. Teaching graduates from James Cook University (Source: National Aboriginal Education Committee, 1984:27).

5. The Norwegian government recognizes that some people in the north are "Sami speaking"; that some "Sami speaking" people can be categorized by economic (not ethnic) criteria as *disadvantaged* etc.

6. Historical documentation from the Middle Ages shows that the Sami people moved freely across the northern parts of Scandinavia and Russia. In 1751 borders were drawn between Norway and Finland/Sweden, and in 1826 between Norway and Russia. In each case the Sami people were ensured freedom of movement across the boundaries which to them are still quite artificial. The boundaries were closed in 1851.

7. "They (the Sami) were bothered by the spite and ridicule ... to which they were exposed ... in interaction with self-confident and arrogant Norwegians. They even had the suspicion that their low standard of living and the lack of industrial enterprises in the fjord might derive from their being inferior race. 'The Lapps must be stupid', they said. Certainly they believed the average Norwegian to be of that opinion. In all details their miserable self-image was a reflection of the Lappish stigma as local Norwegians define it" (Eidheim, 1971:55).

8. In its brochure (1985) the Institute sets out the following goals:

"The Nordic Sami Institute is a research, education and service institute for the Sami people in Finland, Sweden and Norway. The philosophical basis for the Institute is that we, the Sami people, should have the possibility to do research work and develop our own expertise on legal questions, linguistics, education, history, social science and other subjects ... The goals of the Institute are to serve the entire Sami population in the Nordic countries in order to improve the social, cultural, legal and economic conditions."

9. Aboriginal Lands Trust Act, 1965.

10. Prohibition of Discrimination Act, 1966.

11. It should be noted that King made the assumption that the *urban* Aboriginal people possessed a "separate and identifiable Aboriginal

heritage and culture" that they could maintain. This assumption must be questioned. Rather it is an identity that must be *reconstructed*.

12. The Fifth Lapp Conference, 1965, noted that, while Lappish had a rich vocabulary relating to nature and the Lapps' traditional way of life, it was essential to mould Lappish into a means of communication with words and concepts for the ideas which today's Lapps need to articulate.

13. It should be noted, however, that there is a problem endemic to all indigenous people. Creative teachers are drawn away from the classroom to fill other roles in the developing organizations of the indigenous groups.

14. Research on the Sami, rather *for* them, or *by* them, has long been carried out in Universities in Scandinavia and elsewhere. The early Sami movement was supported by some of these intellectuals; today supporters from outside the Sami population are still welcomed.

15. It is supported by the Nordic Council of Ministers (Denmark, Iceland, Norway, Sweden, Finland).

16. The Australian Institute for Aboriginal Studies funds and publishes research on Aboriginal issues. In general, however, the researchers are from the white world.

17. The Australian Aborigines Act legislated in the same way for Aborigines.

18. The Minister of Indian and Northern Affairs revealed in early 1972 that the Quebec Indians were using federal funds to help finance their court action against the Quebec Government and that additional funds would be provided for research (Indian and Eskimo Affairs Program, *Indian News* Vol. 17, no. 7).

    In June, 1972, the Department of Indian Affairs and Northern Development provided $250,000 to meet costs of consultants preparing documentation connected with Indian claims. In 1974 a loan of up to $3.9 million was provided for the Grand Council of the Crees and Northern Quebec Inuit Associations for Legislation.

19. Yoiks have as their themes the affairs of daily life—hunting, the weather and divinations. Personal Yoiks given at birth and adolescence had the social function of bonding an individual to the group. Nils Jernsletter (quoted in Ruong, 1983:120) believed "The Yoik confirms human identity; identity in a Lappish society does not consist first and

foremost in emphasizing one's own individuality, but in the affairs of the clan and to the community".

Bibliography

BERGER, THOMAS, 1977. Northern Frontier, Northern Homeland: The Report of the MacKenzie Valley Pipe-line Inquiry. 2 vols. Ottawa: Department of Supply and Services.

CHRIS-JOHN, ROLAND, ed., 1984. Mokakit. Ourselves Our Knowledge. Establishing Pathways to Excellence in Indian Education. First Annual Conference Proceedings. Mimeo.

Committee on Tolerance and Understanding, 1984. *Native Education in Alberta*, Calgary: Mimeo.

EIDHEIM, HARALD, 1971. Aspects of the Lappish Minority Situation. Oslo: Universitetsforlaget.

ERIKSEN, KNUT, EINAS and EINAR NIEMI, 1981. *The Finnish Menace. Boundary Problems and minority policy in the North* (1870–1940). Oslo: Universitetsforlaget.

FITZGERALD, R. T. 1976. *Poverty and Education in Australia. Fifth Main Report*. Commission of Enquiry into Poverty. A.G.P.S., Canberra.

Federation of Saskatchewan Indians, 1980. The First Nations: Indian Government and the Canadian confederation. Saskatoon: Federation of Saskatchewan Indians.

FRIDERES, J. S. 1978. Education for Indians vs. Indian Education in Canada in *The Indian Historian*. Vol. II, No. 1.

GALE, F. assisted by ALISON BROOKMAN, 1972. *Urban Aborigines*, Canberra: A.N.U. Press.

HASLUCK, P. 1953, A report on the Native Welfare Conference held in Canberra. Sept 1951, *in Native Welfare in Australia, Speeches and Addresses by the Hon. Paul Hasluck, MP*. Perth.

HAWTHORN, H. B., and M. A. TREMBLAY, 1967. A Survey of the Contemporary Indians of Canada: Economic, Political, Educational needs and Policies. 2 Vols. Ottawa: Queen's Printer.

HOEM, ANTON, 1981. The Simple and Complex Society in Educational perspective. University of Oslo: Institute for Educational research. Mimeo.

HOEM, A., 1983. Some reflections on Sami children and education. Oslo: Mimeo.

House of Commons, Canada, 1983. Indian self-government in Canada Report of the special committee. Ottawa: Queen's Printer.

Indian and Inuit Affairs Program Education and Social Development Branch 1982. *Indian Education Paper*. Phase I. Ottawa: Govern Queen's Printer.

Indian and Northern Affairs. Indian News. *The James Bay Agreement*, Vol. 17, No. 7 Special Issue, Ottawa: Eskimo and Indian Affairs Program.

Indian Brotherhood. 1972, Indian Control of Indian Education. Annex A, Indian Education Paper Phase 1 (1982). Indian Affairs Program, Minister of Indian Affairs and Northern Development, Ottawa.

JENKIN, GRAHAM, 1979. Conquest of the Ngarrindjeri. The story of the Lower Murray Lakes Tribes. Adelaide: Rigby.

JORDAN, DEIRDRE F., 1984. *Support systems for Aboriginal students in higher education Institutions, Report to C.T.E.C. and N.A.E.C.* Canberra: C.T.E.C.

KESKITALO, JAN HENRY, 1985. Education and the Native Sami Kautokeino: Sami Council for Education. Mimeo.

KLEINFELD, JUDITH, 1973. A LONG WAY FROM HOME. Effects of public high schools on village children away from home. Fairbanks, Alaska: Center for Northern Educational Research and Institute for Social, Economic and Government Research.

LESLIE, JOHN and RON MAGUIRE, 1978. The Historical Development of the Indian Act. Ottawa: Treaties and historical research centre. Research branch corporate policy Indian and Northern Affairs, Canada. Ottawa: Queen's Printer.

LIPPMANN, L., 1973. *Words or blows: Racial attitudes in Australia.* Ringwood, Victoria: Pelican Books.

——1981. *Generations of Resistance.* Melbourne: Longman Cheshire.

LONGBOAT, DIANNE, 1984. First Nations Jurisdiction over Education. The Path to Survival as Nations. Ottawa: Mimeo.

National Aboriginal Education Committee, 1979. Submission to the National Inquiry into Teacher Education. Mimeo.

1984. *Aborigines and Tertiary Education—A framework for the 1985–87 triennium.*

Ontario, Ministry of Citizenship and Culture, 1983. A Profile of native people in Ontario. Toronto: Queen's Printer.

PAINE, ROBERT, 1982. Dam a River, Damn a People? Saami (Lapp) Livelihood and the Alta/KautoKeino Hydro-electric Project and the Norwegian Parliament. Copenhagen: I.W.G.I.A. Document 45.

POONWASSIE, DEO and D. N. SPRAGUE, 1981. *Funding Research on Native Affairs* Winnipeg, Mimeo.

Rowley, C. D., 1971. *Outcasts in white Australia, Aboriginal Policy and Practice*, Vol. II. Aborigines in *Australian Society*. No. 6, Canberra: ANU Press.

Ruong, I., 1983. The Lapps. *An Indigenous people in Fenno Scandia* in *Ethnodevelopment in the Nordic Sami Region*, working papers at the Unesco meeting on ethnocide and ethnodevelopment in Europe. Karasjok: Mimeo.

Sami Institutuhtta, 1985. Nordic Sami Institute. Kautokeino: Mimeo.

Samiraddi, 1981. Sami Political Program, Ohcejohka: Koillis–Lapin, Kirjapaino, Kemijarvi.

The Nordic Sami Council, 1984. *Information*. Ohcejohka: Mimeo.

The Royal Commission on the Northern Environment, 1978. *Issues Report*. Toronto: Queen's Printer.

Tindale, N. B., 1941. Survey of the half-caste problem in South Australia. *Proc. R.G.S.S.A.*, 42, 66–161.

9 The Pajaro Valley experience

Working with Spanish-speaking parents to develop children's reading and writing skills through the use of children's literature

ALMA FLOR ADA

(To the memory of Elsa Freire)

A young mother, somewhat intimidated in front of a group of nearly a hundred people, is about to read a story written by her daughter. She hesitates, unsure whether the story is appropriate, and apologizes because it contains words which she considers unseemly.

At last, she holds up the title page. It shows a man in field workers' clothing, wearing boots and a hat and holding a long whip in his hand. A small girl is standing next to him, reaching barely to his knee. The mother begins to read: "I am going to tell you a story about a father who returned home from work very angry", and here the mother interrupts the story to explain: "All of this is true. My husband is much older than me, and he comes home from work very tired. And if the children are talking loudly or making noise he gets upset and," she adds with obvious pain, "he sometimes scolds and even punishes them."

She continues reading the story and it is here that the miracle occurs. The story tells us that when the father returned home upset, his daughter asked him what was the matter. Upon finding out that he was tired, she continues: "The old man received a big surprise. His little daughter told him: 'Look, Father I have a cure for your tiredness ... I will tell you a very pretty story that Mother read me from a book ... and the story was so amusing that the father forgot how tired he was and he laughed and hugged his little daughter and gave her a kiss." [1]

Araceli, the five-year-old girl who dictated this story to her older sister Pati, had discovered not only that books can be entertaining but that they offer the possibility of our influencing our immediate reality. Celi faces a problem: her elderly father, exhausted from work, gets angry and upset when he returns home. But Celi learns that she can do something about this problem. By her actions she not only puts her father in a good mood, but has the satisfaction of knowing that reality can be shaped, influenced and improved upon. So strong is the impact of this experience that she turns it into a story and has her sister write it down for her, thus creating a compelling example of what children's interaction with books can produce.

Araceli's mother, who read her daughter the original story which Celi in turn later told her father, is a participant in a discussion-oriented project on children's literature designed around parents.

This programme was developed under the auspices of the Bilingual Programme of the Pajaro Valley School District. This District serves a mostly rural population of 14,497 students in the area surrounding Watsonville, California. Of those students, 7,827 (54%) are Hispanic, mostly of Mexican peasant origins; 3,900 (26.9%) are migrant children; and 5,000 (34.5%) do not speak English fully yet. The percentage of students who do not complete their high school education is 34.5% for the general population and 53.6% for the Hispanic population.

Once a month, since February of 1986, a group of Spanish-speaking parents, varying in number between 60 and 100, meet to discuss children's literature and to read the stories and poems written by the children and, more and more frequently, by the parents themselves.

This activity is in itself unusual, but what makes it even more significant is that these parents themselves have had very little schooling. Many of them had never read a book before, much less thought about writing one. This programme has allowed these parents to encourage their children to write, and to begin to do so themselves.

The programme grew out of an awareness of the importance of parents' involvement in their children's education, the desire to encourage parents' consciousness of the importance of their role and their opportunities and responsibilities with regard to their children's future, and the decision to help parents recover their sense of dignity and self-identity. These, then, were our general motivations and goals when we began the programme. The actual procedures were developed and improved upon as we went along, through the process of our experience and our reflection upon it, in the true meaning of praxis.

The inspiration for the project

The initial spark was provided by the children themselves. Desiring to provide the students with new experiences and to offer them role models of Hispanics who have distinguished themselves in creative endeavours, Paula Cole, specialist in school libraries, arranged for the Pajaro Valley School District to invite me to tell stories and to talk with the children as part of a "Meet the Author" programme which until then had featured only English-speaking authors.

The presentation of the stories was accompanied by dialogue with the children about how a book is made, what a literary work is, what the motivations are that lead an author to write, and my own feelings about my mother tongue and my decision to speak and write in Spanish.

The children's enthusiasm was enormous. Their teachers and school librarians had laid the groundwork: the children had read some of my stories and some of the books I had translated into Spanish, but most importantly, they themselves had written as well. The conversations with the children were delightful. It was made very clear that everybody can write, that what is essential is to observe one's surroundings, to observe one's self, and to let one's imagination run wild. When a third-grade boy asked, "Well, what advice would you give to future writers?" we knew that a spark had been lit which we wanted to keep alive.

The director of the bilingual programme, Alfonso Anaya, decided that the interest which had been stimulated in the children could serve as a base from which to begin working with parents in a project aimed at developing a greater interaction between parents and children. This would strengthen the co-operation between home and school, and in turn contribute to strengthening the reading and writing skills which are essential for all schooling.

Key planning issues

While planning the project, we decided that it was important to take several aspects into account in order to ensure its success.

1. The environment: it was decided to choose a location in which the parents would feel comfortable and at ease. We decided to meet in a library rather than in a schoolroom because, unfortunately, schools often have negative associations of fear and of possible failure, whether because parents often visit a school only when their

children are in trouble or because of their own lack of academic success.

The library offers other advantages: it is a pleasant, roomy, well-lit environment, with chairs designed for adults. It is a "special" place for parents, and it surrounds them with books, thus subliminally reinforcing the message we want to convey.

2. The subject: the subject we chose with which to draw the parents was children's literature. We feared that if we proposed an academic subject, parents would feel unsure or intimidated, whereas the subject of children's books would seem less threatening.

3. The character of the meeting: we insisted upon making the meeting with the parents a special event. Children were sent home from school with invitations in Spanish for their parents to a meeting about children's literature with a writer of children's books. This invitation to an event of interest conveyed respect for the parents. We were careful not to ask something of them, or to tell them what they must do, but rather to invite them to participate.

This participatory tone has been maintained throughout the whole programme, and we consider it to be one of the elements which has contributed to its success.

4. Attention to the children: during every meeting children of all ages are offered a parallel programme, with films, storytelling and other activities in a nearby room, so that parents are not prevented from attending through having to care for their children.

5. Personal contact: before the first meeting, telephone calls were made to the parents to reiterate personally the invitation which they had received in writing. Besides, several teacher's aides offered to give rides to parents who lacked means of transport.

The procedure for the meetings

This is the way in which meetings have been carried out. At the first meeting, we began by talking with the whole group of parents—numbering nearly a hundred—about the purpose of the programme. The basic points covered were:

1. The recognition that children, each and every one of them,

represent the future of the world, and of the need for helping them shape that future and make it theirs.

2. The importance of the relationships between family members.

3. The fact that parents are their children's first and best teachers.

4. The impact that the development of skills in the home has on academic progress, specifically the acquisition of language skills and reasoning.

5. The need to develop these skills in the home language, since this is the language in which the parents can best do so.

6. The recognition that there is nothing negative or pejorative about the use of Spanish. Not only because Spanish is, in and of itself, a language of great international importance, but also because the use of the mother tongue and the transmission of that language to one's children is an inalienable right, no matter what one's language is.

7. The understanding of the pain and psychological harm which is produced when an individual feels obliged to reject his or her language and, along with it, a part of his or her identity.

8. The fact that in the case of minority children a well-developed home language is the best basis for the acquisition of a second language.

9. The value of self-esteem and parents' responsibility in helping their children develop a positive self-image.

10. The importance of communication based on respect, understanding and trust.

Each of these issues was followed by concrete suggestions for their implementation. Parents were given a booklet, specifically designed for this programme, which covered the use of Spanish in the home; the importance of demonstrating affection; and suggestions for the development of language skills, clarity of expression, critical thinking skills, and reading, writing and memory skills.

The results of this initial discussion were overwhelming. It was obvious that the parents were deeply moved. One mother stood up and explained: "What is happening to us is that no one has ever told us that our children are worth something, and no one has ever told us that we are worth something."

This stage of group reflection set the tone for all of the following work. The dialogue on these general themes was followed by a presentation of five picture books. The books had been selected primarily for their appeal, in terms both of literary content and presentation. We wanted to motivate the children to interact with the books, as well as to show parents and children that, just as there are in English, there are beautiful and well-produced Spanish-language books of which they can be proud.

Initially we had thought to present one book at each meeting. Because it was impossible to obtain a hundred copies of the same book on such short notice, we were obliged to present five different titles from which each parent could choose one to take home.

As it turned out, this was an advantage. Not only did it allow parents to appreciate better the diversity of good books which exist in Spanish, but it also contributed to a more active involvement of the participants.[2]

I read each of the books aloud to the whole group of parents as they would be read to children, dramatizing the action and showing the illustrations. The readings were followed by a few comments and a brief period of dialogue. Then each parent was invited to select the book she or he wanted to take home and to join a small group for discussion of that particular book. In each of those groups a teacher facilitated the dialogue.

The teachers, Marina Cook, Yolanda Gutiérrez-Miller, Janet Johns, Terri Marchese, Yida Noguera, Lupe Soltero-Torres and Graciela Rubalcava, are in fact largely responsible for the continued success of this project. In order to make the parents feel comfortable and at ease, they have made it a point to invite each one to participate in the discussion; moreover, they make sure that the group understands what each parent has to say, whether by repeating, paraphrasing or asking further questions if necessary. They know how to accept and validate everyone's participation, upholding the value of different points of view; yet they guide the discussion to more reflective levels of analysis when the parents, as a result of internalized oppression, feel unable to help their children as much as they would like to.

Creative reading

In facilitating the small-group discussions in each of the groups the teachers followed the creative reading methodology.[3] Here the dialogue consists of four phases: the descriptive phase, in which information is identified; the interpretative/personal phase, in which personal reactions to and feelings about the reading are discussed and the information in the story is related to previous personal experience; the critical phase, in which a critical analysis is made of the events and ideas presented in the story, and the creative phase, in which the reading is brought to bear on the discovery of real-life applications.

Besides a copy of the book he or she had chosen, each parent was handed a list of questions organized according to those four phases, as a guide for home discussions with their children. Also provided were a list of suggested activities related to the book and a blank book in which their children might be encouraged to write their own stories.

It was emphasized that the lists of questions and of suggested activities were not to be followed to the letter but, instead, looked upon as a source of inspiration. The parents were encouraged to proceed freely: they might give their children the book and ask them to read it aloud; they might read the story to the children; or they might tell the children the story as they remembered it, using the pictures as an aid. What was essential was that they spend some time every evening with their children and with a book; that at all times they encourage the children to reason and to express themselves clearly; that they listen to the children with interest and with affection; and that they encourage the children to write their own stories in the blank books.

From the second session on, the parents have been meeting first in the small groups according to which book they selected the previous month. There they talk about their experiences over the last month. Then, all together, they read and listen to some of the stories the children have written. Finally, the new books are presented and new small groups are formed to discuss them.

An example of the group discussions

To give an example of the nature and process of the group discussion, we will refer to the book *Arturo and Clementina* by Adela Turin and Nella Bosnia, which was presented at our ninth meeting. We had hesitated to use this or any of the books in the series "In favour of girls" not because we doubted the importance of non-sexist themes, but because we feared that it might create a difficult situation. We did not want to antagonize the parents, especially since we were very pleased by the unusually high level of male participation at the meetings and did not want to discourage it. Nonetheless, the level of awareness demonstrated at previous sessions prompted us to risk broaching the subject.

We chose *Arturo and Clementina* because the theme of the story can be used to generate a broad discussion of insensitivity, dependence and lack of communication as manifested in various circumstances, and not circumscribed to the dynamic between the sexes.

In this extraordinarily illustrated book, two turtles, Arturo and Clementina, meet on a beautiful spring day and promptly fall in love. Clementina talks to Arturo about her dreams of travelling around the world, and Arturo listens, assenting vaguely. But what happens is that Arturo assumes the responsibility of catching enough fish for the two of them, and Clementina is reduced to waiting by the pond for his return. When she begins to feel bored, she decides that she would like to paint or learn to play the flute, but her proposals are emphatically rejected by Arturo, who doesn't believe Clementina has the necessary talent to paint or play. However, he does bring her first a record player, then a painting done by an artist friend of his. Many more gifts subsequently follow and Arturo ties them all on to Clementina's shell.

As the pile of objects grows, it becomes necessary to add more and more floors on to the house. Clementina spends all of her time cleaning and polishing her possessions, and since her home is so heavy, she can no longer move it anywhere.

Then, one day, on another spring morning, Clementina decides to quietly leave her house and go out for a short walk.

Of course she returns right away, before Arturo is due home from work. She keeps taking more walks, however, and since Arturo cannot understand the reason for Clementina's new-found smiles, he does not hesitate to pronounce her a fool—until the day on which he returns to find an empty house.

Arturo still does not understand Clementina's ingratitude. "She had everything. A twenty-five storey house, and every floor filled with treasures!" As for Clementina? She is probably still travelling, painting and playing her flute, in some remote corner of the world.

The questions we used to guide the discussion are as follows:

Descriptive Phase
1. What kind of future life did Clementina dream about when she fell in love with Arturo?

2. What was Arturo's response when Clementina talked about what she wanted to do with their life together?

3. Why was Clementina bored?

4. How did Arturo respond to Clementina when she told him that she was bored?

5. What things did Clementina think she would like to do? How did Arturo respond to Clementina's desires?

6. How did Arturo try to please her?

7. What decision did Clementina make in order to overcome her boredom?

Personal Interpretative Phase
1. Have you ever felt not listened to after telling someone something that was important to you? How did you feel?

2. Have you ever asked someone for something and had them give you something different from what you wanted? How did you feel?

3. How did you feel when someone called you names? Have you ever been called "stupid", "dumb", "foolish"? How did that make you feel?

4. What things do you like to do in order not to be bored?

5. Do you have some wish or dream which you think that others might not understand?

Critical Phase
1. When Clementina told Arturo that she was bored, how could he have responded differently?

2. Do you think that Clementina would have enjoyed sharing the fishing and the food gathering?

3. How do you think Clementina felt when she had to carry so many things on her shell that she could no longer move? Do you think that Arturo would have wanted to own so many things if he had had to carry them?

4. Could Arturo and Clementina have divided the work and the responsibilities better?

5. What is the difference between playing the flute and owning a record player? Is it the same thing to own a picture as it is to know how to paint?

6. Why was Clementina not happy with what she had? What did she really want?

7. What could Clementina have done to change the situation?

8. What different attitudes on the part of Arturo and Clementina would have led to a different outcome?

Creative Phase

1. If you were Clementina, what would you have done to help improve the situation?

2. Are there people in your life that don't listen to you? How can you get them to listen to you better?

3. Could it be that you are not listening well enough to the people around you? What can you do to improve?

4. Do you think that it is possible for two people to live together without having one person's wishes ignored all the time?

The discussion with the parents was full of surprises. Instead of feeling intimidated by the subject, it was an excellent catalyst. Many people reported that it was a common experience for them to feel unappreciated by the people around them. And they were able to share the feelings of frustration and fear which resulted when others did not believe in their potential.

One mother commented that she often feels like Clementina. Although her husband is a very good man, he did not believe in her ability to study and to learn English. "Nonetheless," she said, "I am not remaining silent like Clementina did, but instead I make him see that I *can* do things."

One of the men present quickly make a parallel with his own attitude as a husband, recognizing that he habitually leaves all of the responsibility for the children to his wife. "Maybe what was happening to Clementina was that she was carrying too much weight ..." he said, "this makes me think that maybe my wife needs more of my help, and most of all that I listen to what her problems are ..."

The parents' experience

What parents shared with us about their home experience has been very varied. After the first meeting, one father bought a blackboard and placed it in the garage so that every day he could write a question for his children to answer, in writing, when they came home from school; later they discussed both questions and answers together. Other parents encouraged their children to write answers to the questions we handed out. In general, these have been the principal reactions: parents have begun to read aloud to their children, the children have begun to bring home books from the school library, and parents and children have gone to the public library in search of books. At the first meeting we had a show of hands to find out how many parents had public library cards. None did. At a meeting nine months later almost everyone reported several visits to the library to check out books.

All the sessions have been videotaped. This idea, initially conceived as part of an evaluation process, has turned out to be a highly significant part of the whole project. The teachers' aides borrowed the tapes, on their own initiative, and took them into the community. Thus the children had the opportunity of seeing their parents as characters on the television screen, reading aloud the stories created by the children. This has had several effects. The parents have re-experienced the process and have been able to analyse the dialogue further. The concepts presented have been reinforced, along with the model of how a story can be read or told. The children have felt double pride, both in seeing their parents on the screen and in hearing their own stories being read aloud. This might explain why not only elementary school children but high-schoolers as well have shown great interest in writing stories every month.

The video camera also captures the bearing and level of confidence that parents display as they participate in the group discussions. Clearly, their self-confidence, self-assuredness and self-expression have been strengthened during the course of the project.

These are other signs of the parents' development: they have gradually replaced the teachers as facilitators in the small-group discussions. A number of them petitioned the District School Board for a meeting to talk about the academic future of their children. Another group offered, on their own, to give presentations on the use of children's literature at the Regional Migrant Education Conference.

A very revealing incident was that, after several meetings, the parents themselves said that while they were very happy to receive the books we were giving them, one book a month seemed too little, and they were interested in purchasing additional books for themselves. This led to an invitation to Mariuccia Iaconi, of Iaconi Books in San Francisco, who took several hundred books to the next meeting. The parents—many perhaps for the very first time—bought books for their children.

Of even greater importance is the fact that when, at the end of the summer, we asked the parents what direction the programme should take in the future, they did not hesitate to suggest that, since their children had written such good stories, it would be worthwhile to compile a book of them. The book is under way.

Graciela Rubalcava has taken charge of producing the book. At the eighth meeting, she presented a trial edition to the parents, and asked them to have their children make whatever corrections or additions they wished to their own stories. In addition, since only some of the children had illustrated their stories while others had not, we suggested that whoever wanted to do so could illustrate the stories which had no pictures. This resulted in a new and different kind of creative output.

At the ninth meeting, several parents proudly brought the drawings which their children had made to illustrate the stories. One mother explained that they had first read and discussed the stories, and that then her son had made drawings for several of them. "We've discovered that our son has a talent for drawing," said a father proudly. And, after telling how several people had praised some doves his son had drawn for a poster, which had been inspired by one of the first books presented in the programme, the father added, his voice filled with pride and hope, "Maybe someday he will be an artist."

The words of the parents

Finally, the best evaluation of the programme was expressed by the parents themselves. During the eighth and ninth meetings, when asked to suggest what they had gained through the participation in the programme, the comments offered by participants allow us to see that the growth which has occurred affects the children as well as the adults.

"I feel," said one mother, "that since we began talking every night about the books which they are reading, and since they began writing themselves, our two children have become closer, and we feel closer to them also. This process is so important to my fourteen-year-old daughter," she added, "that even though there is a party tonight [the meeting was the evening before Hallowe'en], she decided to come here instead, because she knew we were going to read her story." Her husband said, "Our children have discovered that from each story, no matter how simple, one can learn something about how to help ourselves and how to help others, and now when they write their stories they concern themselves with understanding and explaining reality." (The younger son of this couple had written a story about a boy who refuses to obey his mother; the older one, about a girl who, following her friend's lead, drops out of school.)

Another mother said: "Ever since I know I have no need to feel ashamed of speaking Spanish I have become strong. Now I feel I can speak with the teachers about my children's education and I can tell them I want my children to know Spanish. I have gained courage."

One mother said: "Thanks to this programme, my son has blossomed. Before beginning this programme I was not aware that he was so special. But seeing how much you have praised what he's written, I have begun to take much more notice of him, and now he has been chosen for a programme for gifted children [GATE Program]." And then she added, with a big smile, "And I have blossomed, too, because I have brought here tonight a story which I have written." The story, an excellent version of a fairy tale which she had heard as a youngster, is an example of the talent waiting to be discovered in these parents.

One father held forth the value of the meetings as an opportunity for getting to know one another better, on a deeper level. After elaborating on how impersonal society has become, and how people tend to perceive one another with fear rather than with trust, he said: "Maybe after seeing each other at these meetings, we might be able to help one another more, offer to lend a hand if anyone needs it. It is very good to have the opportunity to meet each other here."

Another father corroborated that opinion, saying: "I feel a family feeling here." He added an observation about the potential value of the experience for the parents themselves, saying, "In these meetings we can learn to talk without being embarrassed or shy; it is very important to get rid of our inhibitions, because it is very difficult to talk in public."

A mother stated: "My children have become enthusiastic about reading. They are reading a great many books in Spanish and they are learning a lot."

Another added: "I am very happy that my six-year-old boy is very interested in reading and brings books home from school, and this week he read me a story."

One mother said: "I never had any education, I only went to school in Mexico for one year, I don't read or write very well. But I have enjoyed seeing that my children are happy. The children themselves say: 'We brought you the flyer home, it [the meeting] is going to be on such-and-such a day' ... and they mark it for me on the calendar so that I will remember to come. And when the day arrives they tell me 'Hurry up, Mom, it's getting late'. They're learning a lot and they feel happy, because they've told me so."

And a final positive note. One of the fathers said: "I have discovered that my children can write. And I bring another story. But also I have discovered something personal. I have discovered that by reading books one can find out many things. Since my children want me to read them the stories over and over again, I took them to the public library to look for more books. There I discovered books about our own culture. I borrowed them and I am reading, and now I am finding out things I never knew about our roots and about what has happened to them and I have discovered that I can read in Spanish about the history of this country and of other countries."

The girl who discovered that she can influence her reality by using, like a modern-day Scheherazade, a story to entertain her tired father and thus avoid being yelled at or punished, and the father who, through his children's enjoyment, discovered a path to reading and to the wealth of information offered by books—these are examples of why all who have participated in the Pajaro Valley experience feel privileged and want to share with others its message of hope.

Notes to Chapter 9

1. The story as dictated to Pati by Celi:
   "Les voy a contar un cuentito de un Papá que llego muy enojado del trabajo. y la hijita le pregunto. que tepasa biejito y que cres Hermanita lo que le pasaba al biejito. que benia muy cansado de trabajar. y se llebo una sorpresa muy grande el biejito. que su hijita le ba disiendo. Mira, papito llo te boy a dar un Remedio muy bueno para que se te quite lo Cansado. y el papa Sonrrio. Y le contesto asu hijita. aber cual es ese Remedio que me bas a dar para quitar lo cansado. y le contesto la hijita te boy a contar un cuentito muy bonito que me conto mi mamita. de un librito muy bonito que desia asi. y que tiene muchos animalitos Pintados. [Here is the drawing of the pony, the bear and the apple tree, copied from the book, next to them a drawing of a little girl and underneath her name, Araceli.]

   El poni le dijo al Osito no te apures Osito alcabo que el mes que entra cuando todas las hojitas se le caigan alos harbolitos y se les quedaran las puras manzanas. Y entonces comeremos muchas manzanas. para que nuestras barrigas se nos inflen como un globo.

   Y entonses el Biejito empeso a reir y dijo. es berdad mi hijita que con los cuentitos se quita lo cansado. y el biejito muy contento abraso a su hijita y le dio un Besito y le dijo. muchas gracias mi hijita. y otro dia me cuentas mas cuentitos para no sentir lo cansado. Hermanita y quien cres tu quien era ese biejito. ye le contesta su hermanita Pati no lo se. y le contesto. taruga pues ese biejito era nuestro papito. y esa hijita que le conto el cuentito era llo su hijita seli. Colorin colorado el cuentito se a terminado.

Este cuentito lo escribio Pati Cosillaas el dia 7 de mallo 1,986 a las 4 de la tarde. La hermanita se llama Seli tiene 5 años de edad."

"I'm going to tell you a little story about a Father who got home from work very upset. and the daughter asked him. what is wrong old man and what do you think sister was wrong with the old man. he was very tired from working. and the old man had a big surprise. his daughter was telling him. Look, daddy I am going to give you some very good Medicine to take away the Tired. and the father Smiled. And he answered his daughter. let's see what this Medicine is that you are going to give me to take away my tired. and his daughter answered I am going to tell you a very nice story that my mother told me. about a very nice book which went like this. and which has many Drawings of animals. [Here there is a picture of the pony, the bear and the apple tree, copied from the book, and next to it, a picture of a small girl with her name, Araceli, written below.]

The pony told Bear don't worry at the end of next month when all the leaves have fallen from the trees and they will have all apples left. And then we'll eat lots of apples. So that our tummies will be as big as balloons.

And then the Old Man began to laugh and said. It's true my daughter that the stories take away the tired. And the old man was very happy and gave his daughter a hug and gave her a kiss and said. Thank you daughter. and another day you can tell me more stories to take away the tired. Sister and who do you think that man was. and her sister Pati answered i don't know. and I told her. dummy well that old man was our father. and that daughter who told him the story was me his daughter Celi. and this is the end of the story.

This story was written by Pati Cosillas on the 7th of may 1986 at 4pm. The sister is called Seli she is 5 years old."

2. These are the books presented from February through October 1986:

Ada, Alma Flor, and María del Pilar de Olave, *Maravillas*. Lima, Perú: Ed. Brasa, 1975.
Balzola, Asún, *Munia y el cocolilo naranja*. Barcelona: Destino, 1984.
——*Munia y la señora Piltronera*. Barcelona: Destino, 1984.

Bröger, Achim, and Gisela Kalow, *Buenos días, querida ballena*. Barcelona: Juventud, 1978.

——*Historia de Dragolina*. Barcelona: Juventud, 1982.

El cocuyo y la mora. Caracas, Venezuela: Banca del Libro (Ediciones Ekaré), 1978.

Heuck, Sigrid, *El poni, el oso y el manzano*. Barcelona: Juventud, 1981.

Lionni, Leo, *Nadarín*. Barcelona: Lumen, 1982.

——*Frederick*. Barcelona: Lumen, 1982.

Lobel, Arnold, *Sopa de ratón*. Madrid: Alfaguara, 1977.

Loof, Jan, *Historia de una manzana roja*. Valladolid: Miñón, 1974.

——*Mi abuelo es pirata*. Valladolid: Miñón, 1974.

La paloma y la hormiga. Barcelona: La Galera, 1971.

Turin, Adela, and Nella Bosnia, *Arturo y Clementina*. Barcelona: Lumen, 1976.

Paola, Tomie de, *La Virgen de Guadalupe*. Madrid: Ediciones Ecuentro, 1984.

Steadman, Ralph, *El puente*. Valladolid: Miñón, 1972.

Williams, Leslie, and Carmen Solé Vendrell, *¿Qué hay detrás del árbol?* Barcelona: Hymsa, 1984.

3. For additional information on the creative reading methodology see Alma Flor Ada and María del Pilar de Olave, *Hagamos Caminos*. Reading, MA: Addison-Wesley, 1986.

10 Finnish children in Sweden strike for better education

TUULA HONKALA,
PIRKKO LEPORANTA-MORLEY,
LILJA LIUKKA
and EIJA ROUGLE

The background

The school strike in Bredby school in Rinkeby, a suburb of Stockholm, Sweden, started on 16th January 1984, and lasted eight weeks, until 8th March. Bredby school is an ordinary comprehensive school, and a large proportion of the pupils come from different immigrant minorities. Finns, Greeks and people from Turkey and Yugoslavia are the largest groups. Rinkeby itself is the suburb with the highest percentage of immigrants in all Scandinavia.

The strike grew out of the history of the school situation of the Finnish-speaking children. A brief description of this is necessary for an understanding of the strike. The studies of Finnish school children in the early 1970s by Pertti Toukomaa and Tove Skutnabb-Kangas (two studies for Unesco, published in English in 1976 and 1977) clearly showed that something had to be changed in the school situation for Finnish children. They were under-achieving, and they did poorly in language tests in both Finnish and Swedish. It was understood in the early 1970s that nothing could be achieved without the active interest of the Finnish parents. A number of lectures and discussion meetings were arranged to raise the consciousness of the parents, and to give them some of the more theoretical knowledge needed. Finnish-medium classes were started for Finnish children in many places, because the parents thought that the children had the right to understand the teaching.

Because Finns in Stockholm live rather concentrated in certain areas, they were easily reached. Even in the rest of Stockholm the lectures and meetings resulted in demands for Finnish-medium classes in several Stockholm schools. This type of mother tongue medium education was considered disastrous by the Swedish school authorities, and they resisted the classes strongly.

Initially the Stockholm classes had great difficulties. The main reason for this was that many children had almost forgotten their Finnish by the time they reached school age: they came from Swedish-medium day-care centres, and they had had no chance of developing their mother tongue there. Since most parents were hard-working, they did not have enough time during the week to be with their children, who were tired when coming home after a long day in the day-care centre.

The next step was, therefore, the fight for Finnish-medium day-care centres. Information was given to the parents about child development and language development, and about what could be done with the help of Finnish day-care. The parents also got information about how children become bilingual under different conditions.

By the spring of 1981 we had six Finnish-medium kindergartens in Rinkeby, and six Finnish-medium classes in school, with growing numbers of pupils. The results in the schools were improving, as the children who now started school spoke Finnish, and had normal concept development for their age.

"Integration" = forced assimilation

But while all this positive development took place in schools, the school authorities had other plans. In autumn 1981 the headmistress of the Bredby school, Ingrid von Uexkull, had finished her plan for "integrated education for immigrant children", proudly called the "Bredby model". According to this plan,

—the teaching of Swedish as L2 was to begin in grade 1 (instead of grade 2, as earlier)

—the first three grades would have a growing number of lessons in so-called practical subjects, given by a Swedish-speaking teacher

—from grade 4 on, the Finnish pupils would form "integrated classes" with the two Swedish-speaking parallel classes.

The school situation was most difficult for the children in the middle school (grades 4–6, ages 10–12) with the integrated education, a new class teacher and several new Swedish-speaking teachers. Not only were the classes in two integration groups divided, but they could also be divided within their own class for Swedish teaching. So the classes could in the worst case be divided into four different kinds of groups. That meant that the children had to adapt themselves to four different social groups. The children did not always know where and in what language the lessons were going to be.

The first overt justification for integration was "to avoid segregation of the Finnish children". In fact, instead of integration the children were taught by this model that they as minority children were inferior and lacking linguistically and culturally compared with their Swedish-speaking schoolmates. They were identified by the model as socially and culturally handicapped.

In the Swedish classes the Finnish children came to have a minority position within an already formed social group. The situation was bound to be discriminating: the Finnish children were seen as both socially and linguistically inferior. Swedish language was the only allowed medium and to enforce this, Finnish children were physically and psychologically isolated from each other. They were forbidden to use their mother tongue, even punished for using it. They were seated in class next to Swedish-speaking children. All this caused anxiety and insecurity. The Finnish parents thought that it was also not good for the Swedish children to have classmates whose language they did not understand.

As the children were not allowed to use their mother tongue, the medium in which they were most accurately capable of expressing themselves, they were regarded as less intelligent. This perception soon became ingrained in the children themselves. That was the worst damage caused by the model.

Within this system individual children could have up to thirteen different teachers. Schooldays were split into endless intervals of running from class to class, from group to group. Some parents were complaining that their children started to sleepwalk at nights. They took it as a symptom of the daily strain.

Secondly, the integration was aimed at teaching Swedish to our children. According to headmistress von Uexkull the best method of teaching Swedish to immigrant children was imitation, "the aping method" as she called it. "If the children hear Swedish they learn it." She did not believe our children to be capable enough to learn a language through an intellectual process. Both the content and the context of the words were considered less important. The main purpose was to make the children repeat the words with the right accent.

The integration was characterized by conflicts from the beginning. By under-estimating the child's language and cultural identity the child herself was under-estimated. Because the Finnish children had developed their linguistic abilities in Finnish, at this stage they were not yet able to understand fully the language the Swedish teachers used. This naturally caused frictions between the teachers and the children. The teachers were unable to analyse the situation correctly. They regarded the children as naughty and stupid. This wrong analysis led to interpreting "the problem" as a problem within the child and trying to solve the problem by changing the individual child.

This wrong interpretation caused even more disruptive behaviour which, in turn, gave rise to an increase in various kinds of punishments. The situation grew difficult to handle for all the parties: Finnish and Swedish teachers and Finnish- and Swedish-speaking children.

Children felt that they were treated unfairly. Since they naturally could not find the real causes for this they started to seek reasons in the teachers' and the other children's behaviour. This led to unnecessary quarrels and conflicts.

Because the Finnish class teachers met their pupils only for short intervals at a time their relationship also could not develop normally. Children had too many teachers and they could not regard any of them as their own. They had difficulties in coping with so many different kinds of authority.

At home the parents experienced in their children growing restlessness, irritation and lack of enthusiasm for school, and the parents had difficulties in following what the children did in school and in helping their children with schoolwork.

Trying to change by negotiation

Parents' meetings for different classes were organized by the "class mothers" (those responsible for contact between the parents of a class). At these meetings it was found that the situation was intolerable, and that there was nothing comparable going on in other Finnish-medium classes in Stockholm.

Simultaneously with this development, Sweden approved a new

curriculum for Swedish schools, with very liberal and radical plans. A lecture was arranged at the Finnish Club, introducing the new curriculum. Among other things, the curriculum stated that the school not only had to listen to the children and the parents, but it also had to listen to local immigrant organizations when organizing the education of immigrant children.

The Bredby class mothers, representing all the different Finnish-medium classes in the school, had a meeting at which we wrote down all the points where we disagreed with the curriculum in the Bredby model. We requested a meeting with the headmistress, and demanded that the experiment with her plan at Bredby school be stopped.

During the following two years we had a series of meetings and wrote several letters to the administration. In an open letter, "The other Sweden", the parents wrote:

"We know that our everyday life is part of the other Sweden. There is a deep gulf between the reality of the Swedish power holders, those who make the economic and political decisions, and our reality ... Other people decide for us. At the same time we share the reality with millions of Swedes. We work, live and spend our leisure together. In this we have also experienced humanly degrading 'sympathy' and open racism. We have listened to promises and speeches. And we have seen the reluctance of the civil servants to work for our rights. We feel that there is a frontal attack going on in order to narrow down the rights we have achieved. The anxiety grows. We become unemployed 'because there are unemployed Swedes too'. Among the bureaucrats working with day-care and school administration some are looking for means to stop the day-care and education through the medium of our mother tongue. The media tell us to find our supporters from elsewhere—but where? When we are not being listened to, we have to force you to listen to our voice.

For years we have tried to practise the principle of freedom of choice, (one of the three guiding principles in Swedish immigration policy, approved by the parliament, our remark) in our children's education. We have understood 'freedom of choice' so that it also includes the possibility of having mother tongue medium education throughout the comprehensive school."

The letters, meetings and demonstrations had no effect. By autumn 1983 the Bredby model had been made famous all over Sweden, and headmistress von Uexkull was considered one of the important authorities in Swedish immigrant education.

Through connections we had made during the years of struggle, we learned that plans were being made to introduce the Bredby model as The Model for all mother tongue medium classes in the whole Stockholm area.

We had had enough!

This was the final insult. We class mothers once again had a meeting, and after that our representatives met the three largest political parties of the City Council. There we learned that none of the letters we had written had ever reached the politicians, but had been stopped by the civil servants. The politicians told us that the Bredby model was to be chosen specifically because it was so much appreciated by the Finnish children and parents!

At the end of November 1983 there was yet another meeting, arranged by the Finnish Club. All the Finnish parents were personally invited by the class mothers, and the situation was explained. Anger and frustration were the feelings of the meeting. During the evening the frustration grew into a demand for a change in the situation. We had had enough! It was time to take our children away from the school, if our protests were not to be heard. A last meeting with the headmistress was suggested, and a letter, signed by 107 parents, listing our demands, was sent to the school. A committee, preparing a strike, was chosen.

We started collecting money, in case we needed to start the strike. We let the plans "leak" to the mass media. Plans were made for how to take care of the children during a strike. Holidays were not taken at Christmas, but saved for the strike. Volunteers and support groups were sought. The children were prepared for the strike, and they had to work extra hard both in school and at home.

The strike starts

The last meeting with the headmistress did not lead to any results, and so the strike began. Our demands were, first of all, to stop the so-called integration model. We wanted all the new concepts in subject matter teaching to be introduced through the medium of Finnish, during the first six years. We wanted the children to learn Finnish, and to learn to know their own culture and to take pride in their background. We wanted Swedish to be taught as a second language (not a mother tongue), and we wanted it taught by bilingual teachers. We believed that only if the children had a true chance to choose would they grow to feel equal with their

Swedish-speaking schoolmates. We needed more resources for the children with special learning problems. And we wanted, as parents, to be considered as equals when planning the education of our children.

The response to our strike was intense, with people reacting either strongly in favour or strongly against it. From the beginning we felt that our fight was considered as the common fight of all the Finns in Sweden. We received letters of encouragement as well as money (about 25,000 Swedish crowns, 2,500 US dollars). Donations came from both Finland and Sweden. For instance, all the bread for the children during eight weeks came as a gift from a Finnish bakery in Stockholm. Some political parties and other immigrant groups reacted in our favour.

The negative response to our struggle came from the Swedish majority. Our fight was perceived as frightening and immoral. We appeared to them to be ungrateful for all the care we had received. Bilingualism, at any level, appeared to be a threat to the majority. Individual expressions of these negative feelings included numerous suggestions for us to move back to Finland, or to seek psychiatric care. Some of us received threats to our and our families' lives, by letters, postcards and telephone calls.

In the media our demands were misrepresented by the headmistress and even the Swedish Minister for Immigration, to be about a bilingual Sweden, universities in Finnish, etc. In fact we had all the time to fight two battles on two different fronts, one with the school authorities and politicians, and one against the lies and false images of us in the media.

A school for working-class children

In the course of the debate it became clear to us that, in the view of the authorities, the main goal for the education of our children was to learn Swedish. Other subjects were considered less important. This was understandable because the school was striving to educate our children only to become skilled workers.

During the strike it was clearly revealed to us that for the school authorities the primary goals of education are the economic interests of the society, and not the interests of children. The actions and the speeches of the authorities openly showed that the optimal educational situation for children is less important than the need to maintain the status quo of the class and power structure through assimilating minorities. Assimilation ensures continuity of labour supply in the future, and provides the economic buffer needed for unemployment. The numerous quotations by the headmistress of "not wanting to create an A-team and a B-team" made us understand and see that two teams indeed were being educated for the future. And there were meant to be no vacancies in the A-team for our children, unless we changed the system so that the goal would be a true integration on an equal basis, instead of assimilation on the majority conditions.

Means: "to starve us to death"

From the start it was clear that the line of action the headmistress had chosen to take was backed up by the Conservative Party. This line was, as a Communist Party representative from the City Council put it, "to starve us to death". Throughout the strike the Conservative Party openly acted against our interests.

Nothing happened for weeks, and we were starting to feel that it was time to start planning for a private Finnish-medium school, as the only solution. This was a truly unpopular suggestion to solve our problems. We felt that as a part of this society we had a right to Swedish state education regardless of the medium in which the education would be given to our children.

Our prerequisites: nil

What kind of prerequisites did we have, then, for organizing a strike for 118 children for eight weeks? All of it was very new to us. Altogether we were about 30 women and half a dozen men who actively organized everything. Almost none of us had ever before taken part in any political activities, and only four had even worked in the Finnish Club. Most of us were single parents, with long working hours and not much education. Our Swedish was deficient, and we considered ourselves incapable of writing letters to and holding discussions with authorities in higher positions.

That soon changed, though. We learned that we had no choice but to start tackling every problem ourselves. We also found that help was available whenever everything felt as if it was near collapse.

The practical organization

The main challenge concerned the children. We had 118 children (96% of the Finnish children in the relevant classes) on our hands, and they needed food and care all day long. We organized the Finnish Club as a refugee centre. Every day two or three women cooked the food, and the rest of us took care of the teaching. The children had classes every day, as they would have had in school. In teaching we got help from all sorts of people: teachers came in to teach during their breaks, after school hours, etc.; student teachers and students, journalists, all kinds of people came in. Without their help we would not have managed. The mornings were spent on lessons, and in the afternoons visits and excursions of different kinds were organized.

Every Saturday we made a detailed plan for every day of the following week for all six classes. Where would the children have their classes and stay, who would teach which class what, who would cook, what would they eat, etc.? We had to organize people to answer the telephone every evening. At least two big meetings for all the parents had to be arranged and held each week.

The Finnish teachers remained at work all through the strike. Each had one or two pupils to teach. For them the situation was depressing and exhausting. None of their Swedish colleagues took their part or understood their point of view in supporting our action.

On the one hand the Finnish teachers became a substitute against whom the Swedish teachers could direct their aggression and hostility; on the other hand, they had to defend the parents and to explain the reasons for the strike to their colleagues. This was caused by the fact that the Swedish teachers refused to meet the parents. We had called all the teachers several times to a meeting to explain our motives, with no result.

The general meetings were the heart of the strike. There we all met, and got our strength. There we found out what the actual situation was. To these meetings people came from other parts of Sweden, even from Finland (and Denmark and England), to give us their support and encouragement. All the important decisions were taken at these meetings, by democratic vote. The meetings were very informal, and feelings and emotions were openly shown. Women who had never dared to speak in public before gave speeches and were appreciated for them. This led to their also daring openly to confront the highest civil servants in the School Department—and that in a foreign language.

We had chosen a negotiation group, to stand up for our demands in the meetings with the politicians and civil servants. This group could never make a decision on its own, but had to leave the final decisions to the general meeting.

An information group was formed, to take care of contacts with the media, both to inform them and to try to correct the most common misinterpretations. This group also prepared all the information for the parents and for the public, both in Finnish and in Swedish.

All the groups had a very loose organization and gathered informally. Everybody was welcome in any group meeting. All the groups were intertwined, and no group could act on its own, or was considered more important than the others. We grew very close to each other, and became dependent on each other. As we grew tired, quarrels arose, but they were resolved the next day, and forgotten. Some evenings we went home from the meetings crying bitterly and hopelessly. The next morning we picked up the fight again, and even found energy to encourage our children.

Influence on the children

An important aspect of the fight was indeed to explain it to the children, to inform them about why this had to happen. In many ways we learned that the strike helped our children on their way to finding their identities. At the same time the strike was difficult for them. The following account of the strike is written by one of the children, Vesa, then 10 years old:

The strike

"The strike started because there was too much teaching in Swedish. For example, mathematics started slowly but surely to be totally taught in Swedish in the middle school. We in the lower grades had, at least I thought so, quite a good time in the Swedish lessons. Our Swedish teacher sometimes read aloud for us but most of the time we filled in the Swedish books. On the first day of the strike I went to the Finnish Club with a journalist following in my heels. One of the fathers, Jukka, told us children why there was a strike. We ate at the Finnish Club. During the whole strike a Finnish bakery gave us bread. We ate at the Finnish Club all through the strike. In the beginning it was nice to go to the Club in the mornings. After a couple of weeks it felt less nice. During the first days everybody had their lessons at the Club but later on the different classes moved into different flats all over Rinkeby. I think that the teaching we got in these places soon was quite scattered. The strike felt very stressing. All the meetings made it even more stressing. The schoolwork went quite well. When I saw Swedish-speaking children from the same school they mocked us and said that we were totally nuts being on strike. During the strike there were, of course, lots of meetings and loads of telephone calls. For instance, in one evening there was one meeting and about twenty calls. It felt difficult that my mother was all the time at the meetings. When she was at the meetings I stayed mostly at home alone. It was too tiring to follow my mother to all the meetings. I watched TV and wondered when this strike is ever going to end. I think it was a good thing for us Finns to start a strike. It was brave because the Swedes were oppressing the Finns. I want to learn Finnish because it is a beautiful language. And it is nice to be able to speak many languages because then you can speak with many different kinds of people without an interpreter. When the strike was over it felt good. Almost as good as it feels when X-mas holidays begin."

When Vesa was seven, he once pondered on the difference between the mother tongue and other languages like this:

"It is so strange: when you learn a new language, even if you understand what those words mean, deep inside you still don't understand. But with your own language you understand deep inside your innermost self what everything means."

Our own development

In fact, during the strike we found new identities for ourselves. Where before we had been careful, and even full of shame, we now took pride in being Finns in Sweden. We no longer looked back to Finland but wanted positive changes for ourselves here in Sweden. We were not begging. We felt that we, as a part of our new country, had a right to demand human rights for our children and ourselves. We grew to feel equal to our opponents.

In the beginning the media presented us as a pack of misinformed women, led by radical leftist fanatics. That did not work as time passed, and we forced them to see us as we were: cooking food for our children while arguing for a better future for them in Sweden. Often our awareness and arguments were met with lies and attempts were made to sidetrack us, because what we argued for rang a bell of truth even in the ears of our opponents.

During the strike the children learned that the parents and the Finnish teachers were on their side. They learned to know most of the parents in the Finnish classes. They saw that these parents were prepared to fight for all of them. They found out that with a united struggle one can change unjust circumstances. This was the most valuable knowledge they gained to help them in their future lives.

With the strike, in eight weeks, we achieved a total change in the organization of the Finnish classes in Bredby school. Practically all education is now given in Finnish. The "integrated education" lost all its previous glory and was abolished as a possible model for Stockholm immigrant education. A group of politicians was appointed by the City Council to study and plan policy and curriculum for future immigrant education.

During the strike, we women found out that we were capable of taking care of and even changing our own and our children's future. Until the strike we had been objects for authoritarian care. Now we are the subjects of our own lives. Through the strike we grew stronger because we learned to believe in ourselves and trust in other women to stand on our side and fight together with us.

Now we are not afraid to oppose the plans of the government. We have also found out that we have more in common with the other immigrant groups than we have differences. We have formed a group, called "Working group for mother tongue education", together with the Turks, Greeks, Assyrians, Yugoslavs and the Spanish-speaking groups. We will never again give up.

11 Resource power and autonomy through discourse in conflict

A Finnish migrant school strike in Sweden

TOVE SKUTNABB-KANGAS

Introduction

Labour migrants in every country are as a group at the bottom of the power hierarchy. They have very few means of influencing their own situation, because they are a relatively small, often ethnically heterogeneous group, often with little education and often not well organized. To a large extent they lack political rights, which might be one way of exercising influence. The discourse in which they as individuals and as a group engage with representatives of the majority society takes place on unequal terms. If they want to have their fair share of the goods and services of the country where they live and produce, they have to gain more power.

In this chapter[1] I will look at education, both formal and informal, as one of the means for labour migrants and their children to bring about more equitable power relationships with the majority. The empirical example I analyse comes from the experience of Finns, the largest labour migrant group in Sweden. It is important when reading the chapter and trying to see the relevance of the struggle of a white migrant group for other oppressed groups to know that we Finns have a uniquely low position in Sweden, compared with our position as migrants in other countries, for instance, Australia or Canada. This can only be understood in the light of our history: Finland was colonized by Sweden from approximately 1155 to 1809, a period of some 650 years. The economic and ideological consequences of this extremely long colonization, longer than for any African countries, are reflected in the position of Finnish labour migrants in Sweden.

First I will discuss one way of conceptualizing power, building on the work of the Norwegian peace researcher, Johan Galtung (especially 1980). Next I will relate some of the conclusions of this theoretical framework to minority education, in order to see whether mother tongue medium education for minority children can be of more use as an instrument in bringing about more equitable power relationships than can assimilationist submersion models with education through the medium of an L2. The framework will then be applied to an exemplary case, a school strike organized by Finnish parents in Sweden, in order to test its usefulness in analysing how power relations can be altered in a conflict situation. Finally, some tentative conclusions follow.

On conceptualizing power

Power may, of course, be conceptualized in many different ways.[2] According to Galtung (1980), power is both a *relation* and a *quality*. *Power-over-others* is a relation, *power-over-oneself* is a quality, even if its validity is tested in a relation. Galtung distinguishes between three types of power (p. 63). I have summarized them in Table 11.1.

Innate power may be a commanding personality, a charisma of some kind, or simply physical muscular power. It seems to me, though, that what Galtung calls innate is difficult to imagine as completely "innate". Charisma must be partly a result of socialization, and the development or otherwise of muscular power must certainly be at least partly dependent on feeding, i.e. environmental. Innate power will not be discussed further in this chapter, since the other two forms are more fruitful for our analysis, and since the concept belongs to a research paradigm which is inconsistent with the analysis presented here.

Resources can be either material (a gun, books, capital) or non-material (knowledge and skills). Time is also a resource, although Galtung does not mention it separately. But it has been discussed repeatedly in research on women (see e.g. Auvinen, 1977; Eskola & Haavio-Mannila, 1975; Holter *et al.*, 1975; Stören & Schou Wetlesen, 1976; Ås, 1975). Time

TABLE 11.1 *Types of power*

Innate power	being-power	actor-oriented
Resource power	having-power	actor-oriented
Structural power	position-power	structure-oriented

can be used as one example of the fact that material resources (wealth) can be converted into non-material resources (time). Another example would be education, knowledge and skills. Their acquisition is still in most countries dependent on wealth.

Structural power, power on the basis of one's position, also often leads to resource power, and vice versa. One form of power "is convertible to another: structural power into accumulation of resources, resource power into sufficient command of the structure to get into positions of structural power" (Galtung, 1980:64).

Another distinction which Galtung (1980:59) makes is about the means used to exert power. Power can be *ideological* (normative), *remunerative* or *punitive*, depending on whether *ideas* (persuasion), *carrots* (bargaining) or *sticks* (force) are used. In the first case the influence is based on *internal sanctions*, in the last two on either *positive or negative external sanctions*, respectively. Again, I have summarized them in Table 11.2.

All these forms of power can work only if the object, the "power receiver" really "receives" the pressure, "accepts" the "power-sender's" influence. If a person or group has enough *power-over-themselves* so as to be able to withstand what other people or groups may have of *power-over-others*, they can be called *autonomous*. According to the three means of exerting power, autonomy can be discussed in terms of *self-respect* as opposed to *submissiveness*, *self-sufficiency* as opposed to *dependency*, and *fearlessness* as opposed to *fear* (see Table 11.3). In this context Galtung defines (p. 59) self-respect as "confidence in one's own ideas and ability to set one's own goals", self-sufficiency as "the possibility of pursuing them with one's own means", and fearlessness as "the possibility of persisting despite threats of destruction".

Autonomy is important, according to Galtung (p. 59), "in a world where the social context and the powerful define goals for others". This could mean, with our exemplary case in mind, that a minority could, for instance, be told that their language and culture are not worth anything,

TABLE 11.2 *Exerting power: means, processes and sanctions*

Type	Ideological	Remunerative	Punitive
Means	ideas	carrots	sticks
Process	persuasion	bargaining	force
Sanctions used	internal	positive external	negative external

TABLE 11.3   *Autonomy and penetration*

Means	Autonomy	Penetration
Ideas	self-respect	submissiveness
Carrots	self-sufficiency	dependency
Sticks	fearlessness	fear

and that learning the majority language and culture and forgetting about one's own is essential. They could, in other words, be told to assimilate. The minority itself can be made to believe that this is the only feasible goal. The minority would develop a "colonized consciousness". It would thus show submissiveness, not self-respect.

Autonomy is also important in a world where "goal satisfaction depends on supplies from others" (p. 59). Our example could be the minority which cannot organize the education of its children so as to resist assimilation, because it lacks the resources to set up its own schools, and is thus dependent on resources controlled by the majority. Thus it would show dependency, not self-sufficiency.

And last, autonomy is important in a world "where destruction at the hands of others is always an open possibility" (p. 59). With our example it could mean that those minority children who do not conform and assimilate, but who do not succeed in mobilizing enough resources for their own alternative either, may run a risk of at least psychological destruction, combined with a destruction of the basis for their material welfare (i.e. poor school achievement, followed by risk of unemployment). The minority would thus show fear, not fearlessness.

Autonomy is "the degree of 'inoculation' against...power... Autonomy does not mean isolation, nor does it mean equity. Autonomy may mean that one can be self-sufficient any moment one wants, not that one *de facto* is self-sufficient in a given moment" (p. 59). The opposite of autonomy is *penetration*, "meaning that the outside has penetrated into one's self to the extent of creating *submissiveness* to ideas, *dependency* on 'goods' from the outside and *fear* of the outside in terms of 'bads'" (p. 59).

As we know, power is not shared equally between different individuals and groups. Some have more power, some very little. If we want a world with more equity and justice, one of the important questions becomes how those who have less than their fair share of power can get more power. Therefore, we have to have a view about how people gain *access to power*.

Two opposite views can be taken. In an *idealistic, logical-analytical perspective* (which Galtung calls the actor-oriented perspective), *innate power*, strength and superiority, is seen as *basic*. Innate power can then be converted to other forms of power, resource power and structural power (Galtung, 1980:64). This to me represents a social Darwinist theory: those who rule (i.e. who have structural power) do so because they are the fittest to rule (i.e. they have more innate capacities than those who do not rule). Therefore, it is fair that they also accumulate more resources.

In a *materialist perspective*, the structure-oriented analyst "would usually see *structural power* (referred to as exploitation) as *primary* in this conversion process and differentials in resource power as a consequence of having structural power. Differences in innate power would be seen as a propaganda figure, as a rationalization" (p. 64). This could be visualized as in Figure 11.1.

The last two concepts I borrow from Galtung are about two kinds of countervailing power: the *balance approach* and the *autonomy approach*.

"Under the former, the power receiver has the *same resources* for persuasion, bargaining, and force at his [or her, my addition[3]] disposal and can turn them the other way. Under the second formula, she refuses to receive, by developing autonomy or power-over-herself: self-respect, self-sufficiency and fearlessness. She inoculates herself again power-over-others from outside: as she refuses to be a power receiver, power cannot reach her." (Galtung, 1980:63)

Now in many ways the autonomy approach sounds romantic and idealized. We know, though, that it has been used successfully, by Gandhi

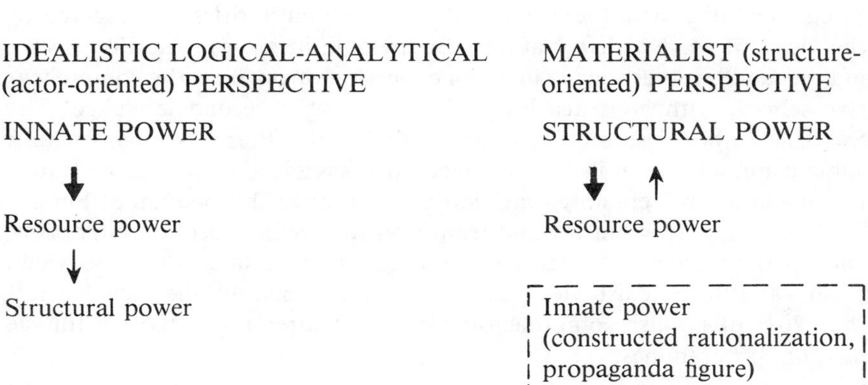

IDEALISTIC LOGICAL-ANALYTICAL (actor-oriented) PERSPECTIVE

MATERIALIST (structure-oriented) PERSPECTIVE

INNATE POWER

STRUCTURAL POWER

↓

↓ ↑

Resource power

Resource power

↓

Structural power

Innate power (constructed rationalization, propaganda figure)

FIGURE 11.1   *Paradigms for analysing access to power*

and others.[4] It seems to me, though, that it might work better when resisting direct physical violence as opposed to structural violence, where the victim may never be confronted face-to-face with the exploiters to show her autonomy.

Next we will see in what ways this conceptualization of power can be used to analyse some of the demands and events in the long struggle of Finns in Sweden to ensure a good education for their children.

Which approach can migrants use to gain access to power?

As indicated initially, the discourse between a migrant minority and the "majority" (represented by the ruling class, here particularly the educational authorities) is characterized by an unequal distribution of power. If we are interested in a discourse where nobody dictates the terms or the outcome, we have to ask ourselves how the unequal power relationships could be equalized. We assume that the Finns, like most parents, want to have a good education for their children (for evidence, see Skutnabb-Kangas, 1986a), and that they have certain views on how this education should be organized. The Swedish educational authorities also claim that they want the Finnish children to have a good education, and they also have certain views on how the instruction should be organized in order to achieve this. If the views coincide, the power relationship does not matter much. But if they do not coincide, then it is likely that the views of the educational authorities prevail, because they have more power than the Finnish migrant minority. And this is in fact the case: the views of the bulk of the Finns in Sweden (represented by the National Union of Finnish Associations in Sweden) conflict with the views of the Swedish authorities (represented by the views of the Swedish National Board of Education). The Finns want maintenance mother tongue medium education throughout the comprehensive school, with good teaching of Swedish as a second language. The Swedish authorities, on the other hand, want either a straightforward submersion education in Swedish-medium classes[5] or some type of transitional education[6]: possibly some education through the medium of Finnish in the lower grades but a rapid transition to Swedish-medium education, with perhaps some mother tongue language arts later on. The views clash—and the Swedish viewpoints prevail, as shown by the fact that less than 20% of Finnish comprehensive school children are in mother tongue medium programmes.

In order for the Finns to be able to decide on the education of their own children in Sweden, they must gain access to more power. But how? First we shall look at the present prerequisites for one or the other of the approaches presented above. Can the Finns use the *balance approach*?

In democratic societies, it is usual that only the representatives of a certain group need to negotiate, not every member of the group. Education is more centralized in Sweden than in many other countries, and ordinary Swedish-speaking parents do not need (and are not in a position) to engage in much negotiation about their children's education: it is to a large extent guided by central decisions. These, in their turn, are guided by results of purposive-rational forms of reasoning (see Habermas, 1971), based mainly on research results (Apple, 1979:8 and Chapter 6). But in minority education encouragement has been given to haphazard experimentation. While waiting for "reliable research results" to emerge (and it has been a long wait), the National Board of Education has come up with recommendations only, not strict decrees. Much of the interpretation has been left to local school districts or schools. That has meant that migrant parents in every municipality, often every school and every class, have often had to negotiate anew each year how the education of their children should be organized. These local negotiations have meant that ordinary Finnish migrant parents have been involved to a much higher degree than they would be in Finland, or than Swedish parents need to.

The *balance approach* would presuppose that Finnish minority parents, when engaging in negotiations with the Swedish school authorities (who decide how the education of Finnish children in Sweden should be organized), would have *the same resources for persuasion* (the same ideological power), *for bargaining* (remunerative power, that they had something to offer, a carrot), and *for force* (a stick, punitive power) at their disposal as the Swedes. Usually a labour migrant minority has none of these.

To be able to *persuade*, you need knowledge and arguments. In this case, where the Finns are arguing about their children's education, the arguments needed are professional and specialized arguments from applied linguistics, psychology, pedagogy, social psychology, sociology, etc. It is not likely that ordinary people with little education (the Finnish minority is roughly 90% working class, with a basic education) have the specialist knowledge needed, or even the means to put across the practical experience and knowledge which they do have, in a way which is convincing enough for school authorities—especially because all this has to be done in a foreign language, Swedish. It is clear that there are people among the minority who can do this, but the bulk of them do not have the means needed for persuasion.

A labour migrant minority has nothing to offer in exchange, either. The only thing most of them own is their labour, and that they have to sell anyway. Besides, their labour is not attractive to school authorities, not even in the form of teachers from the minority group, especially in times of high unemployment among indigenous teachers. Thus there is no *bargaining* power.

Migrants cannot use a stick either. The only *punitive* power they might have *vis-à-vis* the school would be to go on strike, to take their children out of school. That is logically not very efficient. Usually only those strikes are efficient which harm production, or make life difficult for very large groups other than those on strike. But the only production that a migrant minority school strike harms is the production of knowledge in the minority's own children. It has no negative consequences for the majority society. Thus it does not function in a punitive way.

There are no prerequisites, therefore, in educational negotiation between the Finnish minority and the Swedish school authorities for using the balance approach. The structurally unequal relationship between majority and minority has been converted to an unequal access to resources needed for persuasion, bargaining or force.

We are left with the *autonomy approach*. The Finns in Sweden could refuse to be power-receivers, and then, according to Galtung, power would not be able to reach them. In order to become autonomous in this sense, they would need to develop self-respect, self-sufficiency and fearlessness.

Ideological, economic-reproductive and repressive functions of migrant education

Before proceeding to see how this could be done, we have to ask ourselves a few questions. These characteristics (self-respect, self-sufficiency and fearlessness) represent an actor-oriented perspective, regardless of whether one looks at them as innate or acquired resources. They focus on characteristics in *individual actors*. In a materialist perspective, differential resources in individual actors and groups of actors are seen as *results of differences in structural power*. Resource power, especially non-material resource power like arguments and knowledge, then belongs to the superstructure (even if it were to be treated as cultural capital—see Bourdieu & Passeron, 1977). If we believe that superstructure in some way emerges from the relations of production, from the base, should it not follow that the changes have to happen in the base, in the unequal position *vis-à-vis* the relationship to means of production? Is it not a bit naive to believe that changes in people's consciousness can change the world? Should we not rather try to see what should be done within a more structure-oriented perspective? Or can developing self-respect, self-sufficiency and fearlessness be understood as something more than reflections of changes in people's consciousness? All these questions we will have to come back to later, but it seems to be necessary here to hint at ways of conceptualizing the dilemma in a way which differs from Galtung's, or at least to indicate some of the possible limitations of the framework used.

Some of the answers may lie in those dialectic approaches which see changes in the superstructure as being able to influence the base, and which, in addition to this, locate education and changes in consciousness, arrived at through education, in both the base and the superstructure. Like Carnoy (for instance 1982:116) and many others, I see the functions of education as *ideological* (in Althusser's terms, 1971), *economic-reproductive* and *repressive*. Education is *ideological* in that some of its functions, namely the reproduction of labour, division of labour along class lines, and the reproduction of the relations of production, are partly realized *through the ideological relations in school*. Schools are ideological state apparatuses, in other words. In its *economic-reproductive* function education helps to develop a reserve army of skilled unemployed. It helps to increase productivity by producing and reproducing skills, and by producing technocrats (such as school administrators or time-and-motion "experts") who are willing to control other fractions in the work force, speed them up, or throw out those who cannot keep up (like many migrant youngsters, or old people). In addition, education also operates as part of the *repressive* state apparatus. Migrant children are also in quite concrete ways *forced* to stay in school, even if they do not understand much of the instruction if this is through the medium of an L2.

To make this more concrete, we will look at the ideological, economic-reproductive and repressive functions of education specifically in relation to migrant minorities. At the same time we will go back to Galtung's concepts and examine current migrant education so as to see to what extent it enables migrants to change their position. As mentioned earlier, the Swedish authorities recommend for migrant minority children either Swedish-medium education, with a sprinkling of mother tongue language arts (direct submersion), or at the most some type of transitional programmes (see, for instance, Skolöverstyrelsen, 1985). Transitional programmes are a form of indirect submersion. They assimilate children in a way which is slightly more humane than putting the children directly in Swedish-medium instruction from the very beginning (see my analysis of the goals of the different programmes in Skutnabb-Kangas, 1984:125–35). As we saw earlier, the migrants do not have the resources needed to use a balance approach. From the point of view of changing their situation in part through education, we have to examine to what extent the education given to their children in Sweden fosters resources needed for using the autonomy approach. Does Swedish-medium (direct) or transitional (indirect) submersion education produce self-respect, self-sufficiency and fearlessness?

If we see the development of autonomy (self-respect, self-sufficiency and fearlessness) only as changes in consciousness, then all of them belong to the domain of ideology in the analysis of the functions of education. Let us first take this approach, and see what the Swedish school does to migrant minority children from the point of view of ideology. (For details of the claims see Skutnabb-Kangas, 1984).

From an *ideology* point of view, for migrant children, submersion education through the medium of an L2 produces the opposite of autonomy. It educates them to *submissiveness*, not self-respect, because their performance is usually worse than that of the indigenous children (who at least understand most of the instruction) and because their languages and cultures mostly have no place in schools, are worth nothing.

Submersion programmes educate them to *dependency*, not self-sufficiency: they are made dependent on others for both knowledge (cognitively) and acceptance (affectively), because their and their parents' prior linguistic and general knowledge is made to appear useless in schools; and because they are accepted by peers and the school only if they reject what is their own and assimilate to the majority, willingly.

And submersion programmes educate them to *fear*, not fearlessness, because the majority society possesses all the sanctions, both economic (if you don't do what we say, you will not get a job) and psychological (if you don't behave as we do, you will not be accepted by us). Besides, the educational system legitimizes the educational treatment it gives to migrant minority children, by blaming the victims (we give you exactly the same opportunities which our kids get, and in addition to that you get extra help, language lessons, auxiliary teaching, etc. If you still don't make it, it is because you are stupid).

In migrants the *economic-reproductive* function of schools in capitalist societies has found a new group to uneducate. According to Stephen Castles' analysis (1980), migrants are needed as a crisis buffer, to prevent the lowest layers of the indigenous working class from experiencing the worst impacts of the "crisis" so severely. Instead, the migrants are the ones who take the largest cutbacks (because the benefits cut are the ones which the migrants use, partly because of their age structure), suffer the highest unemployment (because the sectors where they work are mostly those most sensitive to economic fluctuation on the labour market), etc. In that way the indigenous working class may still be prevented from becoming too dissatisfied, and too revolutionary. And the migrant discontent is contained, partly by social welfare (which is rapidly disintegrating in many countries, though), partly by the fact that they do not have any political rights such as voting rights in state elections, to voice their discontent. And, of course, by majority hegemony.

But with the present migrant youth, education does not seem to succeed in disciplining at least all of them, so that they can be used as a crisis buffer. Sivanandan's description is a case in point:

"The youth know, viscerally, that there will be no work for them, ever, no call for their labour ... They are not the unemployed, but the never employed. They have not, like their parents, had jobs and lost them—and so become disciplined into a routine and a culture that preserves the *status quo*. They have not been organized into trade unions, and had their politics disciplined by a labour aristocracy. They have not been on the marches of the dis-employed, so valiantly recalled by Labour from the hunger marches of the 1930s. Theirs is a different hunger—a hunger to retain freedom, the life-style, the dignity which they have carved out from the stone of their lives." (Sivanandan, 1982:49)

All this seems *one* way of trying to escape the economic-reproductive force of education (or, rather, non-education): refusing to be educated to *un*employment (which in some way presupposes that one *has* been employed or wants employment, as Sivanandan implies), and to *choose* never to become employed, thereby rejecting the position on the labour market for which education has "prepared" the migrant youth. Refusing to accept the crisis buffer function, in other words. This tendency is further strengthened by the tendency to truancy (staying away from school), which is much more common among migrant than indigenous youth. The push-out rates (or drop-out rates, depending on what is blamed and whether or not truancy can be regarded as a conscious political choice) are much higher for migrant youth as well. Thereby the *repressive* function of schools as one part of the state apparatus is diminished also: youth refuse to be stored in schools which they find meaningless.

Assimilation or rejection—two poor alternatives

But none of these answers—neither submissiveness and assimilation in an L2-medium class, nor the rejection of the school and the shit jobs eventually offered—leads to any kind of positive long-term solution. None of them probably even leads to an accumulation of *resources* which could later be used in a negotiation discourse with the representatives of the powerful majority society.

The former solution, *assimilation*, staying on in an L2-medium submersion class and trying to cope, with massive failure as a result at the group level, leads, from an actor-oriented perspective, to the opposite of autonomy, to *penetration*: submissiveness, dependency and fear, to blaming oneself for failures and to a permanently unequal discourse. To powerlessness. From a structure-oriented perspective it leads to fulfilling the buffer function: shit jobs alternating with unemployment, few opportunities for influencing the situation because of lack of negotiation resources.

The latter alternative, *rejection*, may lead to meaningless violence, bitterness, alienation and marginalization. There is, of course, also one way of looking at rejection as just another form of assimilation. This can be done by using Bourdieu's notion of internalized necessity (1976:111). According to this way of conceptualizing the rejection, we could explain that some migrant youth can see through the nice phrases: they are realistic and can see that they have not got a chance. They accept this as something inevitable, and *choose* to drop out, thereby fooling themselves into believing that they in fact had a choice. Or we could compare them with the "lads" in Paul Willis' seminal book *Learning to labour* (1977). These working-class boys in an all-male comprehensive secondary school in an industrial area of England "skilfully work the system to gain some measure of control over the way they spend their time in school" and "reject a large portion of the intellectual and social messages of the school, even though the institution tries to be 'progressive' " (Apple, 1982c:97). At the same time, the counter-school culture which the lads create, with physicality, masculinity, manual work affirmed and mental labour rejected as effeminate, reproduces their place in the division of labour, links them to an unequal economy. Thus their rejection of a system which has as one of its goals to make them accept the unequal division of power and resources and a place at the lower end of the system, anchors them firmly exactly there, and makes it look as if it was their own choice, a choice which they celebrate. The rejection has thus reproduced the same structural conditions which an acceptance would have produced, too, with perhaps the difference that the contestation of the system by the lads has given them a false sense of choice. This is, of course, a pessimistic and somewhat simplistic interpretation of Willis' book.

But rejection *might* also be a starting point towards preparing for more permanent change. This is, as I see it, only possible if rejection is combined with an analysis which leads to access to alternative resources which can then be used to alter the situation. It means creating, constructing instrument power, in order to gain access to property power, in Mullard's framework (1985). From a theoretical point of view refusing to be a power-receiver, for instance, refusing to be in an assimilationist school, is not enough. It represents only a rejection, without creating alternatives, and *rejection in itself is not enough*, because rejection does not in itself imply that one wants and gets something else instead. Rejection is just saying NO to something, without necessarily saying YES to an alternative. Therefore, rejection must be combined with trying to realize an alternative to what one has rejected. The process of becoming autonomous must at the same time imply the creation of alternative resources, which are not only ideological but which also function at the economic-reproductive and repressive levels.

In the next section I will give a short description of strike action by Finnish mothers (and to some extent fathers) and children in Stockholm, Sweden, where alternatives were created, in addition to a rejection. [7] These alternatives meant, first of all, creating immediate resources, which were then used when trying to negotiate with the educational authorities, in order to organize more viable alternatives for the children within the school system. Secondly, a longer term alternative was also created through the strike, namely, a better educational system for the children, a system which makes them better prepared to fight the unjust conditions of migrant minorities. Again, we shall use Galtung's framework to analyse the alternative resources.

The Rinkeby school strike

Background

The school strike was organized in Bredby school, in Rinkeby, Stockholm. Rinkeby is the suburb with the highest percentage of immigrants in Scandinavia, over 50%. The strike took place in January–March 1984 and lasted eight weeks; 118 Finnish children in grades 1–6, 96% of all the Finnish children in the relevant classes, participated. The parents had, after many years of struggle, succeeded in getting both Finnish-medium preschools and Finnish-medium classes at school. In these classes the children were taught through the medium of Finnish during the first three grades, with Swedish as a second language (L2) from grade 2 on, and then through the medium of both languages in grades 4–6, to be followed by Swedish-only instruction in grades 7–9, with Finnish as a subject. The parents had for a long time wanted to increase the amount of Finnish-medium instruction and to have it continued in grades 7–9 also. At the same time they were dissatisfied with the low level of teaching in Swedish. They wanted the quality of it to be improved, and they wanted bilingual teachers to teach Swedish.

In the autumn of 1981, the headmistress of the Bredby school announced a new plan, a so-called "integration model". According to it, teaching of Swedish would start in grade 1. Many of the practical lessons would be through the medium of Swedish in the first three grades. From grade 4 on, the Finnish children would form "integrated classes" with the Swedish-speaking parallel classes.

From the very beginning both the Finnish parents and the children reacted very strongly against these changes. It was felt that it represented a way to try to assimilate the children completely. The children complained: they could not follow the Swedish-medium teaching; they were punished for using their mother tongue; they became restless and did not want to go to school. The parents could not help their children with school work because it was in Swedish, and they could not follow what the children did in school.

Parents' meetings for different classes were organized: letters of protest sent to the headmistress and the authorities, and through these to the politicians: meetings were held. The new curriculum for Sweden, approved while the struggle went on, stated that the school had to listen to the children and their parents, and also to local immigrant organizations, when planning the education of immigrant children. Parent representatives from each class had a meeting at which they wrote down the points on which they disagreed with the education given to their children. They demanded that the "integration model" be stopped.

Nothing changed. On the contrary, the parents learned that the Bredby school model was to be introduced as the general model for immigrant education in all Stockholm schools. This was because "it was so much appreciated by the Finnish children and parents", they learned! Their letters of protest had never even reached the politicians, but had been stopped by the civil servants. This was at the end of November, 1983. The parents held one more meeting, to discuss the situation. They knew that they had tried, through every possible means at their disposal, to change things, in negotiations with the headmistress and the school authorities. But they were not being heard. They had no power in this negotiation with the representatives of the majority society. All the decisions were being made against their wishes, even if the curriculum stated that they had to be heard. They had tried to persuade with their arguments, but since they had no remunerative or punitive power, the situation was not one of balance in power. The only solution left to the parents was the autonomy approach, a refusal to be power-receivers.

Since the parents did not have power-over-others, meaning they could not make the Swedish school authorities organize the education of Finnish children according to the wishes of the parents, they had to develop power-over-themselves, in order to be able to resist.

What kind of prerequisites did they have, then? Were the parents *self-respecting* (as opposed to submissive), *self-sufficient* (as opposed to dependent) and *fearless* (as opposed to feeling fear)?

Answers to this type of question are of necessity multi-layered. We will look at some indicators in the account written by some of the most active participants, Tuula Honkala, Pirkko Leporanta-Morley, Lilja Liukka and Eija Rougle (this volume, Chapter 10).

From dependency to self-sufficiency

They describe those 30 women and half a dozen men (out of the parents of the 118 children) who were more or less active full-time in organizing the strike:

"Almost none of us had ever before taken part in any political activities, and only four had even worked in the Finnish Club. Most of us were single parents, with long working hours and not much education. Our Swedish was deficient, and we considered ourselves incapable of writing letters to and holding discussions with authorities in higher positions." (p. 246)

The parents elected a strike committee, decided to have one more meeting with the authorities, and then to go on strike if this did not help. It didn't. And so the strike started.

During the whole eight-week strike, the parents took care of the children. Earlier they had been dependent on the school to take care of the children, to feed them (school meals are free of charge in Sweden), and to teach them. Now they are forced to become self-sufficient, and to create the resources needed: time, space for the children to be in, money for food, capacity to teach the children. By doing this, rather than merely rejecting what the school offered, they provided the children with an alternative. The children were taught during normal school hours during the whole strike, in the Finnish Club, in various homes, etc., by the parents themselves and by various teachers, teacher trainees, journalists, etc. who came during their free time or took time off from their jobs to help the striking parents and children. Everything took place in Finnish. The mothers cooked for the 118 children, taking turns, in the tiny kitchenette in the Finnish Club. The money for food came from donations from all over Sweden and Finland. The bread during the whole strike came as a gift from a Finnish bakery in Stockholm.

Now other Finnish parent groups who are planning a strike often contact the Rinkeby group, in order to get advice on how to become self-sufficient ...

From submissiveness to self-respect

The self-respect of many of the parents grew during the strike. All the parents had two general meetings each week, where everything was clarified and decided. There were several open groups responsible for negotiating with the authorities, for information to the media and the parents, for planning the lessons, for cooking, etc. Again, Pirkko Leporanta-Morley (p. 247):

"The meetings were very informal, and feelings and emotions were openly shown. Women who had never dared to speak in public before gave speeches and were appreciated for them. This led to their also daring openly to confront the highest civil servants in the School Department—and that in a foreign language."

"We grew very close to each other, and became dependent on each other. As we grew tired, quarrels arose, but they were resolved the next day, and forgotten. Some evenings we went home from the meetings crying bitterly and hopelessly. The next morning we picked up the fight again, and even found energy to encourage our children ... In fact, during the strike we found new identities for ourselves. Where before we had been careful, and even full of shame, we now took pride in being Finns in Sweden. We no longer looked back to Finland but wanted positive changes for ourselves here in Sweden. We were not begging. We felt that we, as a part of our new country, had a right to demand human rights for our children and ourselves. We grew to feel equal to our opponents." (pp. 248–49)

From fear to fearlessness

There was a tremendous positive response to the strike by other Finns, by many other immigrant organizations, and a few political parties. But there was also a fierce negative reaction

> "... from the Swedish majority. Our fight was perceived as frightening and immoral. We appeared to them to be ungrateful for all the care we had received. Bilingualism, at any level, appeared to be a threat to the majority. Individual expressions of these negative feelings included numerous suggestions for us to move back to Finland, or to seek psychiatric care. Some of us received threats on our and our families' lives, by letters, postcards and telephone calls." (p. 245)

Below follows an example of letters which the Finnish Club received (now stored in their archives). This is not one of the really nasty ones. In translating the letter I have tried to render the over-excited syntax and the shifts of style, which are symptomatic of the strong feelings aroused by the strike.

> "Skogås, February 19, 1984
>
> We have read with dismay the article in Dagens Nyheter about your school strike in Rinkeby school as a protset [*sic*] against that the school does not give instruction in the Finnish language.
>
> Follow, then, a good piece of advice, which is shared by the majority of the Swedish people:
>
> Go back home to Finland again. Why do we Swedish tax-payers with the highest taxes in the world have to pay just because foreigners are swamping our country?
>
> And foreigners who in addition DEMAND all sorts of things. Can we send thousands of Swedish children to finland and DEMAND that Finnish tax-payers pay for the teaching of Swedish for Swedish children in Your country??[8]
>
> We are being drowned by masses of immigrants soon we Swedes are a minority in our own country. Get lost the sooner the better, and don't come here as parasites and DEMAND! We have enough of scoundrels anyway. Go home you bloody Finnish backwoodspeople, and don't come and make demands, we have enough of spongers here anyway, and don't need an addition of good-for-nothings from Finland. Teach the kids their mother tongue at home, but don't come and demand that

we taxpayers have to pay for their education in their mother tongue, here in our Swedish schools.

Actions like the one you perform aggravate further the antagonism between us Swedes and immigrating Finnish backwoodspeople, THAT is probably the only positive thing with the whole action of yours.

Bugger off you bloody carcasses."

In addition to these more personal reactions, there were reactions in the mass media also. Some of these were more harmful for the parents than the type quoted above:

"In the media our demands were misrepresented by the headmistress and even the Swedish Minister for Immigration, to be about a bilingual Sweden, universities in Finnish, etc. In fact we had all the time to fight two battles on two different fronts, one with the school authorities and politicians, and one against the lies and false images of us in the media." (p. 245)

Also some researchers were fooled by the mass media into believing that these were indeed the parents' demands (see, for instance, Paulston, 1985:58, where she repeats these false claims as true).

What the parents demanded, in fact, was that

"—the 'integration model' be stopped,

—all new theory in subject matter teaching be taught through the medium of Finnish during the first 6 years,

—Swedish be taught as a second language (not mother tongue), by bilingual teachers,

—more resources be provided for the children with special learning problems, and

—the parents be considered as equal discussion partners when planning the education of their children." (Skutnabb-Kangas & Leporanta-Morley, 1986).

The parents wanted "the children to learn Finnish, and to learn to know their own culture and to take pride in their background" (Honkala *et al.*, this volume, chapter 10, p. 244). They believed that "only if the children had a true chance to choose would they grow to feel equal with their Swedish-speaking schoolmates" (pp. 244–45).

The children were well prepared for the strike in advance. It was explained to them and discussed with them, and they worked extra hard with their school work before the strike, both in school and at home. They participated in meetings and demonstrations, without fear. They became, according to their parents, much more articulate, much more aware and proud of their language, culture and identity.

What did the strike achieve?

What was achieved through the strike? Partly, after eight weeks, most of the demands for the children's education were met. The results of the teaching that the children now get are good. The Finnish children who were in grade 4 during the strike and only participated in the "integration model" during the autumn semester of grade 4, have now had the benefit of over two years of the type of teaching their parents wanted. Tests given to all school children in Sweden at the end of grade 6 show that the children do as well as Swedish children in all subjects. Their Swedish tests show better results than the Swedish mean. They have also taken standard tests used in Finland, and they are doing as well as Finnish children in Finland, except in English, where they show better results than Finnish children in Finland ... (from an interview with the Finnish and Swedish teachers of that class, Tuula Honkala and Eva Malmvärn, in *Spångan Suomalainen* 4/86, 7).

Partly, and equally importantly, the strike was a unique educational and political experience for the children but especially for the mothers. This is how they themselves summarize it:

"During the strike, we women found out that we were capable of taking care of and even changing our own and our children's future. Until the strike we had been objects for authoritarian care. Now we are the subjects of our own lives. Through the strike we grew stronger because we learned to believe in ourselves and trust in other women to stand on our side and fight together with us.

Now we are not afraid to oppose the plans of the government. We have also found out that we have more in common with the other immigrant groups than we have differences. We have formed a group, called "Working group for mother tongue education", together with the Turks, Greeks, Assyrians, Yugoslavs and the Spanish-speaking groups. We will never again give up." (Honkala *et al.*, this volume p. 250).

Conclusions

Going back to Galtung's concepts, we can summarize the process.

The Finnish women (and some men) were in the beginning in a powerless position in the educational discourse with the Swedish school authorities. They used the autonomy approach to be heard, to make the discussion more equal. They *had* to do this because they lacked the resources for making the power relationship more equal through a balance approach. They had, through their own and their children's experience, and through lectures and meetings organized by the Finns themselves, become confident that their ideas about what was the best type of education for their children were right. Based on this, they set their own goal, which was to change the education. All this means that they showed *self-respect* according to Galtung's definition quoted earlier; they were not submissive.

When they were not able to persuade the authorities by ideological means (as opposed to remunerative or punitive), through argumentation, they decided to pursue their goal by other means, the only ones available to them, thereby rejecting the goals and means, the non-education offered to them by the Swedish school authorities; i.e. they showed *self-sufficiency*. They were not dependent on the school to take care of their children—they created the time resource needed by giving up their holidays. They were not dependent on the teaching given by the school—they taught the children themselves, with the help of friends. They were not dependent on the school to feed their children—they raised the money via donations to the strike fund and did the cooking themselves.

They persisted, despite the fact that they had both the powerful authorities[9] and most of the media against them, and despite severe personal threats, i.e. they showed *fearlessness*.

In that way they forced the negotiations, the educational discourse, to become negotiations between equals. They "grew to feel equal to their opponents", as they themselves put it. And this forced the opponents, little by little, to listen to their arguments:

> "In the beginning the media presented us as a pack of misinformed women, led by radical leftist fanatics. That did not work as time passed, and we forced them to see us as we were: cooking food for our children while arguing for a better future for them in Sweden. Often our awareness and arguments were met with lies and attempts were made to sidetrack us, because what we argued for rang a bell of truth even in the ears of our opponents." (p. 249).

Thus they did develop the power-over-themselves, the autonomy, needed for refusing to be power-receivers. This meant that the Swedish authorities' power-over-others did not reach them.

But is this enough? If the power of the powerful does not reach you, temporarily (in this case while the children were not at school), you are still living in its vicinity. Refusing to be a power-receiver does not in any way destroy the power, it is still there. And keeping out of reach of power in our interlocked world would mean an isolation from others which is impossible, except perhaps for small utopian primitive societies, and not even for them, after Chernobyl. Romantic escapism does not work, and is no solution to the world's problems.

If we go back to Galtung again, there is a way of seeing the autonomy arrived at through the struggle as a more permanent resource. The autonomy is from an actor-oriented perspective a *quality* in the actors, in the women in Rinkeby. But tested in a situation of conflict, this quality is converted into a *relational* concept. The knowledge which the women had gained put them in a different position structurally. They may be more capable of using a balance approach now, since they know that they can mobilize at least some resources *when needed*. Both they themselves and the Swedish authorities know now that they "will never again give up" (ibid.) when new conflicts about the education of their children arise. This has already been tested in a new conflict in February–April 1985, when they, together with others, forced the Swedish government to retreat.

One of the more concrete results of the strike was more and better Finnish-medium education. Through a Finnish-medium education, where their children can get both the analytical conceptual tools and the knowledge needed, in a language they understand, the women give their resources further to their children. The children need the tools to analyse the causes of the powerless situation of all labour migrants, and the role of education in reproducing the relations of the production they are engaged in. That may help the children so that they never become "the never-employed" but become instead fully employed, together with other migrants, in a resistance which works towards changing power relationships: against exploitation and for equity and justice.

Finally, we go back to the three functions of education (ideological, economic-reproductive and repressive). The Finnish-medium education makes the children well prepared for secondary and tertiary education (see Hagman & Lahdenperä, this volume, Chapter 15). They have conscious teachers who work together with the parents and are ideologically committed, partly as a result of the joint struggle. The children *want* to go to school, because they understand the instruction. The Finnish-medium classes may form one of those sites where the majority hegemony is temporarily defeated and where the functions of education can be changed (Apple, 1982a,b; Carnoy, 1982; Wexler, 1982). There may be something here to learn for working class majority members, as well, about how to be incorporated without being subjugated (Dale, 1982:156–57). The Finnish children may succeed in being institutionally incorporated in the Swedish school, without necessarily becoming ideologically incorporated. Thus they may be able to exploit even the discrimination which they encounter, by using it as a weapon when fighting ideological incorporation and racist/ linguistic hegemony.

Thus the strike could be analysed as a positive contribution to the "war of position" (Gramsci, 1971) which is going on in minority education. New educational contradictions keep arising in the Swedish migrant education system, necessitated by the demands for reproducing migrants as a crisis buffer in the base, and the assimilationist policy is constantly being contested. It is part of the continuing resistance of oppressed groups. The autonomy developed by the women carries with it a potential for later use and for spreading to other parent groups, and, through the educational model that was achieved, to children.

There is a vast literature analysing the need for counter-hegemony (see Apple, 1982a; Dale, 1982; Gitlin, 1982; Hogan, 1982 for references). But concrete accounts of how resistance and counter-hegemonies are built are more scarce.[10] Galtung's framework may be useful in trying to trace some of the steps needed when developing resources for the war of position even outside peace research, where Galtung originally developed it. But many more interdisciplinary questions need to be asked about the relationships between the state, the school, power and ideology, before we can even start to understand the dialectic between hegemony and counter-hegemonies in migrant minority education.

Notes to Chapter 11

1. This is a revised version of a paper presented at Colloquium Discourse Power, Utrecht University Summer School on Critical Theory, 9–15 June 1985; previously published in Phillipson, Robert and Skutnabb-Kangas, Tove (1986) *Linguicism Rules in Education*, Roskilde, Roskilde University Centre, Institute VI, 553–577. My thanks for inspiration and encouragement, parties and discussions, go to all the Finnish women in Rinkeby, especially Tuula Honkala, Pirkko Leporanta-

Morley, Lilja Liukka and Eija Rougle. Their continuous struggle for human rights for their children and their perseverance constantly give me and others new hope. Thanks to Robert Phillipson for inspiring discussions about the applicability of Galtung (which we used for a joint article about cultural imperialism and "international English", 1985), to Chris Mullard and Markku Peura for discussions on power and anti-racist strategies in education, and to Duane Campbell, Philomena Essed and Sonia Nieto for asking questions about continued resistance.

2. For references to different ways of conceptualizing power in a minority resistance context, see Mullard, 1985:212, footnote 4.

3. Obviously awareness of many other forms of exploitation and a constant fight against them does not make Galtung aware of sexism in language. I have changed his "he" to "she", letting woman embrace man, and I'm sure Galtung would not have anything against it.

4. The green and other environmental movements (the struggle in Alta, Norway, is the best Scandinavian example where minority and green concerns were joined), women's movement, peace movement, etc. have all used this approach.

5. "A submersion or sink-or-swim programme is a programme where linguistic minority children with a low-status mother tongue are forced to accept instruction through the medium of a foreign majority language with high status, in classes where some children are native speakers of the language of instruction, where the teacher does not understand the mother tongue of the minority children, and where the majority language constitutes a threat to their mother tongue—a subtractive language learning situation" (Skutnabb-Kangas, 1986b:24).

6. "A transitional programme is a programme where linguistic minority children with a low-status mother tongue are instructed through the medium of their mother tongue for a few years and where their mother tongue has no intrinsic value, only an instrumental value. It is used only in order for the children to learn the majority language better, and so as to give them some subject matter knowledge while they are learning the majority language. As soon as they can function in the majority language orally, they are transferred to a majority language medium programme. A transitional programme is a more sophisticated version of a submersion programme, a more 'humane' way of assimilating" (Skutnabb-Kangas, 1986b:24–25).

7. My description of the strike is based on several types of data. I have followed the community closely during the last ten years, since teaching Finnish preschool children there in connection with a Unesco project (partly reported in Toukomaa & Skutnabb-Kangas, 1977), and several of the participating women are my close friends. I was present at the meeting (November 1983) at which the strike committee was chosen, and I attended some of the later meetings during the strike as well. I have participated in numerous discussions about the situation, both before and during the strike, as well as after it, when different participants have discussed the strike. I also followed some of the teaching given by volunteers during the strike. For instance, one morning when I was asleep on a friend's sofa after long discussions the evening before, I was woken up by pupils from grade 4, who were to have their lessons that day in my friend's sitting room, after a change in the plans. I have read much of the documentation relevant to the strike: correspondence between the parents, the school authorities and politicians during several years, media reports about the strike, poems and other accounts written by the participants, etc. A fuller account in English of the strike is in Skutnabb-Kangas & Leporanta-Morley, 1986. Some of the general background for the situation that led to the strike is described in Skutnabb-Kangas, 1984. Since the autumn of 1985 I have taught a voluntary group of parents in Rinkeby, most of them active in the strike, about minority education research.

8. The answer, ironically, is yes. According to Finnish law, Swedish-speakers are not only entitled to have mother tongue instruction in Swedish, but in fact there has to be a Swedish-medium school in grades 1–9 in any municipality where there are 18 Swedish-speaking children, just as there has to be a Finnish-medium school in a municipality in Finland where the majority of the population is Swedish-speaking, if there are 18 Finnish-speaking children. In addition, an elementary school of this kind with minority children "cannot be closed before the number of language minority children falls under thirteen during three successive years" (Hoffman, 1976:4).

9. The authorities in fact used threats both of physical coercion and psychological, moral coercion. There were hints about the possibility that the children might be fetched by force, with police dogs, and taken to school. And in both discussions and documents the parents were accused of being irresponsible and harming the children by keeping them away from school.

10. See (e.g.) Mullard, 1985, which is an inspiring and superbly competent account of resistance, combining thorough empirical evidence with developing a theory of resistance.

References

ALTHUSSER, L. 1971, *Lenin and philosophy and other essays.* New York: Monthly Review Press.

APPLE, M. W. 1979, *Ideology and curriculum.* London: Routledge & Kegan Paul.

——1982a, Reproduction and contradiction in education: an introduction. In M. W. APPLE (ed.), 1982, pp. 1–31.

——1982b, Curricular form and the logic of technical control: building a possessive individual. In M. W. APPLE (ed.) 1982, pp. 247–74.

——1982c, *Education and power.* London: Routledge & Kegan Paul.

——(ed.) 1982, *Cultural and economic reproduction in education. Essays on class, ideology and the state.* London: Routledge & Kegan Paul.

ÅS, B. 1975, On female culture: an attempt to formulate a theory of women's solidarity and action. *Acta Sociologica, Journal of the Scandinavian Sociological Association* 18:2–3, 142–61.

AUVINEN, R. 1977, *Nainen miehen yhteiskunnassa. Historiallinen, teoreettinen ja empiirinen tutkimus naisen asemasta.* Helsinki: Sosiaalipoliittisen yhdistyksen tutkimuksia 25.

BOURDIEU, P. 1976, The school as a conservative force: scholastic and cultural inequalities. In R. DALE *et al.* (eds) 1976, pp. 110–17.

BOURDIEU, P. & PASSERON, J. C. 1977, *Reproduction in education, society and culture.* London: Sage.

CARNOY, M. 1982, Education, economy and the state. In M. W. APPLE (ed.) 1982, pp. 79–126.

CASTLES, S. 1980, The social time-bomb: education of an underclass in West Germany. *Race and Class* XXI, 4, 369–387.

DALE, R., ESLAND, G. & MACDONALD, M. (eds) 1976, *Schooling and capitalism. A sociological reader.* London: Routledge & Kegan Paul.

ESKOLA, I. & HAAVIO-MANNILA, E. 1975, The careers of professional women and men in Finland. *Acta Sociologica. Journal of the Scandinavian Sociological Association* 18:2–3, 174–201.

GALTUNG, J. 1980, *The true worlds. A transnational perspective.* New York: The Free Press.

GITLIN, T. 1982, Television's screens: hegemony in transition. In M. W. APPLE (ed.) 1982, pp. 202–46.

GRAMSCI, A. 1971, *Selections from the prison notebooks*. New York: International Publishers.

HABERMAS, J. 1971, *Knowledge and human interest*. Boston: Beacon Press.

HOFFMAN, L. 1976, School in a bilingual society. In R. LAUKKANEN (ed.), pp. 1–5.

HOGAN, D. 1982, Education and class formation: the peculiarities of the Americans. In M. W. APPLE (ed.) 1982, pp. 32–78.

HOLTER, H., VE HENRIKSEN, H., GJERTSEN, A. & HJORT, H. 1975, *Familien i klassesamfunnet*. Oslo: Pax Forlag.

LAUKKANEN, R. (ed.) 1976, *The position of Swedish-speaking children in the Finnish school system*. Helsinki: National Board of Education, Research and Development Bureau, Information Bulletin 1.

MULLARD, C. 1985, *Race, power and resistance*. London: Routledge & Kegan Paul.

PAULSTON, C. B. 1985, Ethnic and National Mobilization: Linguistic Outcomes. Revue de l'AILA/AILA Review 2, 1985, 49–68.

PHILLIPSON, R. & SKUTNABB-KANGAS, T. 1985, Applied linguists as agents of wider colonisation: The gospel of international English. In J. PLEINES (hrsg) 1985, pp. 159–79.

——1986, *Linguicism rules in education*, 3 volumes. Roskilde: Roskilde University Centre, Institute VI.

PLEINES, J. (hrsg) 1985, *Sprachenkonkurrenz und gesellschaftliche Planung, Das Erbe des Kolonialismus*. Osnabrücker Beiträge zur Sprachtheorie 31.

SIVANANDAN, A. 1982, *A different hunger. Writings on Black resistance*. London: Pluto Press.

SKOLÖVERSTYRELSEN 1985, Timplaneförslag för hemspråksklasser och sammansatta klasser. 1985-03-14.

SKUTNABB-KANGAS, T. 1984, *Bilingualism or not: the education of minorities*. Clevedon: Multilingual Matters.

——1986a, Are the Finns in Sweden an Ethnic Minority—Finnish Parents Talk About Finland and Sweden. In R. PHILLIPSON & T. SKUTNABB-KANGAS (1986) pp. 466–552.

——1986b, Multilingualism and the Education of Minority Children. In R. PHILLIPSON & T. SKUTNABB-KANGAS (1986) pp. 42–72.

SKUTNABB-KANGAS, T. & LEPORANTA-MORLEY, P., 1986, Migrant women and education. In R. PHILLIPSON & T. SKUTNABB-KANGAS (1986) pp. 73–102.

STÖREN, T. & SCHOU WETLESEN, T. 1976, *Kvinnekunnskap*. Oslo: Gyldendal Norsk Forlag.

TOUKOMAA, P. & SKUTNABB-KANGAS, T. 1977, *The intensive teaching of the mother tongue to migrant children at pre-school age.* University of Tampere, Dept of Sociology and Social Psychology, Research Reports no 26.

WEXLER, P. 1982, Structure, text and subject: a critical sociology of school knowledge. In M. W. APPLE (ed.), 1982, pp. 275–303.

WILLIS, P. 1977, *Learning to labour: How working class kids get working class jobs.* Lexington, MA: D. C. Heath.

12 Parents, schools and racism

Bilingual education in a Northern California town

JAN CURTIS[1]

The role of parent involvement in educational programme planning and implementation carries with it a tremendous responsibility to become and to remain well-informed regarding the legislative regulations which bind the school district, the attitudes and positions of local policy makers, and the political activities of opposing community groups. With this information, a parent advisory committee is in a good position to have impact on the planning and development of school programmes in their district. Without this information, no parent group can hope to have any meaningful influence on the instructional programmes in which their children are enrolled.

Even the enactment of legal mandates at the federal or state level provides no guarantee that equal educational opportunity will be available to the children of minority language groups. The power of local policy makers to misinterpret, circumvent and blatantly disregard both the letter and the intent of the law challenges the proponents of change to an ongoing struggle which must continually be reassessed and renewed. The worst enemy of parent groups which oppose racism and bigotry in their children's schools is the complacency which often accompanies political victory. After a difficult fight, success can have a sedative effect. "Resting on one's laurels", however, can be self-defeating in the long run.

A chronicle of the struggle undertaken in one small school district in Northern California provides an example of the way in which the forces of racism can frustrate the efforts of parents and teachers who work together to establish an educational programme which addresses the needs of minority language students. The history of bilingual education in this community can be divided into four phases, each of which is characterized by a major shift in the power relationship between the school administration and the minority community. After a brief demographic description of the community, the major events of each of the four phases will be presented in terms of the actions and reactions of the various groups. Finally, a discussion of the chain of events will examine the necessity to design curriculum in response to the community's educational goals for their children, not just in compliance with legislative mandate.

Calistoga, California, is a rural community with a population of approximately 3,500 in which the major sources of employment are the wine and tourist industries. The dramatic increase in domestic wine production in the mid- to late 1970s, and the need for agricultural workers to tend the vineyards, resulted in an influx of Mexican and Mexican-American immigrants to the area, and a consequent rise in the enrolment of limited-English proficient (LEP) and non-English proficient (NEP) students in the community's schools.

In the academic year 1977–78, the proportion of LEP/NEP students in the Calistoga schools had risen to about 20% (142 students out of the total school population of 735). The percentage was much higher (36%) at the primary level, since many of the immigrant families were young couples with small children.

Phase I: Confrontation

During the spring of 1978, a small group of elementary school teachers, faced with their responsibility to teach children with whom they could not converse and armed with their knowledge of the legal mandates of California State Law,[2] proposed certain changes in the school programme, specifically the implementation of bilingual instruction at the primary level. In addition, these teachers ordered materials for initial reading instruction in Spanish as a part of the regular textbook and instructional supplies requisition process.

The administration and Board of Trustees postponed their response to the teachers' proposal until after school had adjourned for the summer, thereby inhibiting teacher–parent communication and the dissemination of information to community members regarding the progress of the discussion.

During the summer of 1978, the School Superintendent proposed two programme options to the School Board. The first would provide for a programme of bilingual instruction; the second consisted of a programme in which the LEP/NEP students would be pulled out of the regular classroom for twenty minutes each day for English as a Second Language (ESL) lessons. Under this option, all basic skills instruction would be presented in English. In support of the bilingual programme option, members of the elementary school teaching staff made a formal presentation to the board regarding the theoretical basis for bilingual instruction and the description of various bilingual programme models.

Upon the Superintendent's recommendation, the School Board voted to implement the pull-out ESL programme option, and formally adopted a policy in which teachers were forbidden to use Spanish in the classroom. It was made clear to the staff at Calistoga Elementary School by the Superintendent of Schools that the use of the Spanish language by classroom teachers would not be tolerated. When the teachers returned to school in the autumn, they found that their orders for reading materials in Spanish had been cancelled.

During the autumn of 1978, the first official parental request for bilingual instruction for their children was submitted. Encouraged by teachers who met them individually and in small groups at their homes, Mexican and Mexican-American parents began to attend meetings of the District Parent Advisory Committee (a body which was required by State and federal law) and to voice their concerns over the education of their children. Requests by parents and teachers to discuss the issue of bilingual instruction at these meetings were denied. Parents were told that their questions were "out of order" and that the meetings were not the appropriate forum in which to bring up such matters.

In spite of the Board's directives, individual classroom teachers took steps to increase their own proficiency in the Spanish language and began to provide reading instruction in Spanish to the LEP/NEP students, making use of whatever materials they could find. In December 1978, the Superintendent sent a memo to the staff in which he reminded them of the Board policy forbidding Spanish in the classroom. Attached to this memo was a copy of a speech by Senator Hayakawa in which he upheld the supremacy of the English language and warned against the potential dangers of minority language instruction.

At this point, the teachers and parents moved their meetings off the school campus and enlisted the aid of California Rural Legal Assistance (CRLA) lawyers. On the advice of this agency, the parents gave their committee a name, *Los Padres para Mejorar Educación Bilingue* (Parents for the Improvement of Bilingual Education) and elected a chairperson.

Subsequently, this same person was elected to chair the official Parent Advisory Committee (PAC) at the School.

For the next three months, *Los Padres* gathered evidence in support of their claim that the district was engaged in discriminatory educational practices. Beyond the obvious failure to provide bilingual instruction in accordance with the state law, evidence against the district included a history of discriminatory hiring practices. Out of 17 teachers at the elementary school, 14 had been hired in the last two years. Of these 14, not one had any proficiency in the Spanish language nor any training in bilingual-bicultural education at the time they were hired. Other data compiled addressed the issue of academic failure at the secondary level among the Mexican-American students. Of the non-Hispanic student total of 264, some 132 (or 50%) received "cinch notices" in November 1978. These notices warn parents of the likelihood that their child will fail one or more classes unless performance improves by the end of the term. By comparison, 82% of the Hispanic students received these notices.

On 30th March 1979, *Los Padres para Mejorar Educación Bilingue* filed a formal complaint with the Office for Civil Rights (OCR) of the U.S. Department of Health, Education and Welfare, charging Calistoga Joint Unified School District with discriminatory practices in violation of their children's rights to equal educational opportunity under the law.

Coincidentally, during the month of March, 1979, a California State Program Monitor and Review (MAR) team visited Calistoga Elementary School. The MAR process was a regular part of the state procedures for ensuring that schools receiving categorical funds were providing programmes in compliance with the law. Generally, the schools targeted for review were randomly selected, but the rumour of questionable compliance could bump a district forward on the list. When the review team arrived, it became apparent that none of the three members spoke Spanish, although one of the primary duties of the team was to interview parents of children enrolled in the programme. Since many of the parents did not speak English, an additional member was recruited at the formal request of the teaching staff.

The MAR team found the district out of compliance, especially with regard to the instruction of LEP/NEP students. The school was given 30 days to institute changes which would bring the programme into compliance with the specifications of AB 1329.

For the next few months of school, and through the summer of 1979, it became clear to the teachers and parents that even the State Department of

Education either did not have or would not use their power to enforce compliance with State law. The 30-day compliance deadline came and went with no response from the school district. New deadlines were set. The administration asked the State for technical assistance. The Superintendent asked OCR to postpone action on *Los Padres'* complaint until after resolution of the compliance issue, first expressing an intention to negotiate with the parent group for an acceptable programme, later changing his mind and informing OCR of his intention to deny the charges of discrimination and fight the parent group.

In addition, the Superintendent placed negative comments in the personnel files of certain non-tenured teachers (those who had been active with the *Los Padres* movement), potentially threatening the renewal of their employment contracts. As a direct result of intervention by CRLA lawyers on the teachers' behalf, the Office of Civil Rights notified the district that retaliatory action against these teachers would not be tolerated.

CRLA lawyers submitted a request on behalf of *Los Padres* that the parents be allowed to participate in programme planning for 1979–80. In response, the administration invited parents to meetings planned for September, 1979. In the meantime, the plan was written, without parent input, given to the PAC chairperson for her signature and submitted to the State. The following letter was subsequently written to the State Department of Education by the PAC chair:

"September 2, 1979

Dear Sirs,

I, Ramona Canchola, was the chairperson of the bilingual committee at Calistoga Elementary School. I am writing because I am concerned about the Consolidated School Plan that I signed for the school. I really did not know or understand what was in all the forms I signed.

First of all, we the committee were not involved in making the plan, or consulted in this matter at all. The first time I saw this plan at all was when it was mailed to me to be signed.

Also, when our committee met for meetings frequently parents asked if the school was going to have bilingual education, the principal would say they were out of order and that these meetings were not for that purpose. Pretty soon many parents would not even attend meetings because of the fact that when they wanted to discuss Bilingual Ed. the principal would just embarrass them by telling them they were out of order.

I know I signed a lot of forms and documents. The reason I signed these documents without knowing what they were was:

1. I was told by [the principal] that I *had* to sign them because I was Chairperson, I was pressured by [him] into signing them.

2. I signed because I felt if I didn't sign, nothing at all would be done for the children.

I understand that the school has come up with minutes of the meetings we had. There never were any minutes taken at any of the meetings, there was no one at the meeting assigned to take minutes. No one ever read any minutes to us for approval. In fact, this is the first time I have heard of any minutes being taken.

The reason why I am writing this letter is to let you know that if the school is saying that we were allowed to participate in the planning of the Bilingual Program, it's not true.

I apologize if I caused any confusion by signing the forms, letters.

Again, the only reason I signed was because we the committee felt that if we did what he wanted he would try to do a little bit for the children.

Now I understand that this is not true and I don't want you to think that we had anything to do with what the school is saying.

Thank you for your attention,

Sincerely yours,

Ramona Canchola"

The first phase in *Los Padres'* struggle came to a close in the autumn of 1979 with the resignation of the Superintendent of Schools, and the termination of the Elementary School Principal's contract. This was the parents' first major victory. The interesting thing about the accomplishments of the initial phase of the struggle is that none of the significant gains made in terms of programme change occurred as a direct result of action taken by either of the government agencies whose assistance was enlisted by the parents and whose responsibility it was to enforce compliance with the law. The State Department of Education has the power to withhold funds from school districts who fail to comply with programme requirements. In fact, the withholding of funds was never even threatened. The Office continued for months to extend deadlines, offer "technical assistance" and advise the administration on the design of a programme which would *minimally* meet legal requirements, and which was in no way based upon consideration of sound educational practice.

The power relationships before and during this first phase of the struggle can be characterized as a sort of "benevolent patriarchy". The Superintendent of Schools enjoyed almost omnipotent control over policy and decision-making in the district, the Board of Trustees approving virtually every recommendation he made. Officers of the Parent Advisory Committees in the district were easily charmed and intimidated into doing what they were told. When the wisdom of his advice began to be questioned, first by the teachers and parents, and subsequently by Board members themselves, his only face-saving alternative was to resign. However, as will be seen below in the account of the events which were to follow, it is far easier to defeat an individual racist than it is to achieve a lasting victory over racism.

Phase II: vitality

With the appointment of a new Superintendent-Principal, the apparently sincere invitation for parent participation in programme planning and the election of four new members to the School Board, Phase II began. The OCR investigation of the district was terminated.

In the school years from 1979 to 1981, the programme consisted of bilingual classrooms at the kindergarten and first grade levels only. No extra funding was available for specialist personnel during those years. District funds were being used to purchase textbooks and teaching materials in Spanish. There were no credentialled bilingual teachers on the staff at that time, nor were any classroom teachers proficient in Spanish. However, several teachers were enrolled in professional development programmes for the purpose of obtaining their bilingual credentials. The effort was being made to work with the parents to develop as good a bilingual programme as was possible with the limited funds available at that time. The new Superintendent hired by the district was quoted as saying, at the initial faculty meeting of the 1980–81 school year, "I personally hope that Calistoga's bilingual programme will become a model for small school districts in California".

In the autumn of 1980, the district used special programme implementation funding from the State to employ a Bilingual Co-ordinator. In addition to being a very skilful administrator, the Co-ordinator was Mexican-American. Under her guidance, a District Bilingual Parent

Advisory Council was formed. The committee included parents from both the Mexican-American and Anglo-American communities, teachers and other community members. The group met monthly from November until February, 1981. This body had direct responsibility for writing the original application for Federal funding of Calistoga's bilingual education programme.

In the spring of 1981, the application was submitted to the Office of Bilingual Education and Minority Language Affairs (OBEMLA) for Title VII funding of the bilingual programme in Calistoga. A three-year grant was awarded, and the programme thus funded became a model for neighbouring school districts, acclaimed throughout Northern California.

From 1981 to 1984, the bilingual programme enjoyed tremendous growth and vitality. Federal funds made possible the continued employment of the Project Co-ordinator, instructional aides for all the bilingual classes, a resource teacher to work with LEP/NEP students at grade levels where no bilingual class was available and a bilingual secretary/community liaison. Funds were also available for the purchase of materials and for staff development. During the first year of funding, the programme provided bilingual classes at grades kindergarten through to third grade. Each year the project expanded by one grade level, so that by 1983–84, there were bilingual classes at grades K–5.

As early as 1982, however, an undercurrent of anti-bilingual sentiment and opposition to the expansion of the programme became evident. Because the school district was so small, each grade level generally offered one bilingual and one monolingual English classroom. On the one hand, there were plenty of parents from the Anglo-American community who saw the benefit of bilingual instruction for their children to satisfy the legal requirement for bilingual class composition.[3] On the other hand, there was a core of Anglo-American parents whose children were in the monolingual English classrooms who were strongly opposed to the programme. Their objections were expressed in terms of their belief (shared by members of the monolingual staff) that native English-speakers would suffer academically as a result of their bilingual class placement.

In response to the opposition, the bilingual staff launched a community education/public relations campaign. This included radio talk show interviews, newspaper articles, a public forum, and the publication of a pamphlet entitled *Why Bilingual Education? Juntos Mejoramos—Together We Improve* (Appendix). This was written and edited by a team of parents and teachers, specifically in order to avoid the use of academic jargon, and was published in English and Spanish.

Unfortunately, the campaign to enhance the image of the bilingual programme created more problems than it solved. Data were gathered regarding the achievement-test performance of the native English-speaking students. These data demonstrated that there were no significant differences in academic performance between students from the two programmes. In fact, a slight advantage was observed in favour of bilingual class placement in the English-speakers' language scores. Publication of these findings angered the teachers of the monolingual classrooms as well as the parents of their students.

Both the school staff and the community at large were seriously polarized on the issue of bilingual education. The newly elected members of the School Board, who had originally supported the programme, became less enthusiastic. The new Superintendent-Principal, whose double role required that he delegate a great deal of administrative authority to the Project Co-ordinator, withdrew all public support for the programme. In fact, he was unique in the community for his failure to take a personal stand on either side of the controversy.

The second phase of the struggle was a period in which the bilingual programme flourished. The Parent Advisory Committee was a powerful and effective body which exercised legitimate advisory control over programme planning and expansion. The committee was composed of Mexican and Anglo-American parents who worked well together to implement an instructional programme for the benefit of all their children. Because the Mexican community was usually better represented on the committee, meetings were conducted in Spanish. Translation was provided for the English-speaking parents when necessary, but most had sufficient proficiency in Spanish to understand what was being discussed.

The presence on the administrative staff of a member of the ethnic minority group, who was both a competent administrator and an advocate of the programme goals, altered the school–community power relationships in an important way. Decision-making in the schools was for this brief period truly collaborative, in that the parent group had a major impact on programme design and implementation.

Phase III: Backlash

The transition from the second to the third phase of the struggle in Calistoga cannot be pinpointed as coincident with any single event, although several incidents can be cited which contributed to the demise of the programme. The anti-bilingual feelings discussed above smouldered between the years 1982 and 1984, but without any specific target. It was generally felt among the opposition that the bilingual programme was "getting too big", but whether that meant that there were too many classrooms or that the proponents of the programme enjoyed too much power was never made explicit.

In the spring of 1982, it became apparent that the kindergarten enrolment for the following September would include almost 50% LEP students.[3] Legal mandates regulating the implementation of bilingual programmes in the State of California governed the action taken by the district in this matter.[4] In compliance with these regulations, the district was forced to divide the kindergarten enrolment for that one year into three bilingual classes. In previous and subsequent years, the proportion of LEP students allowed for two bilingual classrooms and one monolingual English classroom. Similarly, in the other grade levels where a bilingual classroom was required, it had always been possible to have one non-bilingual class as well.

At a meeting held in the spring of 1982, it was explained to the parents of incoming kindergarteners that they had the choice of withdrawing their child from the bilingual programme, and of specifying that he or she receive an English-only instructional programme, even though there would be no non-bilingual classroom available. Apparently, some of the parents never clearly understood the distinction between bilingual programme and bilingual classroom. (It is acknowledged that the distinction was hazy at best.) Accordingly, their dissatisfaction with the alternatives added fuel to the anti-bilingual fire.

In December of 1983, the question of application for the continuation of Federal funding for bilingual programmes in Calistoga schools was first raised at a regularly scheduled board meeting. The item was tabled until the following month, because the board felt they did not have sufficient information on which to base their authorization to begin the project writing process.

During that month, individual meetings were held between the Project Co-ordinator and members of the board to discuss the project proposal. The Co-ordinator was advised that if the "cultural component" was reduced to the minimum level legally required, the application would have a "good chance of flying". On 4th January 1984, the school board voted unanimously to approve the writing of two proposals, one for continued funding at the elementary school and one for a new programme at the high school. The Bilingual PAC was instrumental in the writing process, and submitted the proposal to the school board two weeks later.

A public hearing was held on 18th January, on the issue of bilingual education. The bilingual staff made a presentation, and input was received from community members. Statements were made both in favour of and opposed to the application for funding, though by all reports the overwhelming majority of public comment heard that night was in support of the re-application. No vote was taken at the time. Board action on the Title VII proposals was scheduled for 1st February, but postponed. In the meantime, a petition signed by more than 300 community members was submitted to the board which asked that they vote "no" on the application for funding. The board scheduled a special meeting the following week to decide the matter.

On 8th February 1984, with a three-to-one vote, the board acted to "scratch" the elementary school proposal for continued Title VII funding of the bilingual programme at the elementary school. Two of the three trustees who voted against the application, the Board President and one other, had been members of the board since the programme's inception in 1979. The board also decided by a three-to-one vote to submit the application for funding at the high school, but only for one year. As fate would have it, the board's action (taken just two days before the application was due in Washington) left insufficient time for the staff to edit a good one-year proposal out of the three-year plan which had been submitted for board approval. For this reason, the district was not awarded federal funds for programmes at either school site.

Analysis of the political processes underlying this decision uncovered an incredible amount of misinformation, misunderstanding and inaccurate perception of the legal realities on the part of everyone involved in the controversy.

The members of the board seemed in large part to be unaware of the role of the Bilingual Parent Advisory Committee in the process of writing and submitting the plan. They also gave no evidence of understanding their own power in designing and approving the "District Commitment and Capacity" section of the Title VII proposal.

The bilingual staff felt that they had been "duped" by the board. They said that they had been led to believe throughout the process that their answers to the concerns raised by the board had been satisfactory and that the proposal would be approved.

The non-bilingual staff were not aware of the potential for reception of their input during the writing process, nor did they seem to understand that different programme administration options had been requested by the board and provided by the project writing staff. They also seemed to feel some threat to their job security, as if they would be required to obtain their bilingual credentials or lose their jobs.

The parents who were opposed to the application had very limited understanding of the differences between the regulations specified by Title VII and the requirements of California State law which would continue to bind district policy on bilingual education even in the absence of federal funding.

The parents in favour of the application, even the members of the Bilingual Parent Advisory Committee, had similar misconceptions about the differences between federal and State regulations. They were also unaware of their own power regarding the State requirement for the chairperson of their committee to sign the school plan for the implementation of all categorically funded programmes in the school, even in the absence of federal funds. If the PAC refused to sign the school plan, the State Department of Education would automatically send in a team to find out why. Funding of all special programmes could be held up indefinitely until a resolution satisfactory to all parties was reached.

Subsequent interviews with members of the various factions failed to uncover any understanding of the reasoning behind the board's decision. Vague reference was made to the "strings attached" to the receipt of federal funds, but no coherent description of these strings was ever offered. Although individual board members denied having been swayed by the petition, it is interesting to note that a petition submitted two weeks after the public hearing apparently had more influence on the policy makers' decision than the comments made at the public hearing itself. At subsequent meetings, the School Board expressed an interest in "healing the wounds" suffered during the controversy, and agreed to district funding of a bilingual resource teacher and community liaison for the 1984–85 school year.

The most important difference between the federally-funded and district-funded programmes was the position of Project Co-ordinator. In the absence of extra funding, the position ceased to exist. This was seen by some as the key towards an explanation of the board's action.

The members of the Bilingual PAC felt personally and collectively discouraged and disenfranchised. The following quotation from the PAC Chairperson at that time reflects the sense of futility generally shared by the Committee members and the Bilingual staff during that period:

"What exactly is needed from the parents? More signatures? The reason the Mexican parents don't come to the meetings is for other reasons than just that they're tired from their work. Simply because the Mexican feels that, 'Why do they have to have so many meetings, so long? They know very well what we will accept, what we want. Why do we have to go to another meeting to say the same thing again if it's the same? Each time, it's the same.' Then they get discouraged. Some always come, but others, no. That's what happens. Then they want to know, so they ask various people, 'What happened? What's going to happen?' And what can I say to them? 'Nothing.' It's for this reason I ask what are the results going to be? What is needed for them to contribute? Because, like I told you, if we're just going to do something the same again, they're not going to come. I know the Mexican people well. I know their feelings. They are very proud, even though poor. But also they will give everything they can, even though they have nothing." (Quotation translated from the original Spanish by the author)

Phase IV: reconstruction

In the years 1984 to 1986, a legally acceptable bilingual programme was provided at the elementary school in Calistoga. By contrast, the high school was reviewed annually by the State and repeatedly found to be out of compliance with legal requirements. However, no action was ever taken by the State to enforce programme changes at the secondary level.

After they had voted to abandon the application for federal monies, the Calistoga School Board expressed the intention to support the bilingual programme with district funds. They also promised to recruit bilingual teachers should any vacancies occur in the staff. (In spite of this promise, out of five teachers hired between 1983 and 1986, only two were somewhat proficient in the Spanish language and none held a bilingual credential.) Bilingual classrooms were provided at each grade level in which they were warranted by the numbers of LEP students. Only one of these classes was taught by a credentialled bilingual teacher.

The real impact of the board's action was the annihilation of the Bilingual PAC. The invitation to parents to be partners in the decision-making process, which had been extended by the Bilingual Project Co-ordinator and staff in all sincerity, but never explicitly sanctioned by the Board of Trustees, had clearly been rescinded. Parent involvement during the following two years was virtually non-existent. Attendance at meetings was poor. The election of officers deteriorated into an effort on the part of the bilingual staff to recruit volunteers to serve. While the situation did not return to "pre-*Los Padres*" levels of parent manipulation, all the fight had gone out of the parents. The district had dealt them a devastating blow. In Spanish, they would say they were *desanimado*.

Conclusion

At the heart of the bilingual education controversies in Calistoga was not so much the issue of whether the school district's legal obligations were being met. Calistoga has, since 1979, been fairly responsive to legal compliance issues. More fundamental was the lack of genuine commitment on the part of the school as an institution representing the dominant values of the community to effectively promote educational success for minority students. In addition, lack of effective communication among the various parties involved and lack of continued vigilance among parents and teachers advocating the educational rights of minority students contributed to the variations in the quality of the educational programme that children were offered.

Interviews conducted by the author revealed that communication was minimally successful among and between parents and teachers on different sides of the issues at the time of the board's rejection of federal funds for bilingual education. Even more important was the fact that no one from any of the various factions felt that they were communicating successfully with the members of the school board. It is remarkable that not one of the many people interviewed by the author understood why the board members had made the decision that they had. Nor would the elected officials provide satisfactory answers to questions about their reasoning when asked.

As suggested in the introduction to this chapter, it is of critical importance that parents who choose to be involved in Parent Advisory Committees and other groups concerned with the educational programmes in their school district be informed not only about the legal realities but also about the attitudes and activities of the local policy makers. Furthermore, it is essential that the trustees of the local School Board continually be made aware of the parents' position on various issues and that parents are aware of their rights and of their power to impact policy.

The parents in Calistoga worked very hard for more than three years towards the establishment of a good bilingual programme at the elementary school. However, they then appear to have assumed, erroneously, that the battle was over. The point is that with an issue as controversial as bilingual education, maintenance and continued development of a good programme requires a long-term commitment. Parents must understand that they are needed at meetings, even if nothing new is going to happen, even if they are only saying the same things they have said before. Given the prevalence of racist values in the wider society which elects school board members, it is essential for parents and anti-racist groups (e.g. some teachers) to assert their commitment to anti-racist education for their children.

Two of the five trustees in Calistoga were appointed by the board within the year before the action to abandon the Title VII plan. This occurred because other board members resigned and no one filed for candidacy. Had the proponents of bilingual education in Calistoga been committed to affecting the programme from a policy level, they would have made certain that someone applied for the appointment who shared their position. They did not.

Epilogue

At the time of this writing, a new Bilingual PAC in Calistoga has begun to make itself heard regarding the implementation of the District Master Plan for Bilingual Education. This document was written by the bilingual staff in the spring of 1985 in accordance with State law (although virtually without parent input) and was approved by the School Board. For some members of the PAC, sufficient time has passed to heal the old wounds. Other members are new. It is a good group, a strong and optimistic group. The task they have undertaken is to rewrite the plan, and then to compare what is said with what is actually done. If discrepancies are found between the two, then either the plan will be changed or the programme will.

Their challenge, the new challenge, is defined by the sunset of the California State bilingual education laws. On 30th June 1987, the provisions of AB507 (which replaced AB1329) ceased to bind school districts around the state, since new legislation on these issues was not passed. And then the proponents of bilingual education in Calistoga are where they really always have been: charged with the responsibility to implement a particular programme because it is best for children, not because it is required by law.

Appendix to Chapter 12

[Editors' note: the authors of this pamphlet permit it to be copied, providing that its source is quoted. They hope that it will inspire others.]

Why Bilingual Education? Juntos Mejoramos—Together We Improve

Answers to the most frequently asked questions about Bilingual Education

1. Why do we need to teach children in the native language if we are trying to teach them English?

Children are taught in the native language so that they will not fall behind academically. The firm academic base which native language instruction provides is important in transferring skills to English. Once a student knows how to read in Spanish he does not have to relearn the reading process for English. If these literacy skills are well developed in the native language first, success in English academics is certain. Studies in Calistoga and elsewhere confirm that bilingual programmes have been more successful in developing English academic skills than programmes in which English only was used. By teaching in the native language, bilingual education programmes also help affirm the importance of the child's cultural identity and sense of community.

Negative feelings coming from the majority culture or negative feelings that children may have about themselves can hinder the student's growth in the second language as well as in academics. Teaching children in the native language makes use of the experience they bring with them. Integrating the children's background with classroom experiences will result in added benefits and will reduce the probability of high early drop-out rates among language minority students. Bilingual education is a positive means by which language minority children can gain access to higher education and professional development.

2. Does a bilingual classroom hurt my child's growth in English?

The Comprehensive Test of Basic Skills (CBTS) is the standardized achievement test given to all children at Calistoga Elementary School each May. The results of these tests demonstrate that native English-speaking students in the bilingual classrooms consistently have made good progress in language and reading. Overall, they have scored at or above grade level as compared with national norms for their grade. While many other reasons could be given for the children's success, the data clearly disprove the assumption that harm is done to their growth in English.

3. Does the teacher say everything twice in a bilingual classroom? How is there enough time for all the subject areas, if the teacher uses both languages?

No, the teacher does not say everything twice in a bilingual classroom.

Experience has taught us that the method of bilingual instruction in which everything is said twice is the least effective in promoting second language growth. Whereas "the basics" (e.g. reading and maths) are generally taught in small groups in the children's native language, all other subjects (such as science, art and social studies) are taught in either English or Spanish according to an alternate day system. Concepts introduced one day in one language are reinforced the next day in the other language. Lessons on both days make use of manipulatives, body language and peer-partners to help make the point for students whose second language is being spoken. In this way, no subject areas are skipped and second language development is facilitated for all students.

4. Will my child receive reading instruction in the second language?

All children first receive instruction in the basic skills of reading, writing and mathematics in their native language. At the same time, children receive systematic instruction in the second language to acquire oral comprehension skills. When children are reading and writing with ease in their primary language and demonstrate receptive and oral proficiency in the second language, reading in the second language is introduced. Students participate in active language-generating experiences which are recorded on charts. After many such stories, children make the transition to reading texts and library books in the second language.

5. How does my child get placed in a bilingual classroom?

If your child has been identified as limited English proficient (LEP), the school will recommend placement in a bilingual classroom so that instruction may be provided in the language best understood, and so that an appropriate second language programme can be offered. If your child is a native English speaker and you are interested in having your child introduced to a second language, you may request placement in a bilingual programme.

State law requires that schools do not practice segregation in a bilingual programme. Therefore, a school must ensure an ethnically balanced classroom. We must make every effort to have an appropriate balance of children from each of the language groups. Children serve as models for each other's second language development.

Placement in a bilingual classroom requires parent notification. If a parent prefers that his child not participate in a bilingual programme, he may request alternative placement.

6. What will my child gain by being in a bilingual classroom?

The best years for learning a second language are the elementary grades. Children are able to internalize sounds and patterns, retain words, grammatical structures and concepts and to develop a flawless accent, when learned in the company of native speakers of that language.

Understanding another language and culture is an enriching experience which will have a positive influence on the study of language and culture at the secondary and college level. Knowing another language, or several languages, will be an increasingly valuable skill in the future. Most European students master several languages while in school. We now have the unique opportunity to encourage similar language flexibility.

7. What does bilingual education have to offer a gifted and talented student?

Teachers in Calistoga are committed to experiences and teaching strategies which challenge the gifted and talented youngsters. We are increasing the kinds of open-ended activities that encourage children to use their creativity, explore their potentials, and participate in lessons which enrich the basic educational programme. In addition, gifted and talented students in the bilingual programme will have the opportunity to study and explore the elements of culture (such as the literature, arts, music, history, community affairs, and world problems) through the use of a second language. Thus, a student can develop the sensitivity and awareness necessary to understand people and their similarities and differences.

8. Grandpa did not have bilingual education and he made it. Why do we need bilingual education?

In Grandpa's day, a great number of states including Florida, New York, Louisiana, New Mexico, Wisconsin, Pennsylvania and California *did* offer bilingual education in many languages. However, in cases where bilingual education was not provided, many grandpas were unable to complete their schooling because they didn't understand concepts being presented in a strange new language. Nevertheless, Grandpa could get work, earn money, and support a family without a high school diploma.

Today, people need at least a high school education even to be considered for employment. Bilingual education provides greater access to meaningful employment since students develop understanding and literacy in two languages. In addition, the bilingual person can utilize his/her second language in any career.

9. Is my tax dollar paying for the education of children who are not citizens or legal residents?

The majority of Spanish-speaking residents of Calistoga are locally employed. Therefore, they too are taxpayers regardless of resident or citizenship status. Their tax dollars are contributing to the cost of public education. These parents are seeking a better future for their children through education. Any student who receives an appropriate education has a better chance of completing school and of being better prepared for a job in the future. Skilled and employable persons will be less likely to need social and government assistance than those who are uneducated. Today's bilingual education programmes will be less costly to all taxpayers in the long run.

Bilingual education serves all U.S. citizens. Any person who wishes to learn a second language has that opportunity through a bilingual programme. Bilingual people in today's job market are twice as employable. This basic education is applicable to any profession a student chooses.

10. Does bilingualism lead to separatism?

No, bilingualism leads to integration. Bilingualism is an important ingredient in an environment where cultures can mix successfully. A primary emphasis in the bilingual classroom is the development of second language skills whether English or Spanish. Our goal is to facilitate communication through which relevant interaction and understanding between children from two cultures can take place. California lifestyle reflects the influence of the Hispanic and many other cultural groups. We have much to offer each other.

There are many countries which have more than one official language. Examples are Finland, Switzerland and Canada. The situation in Quebec is often cited as an example of conflict over language use. To the contrary, the acceptance of official bilingualism in Canada has actually provided a workable alternative to separatism.

11. What is California Law regarding Bilingual Education?

The Bilingual Education Improvement and Reform act requires school districts to provide appropriate educational programmes to language minority students. Assembly Bill 507 includes provisions to identify the primary language of all students, and conduct assessments to determine English proficiency and basic skills proficiency in order to determine language of instruction. When 10 or more LEP students with the same primary language are at the same grade level, a bilingual programme classroom must be provided. When there are less than 10 LEP students at a grade level of the same primary language, a Bilingual Individual Learning Programme must be provided for each child. Yearly academic achievement must be assessed. Standards for reclassification to fluent English proficient must be adopted. Parents must be notified of all assessment results and placement of their children. A Bilingual District Advisory Committee must be established.

12. Why does Calistoga offer bilingual education?

California State law requires bilingual education at the elementary level. Twenty-five percent of the student population at Calistoga is limited English proficient. More than thirty percent of the student population is Hispanic. It is logical, therefore, to offer a programme to all students which would give them an opportunity to learn a second language (Spanish) or to receive basic skills instruction in Spanish while learning English. Calistoga Elementary has made a commitment to ensure appropriate educational opportunities for all our students. We recognize that each child is unique and has special needs. We want to provide the best educationally sound programme possible for everyone.

Notes to Chapter 12

1. The author was a teacher in the school district during the period described and was active in working with parents to pressure the district to comply with legal requirements regarding the education of minority students.

2. California State Assembly Bill 1329, otherwise known as the Bilingual Education Act of 1976, specified programme requirements of school districts which serve language minority students. Of relevance was the requirement that a bilingual programme, including primary language instruction, must be offered at any grade level in which ten or more limited- or non-English-speaking students from the same minority language group are enrolled. Unique to this bill was the feature that the programme requirements were not dependent upon the districts' receipt of funds from the Act. In other words, schools were legally required to offer bilingual programmes whether or not they applied for funds to assist in this process.

3. California Education Code specified that no more than two-thirds nor less than one-third of the pupils should be LEP in any classroom.

4. Specifically, two sets of laws were of relevance: those regarding "Classroom Composition" and those having to do with "Parent Notification". The California Education Code (Section 52167) requires that no more than two-thirds nor less than one-third of the pupils shall be LEP in any classroom. The other pupils participating shall be Fluent English Proficient (FEP) or pupils whose primary language is English. In addition, no programme utilizing consolidated application funds shall sanction, perpetuate, or promote the segregation of students on the basis of race, ethnicity, religion, sex, or socio-economic status (California Administrative Code, Section 3934).

Prior to enrolment in a Basic Bilingual Education Programme or a Bilingual Bicultural Education Programme (the two programme options available to Calistoga), parents of all participants shall be notified in writing about the following:

1. programme being offered the pupil,
2. other programme options available,
3. their right to visit the programme,
4. their right to withdraw their child from the programme, and
5. their right to participate in the school and district bilingual advisory committees.

(California Education Code, Section 52173 and California Administrative Code, Section 4308).

California Administrative Code, Section 4308 goes on to say that the parents of FEP pupils and parents of pupils whose primary language is English must give their approval, orally or in writing, in order to enrol them in a bilingual programme (either programme option mentioned above). If the parents of an FEP pupil or pupil whose primary language is English wish to withdraw the pupil from the bilingual programme, the school must place the pupil in a non-bilingual programme classroom if such a classroom is available, or, if no such classroom is available, in an English-only instructional programme in the bilingual classroom.

13 The Carpinteria language minority student experience

From theory, to practice, to success

S. JIM CAMPOS and
H. ROBERT KEATINGE

Introduction

The Carpinteria Unified School District's Title VII preschool project began in January 1981, during the 1980–81 school year. By the end of the funding cycle, the 1982–83 school year, three groups of Spanish dominant children had been served by the Title VII programme, one for each year of the project.

The primary goal of the project was to bring Spanish dominant children to a level in school readiness skills that matched the skills of the English dominant children in the community upon entrance into kindergarten. Prior to the start of the programme, Spanish dominant children, as a group, had performed far below the English dominant children in the district's testing programme upon entrance into kindergarten. The proposal for the project stated that the children enrolled in the Title VII preschool would receive a strong programme in school readiness skills in their dominant language, while receiving at least 20 minutes a day of English as a second language instruction.

The theoretical rationale for the project was based on the interdependence hypothesis (Cummins, 1984; Skutnabb-Kangas, 1984) which proposes a strong relationship between the extent to which minority children's first language (L1) is developed and their subsequent academic progress in L2.

Carpinteria is a suburban, predominantly middle-class community of about 11,000 people located 11 miles south of the city of Santa Barbara, California. About 30% of the population is of Hispanic origin, consisting mostly of long-time Carpinteria Mexican-American families, and what appears to be an ever-increasing number of new arrivals from Mexico. The new arrivals supply the labour for the large agricultural industry of the city. The school district student population reflects the same ethnic ratio, about 30% Hispanic.

Until the establishment of the Title VII preschool, only about 50% of the children of newly arrived Mexican families attended a preschool programme. A preschool education, however, appeared to confer relatively little advantage on Spanish dominant children. On entry-level measures of kindergarten readiness (administered in Spanish) they performed at virtually the same level as Spanish dominant children who did not attend a preschool. This was − 2 standard deviations from the group mean score of the English-speaking children entering kindergarten.

Students accepted for the Title VII programme were of Mexican descent, between four and five years of age, spoke Spanish as their dominant and home language, and were non- or limited English-speaking. Some 95% came from low socio-economic background; 68% of the students had both parents working; 65% were employed in agricultural work. The average educational level attained by parents was about sixth grade.

Components of the preschool programme

There were three major components of the preschool programme:

1. Development of a strong conceptual foundation in children's L1 through the almost exclusive use of Spanish for interaction

2. Promotion of increased learning opportunities for children at home through making parents an integral part of the programme

3. Implementation of an interactional approach to language/concept development through constantly integrating language with children's preschool experiences.

Students were exposed to new and interesting experiences in the classroom on a daily basis. The experiences required them to "interact" with things both familiar and unknown, make sense out of the experiences, and then talk about them. The emphasis was on student discovery, interacting with both the social and physical classroom environment. For example, on one occasion the teacher provided the students with a broom and a dustpan. The students were then asked to show the teacher how to use the tools to pick up a pile of trash off the floor. Each student was then given the opportunity to solve the problem. Some used two hands on the broom and asked another student to help with the dustpan. Some used one hand on the broom and one on the dustpan. And some used two hands on the broom and their feet to hold the dustpan. During the whole process the teacher was asking the students to talk about the "what" and "why" of their actions. The experience provided the students with the opportunity to think and problem-solve, both individually and as a group, and provided the means for meaningful dialogue and vocabulary building.

The role of Spanish was one of providing the means by which the students and teacher could talk about what was being experienced. The students needed language to tell fellow students and the teacher about what they observed, or what they were doing. Students needed to continue to develop their language skills in order to talk about the many new ideas, things and activities they were experiencing. The result is that language and cognitive growth went hand-in-hand, each assisting the other's development.

Another major facet of the programme was the effort to make the parents an integral part of the preschool programme. Opportunities for participation in the daily programme and monthly workshops were provided for them. Their role as the child's first and "other" teacher outside the school environment was strongly emphasized in the workshops.

Communication with parents was maintained by a variety of means: for example, teachers spoke with parents on the telephone several times a month regarding their child's school progress; monthly parent meetings were held to discuss issues related to the programme and parenting in general; many parent volunteers were active in the programme; a subscription to the preschool magazine *Sesame Street* (with English sections translated into Spanish by preschool staff) was given to each family; parent newsletters were sent home to families on a bi-weekly basis and songsheets were given to parents throughout the year at parent meetings.

Outcomes of the preschool programme

In order to evaluate the effectiveness of the Title VII preschool programme, an evaluation design that focused on three specific areas of comparison with other students was established. First, the Title VII students were compared on skills of school readiness with the English-speaking children in the community and with other Spanish speakers who did not participate in the programme. These other Spanish speakers participated in a Day Care preschool programme, which used some Spanish but placed the primary emphasis on English skills development. Second, they were compared with other Spanish speakers in the USA on a nationally normed test of achievement skills. And finally, they were compared with other Spanish-speaking children in the community on a measure of English proficiency, namely the *Bilingual Syntax Measure*. A survey was also administered to the parents of students to assess parents' attitudes on child development.

The School Readiness Inventory (SRI)

For a number of years, the SRI has been administered to all incoming kindergarten students in the school district during a screening one week prior to the first day of classes. The test is administered in a one-to-one fashion. English dominant students are screened by the teachers of non-bilingual classrooms and the Spanish dominant students by the bilingual classroom teachers, in each case in the dominant language of the child. The purpose of the test is to establish an individual profile for each incoming student in developmental and conceptual skill areas to determine his or her readiness level for kindergarten.

The test is made up of 18 tasks worth two points apiece, which are divided over three areas: Fine Motor, Attending Skills, and Concepts. The Fine Motor area (six points) requires children to demonstrate skills which include cutting with scissors, copying of shapes, and writing of the child's name. The Attending Skills area (14 points) focuses on auditory and visual discrimination tasks and memory skills, such as being able to say one's own name, following three directions, visually discriminating forms and reproducing a design from memory. The Concepts skill area (16 points) requires the naming of colours, shapes, numbers and letters, and problem solving.

The group mean on the test, over the years, has been 23, but a score of 20 or better has been regarded in the School District as indicating a successful year in kindergarten academically and socially.

As shown in Table 13.1, the results of the previous years' administrations of the SRI, from 1979 to the final year of the project, show remarkable consistency for both English- and Spanish-speaking children in the community in all areas of the SRI. In the case of the Spanish speakers, this means two standard deviations below the mean each year in each area

TABLE 13.1   *SRI results for English-speaking children, Spanish-speaking children not in Title VII preschool and Spanish-speaking children in Title VII preschool, 1979–80 to 1983–84*

Year	English-speaking	Non-Title VII Spanish-speaking	Title VII Spanish-speaking
1979–80	23.1	14.0	
1980–81	22.8	15.2	
1981–82	23.1	13.8	17.8
1982–83	23.2	14.6	21.6
1983–84	23.4	16.0	23.3

of the SRI except Fine Motor, which is within one standard deviation for those Spanish speakers enrolled in another preschool programme. Spanish speakers enrolled in the Title VII preschool, however, show steady improvement each year, reaching parity with their English-speaking counterparts in all areas of the SRI in the final year of the project.

The SRI results demonstrate that Spanish dominant children, despite coming from disadvantaged backgrounds, can achieve parity in school readiness skills with the average English dominant child. Parity can be achieved within one year using an approach that fully utilizes the child's dominant language in meaningful contexts.

The El Circo Achievement Tests

The project participants were administered the *El Circo* standardized achievement tests in language and maths in June at the end of each instruction year. The language section is designed to measure the child's receptive abilities in Spanish. These skills include: understanding of verb tense, word order, prepositions and other linguistic structures such as plurals and reflexives. The maths section of the test measures quantitative concepts essential for developing mathematical skills, such as understanding of counting and simple numerical relationships. The test was administered individually in Spanish by fluent Spanish speakers.

The project participants achieved near or at the upper quartile level in each year of the project in both language and maths sections of the test. In the spring of 1982, the *El Circo* tests were also administered to children in the Day Care centre in the community which also served Spanish dominant children, providing them with preschool in English and Spanish. These students scored only at the seventh percentile in language and the 15th percentile in maths. The following year, pre- and post-tests were administered to both groups of Spanish dominant children, with better results for the Day Care children (37th percentile in language and 49th percentile in maths in the post-test). The Title VII participants maintained their high achievement level, scoring at the 85th percentile in language and 88th percentile in maths on the post-tests. It is interesting to note that the Day Care children pre-tested at the 48th percentile in language, which meant that they dropped 11 percentile points during the course of the year. This suggests that the concurrent instruction in English and Spanish in the Day Care programme is not conducive to the continued development of children's Spanish first language skills.

The Bilingual Syntax Measure (BSM)

The BSM is designed to measure children's oral proficiency in English grammatical structures by using natural speech as a basis for making judgements. To elicit natural speech, simple questions are used with cartoon-type pictures to provide the framework for a conversation with the child. An analysis of the child's speech yields a numerical indicator and a qualitative description of the child's structural language proficiency. The five levels of oral language proficiency range from Level 1, where the child neither speaks nor comprehends English, to Level 5 where the child is as proficient as his/her peers who are native speakers of English. The BSM is administered to all incoming kindergarten children who speak a language other than English.

It was found that 76% of the project participants, compared with 42% of the Day Care children, achieved at Level 3 or higher in English upon entrance into kindergarten in the autumn of 1982. This is despite the fact that English usage was stressed in the Day Care programme. The following year 53% of the project participants achieved at Level 3 or higher, compared with 59% of the Day Care children.

A follow-up on the BSM testing for the Title VII and Day Care children was administered upon entrance into first grade for those children who entered kindergarten in the autumn of 1982. The BSM results for these children showed that by first grade 47% of the Title VII preschoolers had achieved Level 5, the highest level, and an additional 23% had achieved Level 4. By first grade, 11% of the Day Care preschoolers had achieved Level 5, and 44% had achieved Level 4. The results of the BSM demonstrate that a preschool programme conducted entirely in Spanish has had no adverse effect on children's acquisition of English.

Parent outcomes

A questionnaire was administered to parents at the end of each school year in order to assess the impact of the programme as seen by the parents. The questions centred on specific skills/behaviours of project participants observed at home, such as singing, story telling, counting, drawing and generally how well the child was expressing him/herself. In addition, two questions dealt with the parents' overall impressions of the programme.

During initial meetings with parents, the project staff detected that the majority of parents were not explicitly conscious of their role as their child's first teacher. They were making no conscious effort to provide a language-rich environment. To the contrary, most parents indicated that they seldom had much oral interaction with their children apart from simple, direct commands. Most of the sustained language interaction for children came from their older brothers and/or sisters.

On the end-of-year parent survey, *all* parents indicated that their children were to some degree singing the songs taught at the preschool and telling them the stories they had learned; they were also drawing better, and in general better able to express themselves than before entering the programme. All parents expressed their approval of the programme and appreciation for the efforts of the preschool staff. These trends were consistent for each year of the project.

Of anecdotal interest was a formal complaint by a group of Spanish dominant parents of preschool graduates that one of the kindergarten bilingual teachers was not a competent teacher. This suggests that these parents are likely to exercise a greater voice in school affairs in the future, and, in fact, school officials have reported that parents of project participants appear to be much more aware of and involved in their children's school experience in kindergarten and grade 1 than was the case in previous years.

Follow-up results in kindergarten and grade 1

Children's progress in academic skills after leaving the preschool programme has been monitored through the regular school district assessment procedures. The kindergarten and grade 1 programmes are bilingual but the major emphasis is on English. Also, the kindergarten and grade 1 programmes initially tended to use a much more teacher-centred instructional approach than that which had been utilized in the preschool, although an interactive approach conducted primarily in Spanish (similar to the pre-school programme) was implemented in the kindergarten for lower-achieving students in the 1983–84 school year. Thus, the philosophy of the preschool programme is only partially maintained in the regular pro-gramme.

In general, children have maintained the high level of achievement demonstrated in the preschool, particularly after the interactive approach was instituted at the kindergarten level. For example, on the California Achievement Test (CAT), administered in Spanish at the end of kinder-garten, students in the 1984–85 and 1985–86 school years obtained mean percentile ranks on Reading Readiness and Maths Concepts ranging from 57 to 71. Scores were considerably lower (range 8 to 25th percentile) in 1981–82 and 1982–83 when children were in the teacher-centred kinder-garten programme. In 1984–85, the year the interactional kindergarten programme was instituted, mean percentiles were 68 for Reading Readiness and 71 for Maths Concepts. First grade reading scores in Spanish have been consistently above the mean for students who attended the preschool programme.

Conclusion

Two basic conclusions can be reached about the Spanish dominant students attending school in the Carpinteria Unified School District since the establishment of the Title VII preschool programme: first, they *can* succeed academically in the public school system; second, the English acquisition process for these children is not impeded by use of their dominant tongue in school instruction. In short, high cognitive achievement can be attained by Spanish dominant students if they are taught in their dominant language, Spanish, using an interactive mode, and it can be attained at no cost to the English acquisition process.

From the data we have gathered to date, it appears to us that English acquisition is the least of the concerns a school district has to contend with in the case of the Spanish dominant student. These students will be communicatively fluent in English within two to three years, whether the student is placed in a situation where English is forced or in a situation where English is rarely used in curriculum instruction, so long as they are developing cognitive skills and school is perceived as a place where learning occurs. On the basis of our findings, attention should be turned to methodologies which develop thinking and problem-solving strategies, hand-in-hand with development of the minority language. Common sense and considerable research tell us that thinking strategies and skills transfer across languages, from Spanish to English. In our opinion, the child who is equipped with more than mere communicative skills in English should have a far better chance of success in the school system.

Programmes such as the Carpinteria preschool programme should be seen in the context of the overall struggle for educational and linguistic rights among minority communities. Although the initiative for this programme came from educators who were familiar with and influenced by research findings, collaboration with the community was an integral part of the entire programme. The programme appears to have empowered the community not only to better develop their children's conceptual skills in Spanish but also to act as advocates for their children within the school system. Through their interaction with educators in the context of the preschool programme, parents began to take initiatives to improve the education their children were receiving.

References

CUMMINS, J. 1984, *Bilingualism and special education: Issues in assessment and pedagogy*. Clevedon, England: Multilingual Matters.
SKUTNABB-KANGAS, T. 1984, *Bilingualism or not: The education of minorities*. Clevedon, England: Multilingual Matters.

14 Beyond cultural inclusion

An Inuit example of indigenous educational development[1]

ARLENE STAIRS

Process: indigenous culture encounters formal education

Typologies of bilingual education are based primarily on the societal aims of bilingual programmes as reflected in language teaching methods and policy *vis-à-vis* the surrounding linguistic community (e.g. Mackey, 1972; Skutnabb-Kangas, 1984:127). The societal aims of bilingual education span the continuum from transition (i.e. shift from minority to majority language use in school and society) to maintenance (i.e. continuing use of minority language within the majority language school and society). In the case of indigenous minorities, the transition versus maintenance issue becomes the much more profound question of assimilation and extinction versus survival and evolution of a human culture. It is proposed here that the range of transition–maintenance aims among indigenous bilingual programmes is best reflected through the *educational development process* rather than through language methods or policy *per se*. Encounters between indigenous cultures and formal schooling are recent in terms of educational history, and the educational development process reflects a vast range of culture contact dynamics in which language is but one element.

Indigenous educational development ranges from an extrinsic *cultural-inclusion* process to an intrinsic *cultural-base* process. The cultural-inclusion process implicitly assumes that cultural universals, at least those worthy of formal teaching, are contained exclusively within the majority culture. Cultural inclusion sees indigenous education as merely the process of adding certain minority cultural specifics to a standard majority programme (Figure 14.1a). Any such development of minority cultural-inclusion elements focuses on cultural knowledge. Little account is taken of indigenous modes of transmitting culture, or of cognitive and interactive styles. The cultural-base process implies that cultural universals are part of all cultures, and that such universals of human perception, thought, language, etc. can be learned through the specific knowledge and transmission style of any indigenous culture (Figure 14.1b). The cultural-base process can extend to educational content outside the indigenous culture, e.g. an Inuk child learns qallunaat (non-Inuit) mathematics as an Inuk.

In the vast majority of indigenous educational development efforts, particularly as documented in Canada and the United States (e.g. Drapeau, 1985; Lowe, 1984:vii–xvvii; St. Clair & Leap, 1982), an extrinsic cultural-inclusion approach has dominated. The process of developing cultural inclusion elements proceeds through three basic stages: (a) gathering of expertise and information by specialists outside the indigenous culture, (b) development of curricula and materials directed by these same external experts, and (c) a blitz training of indigenous teachers to implement the educational programmes. Two main aspects of external expertise are tapped as the basis of programme development. Firstly, there is knowledge of the indigenous culture and language as studied particularly by scholars in anthropology and linguistics (see cell 2, Figure 14.2). Ethnographic information and dictionaries are compiled, often with great haste and

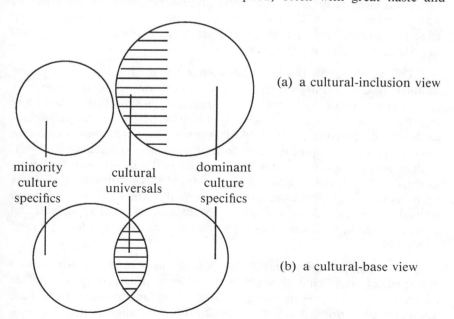

(a) a cultural-inclusion view

minority culture specifics

cultural universals

dominant culture specifics

(b) a cultural-base view

FIGURE 14.1. *Cultural universals and cultural specifics in a bi-cultural context (two views)*

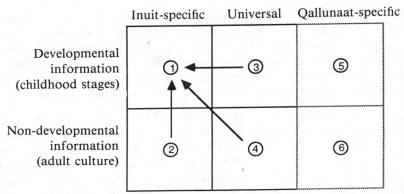

FIGURE 14.2 *Categories of information relevant to Inuit educational development*

emphasis regarding the latter, since language content is still largely equated with formal education by both indigenous populations and outsiders. Linguistic work may extend to grammars, and to efforts at establishing standard orthographies for indigenous languages where literacy has become a cultural element or issue. Secondly, presumably universal principles of pedagogy and child development (cell 3, Figure 14.2), literacy and knowledge taxonomies (cell 4, Figure 14.2) are tapped to incorporate cultural knowledge into school programmes.

This approach to the basic knowledge for programme development seriously risks confusing specifics from the dominant culture of the experts (cells 5 and 6, Figure 14.2) with universal principles, and further lacks any information which is both developmental and specific to the indigenous culture (cell 1, Figure 14.2). Little is known about language acquisition steps or child development stages within particular indigenous cultures. Indigenous people are used only as informants in this information gathering process. Selected individuals are then retaught this information as it has been selected and structured by the external culture. Now considered trained, these individuals are placed in schools, external in operational style, to function as teachers—or sometimes only as teacher-aides—for their own children.

The intent of this chapter is to describe an indigenous educational development situation which essentially reverses this process of outside expert → programme → indigenous teacher. With an intrinsic cultural-base approach, educational development begins through indigenous professional development. Indigenous professionals are then at the centre both of gathering a knowledge base and of programme implementation. The process becomes one of continuous educational development rather than one-shot programme design and teacher training. This intrinsic development process moves towards indigenous education based not just on cultural content, but on the world-view, social roles and interactive style of the indigenous culture. As discussed in the final section, this process integrates educational development with the fundamental survival issues facing indigenous populations: identity, self-determination and cultural evolution in the present world. The two features which seem central to an intrinsic cultural-base educational development process are discussed in the third and fourth sections: indigenous professional development and on-going action research. Specific contextual and historical circumstances which created a conducive setting for these two key development features are described in the following section.

Context: cultural history creates an educational setting

Geographic and demographic context (see Map 1)

The region being described, Nouveau Quebec, is above the 55th parallel in the Province of Quebec, Canada, covering an area of 563,000 square kilometres. Arctic weather and terrain (taiga to tundra) characterize this territory. Approximately 5,700 Inuit, 25% of the Canadian and about 6% of the world Inuit population, inhabit 13 settlements along the Hudson and Ungava Bay coasts. Settlement populations vary from approximately 100 to approximately 1,200 people. The two communities with direct air links to the south (Kuujjuaq, Kuujjuaraapik) have about 25% qallunaat (non-Inuit) population; other communities are 95% or more Inuit. Significant for any consideration of educational development and impact is the youthfulness of this population. The birthrate is about $2\frac{1}{2}$ times that of southern Canada, with half the present population under 14 years of age (compared with a median age of 30 in Canada generally) (Normandeau, 1981; SAGMAI, 1984).

Permanent settlements became established only during the late 1950s and 1960s, and families still spend periods in camps away from the settlements. All communities are now connected by scheduled air transportation and have received satellite television for the past few years. Despite recent increases in communications and mobility, this Inuit population has been more isolated from southern North American culture than has any other indigenous group on the continent. While both wage economy and government subsidy are significant to settlement survival, subsistence off the land remains an element of Quebec Inuit life.

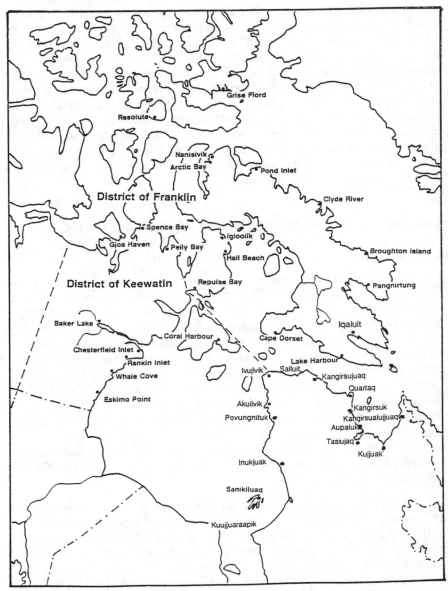

MAP 1. *Nouveau Québec & Eastern Arctic communities*

Linguistic context

The Inuit of Nouveau Quebec speak two mutually comprehensible dialects of Inuktitut, the language family of most Inuit from the Bering Strait, across Canada and Greenland (related Aleut and Yupik languages are spoken by some extreme western groups) (Dorais, 1985). Over 90% of Nouveau Quebec Inuit still claim Inuktitut as their first language—a higher rate than other Inuit regions and any other Amerindian group (Burnaby, 1984; Lowe, 1984). Inuktitut remains the language of communication within Nouveau Quebec communities and within families across all generations. Inuktitut has been described as a flexible language with "a real capacity to deal with new notions and terms" (Brody, 1977:589), and has adapted to recent objects, technologies and concepts introduced by outside cultures (Dorais, 1983).

The rate of basic Inuktitut literacy is very high, with widespread use of the standard syllabic orthography accepted in 1976 by the Inuit Cultural Institute (Harper *et al.*, 1983). Very few adults are unable to write at a level adequate for correspondence, and children are extending the use of written Inuktitut through school programmes. In Quebec, Inuit are confronted by two majority second languages, English and French, perhaps tempering the assimilative pressure of either one. Many of these features, in combination with relative historical isolation and sheer numbers of speakers, makes Inuktitut one of the most viable indigenous languages in the world today (Bauman, 1981; Price, 1981). Among Canada's 53 indigenous languages, Inuktitut is one of only three for which extended survival seems assured (Foster, 1984).

Political and educational context

Preceding the 1970s, the choice between a cultural-inclusion or a cultural-base approach to indigenous educational development was not an issue. Indigenous formal education did not exist. In the late 1940s, the Federal government shifted from a philosophy of isolationism and paternalism towards Canada's native people to a policy of integration with mainstream Canadian society. This policy involved formal education for native children which was as close as possible to the standard curricula of the provinces—the government level constitutionally responsible for education in this country. During the 1950s and 1960s a similar era of assimilationism occurred for indigenous people of the United States and Australia. For many of these years, Inuit children of Nouveau Quebec continued to be brought up and taught in traditional ways by their families as they moved among camps and the growing settlements. In the 1960s, however, Federal schools were established in Nouveau Quebec, and Inuit here were subject to the same assimilationist pressures already faced by western Inuit for some time (Freeman, 1978). Teaching was entirely in English, with Inuktitut forbidden and even a cause for punishment. Children were sometimes removed from home communities to hostel schools for long periods of time.

A first step towards Inuit education came in 1970 with the establishment of a parallel provincial school system in Nouveau Quebec which provided both Inuktitut and French instruction. However, the real beginning of indigenous educational development among Quebec Inuit was the James Bay and Northern Quebec agreement of 1975. This agreement, surrounding massive hydro-electric development in the region, made Quebec Inuit the only native group in Canada with a legal land claims settlement. Combined with considerable political and economic power, the James Bay Agreement also provided for indigenous control of Inuit education through creation of the Kativik School Board.

This board superseded both previous school systems and is unique in its autonomy relative to other school systems in Canada. (Two communities have not yet signed the James Bay agreement, finding even this level of autonomy insufficient.) Kativik is Inuit-controlled through a system of commissioners from each settlement. The board designs its own curricula and determines its own languages of instruction. At present, all but one community teach entirely in Inuktitut for the first three years of school, with second language (English or French) introduced in the fourth year.

Perhaps most crucial in making possible a culturally based process of educational development is the provision for each community to choose its own teachers, unconstrained by formal qualifications, and for the board's subsequent responsibility in teacher training. Under this provision, school programmes are integrated with indigenous professional development and research to a degree impossible under the conventional southern structures of school boards, standard government curricula, and teacher training institutions.

People: indigenous professional development

This description of indigenous educational development rests on the assumption that the intrusion of formal education into indigenous culture is permanent, and is accepted by Inuit as crucial to their survival in the contemporary world (see the final section regarding these assumptions).

However, formal education is not only alien to Inuit culture but, as initially transposed from the south, is in direct conflict with indigenous modes of transmitting knowledge across generations. Formal teaching is characterized by a high level of verbal mediation in a setting removed from daily life, and is carried out by a specialized individual who has no social role relationship to the child. The predominant goals are individual academic achievement and the skill base for a future occupation. Indigenous teaching involves observation and imitation embedded in daily family and community activities, and is carried out by many individuals with particular kinship roles in relation to the child. Awareness and appropriate skills for integration into the immediate social structure are predominant goals. Inuit hunters of the Eastern Arctic give these two modes of teaching radically different concept labels (Wenzel, in press).

In facing the deep differences between formal and indigenous educational modes, cultural inclusion focuses on content goals. From an external perspective this approach attempts to fuse a segment of Inuit content on to the southern school model. In contrast, a cultural-base approach focuses on differences and conflicts in the educator's role, both in the child's life and in society, with content inherent in that role. Cultural-base development seeks resolution of these role conflicts from an internal Inuit perspective. Some features of such development, emphasizing Inuit educators rather than curricula, materials, or research *per se*, can be extracted from Kativik's 10 years of trial and error in indigenous education.

In Nouveau Quebec settlements, Inuit teachers are chosen by community standards, not formal qualification, and begin immediately as "teacher"—not as aides or students. Most remain fully integrated in their communities throughout their training. This avoids (a) depriving settlement life by removal of what are often key members, (b) disrupting personal lives with deep cultural shock, homesickness and family separation, and (c) training Inuit as essentially southern teachers outside of their cultural context. Integration of life and professional development is furthered by rotation of Inuit teachers between years of classroom work and years of home life as new mothers. Those Inuit educators now taking on particular support and development roles (counsellors/master-teachers, instructors, programme designers, etc.) are also part of this three-way exchange between system support roles, settlement classrooms and homes. Resulting from this is a broad base of educators with varied experience, still firmly placed in their cultural setting.

No teacher-training institution exists. Courses and workshops are carried out in the settlements on a rotating basis during times when teachers are free from their regular classrooms. Teachers from throughout Nouveau Quebec gather in a given settlement for a course session, thereby deepening ties among Inuit educators and involving communities in the professional development of their teachers. While the logistics of such events in the Arctic would stun most southerners, Inuit handle the complexity and value the contact. From initial selection, a teacher must participate in these sessions at least until fully qualified (at present 45 Canadian university credits), while she continues to gain experience in her settlement teaching. Depending on initial background, teaching skill and time at home, qualification time varies among individuals.

Courses within the programme differ from conventional southern programmes in several critical ways. (a) Elements of both practical pedagogy and theory are present in most courses, in repeating "horizontal" cycles rather than the frequent vertical separation of these elements. This pattern better meets the immediate need of a newly chosen teacher, and better suits contextualized Inuit learning patterns. (b) Much content for all teachers is special-education in style for several reasons characteristic of the north: little set curriculum exists which can be used with small culturally diverse northern groups; rapid cultural social, economic and technological changes require constant educational adaptation; few specialists in subject matter or individual differences are available. (c) Both material development and basic local research are carried out via teacher training courses and workshop sessions. For example, primary Inuktitut reading booklets designed by groups of teachers in a reading course are then reproduced, used in the field experimentally, revised on the basis of field trial in a subsequent reading course, and likewise through repeating cycles. Similarly, as described below, child observation research is carried out by teachers in their home settlements on the basis of methods learned in child development courses. Thus Inuit educators in the course of their professional development generate school programme rather than simply receive training in it.

From early Kativik days, McGill University and Kativik School Board, with the support of Ministère de l'Education du Québec, co-operated in this apprenticeship-style field-based programme. In 1981, recognizing the results of programme evolution to date, McGill created the Certificate in Northern and Native Education with advanced standing towards a Bachelor of Education degree. To date 28 Inuit teachers are Certificate graduates, and all but one remain as educators. This level of stability is most extraordinary in relation to other northern native training programmes for trades or professions. The cultural integration features of Kativik teacher training may be central to this stability.

Qallunaat (non-Inuit, southern) working with Inuit teachers emphasize professional development, rather than themselves offering direct services to Inuit children. This role structure alone allows for some natural filtering of Inuit teaching mode into the school at early primary levels. A heavy balance of consulting versus career positions among qallunaat further opens the role structure to continuous "step-back" by qallunaat in the system as Inuit roles evolve and expand. Over the course of 10 years, for example, southern consultants have stepped back from teaching Inuit teachers through a translator, to training Inuit teacher-training instructors; from designing local action research, to training researchers. Each step back is not merely a shift from southerner to Inuk in the same job role. The Inuit educators now instructing novices, designing materials, presenting workshops, screening children for specialized developmental problems, studying the impact of native language education through evaluation research—these Inuit progressively redesign their roles to produce a more culturally based education system.

As Inuit teacher-training instructors redesign their roles, training courses evolve continually over time. Each trainee cohort receives a more culturally based programme than the preceding one. Over the years, Inuit teaching and teacher-training have moved through several stages. Initially, one sees little relation between the routines of a new Inuk teacher and the school setting—as if the cultures of the two were in the same room without meeting. Often control of children is a major problem. Later one sees almost "cookbook" rigidity as teachers effectively adopt the formal methods shown them, frequently the model of a favourite consulting master-teacher. Eventually one begins to see new, creative cultural-base approaches emerge as Inuit reconstruct teaching and instructing roles (see Beebe, 1966 for similar stage observations). In this process, the use of Inuktitut is a special and critical issue.

As Inuit educator roles have evolved, the use of Inuktitut has expanded in the training programme until now the Certificate in Northern and Native Education is offered entirely in Inuktitut. Strong monolingual Inuit teachers can be fully trained and are seen by others as a linguistic and cultural base for the education system. Bilingual Inuit teachers extend their confidence in the language and discover Inuit conceptualizations for material once acquired in qallunaat education.

This process of indigenous professional development has now arrived at a very basic issue for higher degree-level education. If, when, how, for whom should second- (dominant) language training in formal southern institutions enter the process; or what range of options should exist? Can and should southern universities adapt to some of the cultural-base features of educational style which Kativik has been exploring, i.e.

 a. integration of study with northern life patterns,
 b. contextualized learning style surrounding work and life activities,
 c. open role structure for professors, tutors, consultants, students?

 These questions concerning the next phase of indigenous professional development are a present Kativik preoccupation.

Information: ongoing action research

 Development of an indigenous educational programme rests on a knowledge basis from various sources, as described above (see Figure 14.2). Formal knowledge concerning the learning patterns of young Inuit children is still very limited (see cell 1, Figure 14.2), and the intuitive knowledge of Inuit teachers concerning these patterns has still not fully entered the school setting. Building an educational development base using both formal and intuitive knowledge must centrally involve Inuit educators themselves. Thus right from the beginning of their professional development, Inuit teachers are involved with information gathering as well as programme development and teaching skills. This three-level role of Inuit teachers can be contrasted with the conventional teacher's role of delivering essentially set programmes to groups of children (Figure 14.3). Indigenous determination of the knowledge base driving educational development is perhaps the most fundamental point of indigenous control over the educational system. Given the pace of change in northern society, basic indigenous research

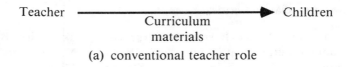

(a) conventional teacher role

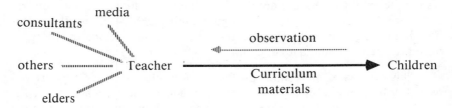

(b) indigenous teacher role (Kativik model)

FIGURE 14.3 *Two models of a teacher's role*

must be a continuous element in the school system and integrated into the educational development process.

Direct emphasis on action research as an integral part of Inuit professional development began in autumn 1978, when the Kativik–McGill teacher training programme recognized the need for content dealing with testing, diagnosis and assessment. Inuit and consultants felt strongly that introducing southern testing and assessment methods to Inuit teachers would be not merely irrelevant, but possibly damaging, both to their own and their student's progress. Only an action research approach, beginning with Inuit teachers' observation of their own children's learning and development, seemed appropriate. The proposed approach would involve (a) collaboration among a multidisciplinary group of southern educators, and experienced Inuit teachers and counsellors, (b) trial and error cycles in developing observation methods and interpreting their outcome, (c) direct involvement and training of Inuit classroom teachers as the observers in this action research, (d) immediate usefulness of the observational work to each classroom teacher herself, and (e) later usefulness of accumulated observations in curriculum and material development, in teacher training courses, and in decisions regarding policy, philosophy and style of Inuit education. A proposal was developed for the Child Observation Project: Inuit Teacher Training (COPITT). This project was accepted and funded by the Ministère de l'Education du Québec for a three-year period. Since then COPITT has been supported as an ongoing function of the Kativik School Board.

Initial COPITT priorities were determined by Inuit counsellors involved in the project. "Why do our children not read until eight or nine years of age, while southern children begin at six years? Is it because our language is difficult, or because of the way we teach?" (Betsy Annahatak). This specific concern led to a general decision at the first COPITT meeting to begin developmental research at the readiness and early primary levels rather than in one specific learning area (e.g. mathematics) across a wide age range.

In the first several years, most progress was made in observation of perceptual and motor skills. The marked strength of visual skills among Inuit children was confirmed, and programme developers began building and refining a reading curriculum capitalizing on this strength. From 1981, there was an increasing focus on language acquisition, involving a combination of Inuktitut linguistic study and developmental study of children's language samples from five to 12 years of age. A hearing-screening project was set up over the same period to begin coping with the very high northern incidence of otitis (middle ear infection) media and related learning disruptions. In a less formal way, thinking skills were studied in designing a basic concept scheme for early Inuktitut mathematics. Similarly, study of the social-emotional characteristics, needs and problems of Inuit children began through a course session, prepared and taught by Inuit instructors, for teachers and school counsellors.

From these beginnings with isolated and analytic study of the child, current COPITT projects as described below are moving into more holistic study of the child's relationships to his educational context.[2] It is felt this is a shift towards a more Inuit research perspective—perhaps from "Child Observation Project" to "Culture Observation Project". This growing attention to contextualized rather than single-feature research is central to a cultural-base process at the research as well as at the development and teaching levels of indigenous education (see Tharp *et al.*, 1984 for comparison). The greatest factor in this evolution of COPITT has been the expanding interest and changing roles of Inuit in education research, and the consequent shifts in consultant perceptions and methods. Inuit are not involved in the following projects only as data-gatherers within externally designed research. Increasingly Inuit researchers and counsellors are centrally involved in the focus (e.g. child and/or context), the methodology (e.g. experimental or descriptive), the interpretation of results, the means of information feedback to all Inuit, and the follow-up implications for next steps in educational development.

Evaluation of early Inuktitut first-language education

Systematic evaluation began during the 1984—85 school year, focusing on children then in grades 3 and 4. These levels include the oldest students who received Inuktitut instruction based on a well-developed language and literacy curriculum for kindergarten and grade 1. Inuktitut instruction has varied greatly among settlements in terms of grade level and percentage of Inuktitut-language teaching, formality of programme, and preparation of teachers. Documentation of these school variables, and of other settlement factors such as second language television, population changes and economic projects, is nearly complete. Writing samples have been gathered from all grade 3 and 4 students and have been analysed for length and complexity indices established in an earlier pilot study (presented at American Speech and Hearing Association, Washington, DC, November 1985). High correlations were found between these linguistic indices and proficiency ratings by experienced Inuit teachers and counsellors. Rating by four Inuit educators was also done with the current writing samples for further correlational study and development of native-speaker language acquisition categories. Among findings of novelty and educational interest is the qualitative rather than strictly quantitative variation among settlements in Inuktitut writing style. Inuit and consultants are now exploring how certain of these differences reflect either positive evolution of Inuktitut or degeneration of the language.

Loss and maintenance of native language and the role of native language literacy

Documentation is under way concerning loss and maintenance of Inuktitut from west to east in Canada and other circumpolar regions, and of language loss experiences among native populations elsewhere in the world (information to date presented to Arctic Quebec communities during Education Services round trip, winter 1984–85). Particular attention is being given to the role of education in the cultural dynamics of native language maintenance. Native language literacy is well-documented as a key factor in language survival, and in both individual development and cultural evolution (see Stairs, 1985a, b).

Kindergarten screening project

During 1984 and 1985, developmental screening was carried out for the first time with all kindergarten children in Kativik schools. This screening was built on the child observation work done in conjunction with Inuit teacher training courses since 1978 (see Stairs *et al.*, 1984). Over the years, observation methods appropriate to Inuit children and teachers have been designed and revised, with further revisions resulting from this first comprehensive screening. Kindergarten screening is being repeated this autumn and is anticipated to continue in following years. Early identification of children with developmental lags or learning disabilities is a primary purpose (12 children identified in 1984–85). Results are accumulated and integrated with past years' observation to provide a baseline for subsequent developmental research with Inuit children; to examine settlement differences and historical changes; and to study cultural specifics in perceptual, motor and language skills preceding formal schooling. Screening results for 1985–86 are now being compiled.

Methods for observing Inuktitut language development and proficiency levels

Attempts to evaluate Inuktitut proficiency (a language which had not been studied developmentally until the COPITT project began) evolved from (a) a fragmentary psychometric (testing) approach (discrimination, articulation and receptive–expressive usage items), to (b) a language-sampling approach using conventional linguistic analysis, to (c) an ethnographic (descriptive) approach. Cultural inappropriateness of earlier approaches in terms of content, testing context and language functions was discovered repeatedly. Currently a major ethnographic study of language acquisition by Inuit children in their home settings is under way (related to doctoral thesis project of the COPITT language consultant). Goals of this study are the development of more appropriate language teaching methods in Inuit schools; more realistic methods for observing language levels, strengths and weaknesses; and some theoretical work concerning accepted language universals which may be confirmed or challenged by the findings. This study will continue for a minimum of two years.

Professional roles and native identity

Over the past year, the conflicts between (a) increasingly demanding professional roles in the educational system and (b) identity in the Inuk world, have become a highly focused concern among Inuit counsellors, consultants and administrators (see Annahatak, 1985). Issues involve differences in style and community role for an Inuk and a qallunaq doing ostensibly the same job; locus of control and decision making; interactive patterns between Inuit and qallunaat; the use of Inuit language and conceptual patterns in originally qallunaat institutions. Background study is beginning concerning mental health problems among Inuit in bridging positions between Inuk and qallunaat cultures, and concerning professional training programmes that have succeeded or failed under various circumstances. Several Inuit counsellors are interested in continuing this documentation work and in beginning interview studies and community observation of these identity issues. This work began systematically during 1986 in the form of tutorials or special projects within the Bachelor level programmes of a few Inuit counsellors. One goal is to work with higher education institutions to design programmes appropriate to the existing professional and community commitments and to the learning style of leading Inuit educators. A second goal is to extend professional training within the school system (teachers, counsellors and others) which incorporates Inuit values, social patterns and language, and reduces the culture conflict of those educating the present generation of Inuit children.

Three further research and development projects have been discussed for the future. The first concerns *Inuit concept acquisition* and cognitive mapping relevant to the presentation of mathematics and science in the northern schools. This work has been proceeding slowly since 1979 in conjunction with development of a primary Inuktitut mathematics programme. More concentrated and systematic study (e.g. verbal and non-verbal classification studies) is now needed. The second project, also in progress but in need of consolidation, is a comprehensive *history of COPITT research work*, and presentation of the model evolving for educational development in a minority native context. Stages of personnel development, native language curriculum and materials development, and categories of continuing research are to be documented. The interaction of these components as they determine the role of education in a culture-contact situation is the fundamental concern. Finally, there is interest in the study of *Inuit child development stages*. Counsellors would explore developmental concepts with adults of various ages, trying to describe an Inuit model of life stages and maturity which they believe exists. This model would serve as an alternative to southern (western) developmental models (e.g. Piaget, Erikson) in guiding some further child observation research.

Philosophy: education and cultural evolution

This description of indigenous educational development should not end with the impression that Nouveau Quebec Inuit are in complete consensus over the place of schools in their culture, or over the process of educational development. In terms of conventional bilingual education typologies, consensus is high concerning a maintenance aim, or a cultural survival aim in the context of indigenous education. A strong Inuk sense of cultural identity combined with competitive ability in the qallunaat world comprise the Inuit educational aim. Viewpoints differ profoundly, however, as to the bicultural balance and dynamics necessary for that survival.

Bullivant (1984:96) has defined two dimensions of cultural survivability that very concisely represent the differences among Nouveau Quebec Inuit groups. One dimension is the ideational base, i.e. ideas, beliefs and social role models of the culture. The second is the economic base, i.e. control of land, money and organizational structures in relation to outside culture(s). These two orthogonal dimensions form a grid on which one can place the cultural survival focus of a given indigenous group. Those Inuit who favour a strong ideational base for survival would also be those favouring a cultural-base approach to educational development. The philosophy of this group is that a strong Inuk cultural base grounds the child for successful second culture learning later on, as well as ensuring the maintenance of Inuk identity. Without such a base, success in second culture learning would be limited and leave children conflicted in identity. Those fewer but very vocal Inuit who favour a strong economic base for survival would advocate a limited cultural-inclusion process of educational development. The philosophy presented by these Inuit is that (a) Inuk culture is learned in family and community, and remains sound enough to survive without formal education and (b) the school's role is preparation for competition on southern terms, for both Inuit cultural success *vis-à-vis* dominant cultures and individual Inuk success within the dominant culture.

Clearly to date, the ideational base for survival, and thus a cultural-base process in education, heavily predominates in Nouveau Quebec Inuit education. This majority group challenges those emphasizing an economic base on two major grounds. Firstly is the overwhelming evidence from the Western Arctic and nearby Labrador of the fragility of Inuit culture, even though superficially strong in the present generation (Dorais, 1985). Passive bilingualism and language loss in one generation, for instance, has been well documented among numbers of indigenous languages (Bauman, 1981). It is noted that dominant language pressures on Inuktitut in Quebec have greatly increased since the formative years of those advocating an economic base policy. Furthermore, indigenous language literacy, as supported through the school system, is seen as a key factor in language survival (Price, 1981).

The second challenge to an economic base emphasis concerns cultural evolution as opposed to cultural survival. The ideal of culturally based educational development is a school system which, although initially the direct transposition of a southern institution, is gradually absorbed and transformed into a new Inuk form of education. This transformation began with Inuit cognitive culture predominating more and more in the school— Inuktitut language and concept patterns as, for instance, in primary mathematics. The current question is whether adaptation at the cognitive level can lead to transformation at the social level—teaching–learning interactive patterns, role structures, school position within the community. It is being asked, for instance, whether or not school should become smaller within an Inuit community, with other institutions taking on certain education roles. Beyond philosophically favouring evolution, those asking such questions fear that unchanging indigenous cultures cannot survive and will be overcome by dominant-culture institutions in their midst— particularly schools.

In specific terms, the cultural-base versus cultural-inclusion controversy centres on language policy in Kativik schools. To date the preponderance of evaluation evidence around the world favours early first language education in minority situations with similarities to the one being described (Cummins, 1983). Proponents of cultural-inclusion, advocating essentially full second language education at all levels, reject similarities between Nouveau Quebec and other minority situations. Inuit here, for instance, grow up in a more totally first-language settlement environment than other minority language groups which have been evaluated. However, Kativik's own evaluation results, as now seen with upper elementary students, begin to support the benefits of early first language education. These results now enter the philosophical-political debate over the role of education in Inuit cultural evolution. However conclusive such evaluation results, or other outcomes of culture contact studies, this formal information will remain but one element in the debate. The same contextual features that stimulated a cultural-base process of educational development in Nouveau Quebec have also kept the philosophy-of-education debate open, dynamic and continuous. The recent Symposium 85 on Inuit Education in Kuujjuaq, Nouveau Quebec witnessed this open involvement. Cross-sectional representatives from all settlements and several circumpolar regions discussed issues ranging from school calendar to parental responsibilities to language teaching. It is perhaps this sense of openness and autonomy among Quebec Inuit which gives most hope for a creative educational future within an evolving culture.

Notes to Chapter 14

1. Many ideas presented in this chapter arose from discussions with Betsy Annahatak, counsellor in Inuit Education.
2. Many of these research ideas have changed their course due to rapid political, financial, and personnel changes during the two years since this chapter was prepared, either moving beyond Kativik or into local Inuit communities, or not being carried further at present.

References

ANNAHATAK, B. 1985, Thoughts of an Inuk teacher. *Education Express*, 1, 2.

BAUMAN, J. J. 1981, *A guide to issues in Indian language retention*. Washington, DC: Center for Applied Linguistics.

BEEBE, C. E. 1966, *The quality of education in developing countries*. Cambridge, MA: MIT Press.

BRODY, H. 1977, Eskimo: A language with a future? *Polar Record* 18, 117, 587–592.

BULLIVANT, B. M. 1984, *Pluralism: Cultural maintenance and evolution.* Clevedon, England: Multilingual Matters.

BURNABY, B. 1984, 1981 census perspective on planning for Native language programs. Paper presented at First Mokakit Conference, University of Western Ontario, July 1984.

CUMMINS, J. 1983, *Heritage language education.* Toronto: Ontario Institute for Studies in Education.

DORAIS, L.-J. 1983, *Uqausigusiqtaat/An analytical lexicon of modern Inuktitut in Québec-Labrador.* Québec: Presses de l'Université Laval.

——1985, La survie et le développement de la langue des Inuit. *Revue de l'Université Laurentienne.* (submitted for publication)

DRAPEAU, L. 1985, Le développement de l'écrit en Montagnais. *Recherches amérindiennes au Québec* 14, 3, 96–101.

FOSTER, M. K. 1984, Canada's first languages. *Language and Society* 9, 7–16.

FREEMAN, M. A. 1978, *Life among the qallunaat.* Edmonton: Hurtig.

HARPER, K. *et al.* (eds) 1983, Inuktitut writing systems: The current situation. *Inuktitut* 53, 36–78.

LOWE, R. 1983, *Kangiryuarmiut Uqauhingita Numiktittitdjutingit/Basic Kangiryuarmiut Eskimo Dictionary.* Inuvik: COPE.

——1984, L'assimilation linguistique des esquimaux de l'arctique de l'ouest. *Recherches amérindiennes au Québec* 14, 4, 54–57.

MACKEY, W. F. 1972, A typology of bilingual education. In J. A. FISHMAN (ed.), *Advances in the sociology of language.* Vol. 2. Selected studies and applications. The Hague: Mouton.

NORMANDEAU, L. 1981, *Les profils due nord du Québec: La population.* Chicoutimi, Québec: Université du Québec à Chicoutimi, Office de la planification et du développement du Québec.

PRICE, J. A. 1981, The viability of Indian languages in Canada. *Canadian Journal of Native Studies* 1, 2, 339–346.

SAGMAI, Gouvernement du Québec, 1984, *Native peoples of Québec.*

SKUTNABB-KANGAS, T. 1984, *Bilingualism or not.* Clevedon, England: Multilingual Matters.

STAIRS, A. 1985a, The developmental context of native language literacy: Inuit children and Inuktitut education. In B. BURNABY (ed.), *Promoting native writing systems in Canada.* Toronto: OISE Press.

——1985b, La viabilité des langues autochtones et le rôle de l'écrit: l'expérience de l'Inuktitut au Nouveau-Québec. *Recherches amérindiennes au Québec* 15, 3, 93–94.

STAIRS, A., CRAGO, M. & HOBBS, C. 1984, *COPITT Report on Child Observation Data 1979–82, Section 1: Perceptual-Motor Development. Section II: Language Development*. Dorval, Quebec: Kativik School Board.

ST. CLAIR, R. & LEAP, W. 1982, *Language renewal among American Indian tribes*. Rosslyn, VA: National Clearinghouse for Bilingual Education.

THARP, R.G. *et al.*, 1984, Product and process in applied developmental research: Education and the children of a minority. In M. E. LAMB, A. L. BROWN & B. ROGOFF (eds), *Advances in developmental psychology*. Vol 3. Hillsdale, NJ: Erlbaum.

WENZEL, G. "I was once independent": The Southern Seal Protest. *Anthropologica*, in press.

15 Nine years of Finnish-medium education in Sweden

What happens afterwards? The education of minority children in Botkyrka

TOM HAGMAN and
JOUKO LAHDENPERÄ

Background

Botkyrka, a municipality in metropolitan Stockholm, Sweden, had 10,000 inhabitants in the mid-1960s. Today there are 65,000, meaning that 55,000 of them have moved to Botkyrka during the last 20 years. Every fourth person has come from another country. Botkyrka has the highest density of foreign nationals not only in Sweden but in Scandinavia. The minority population is concentrated in northern parts of Botkyrka which were developed later, and here some 60–65% are minority members. The population is young, there are many young families with children in day care centres, preschools and schools. The relative percentage of school-children is high compared with other municipalities. In this article we will describe the education of immigrant and minority children in our community.

Towards the end of the 1960s the first attempts were made to "help" immigrant children in the schools. All children, regardless of their mother tongue, were sent to a Greek teacher, because the Swedish teachers did not know what to do with them. Some schools also started to hire Finnish teachers. Their duty was to teach children Swedish, but not Finnish.

In the next phase the parents, in particular, but also the teachers noticed that something was missing. It was natural to start demanding instruction in the children's mother tongue. Mother tongue language instruction was organized for a few hours a week, while Finnish children also received some auxiliary tuition through the medium of Finnish.

In 1971 the municipality hired an *immigrant consultant* who was to work with immigrant children's education in schools. This was also the year when the first *compound class* was set up, a first grade with both Finnish- and Swedish-speaking children, and two teachers, one Finnish and one Swedish. One more first grade of this kind started the following year. In 1973 the process was completed: the *first class started with Finnish children only, who were instructed through the medium of Finnish*. This was done for various reasons:

—The work in the compound classes made the two teachers in them completely dependent on each other. Their capacity to co-operate with each other became a crucial factor.

—Even when they co-operated reasonably well, the children soon learned who was the "real" teacher. Two teachers from different cultures cannot reach equal status when one of them is the representative of the majority, unless something special is done about it.

At this point the Finnish pupils in lower secondary education (grades 6–9) were also gathered into one group, and a Finnish-speaking teacher helped them in Finnish in different theoretical (academic) subjects.

All this development happened in one school district in Botkyrka only, in an area of the municipality where a Finnish-speaking population had been living since the mid-1950s. The positive experience from this district became decisive for the attitudes of the municipality towards immigrant education in general.

At the same time an organization for mother tongue teaching was developed for other language groups. It consisted of both language arts and auxiliary tuition through the medium of the mother tongue. At this point only the Finns had large enough groups to form their own classes, but as soon as other groups became large enough they had the same opportunity to have mother tongue medium education.

During all this time the Finnish immigrant group itself participated actively in realizing these changes, by way of the Finnish Association, the Finnish Home and School Association, and politically. Finns were active in several political parties and were elected to office in them.

The Home Language Reform (see Tingbjörn, this volume) obliged the municipalities to develop an action programme for immigrant education. The School Board in Botkyrka did this in 1977, and this action programme formed the basis for the political decision taken in 1977. According to that decision *every immigrant child in Botkyrka from a group which is large enough must be given the opportunity to attend a mother tongue medium class.* Mother tongue medium classes became the framework for organizing the education of immigrant and minority children in Botkyrka. For the other groups, mother tongue medium education includes grades 1–6 (ages 7–12), and for the Finns (who are the largest group) grades 1–9, i.e. the entire comprehensive school (ages 7–15).

Those groups which are too small to have their own classes attend Swedish-medium classes, but they have as much mother tongue language arts and auxiliary teaching through the medium of the mother tongue as the state allowances permit. Mother tongue medium classes get the same regular allowances as Swedish-medium classes. In addition, all minority children who participate in mother tongue language arts benefit from a special state fund for this. Because children's L1 is the medium of instruction in mother tongue medium classes (where large groups are kept together), the special state funds for mother tongue language arts need not be used for them and can thus be used to provide more L1 instruction for the smaller groups who are taught mainly through Swedish. Besides, if those minority children who are now in mother tongue medium classes were to be distributed in small groups in different Swedish classes, it would be more difficult (because of different timetables) to arrange the instruction in L1 language arts and L1-medium auxiliary tuition. This would also demand more financial resources. Also, the children would have to miss some of the instruction in other subjects in order to be able to obtain their L1-teaching, because children are pulled out from other lessons for it, and this might sometimes lead to difficulties in these subjects.

In 1978 the immigrant consultant's job was changed. Immigrant education got its own administrative unit, which it still has. This administrative unit became responsible for the education of immigrant and minority children, in all schools and districts of the municipality.

The main idea the School Council had was that the directors of immigrant education were to be given the same status as the directors of Swedish-medium education, namely the headmasters/headmistresses. The immigrant education school district has its own budget in the same way as the other districts. It can decide about the use of the state allowances for the actual teaching, materials and in-service education for teachers. It has its own budget for staff and administrative costs. The district has full responsibility for administering the mother tongue medium classes, mother tongue language arts and auxiliary teaching, and Swedish as a second language teaching. It hires the teachers and other staff and is responsible for them. It is also responsible for developing and disseminating the policy on minority education questions.

The municipality regards it as important that those who work for and with immigrants are immigrants themselves, and that it is possible for immigrants to obtain high status jobs in the administration of their own affairs. This ensures that in the negotiations between the immigrant school district and the "territorial" districts the negotiators have the same administrative position, which enhances equality. Co-operation is, of course, never completely devoid of conflict, especially in questions about minority education, and it is not made easier if there is a structural imbalance in power from the start. Positive attitudes have to be formed in structural positions.

The present situation

In 1984–85 Botkyrka had 2,640 pupils in comprehensive school (grades 1–9) and upper secondary school (10–12/13) who participated in mother tongue language arts. *This L1 teaching was given in 50 different languages.* Some 2,100 of these pupils participated in Swedish L2 teaching; 1,000 pupils were in mother tongue medium classes, which exist for the six largest language groups, in Finnish, Spanish, Turkish, Serbo-Croat, Greek and Arabic. Over 300 teachers worked in the immigrant education school district, and the teaching volume was just over 7,000 hours weekly.

All the teaching is organized in order to follow the intentions in the Swedish curriculum, LGR 80 (*Läroplan för grundskolan*, 1980). The weekly hours in grades 1–6 are divided according to the plan in Table 15.1.

In lower secondary grades (7–9) the instruction in theoretical subjects is in the pupils' L1, while L2, Swedish, is used in practical-aesthetic subjects.

There is some variation in the programmes of mother tongue medium classes, of course, in recognition of the fact that the backgrounds and concerns of the different minorities must be respected and used in a positive way. For instance, the Turkish mother tongue medium classes teach a few hours of mathematics and social studies through the medium of Swedish in higher elementary grades. Mother tongue medium classes are organized through grades 1–6, as mentioned earlier, and for the Finnish group through grades 1–9. In the teaching of Swedish as L2 the school district has attempted always to have bilingual teachers.

TABLE 15.1 *Syllabus for Finnish-medium classes in grades 1–6, hours per week*

Subject	Grade	1	2	3	4	5	6	Total
Art		—	—	—	2	2	2	6
English		—	—	—	3	4	4	11
Home economics		—	—	—	—	1	—	1
Sport		1	2	3	3	3	3	15
Mathematics		4	4	5	5	5	5	28
Music		1	1	2	2	2	1	9
Social studies + natural science		5	5	5	7	5	7	34
Wood and metal work		—	—	2	3	3	3	11
Finnish		9	10	9	4	4	4	40
Swedish		—	2	4	5	5	5	21
Optional subject		—	—	—	1	—	1	2
Total		20	24	30	35	34	35	

While the children are in mother tongue medium classes, instruction is actively planned in a way which ensures that children in different classes (mother tongue medium and Swedish-medium) have the opportunity to interact socially and learn together. The teaching in, for instance, woodwork and metalwork for groups that have these subjects in Swedish (e.g. Turkish children) is done so that one mother tongue medium class and one Swedish-medium class are divided, and each half is taught together with a half from the other class. When the schools work with a specific theme for a day or a whole week, all teachers, Turkish, Finnish, Swedish, etc. have the same role and responsibility for *all* children, regardless of language background.

Results and conclusions

Since the Finnish classes are the most comprehensive ones and started earlier than the other mother tongue medium classes, we know more about the long-term results of teaching through the medium of L1 for the Finns than for the other groups. The others seem to follow the same pattern, though. We have had Finnish-medium classes in lower secondary grades (7–9) in their present form since the autumn of 1979. In 1984–85 these classes had 182 pupils in total, divided between three schools.

In autumn 1984, we conducted a follow-up study with those students who finished grade 9. Our aim was to find out to what extent the students from the Finnish-medium classes continue their education in Gymnasium (i.e. the lower secondary education) which encompasses both vocational 2- or 3-year lines and theoretical 3- or 4-year lines (which function as a basis for further studies at the university). We also wanted to know what kind of grades the students gained on leaving the obligatory comprehensive education. The figures for the students from Finnish-medium classes were compared with the corresponding figures for all students from the other 9th grades in the same schools. These classes consisted of both minority students from other groups and all the Swedish students.

Finnish students in Sweden as a group show very low figures for further education (see Skutnabb-Kangas, this volume, Ch. 11). The students from the Finnish classes in Botkyrka show considerably higher figures for further education. In 1982–83, 25 of the 26 Finnish students applied for lower secondary education, and all 25 were accepted. In 1983–84 40 of the 41 Finnish students applied, and 38 were accepted. The percentage of Finnish students who applied for the theoretical 3–4-year lines, leading to university, was somewhat higher than for the students from the other classes. Both types of classes showed the same school achievement pattern, as measured by mean scores in all subjects (3.1 vs 3.0, on a scale of 1–5). Table 15.2

TABLE 15.2   *Students in grade 9 in Alby and Storvret schools, Botkyrka: comparison between Finnish- and Swedish-medium classes*

| | Finnish-medium | | Swedish-medium | |
	1982–83	1983–84	1982–83	1983–84
Number of students in grade 9	26	41	283	237
Applied for upper secondary education	25	40	268	227
Accepted for upper secondary education	25	38	260	222

Type of education for those accepted:	N	%	N	%	N	%	N	%
3–4-year theoretical	10	40	17	45	89	34	82	37
2-year theoretical	3	12	2	5	27	10	15	7
2-year vocational	12	48	18	47	121	47	112	50
other (shorter	—	0	1	3	23	9	13	6
		(100)		(100)		(100)		(100)

shows the proportion of students in higher education programmes from the two types of classes.

The results show that the students have integrated themselves into the Swedish comprehensive school at the same time as they have built up their academic self-confidence and identity.

Our reasons for keeping the minority children together and organizing their education in the way we have described could be summarized in a few points:

1. The minority children experience security and strengthen their self-esteem when they receive their instruction in "theoretical" subjects through their mother tongue (either in mother tongue medium classes, or through auxiliary tuition in L1).

2. The students are able to acquire knowledge in different subjects despite lacking competence in Swedish.

3. The students get structured and well planned teaching in Swedish as a second language, something that is often difficult to organize when minority students are spread out in Swedish-medium classes.

4. The students are given an opportunity to attain functional bi-lingualism, so that when they finish in the comprehensive school they have equal opportunity with Swedish children from a linguistic point of view.

5. We have built up a system which can also cope with newly arrived students.

6. Our experience is that the students, through first being physically segregated in mother tongue medium classes, have the opportunity to develop a capacity for fulfilling the role in society which they themselves choose. The initial segregation makes them capable of integrating, and gives them the confidence to integrate, at a later stage on their own terms. They start from identifying and developing their own strengths and life goals themselves, instead of being given preconditions and expectations by others.

7. Minority parents can, just like Swedish parents, contact the teachers as equal partners, in their own language, without being put in an inferior position.

8. Continuity is important for the students and the parents for long-term planning of schooling and housing. The parents must be able to place their trust in the school administration to take the responsibility

to continue to implement the programme (for the opposite see the chapter about the school strike in Rinkeby by Honkala, Leporanta-Morley, Liukka and Rougle in this volume).

9. Instruction in all the groups/classes where minority children are kept together is voluntarily chosen by the student and the parents.

10. Educational resources are used in the most efficient way through our way of organizing the teaching.

11. Both the parents and the local school administration in Botkyrka agree about the fact that our way of organizing the teaching fulfils a great need, and is done according to strong wishes on each side. Besides, this way of organizing minority education is what all the minority organizations in Sweden that have national unions have demanded from the government.

We believe that this type of instruction is to a large extent independent of which country the children come from and which country they immigrate to. In order to ensure the best possible teaching for all children, we feel that status questions play a decisive role, and this aspect of our model has a high degree of generalizability across countries. Minority children's languages and cultures can be given in every country the same status which Botkyrka has given to them. To some extent a certain variation may be needed in different countries, but the main thrust lies in questions about how to equalize the status and power relations.

Section IV: The global context

The last section, *The global context*, looks at the development and refinement of racism, including ethnicism and linguicism (Mullard, Phillipson), from a global point of view, showing past, present and future trends. It also questions the Eurocentric views in the policies dominant in most of the countries discussed in earlier contributions, by refuting many of the monolingually inspired claims about languages (Pattanayak).

16 Linguicism: structures and ideologies in linguistic imperialism

ROBERT PHILLIPSON

Introducing linguicism

This chapter analyses *linguicism*, "the ideologies and structures which are used to legitimate, effectuate and reproduce an unequal division of power and resources (both material and non-material) between groups which are defined on the basis of language (i.e. of their mother tongue)" (Skutnabb-Kangas, this volume, Chapter 1).[1] Linguicism is similar in its workings and effects to racism, sexism, classism, ageism and similar structures and ideologies which serve to maintain inequality. Like these, linguicism can operate overtly or covertly, at both the individual and the societal levels, and also at the supranational level. But whereas some of the -isms are fairly widely used in both scientific and everyday contexts, linguicism is a new concept and many of the phenomena it refers to seem to be relatively unanalysed. The foundations on which linguistic inequality rests, and the ideologies which legitimate the dominance of one language over others, as manifested, for instance, in beliefs and values in the teaching profession or in "aid" organizations, are relatively under-explored.[2]

The contention here is that the structures and ideologies of linguicism can best be identified and documented by placing them within an explicit theory of *linguistic imperialism*. Linguistic imperialism is seen as an essential constituent of imperialism as a global phenomenon involving structural relations between rich and poor countries in a world characterized by inequality and injustice. The theoretical construct, linguicism, and empirical studies of how linguistic inequality is structurally determined and ideologically legitimated, can serve as a springboard on which to project strategies for contesting such inequality, delegitimating it, and ultimately obtaining more justice for dominated languages.

The exemplification of linguicism in this chapter will be in relation to English, the imperialist language *par excellence* of the past two centuries. The mechanisms of linguicism, however, relate to any situation, nationally or internationally, in which one language dominates at the expense of others.

The chapter begins by considering some of the many forms that linguicism takes. It then outlines the structure of English linguistic hegemony internationally and the consequences for other languages. The way linguicism functioned to secure the dominance of English in colonial times is documented, as is the continuation of the structure of linguistic inequality in the contemporary, neo-colonial world, one aspect of which is the extension and consolidation of the power of English globally. Linguicist structures and ideologies in the professionalism of the language teaching world have contributed decisively to this. The final section attempts to draw conclusions about linguicism as a more widespread phenomenon, and about its relevance to the struggle for more justice for dominated languages.

Forms of dominance

Linguistic imperialism is invariably associated with economic, military, political, cultural and related forms of imperialism. Dominance takes a variety of forms in different historical periods and contexts, and is legitimated in different ways. For instance, religion is in some cases a causal factor in linguistic spread (Catholicism and Spanish have been inseparable in the Americas, as have Islam and Arabic) but not in all (e.g. the imposition of French in North Africa). In colonial times, the dominant powers ascribed to themselves a missionary role which was based on explicitly racist premises. The colonialist ideology is encapsulated in Earl Grey's remarks in 1899:

> "Probably everyone would agree that an Englishman would be right in considering his way of looking at the world and at life better than that of the Maori or Hottentot, and no-one will object in the abstract to England doing her best to impose her better and higher view on these savages ... Can there be any doubt that the white man must, and will, impose his superior civilization on the coloured races?" (quoted in Hodson, 1902:158).

Part of that "civilization" was language. Although empire is now largely vestigial, one of its most enduring legacies is language. And just as colonialism has been superseded by more sophisticated forms of exploitation, the crudely biological racist ideology has been superseded by ethnicism (see Mullard's contribution to this volume) and linguicism. The "higher and better view" of the West is now less represented by the gun and the Bible than by technology and the textbook. Western products still come wrapped in a Western language and in Western thought.

The *forms* that linguicism takes are many. For instance, structural linguicism may be *overt*, e.g. use of a given language is prohibited in institutional settings such as schools. Or linguicism may be *covert*, e.g. certain languages are *de facto* not used in teacher training, or as languages of instruction, or in aid activities, even if use of the languages is not explicitly forbidden. The prevailing ideology may be *consciously* linguicist, e.g. teachers instruct pupils not to use their mother tongue, because they are under the delusion that a ban of this kind will help the learning of another language. Or it may be *unconsciously* linguicist, e.g. English, rather than a local language, is assumed to be the ideal language for education, "development" or "national unity", whatever the local sociolinguistic and cultural context is.

Linguicist ideology has affinities with the way racism is affirmed (Preiswerk, 1980): it essentially involves the dominant group/language presenting an idealized image of itself, stigmatizing the dominated group/language, and rationalizing the relationship between the two, always to the advantage of the dominant group/language.

The international linguistic hegemony of English

The global spread of English has gone through several phases, as the hegemony of English has adapted to a constantly evolving situation. In the *colonialist* phase, the white man's linguistic burden was imposed as the dominant language throughout a far-flung empire. In the *neo-colonial* phase of the past quarter century, the "development" message has been carried overseas through the medium of the "international" language, English. Native speakers of British and American English, and "experts" using English as a second language, whether in business or "aid", in person or on celluloid, have served to secure the establishment or perpetuation of linguistic bridgeheads throughout the global periphery. The hegemony of English is secured and maintained via international organizations (Galtung, 1980:131). These are economic (private or governmental transnational organizations), political (international governmental organizations), military (systems of treaties and alliances), communicational (transport, press agencies) and cultural (entertainment, educational links). In "independent" Third World countries the position of English has been consolidated, for both internal and external purposes. To facilitate learning the language, and thereby entrench it and promote the interests represented by English, the English as a Second/Foreign Language profession has expanded dramatically during this period, in the West and in the Third World. The language has taken on new identities,[3] and linguicism ensures its predominance.

To put things more metaphorically, whereas once Britannia ruled the waves, now it is English which rules them. The British empire has given way to the empire of English. In multilingual contexts, English is seen very widely as providing access to employment, influence, desirable goods, etc. In Kachru's phrase (1986:1), the linguistic power of English is an alchemy:

"English is considered a symbol of modernization, a key to expanded functional roles, and an extra arm for success and mobility in culturally and linguistically complex and pluralistic societies . . . [English] permits one to open the linguistic gates to international business, technology, science, and travel."

The élites in Third World countries owe their position in part to their proficiency in English, and therefore accord a high priority to the learning of English. Even those not proficient in the language can see what it does for those who are, as evidence from oppressed groups in the Third World shows, whether in Kenya: parents "have an acute understanding of the competitive nature of life chances" (Obura, 1986:421) or in the slums of Bombay, where the English-medium school is a prestige symbol (Rajyashree, 1986:46).

The rapid spread of English is not without its *costs*. Those who fail in the quest for the alchemy of English see their life chances reduced. Those who become proficient in the alien language may sacrifice the language of their parents and their own culture in the process. The dominant language partially displaces other languages, through exclusive use of that language in certain domains (for instance in the media, or in the modern sector of the economy), and may replace the other languages totally (Phillipson & Skutnabb-Kangas, 1986b). For well established languages the addition of English should represent no substantial threat, but in many parts of the world linguicist structures and processes have resulted not in English enriching other languages and cultures but in English supplanting them. English is thus in India one of the major symbols of "Indian intellectual slavery" (Pattanayak, 1986:29).

The invariable corollary of the high status of English has been the low status of other languages. There is even worry about the influence of English in Western Europe, in countries with a long tradition of literacy, science and "modern" culture in their mother tongues. The European Parliament has expressed concern that the preponderant use of English in economic life, science and technology, due to the present-day dominance of American civilization, represents a threat to the languages and cultures of the European Community and the concepts and modes of thought embodied in these (European Parliament Working Document 1-83/84/B, 27).

It is of the essence of hegemony that injustices are internalized by both the dominant and the dominated groups as being natural and legitimate. However, neither the structures nor the ideologies are static. Hegemony is lived experience which is in a constant process of negotiation, recreation and adjustment. It is therefore open to contestation. An anti-linguicist strategy presupposes an analysis of what the source of the power of the dominant language is, and what the structures and ideologies are that maintain linguistic inequality. An active anti-linguicist policy in favour of dominated languages is needed at a variety of levels and in each context of linguistic inequality.

Linguicism in colonialism

This section looks at the role of linguicism in the colonial age. English was the language of the British empire. It was official policy to educate subjected peoples through the medium of English from the early nineteenth century. Macauley's educational goal for British India of the creation of a class of persons "Indian in blood and colour, but English in taste, opinions, in morals and in intellect" (Ashby, 1966:52) dovetailed with the demands of the civil service, legal system and all the other means of economic, political and ideological coercion used in colonialism.

The first missionaries operated in local languages, but from the early nineteenth century it was customary for British and American missionaries in Africa to teach and preach through the medium of English. Even if in both India and Africa there was later a policy of using local languages for the initial years of education, this was purely transitional, and languages other than English were stigmatized and incapacitated. Local educational traditions were ignored and marginalized. For those few in school who continued into secondary and higher education, what was offered was identical in content and form to British domestic education.

Macauley's policy was endorsed at the Imperial Conferences of 1913 and 1923. In the words of the head of the British Council's English teaching operations for many years, Macauley "determined what we should do, quite literally, from Hong Kong to the Gambia" (King, 1961:23). The English language was assumed to have the power of "civilizing the natives", a presumption that was articulated and promulgated more pretentiously for French by French colonial ideologists. Despite variation in the educational policies of the European colonial powers, in particular the greater use made of local languages by the British, education had a similar structural role in each empire (for details see Phillipson, 1986, Chapter 3). Acceptance of the "native" into the colonial order implied the adoption of the language of the conqueror and rejection of indigenous linguistic and cultural values. Colonial education embodied an explicitly linguicist structure and ideology, as formulated by a French educational ideologist (George Hardy, 1917, quoted in Taleb Ibrahimi, 1973:12):

> "To transform the primitive people in our colonies, to render them as devoted as possible to our cause and useful to our commerce ... the safest method is to take the native in childhood, bring him into assiduous contact with us and subject him to our intellectual and moral habits for many years in succession, in a word to open schools for him where his mind can be shaped at our will."

Such policies gave language a crucial importance in upholding the imperialist order. In *India*

> "proficiency in English became the gateway to all social and material benefits. If one looked for a job in the government, in educational institutions, in trade, commerce, or industry, knowledge of English was found to be essential. English also became the hallmark of an educated, cultured, and modern man and hence a marker of social position and prestige." (Misra, 1982:150)

In colonial societies, education determined access to influence, and in education "English . . . was the real key to success" (a comment on *Tanganyika* in White, 1980:269). In colonial *Ghana*, "education to many people came to mean simply the ability to speak and write English" (quoted in Mazrui, 1968:186). Success in secondary education in colonial *Zambia* involved "the ability to transpose one's mind from the immediate environment to the European one" (Chishimba, 1981:171). In the entrance requirements at university level in *Kenya* a high grade (a credit) rather than a pass in English was required. "Thus the most coveted place in the pyramid and in the system was only available to holders of an English-language credit card. English was the official vehicle and the magic formula to colonial élitedom" (Ngugi 1985:115)

When the educational provision in the colonies was expanded dramatically in the post-1945 period, as part of an intensive but belated effort to prepare the colonies for "independence", the primary focus was on English and education through the medium of English. The major policy document of this period, "African education: educational policy and practice in British tropical Africa" (Nuffield Foundation & Colonial Office, 1953) identified the need for an increased effort in teacher training colleges to improve the teaching of English and stressed the need for educational research into this subject (ibid.:172). The report argued for priority to be given to English. It made no recommendations for the local languages, apart from expressing the vague hope that some of them might evolve more literature at some point. The establishment of higher education institutions in the colonies did little to strengthen scholarship on African languages. The linguicist policy advocated in the report legitimated the allocation of material resources (teaching posts, timetable allocations) to English alone and reaffirmed the cultural supremacy of English. The *ideological* linguicism of educational planning was converted into the concrete, overt *structural* linguicism of institutions and teacher training programmes. Significantly, the participants at the conference which endorsed this policy were not only colonial administrators and educationalists but also representatives of the colonized countries. These had apparently internalized the norms and attitudes of their colonial masters *vis-à-vis* English, the master language, and its concomitant culture.

Linguicism in neo-colonialism

This section demonstrates how the power of English has been extended and consolidated over the past 30 years. It documents that there has been no significant break with colonialist linguicist practice, and that linguicism has been an essential component of neo-colonialism.

As language exerts a decisive influence on how we see and interpret the world, it is easy to understand that colonial language policies have had a deep, long-term impact. Their influence is still felt. English remains in the post-colonial age as the key language of the multinationals, of administration and justice, of the media, of the military, of science, of internationalism, of aid, of education, etc.[4] The colonial legacy is shared both by the decision-makers in the Periphery (Third World) and by the Centre (Western) personnel who directly or indirectly promote the continued use of European languages. The legacy can be traced in the allocation of resources first to European and then to other languages, which in turn affects the roles and status of each language and attitudes to them.

In sub-Saharan Africa the European languages are still dominant. "The foreign colonial languages are more favoured now than they were before independence", write the Director of the Inter-African Bureau of Languages of the Organization for African Unity, when noting that African languages have been phased out of the education systems, except in such countries as Tanzania and Somalia (Mateene, 1980:vii). The linguicist structural favouring of English and marginalization and displacement of local languages produces the ideological consequence that in countries like Zambia "language teaching, in general, has come to mean English language teaching" (Chishimba, 1981:169).

This state of affairs did not come about by chance. Education in Third World countries has been indelibly marked by the West, as a direct consequence of the Western "*aid*" that followed on the heels of colonialism. For the Americans, English language promotion, as one string of the cultural diplomacy bow, has been an integral part of a foreign policy aiming at global hegemony. Cultural and educational work represents the "fourth dimension" of foreign policy, alongside economic, political and military dimensions (Coombs, 1964). British policy documents of the 1950s explicitly seek the establishment of English as a world second language, and the containment of other languages, in order to protect capitalist interests (Phillipson, 1986, Chapter 4). Both governments have been aware of the integration of language and educational aid with economic, political and military ("security") goals.

In 1961 the British Council foresaw a global linguistic melting-pot, in a policy statement which sees a parallel between the establishment of the hegemony of English nationally and internationally:

> "America, with its vast resources, its prestige and its great tradition of international philanthropy, no less than because it is the largest English-speaking nation, is one of the greatest English-teaching forces in the world today. Teaching the world English may appear not unlike an extension of the task which America faced in establishing English as a common national language among its own immigrant population." (British Council Annual Report 1960–61:16).

The "establishment of English as a common national language" in the United States was achieved by a wealth of pressures over the past century, without formal legislation on national language policy being necessary.[5] English was structurally favoured over other immigrant languages and all indigenous languages. The melting-pot ideology ensured that "no polyglot empire of the old world has dared be as ruthless in imposing a single language upon its whole population as was the liberal republic 'dedicated to the proposition that all men are created equal'" (Gerald Johnson, 1949, quoted in Heath, 1981:19). English became overwhelmingly the first and only language of the citizens of the United States, though ethnolinguistic minorities have tenaciously resisted losing their distinctiveness (11% of Americans declared a language other than English as their mother tongue in 1960 (Fishman, 1972:109), and there have been large numbers of Asian and Latin American immigrants in recent decades).

The "philanthropic" foundations referred to in the British Council policy statement are financed by the profits of capitalism. Their disbursements are intended to perpetuate this system. The massive expenditure of funds in Europe between the two "world" wars (Fisher, 1982) and in the Third World (Arnove, 1982; Fox, 1975) has aimed at securing an extension and consolidation of this imperialist system. Educational aid has lent itself to the achievement of political and economic goals by ostensibly non-political means. A study of foundation "aid" to Africa concludes:

> "There can be little doubt that the Ford Foundation, Carnegie Corporation, and Rockefeller Foundation have used their largesse to insure the controlled growth and development of African societies through the strengthening of strategic cultural and political institutions. The primary means for this has been through support for African education, as well as complementary social science research and public training institutes ... The emphasis on the provision of a commodity which ostensibly had no political overtones and which is in great demand has enabled the foundation personnel to appear in the guise of disinterested humanitarians ... Education was perceived as the opening wedge ensuring an American presence in those African nations considered of strategic and economic importance to the governing and business élite of the United States." (Berman, 1982:225)

The professionalism of English Language Teaching

For the British and Americans to promote their common language successfully worldwide necessitated the urgent creation of expertise in English Language Teaching (ELT, a blanket term for English as Second or Foreign Language). Thus the number of higher education institutions in Britain offering specialist graduate courses in ELT rose from one in 1956 to 28 by the mid-1970s, and has almost doubled since. A similar expansion has taken place in the USA, though the focus here has been more directed towards internal English as a Second Language learning problems. Both countries have been heavily engaged in promoting the learning of English worldwide[6] (for details see Phillipson, 1986, Chapter 4). Scientific and educational imperialism ensured that it was in the Centre that expertise and theory-building evolved, for export to the Periphery and for control of it.

The ELT world has developed its own highly sophisticated professionalism. Innovation in language teaching methods is disseminated along with the language. Those whose business is promoting the language, the ELT profession, tend to see their task exclusively in terms of facilitating a language-learning operation. ELT is largely perceived, both in its own ranks and by others, as being a technical business which is unconnected with cultural imperialism, linguicism, or the global power structure which maintains the Periphery in a state of dependence on the Centre. The professional agenda is overt and highly technical, with its own internal specializations (syllabus development, English for Special Purposes, testing, computers in language learning, etc.) but the foreign policy agenda tends to be covert and imprecise. The professional training of ELT people concentrates on linguistics, psychology and education in a restricted sense. It pays little attention to international relations, development studies, theories of culture or intercultural contact, or the politics or sociology of language or education. The focus in ELT is thus on classroom language learning, materials development, teacher training and related issues. These cultural phenomena are disconnected from structure, the relations of production and societal power, nationally and internationally.

In the Third World, much educational planning has failed to accord due attention to language (Cawston, 1975). This left the door wide open for English to dominate education in post-colonial societies. Most of the educational language planning in the neo-colonial age that has taken place has been inspired by the professionalism developed in ELT in the Centre and, crucially, by a Western ideal of monolingualism. As a result of this, both the aid effort and the investment of newly independent countries primarily went into teacher training and curriculum development in the former colonial language.

The key conference of this period was the Commonwealth Conference on the Teaching of English as a Second Language, held at Makerere, Uganda in 1961. This was held as a direct outcome of a proposal of the First Commonwealth Education conference, held at Oxford in 1959. Linguicism ensured that educational language planning focused not on language learning needs in general, nor on the diversity and richness of the languages of the Commonwealth, but on English.

English is projected as representing "a gateway to better communications, better education, and so a higher standard of living and better understanding" (Makerere report, 1961:47). The way the report argues for an exclusive focus on English is typical of how linguicism operates to promote one language at the expense of others:

"Where a community has decided to participate as speedily as possible in the technological and other advantages of a wider society, a decision to use English as a medium is likely to be inevitable, and a pressure to introduce it fairly early may well be heavy. A society which lays stress on the preservation of a traditional way of life will not introduce English as a medium until later in the life of the child." (p. 21)[7]

Local languages are degraded and marginalized. English is held up as the model for all things good. The idea of any child being educated entirely through a language other than English is not even contemplated.

The legitimacy and political purity of the assembled experts are also explicitly proclaimed. The report claims that the conference was not "in any possible way concerned with politics ... Nor can there be any question of believing that we propose, by our efforts, to supersede or weaken or dilute any of the cultures of Asia and Africa" (p. 46). Drawing a clear dividing line between the technical concerns of the conference and "political" issues is an important premise for the conference, as it is for the ELT profession in general.

At Makerere a number of tenets were given a seal of approval, and these were to guide professional efforts over the succeeding decades. The key tenets can be formulated as follows (Phillipson, 1986:242):

—English is best taught monolingually

—the ideal teacher of English is a native speaker

—the earlier English is introduced the better the results

—the more English is taught the better the results

—if other languages are used much, standards of English will drop.

Although there has been some criticism of adherence to these tenets (Trappes-Lomax in Polomé & Hill, 1980; Pattanayak, 1981), which are in defiance of the UNESCO recommendations on the use of the mother tongues in education (UNESCO, 1953), they have tended to be widely accepted in the ELT profession. The tenets can be seen on closer examination, in the light of research on bilingual education and the available theories of language learning, to be fallacies (the monolingual fallacy, the native speaker fallacy, the early start fallacy, the maximum exposure fallacy, the subtractive fallacy; Phillipson, 1986, Chapter 5). The effect of the tenets is to accord priority to English, to the exclusion of all other languages.

Several other research studies into language-in-education issues indicate that much of the professionalism brought by the Centre to the Periphery was inappropriate culturally, educationally and linguistically (e.g. Widdowson, 1968; Kachru, 1975 and 1986; Mateene, 1980; Chishimba, 1981). The realization that the principles which have underpinned ELT professionalism are false and inappropriate raises serious issues not only about such policy issues as the medium of education but also about the nature of the aid relationship, and long-term accountability for aid projects. The inappropriateness is closely related to the fact that ELT has tended not to be seen in any wider educational and political perspective, implicitly takes the structures and ideologies of the Centre as the norm, and assumes these are universally applicable.

The implementation of policies based on these fallacies has had ideological and structural *consequences*: the Periphery was made dependent on Centre ideology (norms, models, expertise, theories) and products (aid personnel, books, technical support, etc.). These policies have contributed to the former colonial language becoming more secure than ever in the Periphery, and to local languages remaining underdeveloped. Externally, English is the medium for links between the élites in the Periphery and the Centre, in the economy, politics, the military, etc. Internally, proficiency in English represents the watershed between the "haves" and the "have-nots"—or, as Pattanayak more aptly calls them, the "never-to-haves".

The failure of ELT to deliver the goods is part of a general failure of educational aid. A survey of theories of educational aid and dependency and the empirical evidence ends with the bald statement that "there is a good deal of evidence that much Western educational curricula, technology and institutions have failed in the Third World because of their inappropriateness" (Hurst, 1984:33). There seems little dispute about this fact, whereas there is no consensus among the theorists of educational dependency (where a major concern is the contribution of education to the economy) on the causes for the failure, or whether one can conclude that aid is harmful or merely irrelevant (p. 28). However, the evidence of linguicism in education is unambiguous. It can only be interpreted as harmful to the vast majority of the population in the Periphery, and to their languages. Third World education systems which follow a Western model, like their Western counterparts, qualify the few and disqualify the many. The allocation of material resources to English and not to other languages represents a structural favouring of English, which has the following consequences:

- —school in Third World countries is dominated by English, and the vast majority of children get little benefit from schooling, linguistically or content-wise (Mateene, 1980);
- —pupils are taught by teachers with an inadequate command of the language (Afolayan, 1984);
- —the focus on English stigmatizes local languages, prevents them from being regarded as equally valid, and thwarts local cultural and linguistic creativity (Ngugi, 1981);
- —the Periphery looks to the Centre for professional guidance, instead of being self-reliant, but much Centre expertise is of dubious relevance to multilingual countries (Jernudd, 1981; Kachru, 1986; Pattanayak, 1986).

Linguistic imperialism has to do with more than language. Linguistic imperialism in education is intimately integrated with scientific and educational imperialism. Linguicism has served to reinforce and perpetuate the economic, military and cultural dependence of the Periphery on the Centre.

The struggle against linguicism

This chapter has documented linguicism by showing how English linguistic imperialism has spread and been consolidated in colonial and neo-colonial times. The analysis shows that the understanding of situations of language dominance can benefit from placing linguistic imperialism within a general framework of imperialism and by digging down to the historical roots of professional traditions. The case of the spread of English shows clearly that the "development" of this language has been structurally related to and contingent upon the underdevelopment of others. In this respect language is similar to economics. The rhetoric of the contemporary, neo-colonial civilizing mission has stressed altruistic motives and abstract moral principles, but the reality is more muddy. Linguistic imperialism has invariably been associated with other types of imperialism. The professional ideology in English Language Teaching has been linguicist, and harmful to education in general in the Third World and to other languages.

This chapter has focused on linguistic imperialism as one dimension of cultural imperialism, which is itself part of a complex network of relations that together make up imperialism. There is also evidence from many other studies of imperialism which corroborates the analysis here; in particular of educational and scientific imperialism, which are intimately related to linguistic imperialism. Similar structural and ideological forces are at work in media imperialism. The mechanisms of professional transfer to the Third World in media imperialism have been threefold: institutional transfer (in the case of British former colonies, export of BBC principles and practices), training and education, and the diffusion of occupational ideologies (Golding, 1977). The medium for this has, of course, been English. There are thus close parallels between media imperialism and linguistic imperialism. Linguicism in each dimension of cultural imperialism has the cumulative effect of strengthening English *vis-à-vis* other languages.

Although imperialism theory is essentially concerned with relations of dominance between countries, linguicism is a concept which can also be of relevance to the analysis of linguistic dominance within countries. Linguistic dominance is one aspect of *internal* as well as *external colonialism*. As well as spreading worldwide in recent centuries, English has spread throughout the British Isles and much of North America in ways which broadly parallel the consolidation of a national language in most monolingually oriented states. Indigenous and immigrant minorities have been the victims of linguicism. Thus, although the workings of linguicism have been demonstrated here in relation to English, the principles would apply to other dominant languages, nationally or internationally.

Among those who are mother tongue speakers of the dominant language, class differences are maintained by means of sociolects acquired in primary and secondary socialization. These enable the hegemony of the dominant group to be transmitted from one generation to the next. Social structures and ideologies legitimate an unequal division of power and resources between such groups.

Minority language groups can be discriminated against and dominated, or forced to assimilate, in like fashion. In immigrant language education in Britain and the USA, English is the main focus of attention, as is the dominant language in other "host" countries. There are analogies between the way the hegemony of English is maintained *"nationally"* *vis-à-vis* indigenous and immigrant minority language groups, as contributions to this volume show (Jordan for Australia; Stairs for Canada; Tosi for the United Kingdom; Ada, Campos and Keatinge, and Hernández-Chávez for the United States), and *"internationally"* throughout the Third World where English has become the language of power. Linguicist structures and ideologies operate in both contexts. Likewise there are analogies between the operation of linguicism in favour of English linguistic imperialism and linguicism favouring the dominant language *vis-à-vis* indigenous and immigrant minority languages elsewhere, in other contributions to this volume (Dutch in relation to Turkish and Moroccan, Appel; Swedish in relation to Finnish and Sami, in Jalava, Kalasniemi, Marainen, Hagman and Lahdenperä, Honkala *et al.*, Skutnabb-Kangas, Chapter 11).

The structural relations and ideologies underpinning linguistic dominance need identification and critical scrutiny in whatever context they appear. The analysis of linguicism can thus assist in the struggle for increased justice for dominated languages. The next phase is the formulation of anti-linguicist strategies. This struggle is well under way, as the contributions to this book demonstrate.

Notes to Chapter 16

1. The essential content of this chapter is derived from a series of empirical and theoretical investigations brought together in *Linguicism rules in education* (Phillipson & Skutnabb-Kangas, 1986a, 3 volumes, totalling 678 pages). This contains a series of joint articles analysing the spread of English, the role of applied linguists in this process, the links between linguistic imperialism and other types of imperialism, processes of language maintenance, language displacement and replacement, language rights, the legitimacy of the arguments used to promote English, and educational language planning. It also contains a detailed study of official British efforts to promote English, the creation of a worldwide professional cadre of English teaching "experts" and the ideology underlying their efforts. Linguicism, linguistic imperialism and linguistic hegemony are theoretical constructs which permit generalization about both this area of language dominance and the distinct but related area of immigrant and indigenous minority education.

2. In introducing a recent anthology on "Language of inequality", Dell Hymes notes the absence of a unifying theory of linguistic inequality, despite the extensive documentation of pervasive linguistic inequality worldwide (Hymes, 1985:v). He suggests that one reason for this state of affairs is that although scholars know of such matters as multilingualism, language minorities, and the dominance of some languages by others, their awareness is divorced from the professional identity and concerns of disciplines such as "theoretical linguistics" (ibid.). Effectively such professional expertise is disconnected from the sociopolitical contexts within which the expertise operates. Sociolinguists and sociologists of language have, of course, been concerned with the mechanisms by which social differences and privilege are maintained, within monolingual and multilingual speech communities, by means of

language. However, there have been major difficulties in linking the micro level of linguistic description to the macro level of power and societal structure. For Western work in this area, see Calvet, 1974; Cooper, 1982; and the extensive publications of Fishman, e.g. Fishman, Cooper & Conrad, 1977. For a Third World view, see Pattanayak's publications, for example his and other contributions to Annamalai, Jernudd & Rubin, 1986. The ultimate point of linguicism, language death or linguicide, has been of concern to sociolinguists (e.g. Day, 1985).

3. These identities are either geographical (Singaporean English, Kenyan English, etc.) or functional (e.g. computer English, medical English). On indigenization, and the emancipation of the geographical varieties from a British or American norm, see Kachru, 1986.

4. For analysis of the integration of linguistic imperialism with economic, political, military, social and cultural imperialism, and the implications for language maintenance or displacement, see Phillipson & Skutnabb-Kangas, 1986b.

5. See the thematic number of the *International Journal of the Sociology of Language*, 60, 1986 on attempts to bring about an amendment to the American Constitution so as to strengthen the position of English in the USA.

6. The present range of promotional activities of both Britain and the USA covers specialist training in the core English-speaking countries, scholarships, sending teachers of English and experts in teacher training and curriculum work abroad, aid projects, book presentations, libraries, the sale of low-priced books, radio English language programmes, the promotion of technological innovation, e.g. computer-assisted language teaching, etc. Much of this contributes to the displacement of local languages by English.

7. For a detailed study of the type of arguments used to justify the continued use of European languages in Third World education systems see Skutnabb-Kangas & Phillipson, 1986.

References

AFOLAYAN, A. 1984, The English language in Nigerian education as an agent of proper multilingual and multicultural development. *Journal of Multilingual and Multicultural Development* 5:1, 1–22.

ANNAMALAI, E., JERNUDD, B. & RUBIN, J. (eds) 1986, *Language planning. Proceedings of an institute*. Mysore: Central Institute of Indian Languages, and Honolulu: East–West Center.

ARNOVE, R. F. (ed.) 1982, *Philanthropy and cultural imperialism: the foundations at home and abroad*. Bloomington: Indiana University Press.

ASHBY, E. 1966, *Universities: British, Indian, African; a study in the ecology of higher education*. Cambridge, MA: Harvard University Press.

BERMAN, E. H. 1982, The foundations' role in American foreign policy: the case of Africa, post 1945. In R. F. ARNOVE (ed.) 1982, pp. 203–232.

BRITISH COUNCIL Annual Report 1960–61, London.

CALVET, L.-J. 1974, *Linguistique et colonialisme: petit traité de glottophagie*. Paris: Payot.

CAWSTON, F. 1975, The international activities of the Center for Applied Linguistics. In M. FOX 1975, Volume 2, pp. 385–434.

CENTRE OF AFRICAN STUDIES 1986, *Language in education in Africa*. Seminar proceedings 26, proceedings of a seminar at the Centre of African Studies, University of Edinburgh, 29–30 November 1985. Edinburgh: Centre of African Studies.

CHISHIMBA, M. M. 1981, Language teaching and literacy: East Africa. *Annual Review of Applied Linguistics* II, 168–188.

COOMBS, P. H. 1964, *The fourth dimension of foreign policy: educational and cultural affairs*. New York: Harper & Row, for the Council on Foreign Relations.

COOPER, R. L. (ed.) 1982, *Language spread: studies in diffusion and social change*. Bloomington: Indiana University Press, for the Center for Applied Linguistics.

CURRAN, J., GUREVITCH, M. & WOOLLACOTT, J. (eds) 1977, *Mass communication and society*. London: Arnold.

DAKIN, J., TIFFEN, B. & WIDDOWSON, H. G. 1968, *Language in education: the problem in Commonwealth Africa and the Indo-Pakistan subcontinent*. London: Oxford University Press.

DAY, R. R. 1985, The ultimate inequality: linguistic genocide. In N. WOLFSON & J. MANES (eds) 1985, pp. 163–181.

EUROPEAN PARLIAMENT 1984, Working documents 1984–1985.

FERGUSON, C. A. & HEATH, S. B. (eds) 1981, *Language in the USA*. Cambridge: Cambridge University Press.

FISHER, D. 1982, American philanthropy and the social sciences: the reproduction of a conservative ideology. In R. F. ARNOVE (ed.) 1982, pp. 233–268.

FISHMAN, J. A. 1972, *Language in sociocultural change*, essays by Joshua A. Fishman selected and introduced by Anwar S. DIL. Stanford: Stanford University Press.

FISHMAN, J. A., COOPER, R. L. & CONRAD, A. W. 1977, *The spread of English: the sociology of English as an additional language*. Rowley, MA: Newbury House.

FISHMAN, J. A., FERGUSON, C. A. & DAS GUPTA, J. (eds) 1968, *Language problems of developing nations*. New York: Wiley.

FOX, M. 1975, *Language and development: a retrospective survey of Ford Foundation language projects, 1952–1974*. New York: Ford Foundation (Volume 1, report; Volume 2, case studies).

GALTUNG, J. 1980, *The true worlds. A transnational perspective*. New York: The Free Press.

GOLDING, P. 1977, Media professionalism in the Third World: the transfer of an ideology. In J. CURRAN, M. GUREVITCH & J. WOOLLACOTT (eds) 1977, pp. 291–308.

HEATH, S. B. 1981, English in our language heritage. In C. A. FERGUSON & S. B. HEATH (eds) 1981, pp. 6–20.

HODSON, J. A. 1902, *Imperialism, a study*. London: Allen & Unwin.

HURST, P. 1984, Educational aid and dependency. In C. B. W. TREFFGARNE (ed.) 1984, pp. 23–37.

HYMES, D. H. 1985, Preface. In N. WOLFSON & J. MANES (eds) 1985, pp. v–viii.

JERNUDD, B. 1981, Planning language treatment: linguistics for the Third World. *Language in society* 10, 43–52.

KACHRU, B. B. 1975, A retrospective study of the Central Institute of English and Foreign Languages and its relation to Indian Universities. In M. FOX 1975, Volume 2, pp. 27–94.

——1986, *The alchemy of English: the spread, functions and models of non-native Englishes*. Oxford: Pergamon.

KING, A. H. 1961, The nature of the demand for English in the world today, as it affects British universities. In H. G. WAYMENT (ed.) 1961, pp. 22–25.

MAKERERE REPORT 1961, Report on the conference on the teaching of English as a second language. Entebbe: Commonwealth Education Liaison Committee.

MATEENE, K. 1980, Introduction. In K. MATEENE & J. KALEMA (eds) 1980, pp. vi–vii.

MATEENE, K. & KALEMA, J. (eds) 1980, *Reconsideration of African linguistic policies*. Kampala: OAU Bureau of Languages, OAU/BIL Publication 3.

MAZRUI, A. A. 1968, Some sociopolitical functions of English literature in

Africa. In J. A. FISHMAN, C. A. FERGUSON & J. DAS GUPTA (eds) 1968, pp. 183–198.

MISRA, B. G. 1982, Language spread in a multilingual setting: the spread of Hindi as a case study. In R. L. COOPER (ed.) 1982, pp. 148–157.

NGUGI wa Thiong'o 1981, *Writers in politics*. London: Heinemann.

——1985, The language of African literature. *New Left Review*, April–June 1985, 109–127.

NUFFIELD FOUNDATION AND THE COLONIAL OFFICE 1953, *African education; a study of educational policy and practice in British tropical Africa*. Oxford: Oxford University Press.

OBURA, A. P. 1986, Research issues and perspectives in language in education in Africa: an agenda for the next decade. In CENTRE OF AFRICAN STUDIES 1986, pp. 413–444.

PATTANAYAK, D. P. 1981, *Multilingualism and mother tongue education*. Delhi: Oxford University Press.

——1986, Language, politics, region formation and regional planning. In E. ANNAMALAI, B. JERNUDD & J. RUBIN (eds) 1986, pp. 18–42.

PHILLIPSON, R. 1986, English rules: a study of language pedagogy and imperialism. In R. PHILLIPSON & T. SKUTNABB-KANGAS 1986a, pp. 124–343.

PHILLIPSON, R. & SKUTNABB-KANGAS, T. 1986a, *Linguicism rules in education*. Roskilde: Roskilde University Centre, 3 volumes.

——1986b, English: the language of wider colonisation. Paper given at the 11th World Congress of Sociology, New Delhi, India, August 1986. In R. PHILLIPSON & T. SKUTNABB-KANGAS 1986a, pp. 344–377.

POLOMÉ, E. C. & HILL, C. P. (eds) 1980, *Language in Tanzania*. Oxford: Oxford University Press, for the International African Institute.

PREISWERK, R. (ed.) 1980, *The slant of the pen: racism in children's books*. Geneva: World Council of Churches.

RAJYASHREE, K. S. 1986, *An ethnolinguistic survey of Dharavi, a slum in Bombay*. Mysore: Central Institute of Indian Languages.

SKUTNABB-KANGAS, T. & PHILLIPSON, R. 1986, The legitimacy of the arguments for the spread of English. Paper at the post-congress session on Ethnocentrism in Sociolinguistics, Central Institute of Indian Languages, Mysore, August 1986. In R. PHILLIPSON & T. SKUTNABB-KANGAS 1986a, pp. 378–415.

TALEB IBRAHIMI, A. 1973, *De la décolonisation à la révolution culturelle*. Alger: Societé nationale d'édition et de diffusion.

TREFFGARNE, C. B. W. (ed.) 1984, *Contributions to the workshop on "reproduction and dependency in education", part 1*. London: Department of Education in Developing Countries, University of London Institute of Education (EDC occasional papers 6).

UNESCO 1953, *The use of the vernacular languages in education*. Paris: UNESCO.

WAYMENT, H. G. (ed.) 1961, *English teaching abroad and the British Universities*. London: Methuen.

WHITE, J. 1980, The historical background to national education in Tanzania. In E. C. POLOMÉ & C. P. HILL (eds) 1980, pp. 261–282.

WIDDOWSON, H.G. 1968, The teaching of English through science. In J. DAKIN, B. TIFFEN & H. G. WIDDOWSON 1968, pp. 115–175.

WOLFSON, N. & MANES, J. (eds) 1985, *Language of inequality*. Berlin: Mouton, Contributions to the Sociology of Language 36.

17 Racism, ethnicism and etharchy or not?

The principles of progressive control and transformative change[1]

CHRIS MULLARD

The post-war "changes" in and complexities of Western European societies with respect to race and ethnic relations have been fundamental and restructuring in their characterization. Considerations of the inequalities of race, class and gender and what might be called the policies of "legitimate domination" to manage these inequalities (assimilation, integration and pluralization policies) have underpinned and informed these "changes" and complexities since the 1950s.

Whilst much of my research over the last few years has been concerned with trying to describe these changes, it has also been concerned with an attempt to identify and analyse the contemporary configuration of the relations between race and class, especially, with central reference to the role of the state, ideology and power within a social refractionist and anti-racist framework, which in turn has stressed the existence and dialectical nature of the relations between competing definitions of reality.[2] This work is both theoretical and practical in the sense that it has been premissed on endeavours to understand in order to challenge and change the processes, forms and practices of institutionalized racism into those of institutionalized non-racism; and it should be mentioned here that this work is continuing and hence incomplete.

What has emerged to date is therefore only a number of explanatory pieces and the identification of several reformed institutional processes, practices, situations and phenomena. For the purposes of this paper the most significant identifications made so far can be set out as follows:

1. The identification of two challenging and oppositional yet connected social formations: the *dominant class–ethnic formation* versus the *dominated race–class formation* (Mullard, 1985a).

2. The identification of the social emergence and construction of *ethnicism* as the explicit cultural though structurally anchored expression of racism: a representation of the exchange or progression of a racial and largely structurally determined set of ideas and beliefs (bio-structural determinism—racism) to an ethnic and largely culturally determined set of ideas and beliefs (ethno-cultural determinism—ethnicism) (Mullard, 1985a).

3. The identification of the gradual construction of an *etharchy* or a progression from class hierarchies (assimilation), race hierarchy (integration) to *etharchy* (assimilated integration): a representational ordering and combination of the relational features of class, gender and ethnicity which, as an institution, dominates, controls and regulates the relations between dominant and dominated ethnic and racial groups in contemporary European society (Mullard, 1983).

4. The identification of *ethmission* as a qualitatively new kind of cultural transmission which involves a specific and complex hybrid transmission of the relational and ideational bases and the relative values of the class—ethnic construed knowledges of class, gender and ethnicity: a process which entails transmission, manumission (the freeing of ethnicity from race, culture from structure), and, lastly, mission (Mullard, 1983).

5. The identification of two oppositional types of policy and practice: *progressive* policy and practice which, stemming from dominant definitions of reality and the nature of the "problem", progresses from basically structural (race) to cultural considerations (ethnicity) with the object of control; and *transformative* policy and practice which, arising from dominated definitions of reality and the nature of the "problem", attempts to transform or structurally change existing racist and ethnicist policy and practice into non-racist policy and practice (Mullard, 1985b).[3]

Although, as yet, no overall attempt has been made to bring these and other theoretical pieces together into what might look like a social refractionist theory of race and ethnic relations, enough has been completed to suggest the broad contours of such a theory and to expose what constitutes one of the main barriers to its completion. Putting to one side for a moment the shape of the theory which is drawn from the way in which the competing class—ethnic and race—class formations relate to each other, the main barrier to be surmounted here is to be found not in the question of *why*, but rather that of *how* control and change or progressions and transformations have and can occur.

FIGURE 17.1   *Progressive Control and Transformative Change*

In other words, the task at hand is concerned with the unlocking of the internal, actual and ideal dynamics of the control–change relationship as portrayed in the model in Figure 17.1. More specifically it is to pose and try to answer two categories of related questions: the first to do with social control and the management of racism/ethnicism through the adoption of progressive (multicultural) policy and practice; and the second to do with social change and the management of non-racism/non-ethnicism through the adoption of transformative (anti-racist) policy and practice. So the purpose of this paper is to uncover what appear to be the principles of progressive control and the principles of transformative change. For it is only after the completion of this task that it is possible to move towards a fuller understanding of post-war "changes" in race and ethnic relations and to confront constructively both the institutionalized racism and the ethnicism of most Europeanized societies.

Progressive Control

As indicated earlier, there has emerged, certainly in Britain, France, The Netherlands, Scandinavia, Canada, Australia and elsewhere in Europeanized societies, a certain movement or progression from bio-structural to ethno-cultural perceptions, beliefs and definitions of the relations between relatively powerful majority and relatively powerless minority groups: a progression from racism to ethnicism. Similarly, at the level of the institutional order there has appeared a corresponding progression from a class–race to an ethnic–class determined stratification; a

progression from racial hierarchies to etharchies, or an institutional ordering in which ethno-culturally perceived and defined representatives of
dominated and oppressed groups (minority, indigenous, Mediterranean,
ex-colonial and other migrant groups, such as the Finns in Sweden) appear
to occupy high positions in the dominant power structure.

These and other progressions, including those in the whole area of
cultural communication and transmission, all embody several distinct
features. They are, firstly, a notion of movement from one point or
conception to another along a social continuum which in itself is an
expression of the fundamental continuity of the order of things-progress.
Secondly, all progressions in the field appear to exhibit a downward
appreciation of the "problem"; one which, within an implicitly pathological
perspective, explains the "problem" in terms of the social, cultural,
economic, linguistic and religious characteristics of minority groups—an
appreciation which either under-emphasizes (as in the United Kingdom and
France) or neglects altogether (as in The Netherlands, Belgium, Germany
and Scandinavia) the problem of institutionalized White racism (Lawrence,
1982). Thirdly, these progressions, such as the one expressed in the post-war
movement from immigrant-migrant to multicultural-intercultural policy,
embrace a broader objective than that of the tolerance, moral concern or
social assistance they proclaim.

Beneath these social covers of tolerance and pillows of goodwill lurks
an objective of *control*, or in the paraphrased words of senior officials in
The Hague, Paris, Stockholm and London:

> "How can we prevent disturbances, riots and threats to the social
> democratic state from occurring, but at the same time to be seen to be
> doing something about their problems. It is as much in our interests
> (i.e. the social democratic state's) as theirs that we tackle the problems
> in a way which does not upset the consensus, equilibrium and way of
> doing things here (in The Netherlands, France, Sweden and UK)."
> (OECD Conference, 1985)[4]

Thus, unlike any concept of "repressive tolerance", progressive control is
essentially a dynamic process.[5] It is a process which, observed in and
endorsed by policies, practices, official statements and the like, is oriented
and continuously moves towards newer forms of control which, in turn, are
called for as a result of changes in the material and structural conditions,
consciousnesses and resistances that distinguish the character of a
Europeanized society at any specific time in its post-war history.

Transformative Change

The concept and process of transformative change, in contrast to that of progressive control, is anchored in alternative and mainly oppositional definitions of reality. Instead of a movement or apparently logical progression from one point to another along a social continuum, transformative change calls for a break. It entails a special kind of break from former policies and practices and the relations in which they arise. Such a break encompasses not only a qualitatively different perspective from that which dominates, but, in the challenge, there also lives an idea of an opposite conception of approach, policy and practice; one which reflects a transcension rather than a progression from one state to another state of things. In other words, the kind of break which characterizes this kind of change cannot be seen merely as a shift from one position to another within a preconceived or determined framework. It is a break which necessitates the occurrence of a *transformation* of the existing, dominant framework, or, in policy terms, the social transference and exchange of one set of policies based upon one set of beliefs to another oppositional set based upon an oppositional set of beliefs.

Thus the second major feature of transformative change is to be found in the nature of the oppositional and hence alternative beliefs on which it is based. In the case of the field of race, ethnic and minority relations, these beliefs, perceptions and definitions result from an upward appreciation of the "problem"; an explanation which, in turn, is framed within a structural perspective, or one which suggests that the "problem" is located at the level of the institutional bases of society. Moreover, such an explanation is grounded in the premiss that White racism is an institutionalized feature, forming part of the common-sense knowledge of all Europeanized societies dependent upon the labour of Black, ex-colonial, Mediterranean or other migrant workers.

"From this position this alternative and largely dominated definition reflects a view of the world in which Whites, not Blacks, the cultural majority as opposed to the cultural minority groups and the institutional structures and ideologies they fashion and control, constitute the 'problem'. This, of course, is a definition of reality which is inextricably tied up with a critique of the making and continuing of most racist Europeanised societies—the coming into being of the nationalistic capitalisms and states of Europe as a directly related result of slavery, colonialism, imperialism (e.g. Great Britain, France, The Netherlands, Belgium, Portugal); the development of new-world type colonies into Europeanised capitalist economies out of conquest, the

massive extermination of Black, and other indigenous peoples, the
large scale 'forced' migrations (e.g. America, Canada, Australia, New
Zealand, South Africa) and the continuing and restructuring of the
productive capacity and surpluses of all these societies, in especially the
post-war period, through the encouragement of migration and the
exploitative employment of largely Black or, descriptively speaking,
non-White labour." (Mullard, 1985b)

The meaning of change

Although the above perspective is clearly different and in most respects
oppositional to that held by the advocates of progressive, piece-meal or
reformist policy, at first glance, the same thing cannot be said about the
third characteristic of transformative change—namely the objective of
change itself. The reason for this is due in part to the ambiguity of the
concept of change in so much that it can be argued that all progressions, as
well as transformations, constitute a change of some sort. On the plane of
literal description this, of course, is indisputable: all movements from one
point to another represent a literal change. But the difference between literal
and essentially horizontal change (progression) and a change which calls for
a break and a social repositioning into the vertical (transformation) is to be
seen not just in terms of this kind of conceptual distinction. It is also to be
found in the socially organized interests and objects which underpin and
inform both the type and quality of movements; or to put this observation
in another way, it is to be found in the question—a movement for what?

While the pure answers to such a question are obviously those of
control (progression) and change (transformation) with the latter embody-
ing the object of the movement itself, the hybrid responses include both a
concept of control–change and change–control. Whereas the former more
closely approximates to reformism as a masked type of progressive control,
where the movement or progress seems to conceal the object of control and
in so doing appears to become the object, the latter signifies radicalism as an
eclipsed type of transformative change. But whatever the designations
chosen to describe the variations and manifestations within the two basic
orientations, the control–change forms, along with the primary object of
control, are all part of progressive control and, conversely, all change–control forms fall within the category of transformative change.

Although slightly distanced from the immediate aim of this paper (i.e.
to set out the principles of progressive control and transformative change)
this definitional detour has been necessary for a number of reasons. Firstly,

it has helped to clarify a basic confusion that nearly always surrounds discussions on the usage of the concept of change. Secondly, it has introduced here another level of complexity, which addresses not only the designation of policies and practices as reformist or radical, but which also suggests where, for instance, reformism and radicalism as specific policy types might be located in relation to each other and the broader social objectives of policy and practice. Thirdly, it has helped to indicate outside of the realm of discussing things as they are, the here and now in society A or society Z, that progressive control is not some immutable description or conceptual apparatus for the understanding of, say, the policies and practices of the political and ideological right, or that transformative change is somehow inalienably the prerogative of the political and ideo-logical left. Indeed, this detour has released, in admittedly an unworked-out way, any direct associations that might be made between right and left and progressive control and transformative change—for the reality is that societies can be changed (transformation) from socialist to capitalist, capitalist to socialist and, likewise, within any given society control (progression) can and does exist.

The "PC" principles

To return to the purpose of this paper within the field of race, ethnic and minority relations, and given the qualifications alluded to above, the main questions can now be restated as follows: How has the progression from racism to ethnicism occurred, and what are the principles which underpin such a progression? And in the light of the answer to this question, what then are the probable principles that underlie a transforma-tion from racism and ethnicism to non-racism?

In the case of the first question a systematic study of racial policies and practices (with particular reference to education) in the United Kingdom and a critical acquaintance with general racial policy and practices in, for instance, Canada, Australia, Sweden and The Netherlands have revealed that there exist four chief principles of control progression (see Mullard, Bonnick & King, 1983a, 1983b, 1984a, 1984b). They are: (i) disconnection; (ii) reconstitution; (iii) affirmation; and (iv) legitimation.

(i) Disconnection

This principle involves the disconnecting or separating out of the various parts of an explanatory perception and definition of the "problem". That is to say, the biologically and intrinsically structural in race is disconnected from the ethnic and predominantly cultural. For instance, as can be seen in the progression from immigrant to multicultural education or migrant-assimilationist to multicultural pluralist policies, the official discourses in which this principle can be observed undergo an alteration. They move from centring on biological and physical references as justifications for acts and patterns of discriminatory behaviour to ethnic and cultural references. Though theoretically false the disconnection that occurs here is a separating out of culture from structure in such a way as to suggest not only that it is possible to do this, but that the structural bases and reasons for the attraction of migrant groups in the first place were hardly, if at all, connected to the process of and need for labour exploitation and capital maintenance or accumulation. Thus the disconnection that takes place is a little more than the disconnecting of culture from structure: it encompasses a disconnection of a certain array of historically experienced conditions such as oppression, exploitation and discrimination (structural) from what might be termed a range of rationally acceptable characteristics such as language, religion, customs, dress and food (cultural).

In the case of the Finnish migrants in Sweden, the Turkish *Gästarbeiters* in Germany and The Netherlands, and, for example, the Asian migrants in Britain, this kind of disconnection has become almost a statement of the obvious. Despite the differences in the historical antecedents and dating of the afore-mentioned migrations, it is clear from national policy reports, press accounts and other sources that what van Dijk terms an ethnic discourse has become almost totally disconnected from any structural basis in the economy (van Dijk, 1982, 1985, 1986). Focusing on the so-called "ethnic and cultural" features of migrant populations and imputing the existence of a massive sociocultural distance between migrant and non-migrant groups, this discourse in the 1980s is built up without reference, in order, possibly, to deny the value of the economic role of migrant workers in Europeanized societies. Hence the conditions under which migrants survive and the racism and ethnicism they experience are similarly denied in part, as in Britain, or in whole, as in The Netherlands or Sweden (Essed, 1984; Skutnabb-Kangas, 1984, 1985).[6] The disconnection and, of course, with it all forms of moral responsibility, obligation and, in the last analysis, acceptance of migrant groups as "being equal to" become negated in the very principle, process and actions of disconnection—for in Europeanized societies the reality of disconnection become *the* reality.[7]

(ii) Reconstitution

Once the disconnection has taken place a problem, however, still remains, namely that of how to maintain the historical conditions required to secure capital maintenance or acquisition or, in situations of economic recession and unemployment, to maintain differentiations between majority and minority groups and between the various minority groups themselves. In short, this calls for and makes evident the principle of reconstitution. At one level what this means is the reconstituting of the structural in terms of the cultural, the equating of structural conditions with rationally acceptable ethno-cultural as opposed to bio-structural characteristics, and the almost complete elevation of a discourse informed by cultural influences, considerations and characteristics over that of an earlier and structurally informed discourse. Yet, as the cultural characteristics are far more numerous than the structural and as they appear to be more rationally acceptable, the possibilities of creating more sophisticated and fuller patterns of differentiation are then that much greater. Indeed, the actual political effect and use of reconstituted reality is to be witnessed in the making and ordering of cultural differentiations into what amounts to an ethnically prescribed cultural hierarchy—which together with the cultural features of class and gender forms the foundations and brickwork of the etharchy.

In other words, the principle, process and actions of reconstitution are in essence the reality forming and shaping materials and social clothing of the primary and ideologically managed disconnection of culture from structure. As new forms of "punishment and discipline" in Europeanized, capitalist societies required the disconnection of "body" from "soul", and later "mind", then new forms of differentiation have likewise presaged new hegemonic relations and forms of social organization or probable stratification—and vice versa (Foucault, 1979). Seen in this way, reconstitution as the symbolic re-ordering of the structural into the cultural, the material into the non-material becomes as a principle as well as a process the archway that bridges reality before and after disconnection.

(iii) Affirmation

Clearly the principles of disconnection and reconstitution and the processes and actions in which they are embodied remain merely hypothetical discoveries unless they can be observed in operation. This again is possible to do in the international, national and local debates on race, ethnic and migrant issues. For what can be observed in such debates is not just the content, which is heavily culturalized, ethnicized and prejudiced, but also the projection and affirmation of the disconnected-reconstituted reality. The perceptions or voice of dominant, non-migrant groups then in essence constitute an affirmation of both a new reality which equals a shift or progress from structural to cultural definitions, and a way forward for the re-patterning of broad sociocultural and specific race, ethnic and migrant relations. So discussions on inequality, exploitation, disconnection as were heard a decade or more ago, and which led to tokenistic, anti-discrimination legislation in, for example, America, Britain, Canada, Australia and The Netherlands, have now been more firmly replaced with discussions on language, scholastic underachievement, religious differences, ethnic crime, cultural (family) disadvantagement, and so on.[8] These and many more ethnicized topics have come to form, therefore, the content of a fairly integrated discourse in and through which is affirmed not only a pluralistic (*qua* etharchical) as opposed to a class- and gender-ordered society but, more subtly, the discourse itself has become both a producing and reproducing medium and a social conduit for the affirmation and preservation of the culturally reconstituted relations of power.

This is to say that the principle of affirmation is an essential part of the expressive apparatuses of power. Whether what is affirmed or not is dominant or otherwise is naturally dependent upon the ownership of and access to the media and other sites, agencies and institutions where affirmations can be made and heard. But given that these sites, agencies and institutions, including education, are controlled if not solely owned by dominant non-migrant groups, then it is to be expected that what is currently being affirmed in Europeanized societies is in fact a cultural rather than structural, an etharchical rather than a class definition of the relations between race, ethnic and migrant/non-migrant groups.

(iv) Legitimation

Closely connected to, but qualitatively different from the principle of affirmation, the principle of legitimation is to be found in the arenas, practices and actions which are at least officially, if not always legally, sanctioned by the governments of Europeanized societies. Thus, the multi- and intercultural policies of these societies, enshrined often in constitutional law, such as Canada's multiculturalism, formal and governmental statements of policy as in the case of The Netherlands, or as a mixed set of legislation and statements which characterizes Britain's position, appear then to sanction and hence help to legitimate or provide validity for the apparent progression of changes—from racism to ethnicism, class–race to ethnic–class formations, and racial hierarchy to etharchy.

Even more than this, the way in which the principle of legitimation is articulated (that is the actual practices, actions and statements endorsed and sanctioned by the state) is at all times located in a legislative and policy discourse, which continuously propounds a notion of progress and change. By its powerful advocates such a development is seen to be more progressive, liberal and moral; one which is sensitized by a concept of culture difference rather than structural similarity, by individual ethnicity and cultural biographies rather than by fundamental social classifications and histories. It is thus a development which stretches back along the well-trodden traditional Europeanized route of individualism and forward towards a state of affairs in which individuated reality approximates social reality and hence where individual differences, needs and experiences triumph over collective similarities, objectives and conditions. Thus unlike the principle of affirmation, which is necessary for acquisition and the mapping out of the intentions of power, the principle of legitimation is required for the actual rationalized confirmation of power and dominance. But like the other principles of disconnection, reconstitution and affirmation, it, too, is to be found in the same overall discourse on race, ethnic and migrant relations, existing alongside and as part of others as well as in its own supreme right vitalized in the legislation and governmental policy statements of Europeanized societies.

The "TC" principles

Also four in number, these principles (in reverse order to those discussed above) are: (i) legitimation; (ii) affirmation; (iii) deconstitution; and (iv) connection.

(i) Legitimation

If the legitimation principle within progressive control policy and practice is to be found clearly operating and symbolized in legislation and governmental policy statements, then it is, perhaps, clear that such a principle is not completely detectable within transformative change policy and practice. This is not to say that it does not exist, but it is to suggest that full legitimation can only take place once the advocates of "TC" policy and practice occupy positions of dominance, through takeover or conversion in ideological struggle, and thus constitute either the government or those sections within it, including national and international governmental agencies, responsible for influencing and changing race, ethnic and migrant-oriented policies and practices. Indeed, any argument which purports that the legitimation principle is absent within the "TC" perspective is at the same time discounting not only the anti-racist and non-ethnicist struggles currently being waged in Europeanized societies by White and Black, migrant and non-migrant, but just as seriously is overlooking the effect and influence of these struggles on the formulation of local, national and, as partly stated in the EEC statements on human rights and migration, international policy (if not, entirely, practice).[9] In other words, the legitimation principle, varying only in degree of operationalization (which in turn is understandable only within the relations of dominance and domination) is common to both "TC" and "PC" positions on policy and practice in the field.

(ii) Affirmation

Similarly, the principle of affirmation occupies an almost parallel social and theoretical status to that of legitimation. Where it differs is in respect to the relationship between "intention" and "confirmation". Or to put it rather bluntly, the intentions of dominant groups within a power structure are more likely to be confirmed and instigated, whilst the intentions of dominated groups in their affirmations of "TC" policy and practice either become partially incorporated or are dismissed altogether as militant rhetoric (UK), Communism (USA/Canada, Denmark, etc.), or, rather quaintly, as being "unscientific" (Germany, Sweden, The Netherlands).

Although these and other strategies of dismissal provide considerable scientific interest in their own right, they also, of course, indicate the presence of an affirmation principle within "TC" policy and practice—one which is as discernible in the alternative academic and non-academic media, the statements produced by race, ethnic and migrant groups, organizations and movements, and the reports and papers delivered within the consultative framework of government policy, as it is in the struggles fought and the positions taken by migrant groups, Black and White, in the workplace, in schools and on the streets. It is consequently in the processes, practices and actions of the continual affirmation of oppositional and alternative values, beliefs and definitions of the "problem" outlined earlier in this paper that a significant step can be taken towards the creation of non-racist, non-ethnicist and non-etharchical societies.

(iii) Deconstitution

Unlike the principle of reconstitution, this principle of deconstitution is always to be found at work in the actions and practices of those groups who oppose dominant definitions of reality. As a principle associated with and observable in the struggles of dominated groups, it operates to see through, break down and unpack constituted reality which, as argued elsewhere, is a form of refracted reality (Mullard, 1985c). This means, in essence, that the various media of refraction, based upon interest-governed conceptions and definitions of reality (the "problem") and involving all the ideological apparatuses of the Europeanized state, are identified and ultimately analysed within the framework of the alternative perspectives that promote "TC" policy and practice as the only effective restructuring instrument of change.

On one level deconstitution then involves a questioning, analytical and resistive programme of intellectual and counter-ideological or, utilizing Mannheim's classic insight, "utopian" work, digging beneath the pragmatic to reveal the paradigmatic, scouring the bundle of "good intentions" and statements of "goodwill" to expose interests (Mannheim, 1936). On another level, and on one which relates directly to the experiences of race, ethnic and minority groups, deconstitution as a principle in practice calls for a deconstituting of the dominant images about ourselves that dominant racist and ethnicist groups possess. This is not a question about debunking lazy, slave-working, flighty, sexual, cunning or Uncle Tom-ish stereotypes, but rather a question of retrieving the subject from the object, the object from the subject, which dominant groups in the process, practices and actions of disconnection and reconstitution have separated out and re-ordered in accordance with dominant definitions of interests and reality.

But yet on a third, far more penetrating level, the principle of deconstitution operates to establish how structural relations, conditions and histories have been reconstituted culturally, and thus how new forms of control and reconstituted relations of power, dominance and hegemony have been constructed over time, under specific conditions and within a realm of both stable and shifting interests. It is in this respect that the principle itself is one which, along with that of connection, truly characterizes the "TC" position and, accordingly, the detailed strategies of anti-racist struggle (see Mullard, 1984 for a more detailed account of such strategies).

(iv) Connection

This final principle, of course, corresponds oppositionally with that of connection. It is a principle which in operation rejoins all that which has been disconnected, structure with culture, culture with structure, in a way which demonstrates the actual inseparability of structure and culture— other than as an heuristic possibility in order to subject specific phenomena to one form or other of analysis. As a principle, connection not only shows that culture lives in and springs from structure, material or structural-culture, and that culture, too, however remote, always possesses or gives rise to a structural base, namely a notion of "cultural materialism". But, less abstractly, the principle of connection—unlike that of deconstitution—leads to a holistic approach, perspective and an eventual understanding and explanation of social reality. It is the key principle which unlocks the social safe built out of the processes, practices and actions of "PC"-oriented dominant groups: it is the principle which connects history with contemporary experience, consciousness with action, object and subject with identity, dominant languages with control, dominated languages with resistance, oppression with liberation, and so forth.

Therefore, as a principle which exhibits in the historical and theoretical text of "TC" policy and practice a basically non-fractional and non-refracted view of the world, it is able to allow for the dialectical combination of old and new dichotomies as well as the sequential development of one action after another within the frame of reference in which it is embedded. In other words the principle of connection, in juxtaposition and opposition to that of disconnection, operates to combine both the normally uncombinable and the combinable within an explanatory framework, whose immutable references are those of justice, equality and freedom.

Although the degree to which this is achieved is largely dependent upon the quality of consciousness employed to actualize the principle, the existence of such a principle is almost indisputable, as can be readily seen from the numerous references made by race, ethnic and migrant groups in Europeanized societies to, for example: the historical experience of slavery or contract labour and the contemporary experience of racism (the Afro- and Asian-Caribbean migrants in Britain, France and The Netherlands); the colonial and imperial experience and the current experience of race and ethnic subordination (all colonial, ex-colonial migrants, including the Finns in Sweden, the Irish in Britain and the Algerians in France); and, lastly, the relatively recent experience of *Gästarbeiters* and their present experiences of ethnicism (the Turkish migrants particularly in Germany and The Netherlands, the Greeks and Italians in Germany, the Moroccans in France, and other smaller migrant groups in Europeanized societies).

The "PC" and "TC" principles summarized

The principles outlined in the last two parts of this paper cannot, of course, be separated out in the normal course of social activity in the field of race, ethnic and migrant relations. To a greater or lesser extent they exist in most policies, practices and actions. Although it is obvious that the "PC" principle of disconnection and the "TC" one of connection have to precede in a sense those of, say, legitimation and delegitimation it is, however, also clear that in the main policies and actions, which embody the latter, the former and other principles are evidently present. Thus each action, policy or practice displays at least one, often more, and sometimes all of the principles discussed and set out in Figure 17.2.

Even though the principles, as discussed here, might lend themselves to the specific description of a particular political and ideological stance, the point made at the beginning of this paper must be re-emphasized. Namely, the principles themselves transcend political or ideological positions: they are located in and result from dominant and dominated structures and relations of power and, particularly, the way in which these structures and relations face each other. Thus in societies which are dominantly socialist, the kind of progressive control policies pursued appear to rarify and disconnect structure from culture, as opposed to the other way round, which, as already shown, is a characteristic of non-socialist (Europeanized) societies. So in these socialist societies the thrust of transformative change policy is still based upon the principle of connection: to connect culture to structure and in the act of doing this to de-constitute or break down and unpack constituted or refracted reality. Not only then are the principles the same in socialist or capitalist societies, but the main question to be asked in order to account for the deep differences between these two types of society is the one of—"what?" This is to say, what is disconnected, connected; what is reconstituted, deconstituted, and what is affirmed and legitimated in each main type of society? In other words, the point being made here is not one which concerns the existence or otherwise of the principles in societies

P R I N C I P L E S	Progressive Control	Transformative Change
	1. Disconnection 2. Reconstitution	1. Connection 2. Deconstitution
	3. Affirmation 4. Legitimation	

FIGURE 17.2 *The principles of Progressive Control and Transformative Change*

of different ideological persuasions—as they exist in *all* societies. Instead it is one which concerns contents and relative values, judgements and opinions made about these contents.

A final interesting rounding out point to be made before concluding in effect calls for a return to the very notion of progressive control ("PC") and transformative change ("TC"). It will be recalled that at the outset the two types of policy and policy directions were introduced as existing on two qualitatively different planes: with progressive control on a horizontal plane and transformative change breaking the horizontal to form a vertical plane. The question this begs cannot be fully addressed here, of course, but it is one which relates to the starting points of "PC" and "TC", the possibility of moving backwards as well as forwards at any given point of time in history, and, in fact, to the existence of another "ideal" type of control and change. For the purposes of descriptive rather than analytical completion it is possible to refer to one as being a form of *regressive control* ("RC") and the other a form of *subvertive change* ("SC").

Whilst neither term is over-precise, both, nevertheless, indicate the kind of polar opposites associated with the two main types of policy and practice. Regressive control, for instance, holds an idea that policies can move backwards to a point at which they are openly and incontrovertibly racist, fascist and bordering upon absolute authoritarianism, such as those implemented in Nazi Germany and Stalinist Soviet Union in the past and the apartheid policies of South Africa today. And subvertive change also contains a similar notion of going back from open policies of changing societies which can or are willing to be changed, to closed or clandestine policies of undermining, from within an alternative perspective, the highly repressive and authoritarian policies of regressive control societies.

Lastly, as can be seen from Figure 17.3, it is also possible to have both kinds of change policies existing in "RC"- and "PC"-oriented societies. But it would be a contention here, as symbolized by the broken lines in the figure, that severe repressive control precludes any full expression of transformative change policies and practices because, as the fates of Steve Biko, Nelson Mandela and many others in South Africa clearly demonstrate, the advocates of such policies and practices are either imprisoned indefinitely or murdered by the state.

In this kind of situation policies and practices of subvertive change are then the only feasible or realistic ones to follow.

But in progressive control situations and societies subvertive change is made more or less redundant by the degree of "progressiveness" that

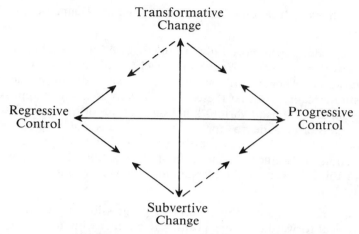

FIGURE 17.3   *Transformative Change versus Progressive Control, Subvertive Change versus Regressive Control*

pertains; for as witnessed in the already quoted paraphrased words of senior officials in The Hague, Paris, Stockholm and elsewhere, one of the main content features of progressive control is "to be seen to be doing something about their problems".

Thus, in these mainly Europeanized societies there exists a need to move forward along the vertical plane to a point where the policies and practices of transformative change are worked out, embraced and, as an outcome of struggle, implemented.

In academic and theoretical terms this calls for far more searching, critical and experientially sensitive and sensitized studies into precisely how the principles of disconnection, reconstitution, affirmation and legitimation work. These studies are not only necessary for understanding how forms of progressive control manifest themselves, but they are of overwhelming importance for the understanding of what needs to be connected, deconstituted, affirmed and, finally, legitimated if the object is to transform Europeanized societies—from racist to non-racist, from ethnicist to non-ethnicist, and from etharchical to non-etharchical societies.

Notes to Chapter 17

1. The first draft of this paper was presented as the principal plenary paper for the International Symposium on Minority Languages in Academic

Research and Educational Policy, Sandbjerg Slot, Denmark, 1–3 April, 1985.

2. Although developed more fully in Mullard (1985c) a social refractionist framework here means a framework which is built upon the basis of four propositions. They are: (i) that images of reality do not in themselves constitute reality; (ii) that these images or representations approximate to social distortions of various kinds and various degrees; (iii) that these distortions are made to appear "real" in ideological practices and accounts of situations; and, lastly, (iv) that it is through the study of refractions, a specific kind and form of social action, that it is possible to move towards a greater understanding of what might be "real" and "true".

3. In this present chapter the concept of progression is used to denote a movement forward from one position to another without a fundamental break or change in values, beliefs or ideology. Thus, it is to be distinguished from the idea of "progressive" as a euphemism for "revolutionary" forces.

4. Heard expressed at an OECD Conference, January, 1985, this quotation not only paraphrases the viewpoint of many senior officials in parliamentary capital cities, but it is also reflected at regional, local and individual levels amongst administrators, teachers, social workers, etc.

5. The distinction that is being made here is that often notions of repressive tolerance, since Herbert Marcuse's own formulation, have tended to be used to describe a condition or a fairly fixed set of relations of the state, whereas progressive control is far from fixed; moving from and sometimes back towards (as will be shown later) "regressive control", it needs mobility in order even to warrant its "progressiveness"!

6. For a perceptive recent account of the experiences of, in particular, Black women in The Netherlands see Philomena Essed (1984). And for similarly penetrating accounts and analyses of the racism and ethnicism experienced by migrants and often expressed in the debates on bilingualism, see Tove Skutnabb-Kangas, 1984a, 1984b, and this volume, Chapter 11.

7. For a critically important account of socially reconstructed reality and one example, mugging, of a socially constructed phenomenon—only possible after disconnection and hence when the phenomenon becomes a "reality", see Stuart Hall *et al.* (1978).

8. Indeed, in the mid-1980s it is education and related fields such as language, cultural identity, youth and the "migrant family", which are

now demanding the most funding and attention by national, international and government bodies. The argument here, of course, is that this state of affairs is no mere coincidence, for as the title of the 1985 *Swann Report* (London: HMSO) in Britain suggests, an *"Education for All"* symbolizes the cultural control and reproductive significance of education.

9. This influence can be seen in Britain, where several local authorities, in addition to the Inner London Education Authority, are beginning to respond to the anti-racist struggle by producing anti-racist policy statements. The same thing is also emerging in The Netherlands, where the Amsterdam City Council, teachers and other groups are in the process of producing anti-racist policy statements. It can also be seen in statements like the Programme of the National Union of Finnish Teachers in Sweden.

References

ESSED, P. 1984, *Alledaags Racisme*. Amsterdam: Feministische Uitgeverij Sara.

FOUCAULT, M. 1979, *Discipline and punish: The birth of the prison*. Harmondsworth, Middlesex: Penguin Books.

HALL, S. *et al.* 1978, *Policing the crisis: Mugging, the State, and law and order*. London: Macmillan.

LAWRENCE, E. 1982, In the Abundance of Water the Fool is Thirsty: Sociology and Black 'pathology'. *The Empire strikes back: Race and racism in 70s Britain*, Centre for contemporary Cultural Studies. London: Hutchinson.

MANNHEIM, K. 1936, *Ideology and utopia: An introduction to the sociology of knowledge*. London: Routledge & Kegan Paul.

MULLARD, C. 1983, *Racism, education and the state: The class-ethnic formation*, unpublished lecture in the Sociological Research Unit Lecture Series, University of London Institute of Education, London.

—— 1984, *Anti-racist education: The three O's*. London: National Association of Multiracial Education/National Anti-racist Movement in Education.

—— 1985a, *Race, class and ideology: Some formal notes*. Race Relations Policy and Practice Research Unit, University of London Institute of Education, London.

—— 1985b, *The social dynamic of migrant groups: From progressive to transformative policy in education*. Paris: OECD.

—— 1985c, *Race, power and resistance*. London: Routledge and Kegan Paul.

MULLARD, C., BONNICK, & KING, 1983a, *Racial policy and practice in education: A letter survey*. Working Paper I, Race Relations Policy and Practice Research Unit, University of London Institute of Education, London.

—— 1983b, *Local Education Authority policy documents: A descriptive analysis of contents*. Working Paper II, Race Relations Policy and Practice Research Unit, University of London Institute of Education, London.

—— 1984a, *Process, problem, and prognosis: A survey of Local Education Authorities' multicultural education policies and practices. Part One: The multicultural process*. Working Paper III, Race Relations Policy and Practice Research Unit, University of London Institute of Education, London.

—— 1984b, *Process, problem, and prognosis: A survey of Local Education Authorities' multicultural education policies and practices. Part Three: The prognosis*. Working Paper V, Race Relations Policy and Practice Research Unit, University of London Institute of Education, London.

SKUTNABB-KANGAS, T. 1984a, *Bilingualism or not: the education of minorities*. Clevedon: Multilingual Matters.

—— 1984b, Why aren't the children in Nordic countries bilingual? *Journal of Multilingual and Multicultural Development* 5, 301–315.

VAN DIJK, T. A. 1982, Prejudice in discourse: An analysis of ethnic prejudice in cognition and conversation. *Ethnic prejudice in cognition and discourse*, Working Paper No. 4, University of Amsterdam, Amsterdam.

—— 1985, *Elite discourse and racism*. Unpublished paper.

—— 1986, *Reproducing racism in cognition, conversation and communication*. Beverly Hills, CA: Sage.

18 Monolingual myopia and the petals of the Indian lotus

Do many languages divide or unite a nation? [1]

DEBI PRASANNA PATTANAYAK

What is the national language of India?

All languages of India are national languages. No language is anti-national.

People have no idea about the number of Indian languages. That is one reason for anxiety. Could you say something about the nature of Indian multilingualism?

According to the 1961 Census there are 1,652 mother tongues. Depending on how people count, there are between 200 and 700 languages. It is not only that the Indian Union has many languages; each constituent state has many languages as well. The thirteen major Indian Constitutions have history and literature of about 1,000 years and are communicationally heterogeneous. They have dialects, sociolects, styles and registers. These languages belong to four language families. There are eight major script systems, not counting Roman and Arabic. All these eight belong to a single script family and are derived from Brahmi. It must, however, be remembered that during the thousands of years of interaction India has emerged as a single linguistic, sociolinguistic and semantic area.

Don't you think that many languages lead to national disintegration?

No. Many languages are like petals of a lotus. Many languages form a national mosaic. If some petals wither and fall off or some chips are displaced from the mosaic, then the lotus and the mosaic look ugly. With the death of languages the country will be poorer.

Don't you see that quarrelling among languages threatens to break the country?

One can say that quarrelling among languages has the same potentiality of breaking a nation as quarrelling among members of a family has the potentiality of breaking a home. Moreover, "languages" do not quarrel. When representatives of languages do, the reasons are mostly extra-linguistic.

Don't you agree that one language is essential for the nationhood of a country?

No. English- as well as Chinese-speaking regions are each divided into many nations. The Soviet Union is a nation with many different languages. Canada has two official languages and Switzerland has four.

You seem to be talking of a different kind of nation from what we find elsewhere in the world.

Yes. In the West, the notion of nation revolves around a single language, a single religion, a single culture and in its extreme manifestation one party and one leader. Countries like India, which are multilingual, multi-ethnic and multicultural are nations in a different sense of the term.

You may be right. But don't you see that a country of many languages is always threatened by disintegration?

Yes. It is in the same sense that a plural world is always threatened by disintegration. No more, no less. If this leads one to the position that all languages of the world should give way to a single language, all religions should merge into one, all ethnicities should merge and fuse into one, one is arguing in favour of a reductionism which is fraught with serious consequences for the survival of humanity.

Ecology shows that a variety of forms is a prerequisite for biological survival. Monocultures are vulnerable and easily destroyed. Plurality in human ecology functions in the same way. One language in one nation does not bring about equity or harmony for the members or groups of that nation.

Do you believe in the Three Language Formula?[2]

It is not a question of belief. The Three Language Formula has emerged as a consensus after wide consultations and after it was adopted by the Chief Ministers of States and the Indian Parliament.

Don't you think that many languages are a burden?

As a donkey considers a load of sandalwood a burden, so education is a burden for any one who considers it an unwanted imposition. Many languages are used for differing purposes. As local history, regional history, national history and world history are not burdens, a language for intimate communication, one for proximate communication and one or more for distant communication need not be considered a burden.

Aren't too many languages economically wasteful?

This is an attitude born of the assumption that one language is more economical. Such a view considers more people uneconomic as there are many to claim the economic cake. It considers many cultures, many ethnicities, many religions as inconveniences and burdensome. Such an attitude does not plan for all components of political activity, but plans the removal of the weaker sections in the name of economic development. Each language is equally economic for the group speaking it. The hidden social costs of denying a language to its speakers are enormous. In any case, the economy has to be planned to suit people, and not people manipulated in pursuance of economic efficiency.

Don't you think many languages take away time from the study of science and technology?

This is based on a false understanding of education and science. Language education is a necessary component of education. It is, however, necessary to distinguish between language as subject and language as medium. No subject can be taught without a medium and no language can be taught without content. Many languages can be taught as media of many subjects. Many languages provide many windows for perception of the wide world and give ability to the young to meet the challenges of a plural world. Language study is as important as the study of science, not only because language is the basis of conceptualization, but also because it is the medium of study of science and technology and the only instrument for internalization of science and technology in culture. Therefore there is no question of language taking away time from science.

You seem to be equating language education with science and technology education.

Not really. In some sense language is basic to both. Without clarification through language, it is difficult to teach mathematics. *Mathematics is the most logical language.* Even graphs and formulae are languages. It is important to know that technology is what results from the interaction of science with society. *Science cannot interact with society in foreign languages.*

Don't you believe in a language of wider communication?

I believe in many languages of wider communication. Take any major-language-speaking State of India. The major language is the language of wider communication for all the linguistic elements in the State. Sadri in Madhya Pradesh, Bihar-Orissa border and Desia in Andhra Pradesh–Orissa border areas are languages of wider communication in so far as they are media of communication, not only among the tribal peoples speaking different languages, but also between the tribal and non-tribal peoples of the region. So is the Pidgin in the North-East which is variously known as Nagamese, Arunachalese, etc. Hindi and English are languages of wider communication linking different categories of people and for different purposes. Besides these, there are many languages of wider communication in the international arena which are languages of wider colonization.

Then you do not think that one language is needed for communication in the country?

One language is an impractical proposition for a multilingual country. Asking for one language in India is like asking for one language for Europe. In any case, the proper implementation of the three language formula will give not only one but two languages for communication in the country outside one's home state.

I am now confused. Could you summarize the state of language and communication in the country?

If one looks at the linguistic demography of the country, one will find that (a) there are some States where the majority language is spoken by between 85 and 95% of the population; (b) there are some States where the majority language is spoken by between 45 and 65% of the population; and (c) there are States where no language is spoken by more than 20% of the population. In the first category of States the majority languages are not communicationally homogeneous. The States in the second category are constantly under pressure from the minority language speakers. The third category of States often chooses an outside language as the language of education, administration and mass communication. As a result there are problems of communication everywhere. The problems vary in degree and complexity.

No wonder that India is so backward!

Backwardness is not necessarily due to many languages. Parts of many English-speaking countries are backward. Parts of America are backward. The Swiss franc is the strongest currency in Europe in spite of Switzerland having more languages than most countries of Europe. The Soviet Union, with so many languages, is not backward.

What about India?

India, in spite of its many languages, is the third country in the world in scientific and technological manpower. It is the eighth country in the world in publishing. Economically it is ahead of many third world countries. Western sociolinguists claim that countries which are economically poor are also linguistically poor. This is not true. If it is true, India is an exception. Even if India is economically poorer in comparison with many technologically developed countries, it is culturally and linguistically rich.

All the development you referred to is because of the English language.

On the contrary, English stands as a barrier between the common person and development. It has created a great divide between 96–98% of the population who do not know English and 2–4% of the population who know some English. It has created greater inequality, because the 2–4% of the population have greater access to knowledge, information, rank, status and wealth. As a substitute for other Indian languages in education it creates alienation from culture, develops blind spots in cultural perception and curbs creativity and innovativeness.

I never knew that the English language has so many inherent disabling properties.

I am sorry, you have misunderstood the entire issue. No language has inherent abilities and disabilities. All languages have the same potential for meeting communicational needs. It is the role and function of a language in society that give it power. If we assigned wider role and function to Indian languages, English would be needed more for inter-regional communication. But by casting English in an adversary role with other Indian languages, we are doing harm to both.

English is an international language and cannot be compared with Indian languages.

English is not the only "international" language. Russian, Chinese, French, German, Spanish and Hindi are all "international" languages. There are more people speaking Hindi internationally than German. The

British are a trading people. They treat English as a commodity to be sold. "English fairs" are organized by the British Trade Authority. We could project our languages if we wanted to.

You seem to be anti-English.

We treat English as one of the languages of India. We have given it the status of associate official language of the Union. It is the language of some states. It has been the language of academic study for my generation, although now the situation is changing. I am not anti-English. I believe that English as an ally of Indian languages is a strength, as an adversary of Indian languages it debilitates.

What about Hindi?

I have the same view about Hindi. If Hindi grows in alliance with the other Indian languages, all languages will be enriched. But if Hindi grows to be a substitute for other Indian languages it will be resisted by non-Hindi interest groups and in the process all the Indian languages will be weaker.

Why do Indian languages oppose one another?

Languages belong to a happy family. They do not oppose one another. It is only interest groups which oppose one another, sometimes in the name of language, sometimes in the name of ethnicity, sometimes in the name of religion. The fact that some languages and scripts are identified with specific religions aids this process. Those who are not sympathetic to multi-lingualism and see relations in linear and binary terms always see pairs of languages at loggerheads. Thus they see Hindi/Urdu opposition as Hindu/Muslim opposition, Hindi/English opposition as opposition between nationalism and internationalism, Regional Language/Hindi opposition as opposition between regionalism and nationalism and Regional Language/English opposition as opposition between forces of localism and internationalism. They are so wrong that it would be a waste of energy to refute them. One example will suffice. Urdu is an Indo-Aryan language written in Perso-Arabic script. It is developed by both Hindu and Muslim writers. In actuality, Hindi and Urdu are two styles of the same language. Urdu is claimed as mother tongue by less than 50% of Muslims in India. Yet those interested want to keep this controversy alive.

What is happening in Goa, if not two languages opposing one another?

In Goa the division of linguistic and communal lines is the handiwork of vested interests. For over fifty years there has been a scholarly debate as to whether Konkani is a dialect of Marathi or a separate language. Translating the scholarly debate into political action marks the failure of both intellectuals and politicians. Konkani is a fine example of integration. It is written using four scripts, Nagari, Kannada, Malayalam and Roman. There is no question of opposition.

How can one language become a dialect of another? Is it not a question of Marathi chauvinism?

Language and dialect are not immutable entities. A dialect, when it remains focused for a long time, assumes the status of a language. A language when faded assumes the status of a dialect. Take, for example, Hindi. At different times and places it has been known as Bhojpuri, Awadhi, Maithili or Braj. Literatures of quality have been written in these, and they are recognized as languages. Later they fade away and are subsumed under the macro-identity "Hindi". The same is the case with English. American, British and Australian English can be seen as three different languages, or they can be seen as three dialects of the *English* language. It is not so much a question of chauvinism as a question of identity.

Do you refuse to accept that dialects are inferior?

There is no question of inferiority as far as language varieties go. The standard is also a dialect. All dialects have the same potential for communication. Sociologically, however, once a particular dialect is accepted as standard, either other varieties are treated as unequal or they are forced to develop a sense of inferiority. It is necessary to know that, contrary to popular belief, standard is a spectrum. The broader the spectrum the greater is the acceptance of the standard and greater the amicability among dialects.

Then why do you think there is conflict among dialects and the standard in our country?

First of all, this is not a problem confined to our country. The relationship of Mandarin with Hakka or Nokkien, the relationship of Venetian with Italian or Black English with standard White English can be taken as examples of the dialect/standard conflict. If all the dialects of a language, instead of acting as members of a joint family, start building walls around themselves, there is bound to be identity assertion movements.

In your enthusiasm, you have equated dialects with languages. You will now champion their cause in education.

Any education which aspires to excellence and equality must take the home language of the child as the point of departure. There is a theory which seems to claim that the child's mind is an empty bucket which needs to be filled by the wisdom of the teacher. This has resulted in the utter neglect of the child as a resource in the classroom. There are several Scandinavian studies showing that those children who start their reading instruction in their own dialect become better in reading and writing the standard than those dialect-speaking children who start directly with the standards. Unless strategies are developed to link the dialects with the standard and the home language with the school language, it is hard to fight educational inequality.

So you are against English-medium education?

I am not against English-medium education as such, but I am certainly against English-medium pre-primary and primary education for those whose mother tongue is not English. When a child from a tribal or working class home starts with English, the first alienation from work ethics and cultural ethos has taken place. The work, culture and environment related terms not being available in the new language, the learning child develops cultural perception blind spots. The child's intellectual and linguistic development does not get maximal opportunities either.

Many things in those cultures are irrelevant. If these children learn science and technology through English why do you stand in their way?

If they cannot learn sufficient English, how can they learn subjects through it? By the age of four or five, the child has acquired proficiency in the basic structure of his or her mother tongue. There must be some way of making progression from the existing base rather than both pretending that it does not exist, and at the same time eradicating it. Secondly, learning science is not learning scientific terminology, i.e. it is not learning empty labels only. As one cannot speak the language even if one has memorized the entire lexicon, one may not know science even if one has memorized a lot of *terminology*. Terminology represents a concept. If the concept is not clear, then whether the terminology is Hindi, English or Chinese makes no difference. One has learned a label but not understood the content. One can look at it from yet another perspective. Supposing the people of a certain culture count in fours, they have no word for dozen or twenty, they have special markers to distinguish flat, round, sharp and pointed objects and English operates on a different system, then substitution of English will create cognitive imbalance, whereas linking would provide greater abilities to cope.

Are you suggesting that education should be imparted through dialects and mother tongues?

It is a well-known pedagogical principle to proceed from the familiar to the foreign. I am only reiterating that principle. Start from the familiar and the known and move to the foreign and unknown. If both the form (i.e. the language) and the content (for instance, scientific concepts) are foreign at the time of the presentation, you make the task impossibly difficult for the child, and defy the pedagogical principle. Learning occurs if you talk about unknown phenomena in a familiar language (the child learns the content, for instance science, through the medium of the mother tongue) or if you talk about known phenomena in an unfamiliar language (the child may learn some English but does not learn any additional science, only what she/he knew earlier). Why are you horrified at using the mother tongue as the point of departure? If someone forced you to give up your own language and study through a foreign language, how would you feel about it?

How can anyone ask me to give up my language, which is so advanced? You are avoiding answering the question about dialects and mother tongues by asking me this question

Languages are born, they develop, and they also die. Your language is no exception. Those whose languages are not "developed" (in the sense that they may not have a large vocabulary for Western technology, even if they do have a well developed vocabulary for areas where most Western languages are poorly developed) want them to be developed. You are afraid because the limited resources available for the development of languages will be shared by the new claimants. If this is so, instead of condemning them, convince them that the progress of all lies in linkages and not substitution of one language and script for another.

All dialects are mother tongues. But a mother tongue is more than just language. It is linked with social memory and individual and collective dream. Mother tongue is that language in which one is most creative and innovatory and without which one grows intellectually sterile. I know of an Oriya married to a Tamil, speaking English at home, living in a Bengali neighbourhood with the children taken care of by a Hindustani Ayah and a Nepali loon man. I always say that those children have six mother tongues.

What about education?

For such children early education can probably take any of these languages as the point of departure. It is not necessary to put all dialects to use as the medium. There are many experiments available. I have designed a model by which a child begins reading and writing the mother tongue using the script of the language which will be the medium at higher stages, and by using different strategies, makes a transition to the higher medium language by the post-primary stage. Orissa has grouped tribal languages into five groups for purposes of education. There is no single procedure valid for all people at all times. Once it is agreed that it is the responsibility of the formal system to link home language with school language, first language with second and further languages, search for appropriate methods and materials will begin.

I am still not convinced. How can you have national integration in a country divided by so many languages?

You must know of the philosophical argument, whether half a glass of water is half full or half empty. One can have a similar argument about your question. Given 50 languages, is the country divided by them or linked by them? India has been a country of immense variation from the dawn of history. For a Shankara to go from Kanyakumari to Kashmir, from Gujarat to Assam and for an Agastyas to come from the Himalayas to the Cape Comorin, language does not stand as a barrier. The Bhakti movement, which binds the country, found expression in diverse ways in different languages. The Tamil stone carvers built temples in Gujarat and Kalinga and the traders and artisans of Kalinga went to far-off places. There is no reason why today the country would become disintegrated if we hear the inner voice of India.

What is this inner voice?

The Upanishads have proclaimed that one who sees the wood but not the trees is as much wasted as the one who sees trees but not the wood. India has always stood for a holistic view of life and respect for the different. This is why for the survival of a plural world intellectuals of the world have looked towards India. Only people who respect the different can say Vasudheiva Kutumbakam or Yadum ure Yavarum kelir: "The world is my village and all the people my brothers and sisters." Those who consider different as deficient would consider many languages, many ethnicities, many religions, many cultures and many identities as inconvenient and therefore untenable. It will take considerable re-education to convince them that life is rich and beautiful because it is varied, and equalitarianism presupposes acceptance of plurality as a point of departure.

Notes to Chapter 18

1. This paper is based on an interview in which academics and journalists put questions to Dr Pattanayak.

2. India has accepted the Three Language Formula as a basis for its language education. Each child is expected to learn three languages in school: the state language, Hindi and English. In those states where Hindi is the state language, another Indian language is taught instead of Hindi.

19 Concluding remarks: Language for empowerment

TOVE SKUTNABB-KANGAS and
JIM CUMMINS

When discussing the name of this book, we first thought of "from shame to power". Power is, after all, what it all is about. The education of minorities is organized the way it is, by others, precisely because the minorities lack the power to decide themselves. But minorities do not want "power-over-others" (Galtung, 1980), only "power-over-oneself" The minorities this book talks about do not want to exchange one set of rulers (the present ones) for another set of rulers (themselves). What they/we want is to have the power to decide about one's own destiny, without encroaching on other people's right to decide about their destiny.

It would be foolish to believe that those who have the power to decide over others in the present world would give away that power voluntarily —South Africa is a good example. Therefore, the power has to be won through struggle, in every field. We are in the middle of the educational part of this struggle—we do not have the power yet to organize minority education in the way the minorities think would be good for their children. Therefore, "from shame to struggle".

But the struggle has to be well informed. It has to be based on an adequate description of the past and present—some chapters in the book give that. It has to be based on a thorough analysis of what happens and why, at both a local and a global level—other chapters in the book have started that analysis. It has to be based on a deep and profound intellectual and emotional understanding of what happens—there are many examples in the book of this understanding. We also need accurate accounts and analyses of ongoing struggles, with shortcomings and successes, to learn from each other—and that has been largely lacking in the literature on mınorities (for exceptions see, for example, Kohl, 1971; Kozol, 1967; Mullard, 1985; Simon, 1982). Many of the chapters in this book tell of the struggles and the strengths and weaknesses of specific approaches.

We have tried to combine perspectives in this book which are not always linked, in at least two ways. Firstly, the book links more traditional academic research with other ways of describing and analysing the same phenomena, thereby providing a fuller picture of the world. We have tried to show that some of the basic questions in minority education are either difficult or impossible to conceptualize in all their subtlety, with the tools that traditional research has developed until now. We must use different types of data and analyses, in order to create a more variegated picture— therefore the link between different approaches. Most of the authors come themselves from the immigrated or indigenous minorities they describe. We believe that this insider's perspective is an extremely important one.

Secondly, the book also links together the experience of very different types of minorities, indigenous and immigrated, black and "white", showing what is common, despite the many profound and real differences. This global perspective is, in addition to the insider's perspective, decisive for the struggle to succeed. We have to join forces, and to counteract the research imperialism which prevents marginalized groups from acquiring knowledge about each other.

But description and analysis are not enough. Not even understanding. "It cannot be said enough that the dawn of the nuclear age may signal the end of our species," says Paul W. Hoag (1986:5), and continues:

"Somehow, though we have made our best individual efforts, we are collectively a failure. Somehow, the scientific and technical knowledge to which we have devoted our lives, as scientists, scholars and intellectuals, have produced an ominous era of human history. Therefore, we bear a special responsibility to rectify and alleviate the undesirable and unforeseeable consequences of science and technology. Since we are scientists, we will proceed scientifically. We will identify the problems, together analyse the problems, share our insights openly, and enter into objective debates. The scientific method can produce knowledge and so each of us will contribute to the thorough understanding of present circumstances. But that is not enough. It is essential that we acknowledge individually and collectively the need for good will and political action. Knowledge of disaster is not enough; prevention is the point ... So we must act, but to act we must understand."

Researchers in the humanities and social sciences have equally many reasons as researchers in technology and science to "bear a special responsibility". A prerequisite for "good will and political action" is that we form value judgements on the basis of the knowledge and understanding which we acquire through our research and experience.

We have tried to show in this book that research, in order to empower, must also take seriously the questions of value judgements. They are a legitimate part of research. In order for research to be "objective", the value judgements must be made explicit. Instead, in the same way as racism is becoming increasingly covert, value judgements are being hidden. Still they exist under the surface, like racism, but perhaps more unanalysed than earlier.

School helps to maintain this lack of analysis. At present we educate whole generations to be the same type of *value invalids* that our own generation in the West is, says Professor Matti Bergström, a Finnish neurophysiologist (Bergström, 1986: 4, 6, 8):

> "In the present information society where everything centres around knowledge and information, we think that the one who *knows* much is intelligent. Because we think knowledge is all that is needed, our educational philosophy is based on the argument: if you know enough, you will manage everywhere in the world. *Energy* is also needed, and *the combination of knowledge and energy is—technology.* The argument for our educational ideology would then be: if you have enough technology, you will manage everywhere in the world. But it is here that the mistake is made. We have in our brain a system which chooses, samples, evaluates. It is this apparatus which reflects, which sees the larger contexts, and gives us the opportunity to compare. In order to be able to develop our societies, *we need all our resources, the knowledge resource, the energy resource and the evaluating resource.* And it is the third resource which is the decisive one, the one which guides all our behaviour ... In the schools which usually are thought of as knowledge centred, the students are being stuffed with information constantly. There is no time for evaluation. We neglect the development of the very capacity which criticizes, evaluates, turns things up and down. The result is that we perhaps create whole generations who have knowledge and energy but who lack the capacity to know how to use the knowledge and what to do with the energy. And so we educate whole generations to become *value invalids*. Science has tidied away the concept of values. Research is now geared towards knowing, towards getting knowledge. Research is not supposed to contain value

judgements, they say, and this is where the danger lies ... If we choose value invalids to have power, if we have given away the power to decide about knowledge, energy and technology to value invalids, which I fear we have, then we are threatened by a general catastrophe." [our translation]

What are the values, then, which underlie the contributions in this book? Obviously each author would give a different answer. But we can see common threads, too.

All those who contributed to this book have distanced themselves from the "liberal", "culturalist" discourse of multiculturalism and pluralism. This discourse emphasizes "such things as the need to safeguard ethnic identity, ethnic pride, and in particular the right to assert and maintain one's cultural heritage" (Jayasuriya, 1986:5). This is an emphasis which we do *not* dispute. But at the same time—and this is what most of the authors in this volume dispute—it also sees the problems which minorities encounter

> "not as structural problems but as personal, individual problems whose solution lay largely with the migrants themselves with appropriate assistance from the State ... These policies were designed to help migrants to help themselves to overcome their difficulties, which were seen largely as of their own making." (p. 5)

We agree with Jayasuriya when he argues that "a model of multiculturalism, concentrating on the private domain, may be dysfunctional in that it diverts attention from the real issues of inequality, deprivation and discrimination facing ethnic minorities in the public domain" (p. 8).

The dilemma of pluralism is, as Jayasuriya forcefully argues, how to "reconcile the rightful concerns of cultural diversity and identity with the socially legitimate desires and claims to achieve equality" (p. 8); or, to state it differently,

> "to recognize the competing pressures of the expressive and instrumental dimensions of ethnicity—the latter being concerned with the more material aspects of living, especially the need for economic, social and political power on the part of ethnic minority group members." (p. 8)

Social justice is not a question of "equality of opportunity"—which is the liberal view—but of "equality of outcome", and beyond.

The dilemma when emphasizing the learning of the minority mother tongues (and second languages) as the authors do in this book, is that it can be done with at least three completely different purposes. Firstly, the mother tongue can be emphasized to the *exclusion of the learning of both the second language and other skills*, as is done in segregation programmes (Bantu education in Namibia and the education of many Turkish children in Bavaria are cases in point; see Skutnabb-Kangas' first chapter in this volume). Secondly, the mother tongue can be emphasized as a part of ethnicity, to the *exclusion of societal questions of economic and political power*, as is done in most of the multiculturalism discourse. This is a *therapeutic* approach, which builds on *deficiency theories*, and is used as a form of *pacification* (as satirized in a cartoon in Australian *Mentor* 1, 1986:7: A: "I want this to be a multicultural society"; B: "Ah—where each ethnic group can make its unique contribution"; A: "Right ... while us White Protestant Anglo-Saxons get on with running the country").

Or thirdly, the mother tongue can be emphasized partly in its own right, as *a self-evident human right*, and partly in order to be able to give a *better instrument* for coping with both the learning of the second language and the learning of other skills, and to include *analysis, understanding, evaluation and action in relation to societal questions of economic and political power*.

An emphasis on minority mother tongues can thus be for *exclusion*, for *pacification* or for *empowerment*. It is the last of these approaches, advocating language for empowerment, that this book stands for.

References

BERGSTRÖM, M. 1986, Den glömda resursen. *Fredsposten* 6, 4–8.

GALTUNG, J. 1980, *The true worlds: a transnational perspective*. New York: The Free Press.

HOAG, P. W. 1986, Current prospects for the increasingly dangerous arms race: one perspective. *Scientific World* 4, 5–12.

JAYASURIYA, D. L. 1986, Ethnic minorities and issues of social justice in contemporary Australian society. Keynote address at the Australian Adult Education Conference 'Learning for Social Justice', Australian National University, Canberra, 7–9 December 1986.

KOHL, H. 1971, *36 children*. Harmondsworth, Middlesex: Penguin.

KOZOL, J. 1967, *Death at an early age*. Boston: Houghton Mifflin Company.

MULLARD, C. 1985, *Race, power and resistance*. London: Routledge & Kegan Paul.

SIMON, J. B. 1982, *To become somebody. Growing up against the grain of society*. Boston: Houghton Mifflin Company.

Notes on Contributors

Alma Flor Ada, born in Cuba, has lived in the USA since 1958. Author of *Pedro Salinas: El Dialogo Creador* (1969); *Iniciacion Literaria* (1974); *Ver y Describir* (1974); *Oir y narrar* (1974); *Maravillas* (1975), *Tecolote* (1983) and *Hagamos caminos* (1985), the last three with Maria del Pilar de Olave.

René Appel (Institute for General Linguistics, University of Amsterdam, The Netherlands) has published on bilingualism and second language acquisition. Author of *Immigrant children learning Dutch; sociolinguistic and psycholinguistic aspects of second language acquisition* (Foris), and co-author (with Pieter Muysken) of *Language contact and bilingualism* (Edward Arnold).

S. Jim Campos, born in California, USA. Currently works in the Carpinteria Unified School District, California. Is a Ph.D. candidate at the University of California at Santa Barbara.

Jim Cummins, born in Ireland, has lived in Canada since 1971. Author of *Bilingualism and special education: Issues in assessment and pedagogy* (Multilingual Matters) and *Bilingualism in education: Aspects of theory, research and policy* (Longman; with Merrill Swain). Currently works in the Modern Language Centre, Ontario Institute for Studies in Education, Toronto, Canada.

Jan Curtis was born and lives in Northern California, USA. Has taught in the bilingual primary classroom since 1978. Studied bilingual education in Mexico, California and Canada, and the acquisition of literacy among bilingual and monolingual children in California and Canada. Published a collection of stories written by bilingual children, *One Day I Lost My Head and other Stories*.

Tom Hagman, born in Finland, has lived in Sweden since 1972. Headmaster of Immigrant Education in Botkyrka.

Eduardo Hernández-Chávez is Co-ordinator of the Migrant Farmworker Rights Project in Sacramento, California. A former farmworker himself, he was active in the Third World Movement of the 1960s and 1970s at

Berkeley. He has taught Chicano Studies at the University of California, Berkeley, and Chicano sociolinguistics at Stanford University and the University of California, Davis. His research has focused on Spanish–English bilingualism in the USA among Chicanos.

Tuula Honkala, born in Finland, has lived in Sweden since 1976. Teacher in Rinkeby.

Antti Jalava, born in Finland in 1949, has lived in Stockholm, Sweden, since 1959. Author of: *Matti*, 1974, Cavefors; *Jaq har inte bett att få komma* ("I did not ask to come"), 1976, Bonniers; *Asfaltblomman* ("Asphalt Blossom") 1980, Askild & Kärnekull (Finnish translation: *Asfalttikukka*, WSOY, 1982).

Deirdre Jordan, Adelaide, Australia, has been engaged in research for Aboriginal people in Australia for the last fifteen years. Her work has been particularly concerned with the maintenance and construction of Aboriginal identity and access to higher education.

Jukka Kalasniemi, born in Kemi, Finland, in 1968. Has lived in Stockholm, Sweden, since 1970. Nine years of Finnish-medium education in Botkyrka, now in his third year of upper secondary school in an Engineering & Science track.

Theodor Kallifatides, born in Greece in 1938, has lived in Stockholm, Sweden, since 1964. Author. Has published two collections of poems, eight novels, film manuscripts, travel books.

H. Robert Keatinge, born in California, USA. Currently works in the Carpinteria Unified School District, California. Is a Ph.D. candidate at the University of California at Santa Barbara.

Binnie Kristal-Andersson, born in New York, USA, has lived in Stockholm, Sweden since 1967. Psychologist/author. Books: *Svenska för invandrare* ("Swedish for immigrants"), Immigrant-institutet, 1975; *Dikter vid köksbordet* ("Poems at the kitchen table"), 1979; *Inför Dig* ("Facing you"), 1981; and *Ett annat språk* ("Another language"), 1981, all Raben & Sjögren; and *Psykoterapi och social förändring—går det att förena*? ("Psychotherapy and social change—can they be combined?"), 1980, Wahlström & Widstrand.

Mazisi Kunene, born in South Africa, educated at the University of Natal and the School of African and Oriental Studies, University of London. Proscribed in South Africa under the Suppression of Communism Act. Professor of African Language and Literature, University of California, Los Angeles. Author of *Zulu Poems* (1970), *Emperor Shaka the Great*

(1978), *Anthem of the Decades* (1981) and *The Ancestors and the Sacred Mountain* (1982).

Jouko Lahdenperä, born in Finland, has lived in Sweden since 1960. Headmaster of Immigrant Education in Botkyrka.

Pirkko Leporanta-Morley, born in Finland, has lived in Sweden since 1978. Preschool teacher. Head of a Finnish-medium preschool in Rinkeby. Has published poems and articles on minority education and on the situation of immigrant women.

Lilja Liukka, born in Finland, has lived in Sweden since 1966. Six years of education. Has worked mostly in hospitals. Works since 1979 in the Finnish Club in Rinkeby. Has published poems and articles. (She is the soul of Rinkeby: editor's remark.)

Rauni (Ravna) Magga Lukkari, Norway, born in Finland in 1943, moved to the kingdom as adult because of marriage. Mother Sami from Norway, father Sami from Finland. Author of three books of poems in Sami: *Jienat vulget* ("the ice cracks up"), 1980; *Baze dearvan Biehtar* ("Good-bye, Biehtar"), 1981; *Losses beaivegirji*, 1986 (Norwegian translation *Mörk dagbok* ("The Dark Diary"), 1987).

Johannes Marainen grew up in a nomad Sami family in Sweden. After nomad school he continued his studies and eventually became teacher of Swedish and History in a high school in Gothenburg. During the last few years he has been engaged by the Nordic Sami Institute in Kautokeino, doing research in Sami history at the Dept. of History, University of Gothenburg.

Chris Mullard, born in the UK, has lived in The Netherlands since 1984. Director of the Institute for Race and Ethnic Studies, University of Amsterdam. Author of *Race, power and resistance* (1985).

Debi Prasanna Pattanayak, India. Director of the Central Institute of Indian Languages, Mysore. Author of *Multilingualism and mother-tongue education* (1981).

Robert Phillipson, born in the UK, has lived since 1974 in Denmark, where he teaches at the University of Roskilde. Prior to this he worked for the British Council promoting English in Algeria and Yugoslavia. Author of *Learner language and language learning* (with Claus Faerch and Kirsten Haastrup), Multilingual Matters, 1984, and of *Linguicism rules in education* (with Tove Skutnabb-Kangas).

Eija Rougle, born in Finland, has lived in Sweden since 1969, moved to the USA in 1987. Teacher and school administrator in Rinkeby. Works with acquisition of bilingual literacy and reading materials.

Guilem Rodrigues da Silva, born in Brazil, has lived in Sweden since 1966. Collections of poems: *Jag söker gryningen* ("I seek the twilight"), Cavefors; *Innan natten kommer* ("Before the night comes"), Invandrarförlaget. Poems in several anthologies in Sweden, Norway, Cuba, USA.

Tove Skutnabb-Kangas, born in Finland, has lived in Denmark since 1979. Author of *Tvåspråkighet* ("Bilingualism"), 1981; *God, bedre, dansk? Om indvandrerbörns integration i Danmark* ("Good, better, Danish? On the integration of immigrant children in Denmark"), 1983 (with Birgitte Rahbek); *Bilingualism or not: the education of minorities*, 1984; *Minoritet, språk och rasism* ("Minority, language and racism"), 1986 (in collaboration with Ilka Kangas and Kea Kangas, Tove's daughters) (Finnish translation *Vähemmistö, kieli ja rasismi*, Gaudeamus, 1987); *Linguicism rules in education*, 1986 (with Robert Phillipson).

Arlene Stairs, born in Canada, has worked as school psychologist and educational development consultant since 1972, the past eight years in the northern Inuit region. Recent projects and reports focus on (a) teacher education, as a member of the Faculty of Education of McGill University (Montreal), including local child development research, and (b) the role of native language in formal education.

Gunnar Tingbjörn, Sweden. University lecturer, director of the SPRINS (The Linguistic Development of Immigrant Children in Sweden) research group at the University of Gothenburg. He has taken an ardent interest in planning an adequate teacher education for teachers in the new subject Swedish as a Second Language. Tingbjörn has published about 50 titles, including books, reports and articles on bilingualism, Swedish as a Second Language, and the linguistic development of immigrant children.

Arturo Tosi teaches at Oxford Polytechnic and is Research Associate at the London University Institute of Education. He is the Chairman of the Royal Society of Arts Scheme for the Training of Teachers of Minority Community Languages, and his published works include *Immigration and bilingual education*.

Index

Note: L1 = first language, mother tongue; L2 = second language

Aboriginals, Australian
—education 191, 193, 198–9, 200, 208–11
—problems facing 212–13, 216
—status 195, 199–201, 214
Accent, emphasis on 242
Acculturation, linguistic 47–8, 66–7
Achievement, minority children 4, 23–7, 67, 131, 192, 202, 239, 286, 305–6, 333–4
—and identity 4–5, 137–9, 193, 242
Acquisition
—L1 319, 322
—L2 88–9, 115–16, 123, 227, 306
Ada, Alma Flor 4, 223–37
Advocate, for minority students 142, 148, 152, 307
Affirmation, and racial policy 367–8, 369–70, 375
Africa, languages 37, 345–6
Aid organizations, and linguicism 339, 341, 346–7, 348, 350
Alaska, education 217n.
Alienation 165–6, 193, 197, 262, 386
Alopeus, Marianne 177
Altena, N. & Appel, R. 70, 74
Altena, N. & De Haan, D. 70–1
Anaya, Alfonso 225
Anglo-conformity, Canada 127, 129, 133, 136, 138–9, 141, 151–2
Annahatak, Betsy 319
Anti-racist movement 4, 95–6, 97, 128, 135–6, 138–9, 149–52, 369–71, 377n.
—United States 278–97

Appel, R. 57–77, 130
Appel, R., Everts, H. & Teinissen, J. 74
Apple, M.W. 262
Arabic
—in Netherlands 61, 70
—in Sweden 331
Arithmetic, immigrant children 73, 75, 76
Aronwitz, S. & Giroux, H.A. 3
Ashby, E. 345
Assessment
—indigenous minorities 319, 321
—in L1 147
—multicultural 130, 141, 145–9, 297
—preschool 302–6, 321
—and racism 132–5, 138, 150
Assimilation
—of indigenous minorities 190, 192–3, 194–5, 197–9, 211, 308, 313–14
—integration as 240–2, 245–6, 271
—linguistic 27, 32, 38, 69, 79, 107–9, 129, 139, 148–9, 252, 352, indigenous minorities 191–2
—social 64–5, 68, 83, 194, 254, 259–61, 262–3, 360
Attitudes
—language 12, 48–51, 62, 66, 70–1, 151, 162–4, 343, 349, and linguicism 343, 345–6
—to bilingual education 285–7
—to education reform 2

—to immigrants 64, 81–2, 129, 149, 162–3, 266–8, 366
—to indigenous minorities 181–2, 194–5, 214, 218n.
Australia
—Aboriginals 191–3, 195, 198–201, 208–11, 212–13, 214
—and monolingualism 12
Autonomy 198–201, 253–6, 258, 260, 264, 265, 269–71, 314, 325

Ballot, bilingual 46, 51, 54–5
Bantu education 23, 30, 394
Barnes, D. 143
Base, cultural 309–11, 313, 315–17, 320, 323–5
Bedfordshire Education Authority, and mother tongue teaching 87–8, 89
Beleidsplan 61, 66
Berger, T. 189–90, 197
Bergstrom, M. 392–3
Berman, E.H. 347
Bernstein, B. 93
Bidialectism 94–5
Bilingual Education Act 1976, California 279, 297n.
Bilingual Syntax Measure 302, 304–5
Bilingualism
—active 107–26, 334
—additive 47, 139–40
—advantages of 139, 141
—attitudes to 12, 48–55, 145, 245, 266–7, 285–7
—definitions 20–2
—and education 13, 15, 33, 35–7, aims of 308, England 86–9, 90, 92–8, Netherlands 61–2, opposition to 285–7, programmes compared 22–7, Sweden 106–26, 177, 266–7, USA 51–4, 278–97
—encouragement of 10, 14–15, 47–8, 94
—passive 324
—subtractive 139, 141, 145, 274n.
—transitional 52, 72–5, 88–9, 113, 308, 343
Botkyrka, minority education in 328–35

Bourdieu, P. 262
Bradford, mother tongue teaching projects 88–9
Bredby school, Stockholm 239–50, 335
Britain, *see* UK
British Council 344, 346–7
Brumfit, C. 96
Bullivant, B.M. 323
Bullock Report, 1975 86, 143–4

California Achievement Test (CAT) 306
California Rural Legal Assistance (CRLA) 280, 282
CALP (common underlying proficiency for all languages) 29, 35
Calvet, J. 9
Campos, S.J. 299–307
Canada
—immersion programmes 24–5
—indigenous minorities 189–91, 194–5, 201–4
—minority education in 3, 27, 112, 127–55
see also Native Canadians
Carnoy, M. 259
Carpinteria, minority students in 299–307
Castillo, G.R. 38–9
Castles, S. 260–1
Change
—subvertive 374–5
—transformative 33, 359–61, 363–5, 369–75
Change, educational
—realities of 128, 149–52
—and social control 2–4, 90–2, 93
Chicano
—and language policy 26, 47, 53, 55
—minority education for 28
Child Observation Project: Inuit Teacher Training (COPITT) 319–23
Chishimba, M.M. 344, 346
Chretien, Jean 197
Churchill, Stacy 32

Civil Rights, Office for (OCR) 52–3,
  281–2, 284
Civil rights movement, USA 51
Classes
  —bilingual 287, 290, 293–4, 297,
    329
  —composed 117–18
  —compound 329
  —home language 117–19
Co-ordinator, bilingual 284–7,
  289–90
Codes, language 94
Cole, Paula 225
Collaboration, minority communities
  and educators 4, 139–40, 144–5
Colonialism, and language
  dominance 37, 340–5, 352
Commonwealth Conference on the
  Teaching of English as a Second
  Language 348–9
Commonwealth Immigrants Advisory
  Council 82, 94
Communication, and language 14,
  45, 134, 382
Compensation, see education,
  compensatory
Competence
  —bilingual 21–2, 87, 95, 97, 109,
    119, 120, 126
  —L1 17–18, 19, 22, 88, 90, 93–4,
    107, 110, 121, 123
  —L2 123, 125
Comprehension, immigrant children
  76, 294
Conflict, cultural 322
Conflict, social 2–3, 76, 92
  —and minority languages 62
Confusion, language 136
Connection 371–2, 373
Conscientization, need for 4
Consent, and social control 91–2, 95
Conservative Party, Sweden 246
Conservative Party (UK)
  —and immigration 81
  —and mother tongue teaching 88
Contact, culture 323, 325
Contrastivity, see methods, teaching
Control, educational 143–4, 202–4,
  212–13, 214, 314, 318–19, 368
Control, social 90–2, 361

  —progressive 361–2, 364–9,
    372–5
  —regressive 374–5
Core-periphery thesis, and language
  dominance 348, 350–1
Couwenberg, S.W. 64–5
Cramer, T. 212
Culture, indigenous 139, 193, 197,
  200, 204, 215, 308–9; see also
  base, cultural; universals, cultural
Cummins, J. 127–55, 390–4
Curriculum
  —hidden 127
  —and indigenous cultures 197,
    202–4, 206–7, 210, 309,
    314–15, 319–20
  —and language diversity 83–9, 94,
    96–7, 130, 141, 144, 243, 250,
    265
Curtis, J. 150, 278–98

Da Silva, Guilem Rodrigues 173–5
Darwinism, social 192, 198, 255
Day-care, mother-tongue 240
Deconstitution 370–1
Deficit views of minority education
  3–4, 32–6, 52, 82, 85–7, 89, 95,
  133, 394
Deprivation, and minorities 82, 85
Derrick, J. 84
Development
  —educational 308–25
  —socio-cultural 74–5
Dialect 385–7
Van Dijk, T.A. 366
Disadvantage, mother tongue as 85,
  86–7, 94; see also handicap
Disconnection, and racial policy
  365–6, 367, 369, 371, 373, 375
Discrimination
  —positive 200
  —racial 82, 91, 95, 132, 146–8,
    198, 200, 241, 271, 281–2,
    352
Dispersal
  —of indigenous minorities 198
  —in minority education 83
Disruption, social, and miseducation
  1

District Bilingual Parent Advisory Council 284–5, 297
District Parent Advisory Committee 280
Diversity, language, as educational problem 83–4, 97
Dominance, language 26–7, 339–42, 352–3; see also linguicism
Dosen, R. 69
Drop-out rate, indigenous minorities 193, 202, 208, 210, 213, 261, 293
Dutch
—extra-school use 68–9
—as L2 59–61, 63, 65, 67, 73

Education
—adult 200
—behavourist model 144
—compensatory 83, 84–6, 94, 95–6, 133
—as economic-reproductive 259, 260–1, 265, 272
—higher 60, 204, 209, 210–11, 293, 317–18, 333–5, 345
—as ideological 259–60, 264, 272
—for indigenous minorities 190–3, 196–7, 200, 201–11, 212–14, 216, 308–25, 352
—intercultural 57, 61, 66–8, 71, 151
—and language dominance 343–5
—and linguicism 347–51
—and power relationships 239–50, 251–74, 348, 390–1
—reciprocal interaction model 143–5, 149–50, 300–1, 306
—remedial 86, 116–17, 121, 123, 141
—as repressive 259, 261, 264
—"survival" 204
—transmission model 143–5, 155n., 385–6
see also control, educational
Education, minority
—functions of 258–61, 270
—goals of 14–16, 20–2, 35, 107–10, 119, 120–2, 124, 131, 245–6, 254, 315, 323, success rates 22–31
—history 18, 32–6

—new trends 63–8
—private 246
—and special needs 82–6, 94, 146–7, 268
see also Netherlands, the
Education, multicultural
—Canada 127–8, 140–1, 144–6, 151–2; history and context 128–31
—England 83–6, 89–98
—support for 2
Education, multilingual, India 381–8
Education and Science, Department of 83, 85, 87–8, 93, 97
Educators, role of 130, 135, 138–9, 141, 149–50; see also teachers
Eidheim, H. 191–2, 214, 218n.
El Circo Achievement Tests 303–4
Elicitation techniques 304
Élites, power 14, 26, 39n.
Employment
—and bilingualism 139, 295–6
—for minorities 1, 207, 213
England, decentralized education system 87, 90, 92–3, 96
English
—as international language 383–4
—as L2 26, 28, 47–8, 106, 210, 280, 299, 342, 345, 383, 386, professionalism of 347–51
—and linguicism 340, 341–3
—in United States 2, 46–7, 48–55, 304
—"US English" movement 2, 48–9, 153n.
Enrichment theories 33–4, 35–6, 141
Enschede, experimental school 75–7
Equality, ideologies of 93–4, 194, 278, 393
Van Esch, W. 66–7, 68
Essed, Philomena 376n.
Etharchy 360, 362, 367–8
Ethnicism, institutionalized 3, 18, 33, 341, 360–1, 365, 372
Ethnicity 129, 211, 369, 393–4
Ethnocentrism 54, 64, 149, 211
Europe
—minority education 32–3, 37
—and monolingualism 12, 14–15, 17, 20

European Economic Community
(EEC), and minority language
teaching 87–8
Evolution, cultural 324–5
Expectation, teacher 29, 130, 193
Exposure, in L2 learning 25, 30,
40n., 133–4, 140

Failure, educational 22–3, 28,
132–4, 139, 145, 165, 262
—and inequalities of power 2, 4,
10
—student seen as cause of 10, 82,
138, 148, 244, 262
—US Hispanics 281
Faries, G. 191
Fear–fearlessness 253–4, 258–60,
267–9, 271
Finance, of mother tongue education
209, 330–1
Finland
—minorities in 41n.
—minority education in 1, 275n.
Finnish
—in education 162–4, 177–8,
239–40, 242, 328–35
—maintenance of 24–5, 26, 28,
33, 107, 117, 119, 124, 164–5
Finnish Club, Stockholm 244,
246–7, 266
Finns, in Sweden 36, 103, 112–13,
154n., 161–6, 177–8, 239–50,
252, 256–8
—status of 251–2, 366
Fitzgerald, R.T. 193
Fokstad, Per 196, 206, 215
Freire, P. 4
French, and colonialism 344
Frisians, and L1 teaching 62

Galtung, Johan 153n., 252–5,
258–9, 264, 270–1, 273
Gastarbeiters, *see* guestworkers
German, in United States 49–50
Ghana, linguicism in education 344
Giddens, A. 39n.
Gramsci, A. 90–2, 95, 271
Greeks
—in Canada 146
—in Sweden 239, 250, 331

Grey of Falloden, Lord 340
Guest worker 108–9, 366, 372

Haanen-Thijs, M. 67–8
Haast, M. & Van Haastrecht, T. 68,
69
Hagman, T. 328–35
Hall, S. *et al.* 376n.
Handicap
—L1-related 32, 35, 82–3, 132,
241
—L2-related 32–3, 34
Handicrafts, and indigenous identity
206–7
Hardy, George 344
Harney, R. & Troper, H. 129
Hasluck, P. 198
Hawthorn, H.B. & Tremblay, M.A.
196
Hayakawa, Senator 280
Hegemony theory 90–2, 93, 343, 367
Hernández-Chávez, E. 45–55
Hindi 382–4, 385
Hispanics, in United States 224–5,
279–97, 299–307
History, minority 183–5, 190, 195,
197, 205, 311–14
Hoag, Paul W. 391
Hodson, J.A. 340
Holmes, Justice 46, 48
Home Language Reform, 1977
(Sweden) 116–17, 329–30
Honkaala, T. 239–50, 265, 269–70
Hymes, Dell 353n.

Iaconi, Mariuccia 233
Ibrahimi, Taleb 344
Iceland, as monolingual country 11
Identification, Placement and Review
Committee (IPRC), Canada 147
Identity, minority 10, 59–62, 65,
69–72, 129, 164, 177, 184, 227,
249–50, 293
—indigenous 189–90, 193, 194–6,
198–9, 203–5, 206, 208–16,
218n., 311, 322–4
see also achievement, minority
children, and identity
Identity, shift 18–19, 164–6, 182–5

Ideology
—and education 259–60, 264, 271
—liberal 2–3, 33, 393
Imitation, as teaching method 241–2
Immersion programmes 23, 24–5,
    27, 29–30, 40n.
Immigration
—Canada 1, 129, 214
—England 79–83, 366
—Netherlands 57–77, 366
—policies towards 194
—Sweden 103–6, 107–26, 161–76,
    239, 243, 250, 267, 328–31,
    366; differences between
    groups 112–14
—United States 1, 47–51, 54, 279,
    300
Immigration Act 1971, UK 80–1
Imperialism, linguistic 339–54; see
    also linguicism
Inclusion, cultural 308–10, 313, 315,
    324–5
India
—extent of multilingualism 11,|379
—linguicism in 342, 344
—minorities in 36
Indians, Canadians, see Native
    Canadians
Inspectorate, schools, England 92–3
Integration
—assimilated, see etharchy
—educational 59–61, 65, 72–5,
    240–2, 244–6, 250, 268, 296,
    313, 334
—political, economic 53, 71,
    74–5, 82, 199, 214, 360
Interaction, adult–child 134,
    149–50, 225, 227
Interculturalism 2, 33, 38, 131,
    135–6, 151
Interdependence hypothesis 299
Interlanguage 30
Intervention, educational 136–49,
    141
Inuit 202–3, 213
—child development 323
—concept acquisition 322–3
—educational development 308–25
—geography and demography
    311–13

—language 313
—politics and education 313–14
Inuktitut 313, 314, 316–17, 319–22,
    324
Italian, in Canada 140, 146

Jalava, Antii 161–6
James Bay Agreement 204, 213, 314
Jayasuriya, D.L. 393
Jernsletter, Nils 219n.
Johnson, G. 346–7
De Jong, M.J. 65
Jordan, D.F. 189–220

Kachru, B. 342
Kalasniemi, J. 177–8
Kallifatides, Theodor 167
Kativik School Board, Canada 314,
    315–16, 318–19, 321, 324–5
Kaymak, A. 71
Keatinge, H.R. 299–307
Van Kemenade, J. 65
Kenya, linguicism in education 342,
    344
Kiers, T. 70
King, 199, 218n.
King, A.H. 344
Kleinfeld, J. 217n.
Knowledge, transmission of 90–2, 96,
    139, 216, 308–9, 315
Konkani 384–5
Kool, C., Konings-V.D.M., Snoek
    and Van Praag, C.S. 58
Kristal-Andersson, Binnie 168–72
Kunene, Mazisi 176

L1, see language, minority; mother
    tongue
Labour Party, Australia 198–200
Lahdenpera, J. 328–35
Lalleman, J. 68–9, 70
Language
—community, in education 94, 97
—heritage 130–1, 139–42, 148,
    151–2, 152n., 153n.; see also
    mother tongue
—international 341, 383–4
—national 379
—official 10, 48–50, 205, 296, 384
—oral, see talk

—primitive 12
Language, foreign
—minority language taught as
94–5, 97–8, 120
—teaching of 106–7, 110
Language, majority
—in education 15–16, 20, 65–6
—as goal for minorities 32
—use by immigrants 68–9
Language, minority
—differences within 114
—in intercultural education 67–8
—prestige of 111–12, 117, 119,
124, 343, 349, 351
Language, minority, and culture,
teaching (MLC) 61–3, 65–6,
67–77
—experiments in 72–7
Language-learning
—additive 30, 47, 139–40, 145
—subtractive 30, 139, 141, 145,
273n.
Law, indigenous 212–13
Legitimation, and racial policy
368–70, 373, 375
Leporanta-Morley, Pirkko 172–3,
239–50, 265–6
Leyden, experimental school 72–5
Liaison, school-community 142, 289
Liberal Party, Australia 199, 200
Lindfors, J.W. 143
Linguicism 10, 13–14, 16–18, 20,
22, 33, 36–8, 339–54
—and colonialism 340, 341, 343–5
—effects of 350–1
—forms of 341, 345
—and neo-colonialism 345–7
—results of 18–19, 31
Linguistic Minorities Project 88–9
Lippmann, L. 193
Literature
—children's 223–37
—indigenous 206, 215
Liukka, L. 239–50, 265
Llewellyn, Richard 5
Longboat, D. 190, 197, 202–3, 212
Lukkari, Rauni Magga 175

Macauley 343–4

McGill University, and educational
development 316, 319
Machiavelli, N. 92
McLeod, Judy 153n.
Maintenance, see mother tongue
Mannheim, K. 371
Marainen, Johannes 179–85
Marathi 284–5
Marcuse, Herbert 376n.
Marginalization, of minorities 27,
72, 211, 262
Materialism, cultural 372
Materials
—bilingual 29
—indigenous language 205, 206,
279–80, 284–5, 309
—multicultural 127
Mathematics, Inuit schools 323
Media, ethnic 216
Methods, teaching 322, 348
—contrastive 106, 125
Metropolitan Separate School Board
(MSSB) 140
Miedema, W. 57–8, 66–7
Minorities
—empowerment of 130, 136,
137–41, 143–4, 149, 152, 251,
307, 390–4
—future of 32
—indigenous 179–85, 189–220,
group size 213, and pluralism
214–16, survival of 308, 311,
314, 323–4, see also
Aboriginals; education;
identity; Native Canadians;
Sami
—and school 141–3
—status of 48, 335
Misra, B.G. 344
Missionaries, use of native languages
190–1, 217n., 343
Mixing, language 124–5
Moluccans, in Netherlands 62
Monitor and Review (MAR) team,
California 281
Monoculturalism 13, 96
Monolingual, definition 11
Monolingualism
—extent 11–12, 348–9
—individual 13

—official 9–11, 13, 14–15, 95–6,
    107
Moroccans, in Netherlands 58, 61,
    69–71, 72–7
Mother tongue
—definitions 16–18
—deprivation 33, 35, 53, 108,
    162–7, 172–5, 183–5, 241
—as educational medium 14, 16,
    23, 26, 27–8, 31, 33, 37, 54,
    227, 252, 349, 386–7, 393,
    Canada 139–40, 314–18,
    320–1, 325, England 86–9,
    93–5, 97, Netherlands 59, 60,
    72–3, Norway 205–6,
    Sweden 104, 108–9, 112–13,
    116–19, 120–2, 177–8, 180,
    239–44, 250, 256, 264–5, 268,
    271, 328–34, United States
    279–80, 293, 300, 306
—extent of use 69–70
—and identity 10, 19–20, 60–1,
    195–6
—language arts, Sweden 329–30,
    331
—maintenance 23, 24–5, 26, 29,
    53–4, 62, 70–1, 308, 321, 323
—proficiency, see proficiency, L1
—proscription of 5, 191–2, 314,
    341
—role of 86
—sanctions against 5, 241, 314
—teaching in UK 79
see also language, heritage
Mother Tongue and Culture Pilot
    Project 87–8
Mother Tongue and English Teaching
    Project 88–9
Mother Tongue Teaching, National
    Council for 87
Motivation
—L2 learning 24, 29, 106, 109,
    111, 124, 138, 144
—for mother tongue use 69–70,
    228
Mullard, C. 67, 263, 275n., 359–77
Multiculturalism 194, 214–16, 361,
    393–4
—Australia 201
—Canada 127, 128–31, 141,

144–6, 151–2, 214, 368
—England 83–6, 93–8
—Netherlands 61
Multilingualism
—attitudes to 12, 13–15
—as educational goal 14–15, 61
—extent of 9, 10–11, 379–80
—India 379–89
Music, indigenous groups 206, 215

Nalbantoglu, Papatya 63, 71
Namibia, education 23, 31, 394
National Aboriginal Education
    Committee 208–9, 216
National Indian Brotherhood
    (Canada) 196, 197–8, 201, 203
Native Canadians
—education 190, 197–8, 201–6,
    213
—problems facing 129, 212–13,
    216
—status 194–5, 196–8, 214
Neo-colonialism, and language
    dominance 37, 341–2, 345–7,
    351
Netherlands, the
—minority education in 3, 57–77
see also policy, educational; policy,
    language
Ngugi wa Thiong'o 344
Nigeria, extent of multilingualism 11
Northern Environment, Royal
    Commission on (Australia) 193
Norway, Sami in 189–90, 205–8
Norwegian 191–2
Nouveau Quebec, Inuit of 311–16,
    323–5
Novogrodsky, Charlie 154n.

Observation, indigenous minority
    children 319–22
Obura, A.P. 342
Ontario, minority education in 127,
    129–31, 139–46, 150, 152
Oppression, minorities 31, 72
Organisation for Economic Co-
    operation and Development
    (OECD) 1, 32, 362
Orthography
—Inuit 313

—Sami 195, 206
Ortiz, A.A. & Yates, J.R. 148
Out-station movement 209–10

*Padres para Mejorar Educacion
    Bilingue, Los* 280–3, 291
Paine, R. 189–90
Pajaro Valley Bilingual Project
    223–37
—evaluation 234–6
—group discussions 229–32
—parents' experience 232–4
—planning 225–6
Pareck, B. 95
Parent Advisory Committee (PAC),
    United States 281–4, 286–9,
    291–2
Parents
—and children's literature 224–9,
    232–4
—and education 66, Canada
    141–2, 147, 150–2, Sweden
    122–3, 242–50, 257, 265–9,
    328–9, 334–5, United States
    224, 227, 239, 278–97, 300–1,
    305, 307
—indigenous groups 191, 197,
    205, 207
—and language use 5, 69, 71–2,
    134, 140
Pattanayak, D.P. 13, 15, 342, 350,
    379–89
Penetration 254, 262
Phillipson, R. 339–54
Phillipson, R., Skutnabb-Kangas, T.
    & Africa, H. 23
Piaget, J. 144
Pluralism 194, 214–16, 368, 388,
    393
Policy, anti-linguicist 343, 351–3
Policy, educational 41n. 348–50
—Canada 128, 138–9, 145–8,
    150–2, 201–3, 324–5
—England 84–6, 365
—indigenous minorities 194–201
—Netherlands 59–61, 368
—Norway 206
—Sweden 106–12, 116–17
—United States 278–97
Policy, language 360

—colonial 343–5
—India 380, 389n.
—Netherlands 61
—USA 45–55, 146, 346–7
Polish, teaching of 80, 81
Portuguese, in Canada 140, 146
Powell, Enoch 81
Power, social 2–4, 11–14, 36–8,
    39n., 90–2, 128, 130, 131–2,
    137, 152, 252–6, 279, 284, 286,
    352
—access to 254–5, 256–8
—and minority communities
    245–6, 264, 265, 269–71, 335,
    367–71, 373, 390
    see also hegemony theory;
    linguicism; minorities,
    empowerment of
Preschool project 299–307
—evaluation 301–5
Problem, language diversity as 83–4
Professionals
—indigenous 310–11, 314–23, and
    identity 322–3
—and L2 teaching 97–8, 347–51
Proficiency
—L1 69–70, 72, 177
—L2 74, 76, 84, 304
—limited-English (LEP) 279–81,
    285, 287, 290, 294, 296–7
—non-English (NEP) 279–81, 285
Programmes, L2 learning
—learner-related affective factors
    24, 29
—linguistic, cognitive and social
    factors, L1 25, 29–30
—organizational factors 24, 27–9
Pronunciation 123
Push-out, minority students, *see*
    drop-out rate

Qallunaat 311, 316–17, 322–3

Race relations
—Canada 154n.
—England 81–2, 83
Racism
—biological 33, 341, 360–1
—institutionalized 3, 4–6, 10, 18,
    28–30, 38, 64, 271, 359,

362–3, 365, Canada 127–9,
131–6, 145–52, 154n.
—UK 81
—United States 284, 292
see also anti-racist movement
Reading
—creative 228–9
—immigrant children 60, 76
—L1 122–3, 225, 293, 294, 306,
316
—L2 60, 63, 294
Reception education, for immigrant
children 59–60
Reconstitution, and racial policy
366–7, 369, 371, 375
Rees, O. & Fitzpatrick, F. 89
Rees, T. 80, 83
Reforms, liberal 2–5, 33, 393
Refractionism, social 359–60, 371–2,
376n.
Refugees
—in England 80–1
—in Sweden 104–5
—US 48, 54
Rejection, of education 262–3, 269,
270
Religion, and language dominance
340
Repression, and education 259, 261,
264
Research, indigenous communities
208, 318–23
Resources, control of 131, 252–5,
257–8, 262–3, 273, 339
Rex, J. 82
Reynoso, Cruz 47
Rights, educational, of indigenous
minorities 190–3, 194, 291
Rights, land, of indigenous
minorities 189–90, 195, 198,
200, 205
Rights, linguistic 31, 36, 45–6, 227
—of children 10, 14, 19–20, 249,
394
—Sami 205–6
—in United States 46–55
Rinkeby school, see Bredby school
Rodriguez, R. 153n.
Rougle, E. 239–50, 265
Rowley, C.D. 192–3

Rubalcava, Graciela 233
Ruong, I. 192, 195, 196, 205–6, 208,
212, 215
Ryan, S. 209

Sami
—education 179–82, 191–2,
195–6, 206–8
—in Norway 189–90, 194, 195–6,
205–8
—problems facing 212, 213,
214–16
—status 194–6, 205, 214
—in Sweden 103, 175, 179–85,
195, 206
Sami Educational Council 206, 207
Sami Institute 196, 208, 216, 218n.
Sami (language) 191–2, 195, 205,
219n.
Samuda, R.J. 148–9
Samuda, R.J. & Crawford, D.H.
147
Saudi Arabia, minorities in 41n.
Scandinavia, minorities in 31, 32
Scandinavian Lapp Council 195–6
School boards
—Australia 210
—Canada 142–3, 144–8, 150–2,
197, 202–4, 314
—Norway 207
—Sweden 237–8
—United States 279–80, 284,
286–92
School Readiness Inventory (SRI)
300–1
Schools, community 210
Segregation
—in education programmes 23–6,
28–9, 63, 72, 108, 196, 241,
294, 334, 394
—of indigenous minorities 198
Self-confidence, and L2 learning 24,
29, 32, 34, 52, 60–1, 123, 227
Self-determination, indigenous
minorities 4, 194, 196–7, 200–4,
209–14, 311
Self-management 200, 213
Self-respect 4, 253–4, 258–60,
265–6, 269

Self-sufficiency 253–4, 258–60, 265,
    269–70
Separatism, and minority language
    53
Serbo-Croat, in Sweden 117, 331
Shame 4–5, 18, 134, 164–6, 182,
    184, 249
Shelter, language 23, 26
Sivanandan, A. 261
Skills, school readiness 299–301,
    302–3, 306–7
Skills, language, development of 227
Skin colour, prejudice 192–3
Skutnabb-Kangas, Tove 9–41, 152n.,
    239, 251–73, 339, 376n., 390–94
Socialism, and progressive control
    373
Solidarity, indigenous minorities 38,
    216
South Africa, institutionalized
    violence 5
Spanish
    —in Canada 141
    —in Netherlands 69
    —in Sweden 111, 117, 250, 331
    —in United States 26, 46–54, 150,
        224–37, 279–81, 284, 299–307
Special education bill (Bill 82),
    Canada 146–7, 150
Stairs, A. 308–25
Stone, M. 67
Streaming, minority students 146
Strike, by children 244–50, 252, 258,
    266, 273n.
    —results of 267–8
Submersion programmes 23, 24–5,
    26–7, 28–30, 40n., 252, 256,
    259–60, 262, 273n.
Surinamese, in Netherlands 58
Swann Committee on the Education
    of Children of Ethnic Minorities
    94, 95, 97, 376–7n.
Sweden
    —bilingual education 103–26, 244
    —minority education 1, 3, 26, 28,
        32–3, 36, 239–50, 328–35
    —minority experiences 161–76,
        177–85
Swedish 106–7
    —and immigrants 104–6, 111,

        113–14, 116–17, 119–20, 164,
        177, as L2 123–6, 162–3,
        240–1, 244, 248, 256, 259–60,
        264, 268, 328–33
    —and Sami 180
Switch, language 134, 136

Talk, in reciprocal interaction model
    144, 145
Teachers
    —bilingual 28–9, 30, 37, 89, 113,
        124, 125–6, 244, 264, 268,
        284, 288–90, 331
    —discrimination against 281–2
    —indigenous 310, 314–18, role
        of 318–23, 324
    —and indigenous minorities 207,
        209–10, 219n., 314
    —language attitudes 53, 149, 151
    —and linguicism 339–40, 345
    —training 28, 125–6, 149–50,
        207–8, 209–10, 284, 309,
        314–16, 319–21
    see also educators
Tests
    —Comprehensive Test of Basic
        Skills (CBTS) 293
    —psychometric 322
    see also Bilingual Syntax Measure;
        School Readiness Inventory; El
        Circo Achievement Test
Three Language Formula 282, 380,
    389n.
Time, as resource 252–3
Tindale, N.B. 198
Tingbjorn, Gunnar 103–26
Tolerance, repressive 362, 376n.
Toronto Board of Education 142,
    146, 152, 153n.
Tosi, Arturo 79–98
Toukomaa, P. 239
Transfer, of skills 29, 293, 307
Transition, language, programmes
    27, 40n., 52, 88, 113, 256,
    259–60, 273n., 308, 343
Transmission, of education 143–5,
    155n., 385–6
Triesschijn, T.M. 71
Troper, H. 128–9, 131
Truancy 261

Trudeau, P. 127
Truman, Roy 85
Turin, A. & Bosnia, N. 229–32
Turkish Teachers in The Netherlands,
    Society for 71–2
Turks
    —in Netherlands 58, 61, 63, 68–9,
        70, 72–7, 366, 372
    —in Sweden 104, 107, 117, 239,
        250, 331
    —in West Germany 23–6, 30–1,
        33, 366, 372, 394

Von Uexkull, Ingrid 240–1, 243–6
UK
    —bilingualism in 79–98
    —and English as L2 347–8
    —L2 learning programmes 26–7,
        33
    —and linguicism 346–7
    —minority education 3, 79–98
Ukrainian, in Canada 140
UNESCO, on mother tongue
    teaching 349
United States
    —and English as L2 347–8
    —and linguicism 346–7
    —minority education in 2, 3, 28,
        141, 278–97
    —monolingualism 11
    see also policy, language
Universals
    —cultural 308–10
    —education 322
Urban Aid Programme (UK) 82
Urdu 384
Use, language 120, 133, 144
USSR, minorities in 36
Utsi, Paulus 185
Uzbekistan, L1 maintenance 24–5,
    26, 28

Value judgements 392–3
Violence, educational 5
Vocabularies, indigenous, extension
    of 205
Vygotsky, L. 144

Wechsler Preschool and Primary
    Scale of Intelligence (WPPSI)
    132–3
Wells, G. 143
West Germany
    —L2 learning programmes 26–7
    —minority education 23–6, 30–1,
        33
Van de Wetering, S. & El-Koundi,
    M. 69–70, 71
Williams, R. 90
Willis, P. 262–3
Winnipeg Centre Programme 204
World Conference of Indigenous
    People 216
Writing
    —children's, see literature,
        children's
    —L1 222–3, 224–5, 294
    —L2 60, 63
    —in reciprocal interaction model
        143–4, 145

Yoik, Sami 206, 215, 219n.
Yugoslavia, minorities in 36
Yugoslavs
    —in Netherlands 69
    —in Sweden 103–4, 239, 250

Zambia
    —L2 learning 24–5, 26, 28, 30, 37
    —linguicism in education 344, 346